4/2000

THE COMPLETE
TITANIC

Other books by Stephen J. Spignesi

The Beatles Book of Lists
The Celebrity Baby Name Book
The Complete Stephen King Encyclopedia
The ER Companion
The Gore Galore Video Quiz Book
The Italian 100
The J.F.K. Jr. Scrapbook
The Lost Work of Stephen King
Mayberry, My Hometown
The Odd Index
The Official "Gone With the Wind" Companion
The Robin Williams Scrapbook
The Second Stephen King Quiz Book
The Stephen King Quiz Book
The V. C. Andrews Trivia and Quiz Book
What's Your "Friends" IQ?
What's Your "Mad About You" IQ?
The Woody Allen Companion

THE COMPLETE
TITANIC

FROM THE SHIP'S
EARLIEST BLUEPRINTS
TO THE EPIC FILM

STEPHEN J. SPIGNESI

A BIRCH LANE PRESS BOOK
PUBLISHED BY CAROL PUBLISHING GROUP

A Birch Lane Press Book
Published by Carol Publishing Group
Birch Lane Press is a registered trademark of Carol Communications, Inc.

Editorial, sales and distribution, and rights and permissions inquiries should be
addressed to Carol Publishing Group, 120 Enterprise Avenue, Secaucus, N.J.
07094.

In Canada: Canadian Manda Group, One Atlantic Avenue, Suite 105, Toronto,
Ontario M6K 3E7

Carol Publishing Group books may be purchased in bulk at special discounts for
sales promotion, fund-raising, or educational purposes. Special editions can be
created to specifications. For details, contact Special Sales Department, Carol
Publishing Group, 120 Enterprise Avenue, Secaucus, N.J. 07094.

Manufactured in the United States of America
10 9 8 7 6 5 4 3 2 1

Library of Congress Cataloging-in-Publication Data

Spignesi, Stephen J.
    The complete Titanic : from the ship's earliest blueprints to the
epic film / Stephen J. Spignesi.
        p.   cm.
    Includes bibliographical references and index.
    ISBN 1-55972-483-8
    1. Titanic (Steamship)—History—Chronology.   2. Shipwrecks—North
Atlantic Ocean—History—Chronology.   I. Title.
G530.T6S65   1998
910'.91634—dc21   98-29132
                                                                        CIP

For my brother Paul

THE TEXT OF THE *TITANIC* "DEATH MESSAGE"
SENT BY THE R.M.S. *OLYMPIC*
ON MONDAY, APRIL 15, 1992

Carpathia reached Titanic position at
daybreak. Found boats and wreckage
only. Titanic sank about 2:20 a.m.,
in 41.16 N; 50.14 W. All her boats
accounted for, containing about 675
souls saved, crew, and passengers
included. Nearly all saved women and
children. Leyland Liner Californian
remained and searching exact position
of disaster. Loss likely total 1800
souls.

CONTENTS

PART III

MYSTERIES OF THE *TITANIC:*
A CENTURY OF SECRETS

ACKNOWLEDGMENTS

I'd like to thank my editor, Mike Lewis, who carefully helmed this project all the way to its berth, deliberately steering it away from icebergs of all kinds; my sister-in-law Linda Fantarella and her best man, Steve, for their research help; the Titanic Historical Society for being an incredible source of all things *Titanic* (not the least of which is their fabulous journal, the *Titanic Commutator*); the University of New Haven Library; Albertus Magnus Library; Merilee Choquette, and Sue and Bob Leen at Minuteman Press in East Haven; Jennifer Eldridge and Joanna Bell for their help with the *Titanic* musical playbills; Cody Grater; John White; Steven Schragis; my always hopeful mother, Lee; my dear friend, Toni Capelli; and of course, Pam and Carter.

White Star Liner, "TITANIC"

INTRODUCTION

R.M.S. *TITANIC:* DOOMED SHIP OF DREAMS

Nothing had really happened since the days of Napoleon
to destroy man's faith in continued progress.
—Walter Lord, author of *A Night to Remember* and
The Night Lives On

To my mind, the world of today awoke April 15th, 1912.
—Jack Thayer, *Titanic* survivor

Titanic. Since April 1912, her name has become a metaphor for many
things. Her sinking on her maiden voyage probably would not have
spurred such ongoing interest and fascination throughout the years had
she not been launched with everyone—from the most seasoned commander to the lowliest third-class passenger—believing the *Titanic* quite
simply could *not* sink. Tempting fate has never had such dire and pro-
foundly far-reaching results.

But the continuing interest in the *Titanic* is more than a detached,
clinical assessment of the symbolic significance of her planning, construction, sailing, and death. The drama and irresistible appeal of the
Titanic's story results from a myriad blend of emotionally powerful,
interconnected elements that include the social arrogance and strict, dis-
criminatory class structure of the times; the optimism and hopes of the
hundreds of emigrating steerage passengers headed to America; the
unparalleled luxuriousness and unprecedented grandness of the ship; and
the chain of fatal misjudgments that ultimately doomed the *Titanic* and

over 1,500 of her passengers—ranging from too few lifeboats to the wrong order being given after hitting the iceberg.

At one point when working on this book, I was listening to Mozart's *Requiem* through headphones while writing about Emily Ryerson leaving her husband and several other men standing on the deck of the *Titanic:* they "were all standing there together very quietly," she later recalled, as she and her children were lowered into the water in a crowded lifeboat. There was a sudden moment when the dark majesty of Mozart's "Introitus" and the surreal image of the men standing on the deck watching the lifeboat be lowered blended into a feeling I can only describe as emotionally overwhelming.

The problem every writer faces when trying to write about the *Titanic* is that we are all shackled to using mere words to describe something that is beyond language. The *Titanic* sinking is a historical event so primal, so visceral, and so horrible that it soon becomes obvious to the chronicler of such an event that language has not yet evolved to the point where words can truly convey the tragic essence of the disaster.

Ever since 1955, when Walter Lord published his seminal *Titanic* chronicle, *A Night to Remember,* interest in the *Titanic* disaster has grown annually, as more and more people become interested in this abominable, yet memorable night.

In 1997, James Cameron's epic film *Titanic,* seemingly overnight, transformed a subject of interest to some into a phenomenon of interest to millions. Within days after the film's opening, *Titanic* fever raged through the popular culture of the planet. *Titanic* books planted themselves on the bestseller lists; the *Titanic* soundtrack became the biggest selling movie soundtrack in history; the *Titanic* Historical Society signed up hundreds of new members; and by spring, Jim Cameron's magnum opus was the highest-grossing movie in history. Records were being set everywhere, and in late March 1998, the media was abuzz with the rumor that an extremely grateful Twentieth Century–Fox and Paramount Studios were planning on bestowing a bonus on James Cameron—of approximately $110 million. (In order to complete the film, Cameron had waived his profit participation until the movie grossed $200 million at the box office.)

Yet another book about the *Titanic?* Yes, because *The Complete Titanic* is unlike any other book about the *Titanic* ever published. At once a *Titanic* companion, anthology, browsing book, encyclopedia, and reference, *The Complete Titanic* is a *Titanic* time capsule that contains articles, essays, and even a complete novella; as well as lists, charts, photos, survivors' accounts, court documents, Senate testimonies, a who's who, a massive time line, and much more.

I especially want to note that in the preproduction stage of this book, the author and editors decided to retain the grammatical and syntactic inconsistencies and spelling irregularities found in the original 1912 public records documents, magazine and newspaper articles, and miscellaneous documentation, such as menus, insurance claims, and advertisements, when reprinting them in these pages.

Keeping the orthography of the original material was done out of respect for the memory of the *Titanic,* her passengers, and the original authors of these documents, and not out of indolence or negligence. At times this does result in a somewhat jarring juxtaposition of words or an odd or obsolete spelling or word usage.

So be it.

This book is meant to serve as a complete chronicle of the entire *Titanic* phenomenon; a comprehensive companion to all things *Titanic.*

The R.M.S. *Titanic* holds a hallowed place in the consciousness of the world. Ships like the *Titanic* come alive to the people who build her, who pilot her, and who travel on her. It is not an exaggeration to say that many people would have been greatly saddened to lose such a magnificent ship in a freak accident—even if not a single life had been lost.

The Complete Titanic: From the Ship's Earliest Blueprints to the Epic Film is an ode to the *Titanic.*

As the final lines of the moving *Titanic* musical so aptly put it, "Sail on, sail on, great ship Titanic! Fortune's winds sing Godspeed to thee!"

Engineering News

January 12, 1911

This article from the respected journal *Engineering News* provides a glimpse into the *Titanic* in its earliest stages: the completion of the liner's construction and the subsequent concern about the inadequate length of the New York harbor docks (expressed along with a surprisingly negative view of the grandiosity of these new "marine monsters").

The *Olympic* and *Titanic* Near Completion

The White Star Steamship Co. is about completing the two largest vessels in the world, the *Olympic* and *Titanic*. The hulls of these vessels are 882½ ft. long over all. The *Olympic* is expected to be in commission and begin regular trips in June next. The question arises, however, where these monster vessels can be docked.

It is necessary, for safety of course, that a pier should be provided at least as long as the vessel herself. The great new piers which New York City has just completed on the North River near 23rd St., however, lack by nearly 100 ft. the length necessary to fulfill this requirement. If the *Olympic* were to be docked at the White Star pier, therefore, her stern would project nearly 100 ft. out into the stream and be subject to risk of injury by passing vessels. The Steamship Co. is therefore asking the New York Harbor Line Board to permit two of the Chelsea piers to be extended out into the North River

about 100 ft. to provide berth room for the *Olympic* and her sister vessel.

It is, of course, easily seen that this is only the beginning of such applications. The Hamburg-American Co. has begun work on a vessel which will be about 40 ft. longer than these White Star steamers, and will doubtless be coming forward shortly with an appeal for permission to lengthen its piers in Hoboken. The Cunard Co. has also announced the undertaking of a vessel which will exceed the Hamburg-American boat in length, and the Cunard piers also will then need extension.

There are two questions of moment connected with this application. One is whether it is really for the public interest and the interest of safe navigation that the free navigation width of the North River should be decreased. The other question is whether the overburdened taxpayers of New York City can equitably be asked to shoulder a load of additional bonds for dock extensions simply because two or three steamship companies have built some vessels far larger than anything hitherto attempted.

If these latest marine monsters represented a real advance in economic transportation—if their construction meant cheaper transatlantic freight transportation—it would be easy probably to answer both of these quetions in the affirmative. We know of no reason, however, to suppose that these huge vessels really represent any such advance. They are built primarily to furnish the acme of luxury in passenger travel. Instead of representing an advance in economic transportation, they probably represent an actual increase in cost. That is to say, taking the year through, it is probable that passengers can be carried with reasonable comfort on vessels of moderate size more cheaply than they can by these latest marine monsters.

It is urged by those who are appealing to have the North River narrowed, and to have New York City undertake the burden of providing these dock extensions, that these vessels will go somewhere else if they cannot be provided with proper pier accommodations at New York. The best answer to this is that there is no other place where they could go. No other city anywhere can furnish a transatlantic passenger traffic sufficient to make these huge vessels pay.

The curious thing is that these steamship companies should undertake to build these huge vessels without knowing beforehand where they could dock them at this end of their voyage. As the companies have put themselves into a dilemma, it would seem to be a good plan to let them find their own way out. At least, if piers must be provided for these new monsters, we see no reason why the companies who own them should not furnish the money.

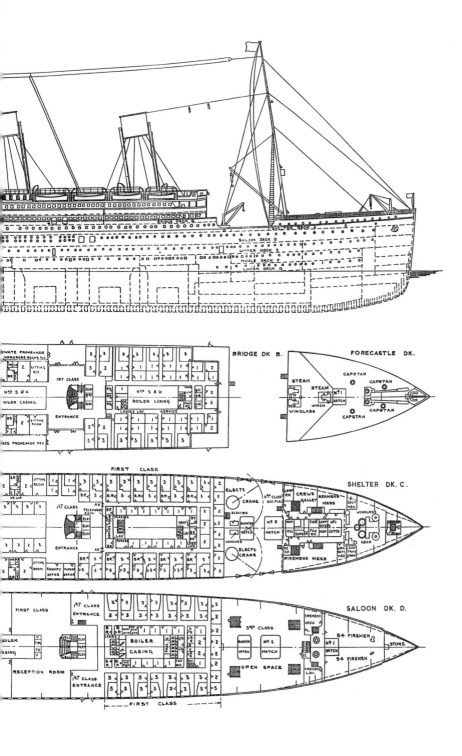

PART I

The *Titanic* Files:
A Complete Chronicle
of the *Titanic* Disaster

Titanic Haiku

Still vast black water
Jet face of ancient iceberg
Quiet of new dead.

1

TITANIC ON THE RECORD

These three documents—*Titanic*'s Transcript of Register, Certificate for Clearance, and Survey of Emigrant Ship—chronicle *Titanic*'s attainment of official sea-going status and provide a fascinating look at her transformation from the biggest ship ever built by man to the biggest ship ever to sail the seas.

Reading through the particulars of these documents with over eight decades of hindsight to draw from is fascinating and sad; how can we not be moved by the clinical comment at the conclusion of the transcript that reads, "Vessel wrecked in the Atlantic Ocean 14th April 1912. Certificate of Registry lost with the vessel"?

Two lines from the Survey of Emigrant Ship also stand out as well: The inspector writes, "I have inspected the boats and their equipments, and have seen *sixteen* swung out and lowered into the water," and then, a few lines later, he states, "I was on board this ship immediately before she sailed. I saw *two* boats swung out and lowered into the water." This seems to confirm that the crew did not have a boat drill before its maiden voyage, other than a perfunctory swinging out and lowering of only two boats. The inspector states that he did see sixteen boats swung out and lowered, but this was apparently well before sailing day, considering that he then makes the point that he only saw two lowered before sailing.

These official records paint a poignant portrait, and reading through them takes us back to the days when *Titanic* was new and believed to be unsinkable.

THE REPORT THAT OFFICIALLY REGISTERED *TITANIC*

Selected Items From the Liverpool Transcript of Register for
Transmission to Registrar-General of Shipping and Seamen
Dated March 25, 1912

Signal Letters (if any): H. V. M. P.

Official Number: 131,428
Name of Ship: Titanic
No., Date, and Port of Registry: 24/1912, Liverpool
No., Date, and Port of previous Registry (if any): New
   Vessel
Whether British or Foreign Built: British
Whether a Sailing or Steam Ship; and if a Steam Ship, how
   propelled: Steamship Triple Screw
Where Built: Belfast
When Built: 1912
Name and Address of Builders: Harland and Wolff, Ld,
   Belfast

Number of Decks: Five and two partial
Number of Masts: Two
Rigged: Schooner
Stern: Elliptical
Build: Blencher
Galleries: —
Head: —
Framework and description of vessel: Steel
Number of bulkheads: Fifteen
Number of water ballast tanks, and their capacity in tons:
   Seventeen; 5,726 tons

Length from fore part of stem, under the bowsprit, to the
   aft side of the head of the stern post: 852.5 feet
Length at quarter of depth from top of weather deck at
   side amidships to bottom of keel: 849.2 feet
Main breadth to outside of plating: 92.5 feet

4

Depth in hold from tonnage deck to plating at midships:
31.6 feet
Depth in hold from upper deck to ceiling at midships, in the case of three decks and upwards: 59.58 feet
Depth from top of beam amidships to top of keel:
64.91 feet
Depth from top of deck at side amidships to bottom of keel: 65.33 feet
Round of beam: .25 feet
Length of engine room, if any: 123 feet

PARTICULARS OF DISPLACEMENT
Total to quarter the depth from weather deck at side amidships to bottom of keel: 77,780 tons
Ditto per inch immersion at same depth: 150 tons

PARTICULARS OF PROPELLING ENGINES
No. of set of engines: Two reciprocating and one turbine
No. of shafts: Three
Description of engines: Four cylinder triple expansion inverted vertical direct acting surface condensing cylindrical multiboilers
Particulars of boilers:
  Numbers: 24 D. E. and SSE
  Iron or Steel: Steel
  Loaded Pressure: 215 lbs. per square inch
Whether British or Foreign Made:
  Engines: British
  Boilers: British
When made:
  Engines: 1912
  Boilers: 1912
Name and address of makers:
  Engines: Harland and Wolff, Ld.
  Boilers: Belfast
Reciprocating Engines:
  No. and Diameter of Cylinders in each set:
  1–54″; 1–84″; 2–97″
  Length of stroke: 75″
Rotary Engines:
  No. of Cylinders in each set: One

N. H. P.: 6,906
I. H. P.: 50,000
Speed of Ship: 21 Knots

PARTICULARS OF TONNAGE

Gross Tonnage:
  Under Tonnage Deck: 14,840.66 tons
  Space or spaces between decks, Salon, Upper &
    Middle: 14,142.81 tons
  Turret or Trunk: - 0 -
  Forecastle: 240.39 tons
  Bridge space: 3,633.45 tons
  Poop: 294.21 tons
  Side Houses: - 0 -
  Deck Houses: 5,902.89
  Chart House: - 0 -
  Spaces for machinery and light, and air under
    Section 78 (2) of Merchant Shipping Act, 1894:
    1,184.16 tons
  Excess of Hatchways: - 0 -
Deductions Allowed:
  On account of space required for propelling power:
    21,689.68 tons
  On account of spaces occupied by Seaman or
    Apprentices, and appropriated to their use, and
    kept free from Goods or Stores of every kind,
    not being the personal property of the crew.
    These spaces are the following, viz.: In lower
    middle upper and saloon tween decks poop
    forecastle bridge and round houses: 2,628.96 tons
  Deductions under Section 79 of the Merchant
    Shipping Act, 1894, and Section 54 of the
    Merchant Shipping Act, 1906, as follows:
    Fore Peak water ballast tank: 44.43 tons
    After Peak water ballast tank: 30.95 tons
    Master's Accommodation: 21.98 tons
    Boatswain's Stores: 45.00 tons
    Chart Room: 6.23 tons
    Total: 148.59 tons
Total Deductions: 24,497.23 tons

	No. of tons	Cubic Metres
Gross Tonnage:	46,328.54	131,109.85
Deducations, as per Contra:	24,497.23	69,324.16
Register Tonnage:	21,831.34	61,482.69

NOTE.—1. The tonnage of the engine room spaces below the upper deck is 11,209.94 tons, and the tonnage of the total spaces framed in above the upper deck for propelling machinery and for light and air is 1,184.16 tons.

NOTE.—2. The undermentioned spaces above the upper deck are not included in the cubical contents forming the ship's register tonnage:
Open space in front of poop 16 feet long—65.24 tons. Open space abaft 2nd class smoke room 6 ft. long = 15.84 tons. Open space on Promenade Deck, abreast windows, port side—198 feet long = 343.24 tons. Open space on Promenade Deck, abreast windows, starbd side—198 feet long = 344.24 tons.

Names, Residences, and Description of the Owners, and Number of Sixty-fourth Shares held by each:
Oceanic Steam Navigation Company Limited having its principal place of business at 30 James Street Liverpool—Sixty-four Shares.

Harold Arthur Sanderson
30 James Street, Liverpool
designated: Manager
Advice received 25th day of March 1912
Under the seal of the owning company

Copy of Transactions Subsequent to Registry

Registry closed 31st May 1912.
Vessel wrecked in the Atlantic Ocean 14th April 1912. Certificate of Registry lost with the vessel. Advice received from the registered manager.

CORRESPONDENCE RECEIVED 3 JUNE 1912

SURVEY OF AN EMIGRANT SHIP
CERTIFICATE FOR CLEARANCE
Selected Items From the April 11, 1912 Queenstown Document
That Cleared the *Titanic* to Carry Passengers and Recorded Her
Boardings in Southampton, Cherbourg, and Queenstown

Ship's Name and Official Number: "Titanic": 131428
Port of Registry, and Tonnage: Liverpool
  Gross Tonnage: 46,328
  Register Tonnage: 21,831
Name of Master: E. J. Smith
Port of Departure: Southampton
Ports of Call: Cherbourg and Queenstown
Destination: New York

CABIN PASSENGERS
ADULTS (12 YEARS AND UPWARDS):
  Married:
  Male: 52   (Southampton)
            29   (Cherbourg)
  Female: 52   (Southampton)
            29   (Cherbourg)
  Single:
  Male: 196   (Southampton)
            51   (Cherbourg)
             5   (Queenstown)
  Female: 101   (Southampton)
            58   (Cherbourg)
             2   (Queenstown)

CHILDREN:
  Between 1 and 12:
  Male: 10   (Southampton)
             3   (Cherbourg)
  Female: 12   (Southampton)
             2   (Cherbourg)

8

Under 1 Year:
  Male: 4   (Southampton)
  Female: -0-

Total Cabin Passengers: 427 (Southampton)
                        172 (Cherbourg)
                          7 (Queenstown)

Equal to Adults computed by
Part III, M. S. Act, 1894: 412 (Southampton)
                        169 1/2 (Cherbourg)
                          7 (Queenstown)

STEERAGE PASSENGERS

ADULTS (12 YEARS AND UPWARDS):
  Married:
  Male: 25 (Southampton)
             4 (Cherbourg)
             2 (Queenstown)
  Female: 25 (Southampton)
             4 (Cherbourg)
             2 (Queenstown)
  Single:
  Male: 315 (Southampton)
           59 (Cherbourg)
           50 (Queenstown)
  Female: 74 (Southampton)
           18 (Cherbourg)
           54 (Queenstown)

CHILDREN:
  Between 1 and 12:
  Male: 22 (Southampton)
            7 (Cherbourg)
            5 (Queenstown)
  Female: 28 (Southampton)
            7 (Cherbourg)
  Under 1 Year:
  Male: 3 (Southampton)
            3 (Cherbourg)
  Female: 3 (Southampton)

Total Steerage Passengers: 495 (Southampton)
                             102 (Cherbourg)
                             113 (Queenstown)

Equal to Adults computed by
Part III, M. S. Act, 1894: 464 (Southampton)
                                 92 (Cherbourg)
                                110 1/2 (Queenstown)

CREW

Deck Department: 73
Engine Department: 325
Stewards' Department: 494

Total Crew: 892
Equal to Adults computed by Part III, M. S. Act, 1894: 892

                  • • • • • • • • • • • •

Total Number actually on board, including Crew: 2,208
Equal to Adults computed by Part III, M. S. Act,
  1894: 2,147

Total Number of Statute Adults (as Steerage Passengers),
  exclusive of the Master, Crew, and Cabin Passengers,
  which the Ship can legally carry according to space
  allotted: 1,735
Clear Space in Sq. Ft.: 26,992
Number of Beds fitted: 1,134

I hereby certify that the particulars inserted in the
above form are correct. I also certify that all the
requirements of the Merchant Shipping Acts relating to
emigrant ships, so far as they can be complied with before
the departure of the ship, have been complied with, and
that the ship is, in my opinion, seaworthy, in safe trim,
and in all respects fit for her intended voyage; that she
does not carry a greater number of passengers than in the
proportion of one statute adult to every five superficial
feet of space clear for exercise on deck; and that her
passengers and crew are in a fit state to proceed.

                                  Dated at Queenstown
                             this 11th day of April 1912

                                      E. J. Sharpe
          Emigration Officer, or Assistant Emigration Officer

THE REPORT THAT CERTIFIED THE *TITANIC* SEAWORTHY AND READY TO SAIL

Selected Items From The Queenstown Board of Trade, Surveyors' Office Report of Survey of an Emigrant Ship M23780 No. 403., Dated April 12, 1912

SHIP

Name and Official Number	"Titanic" 131,428
Port of Registry	Liverpool
Single, twin, triple or qaudruple screw	Triple screw
Where and when built	Belfast 1912
Date of expiration of passenger certificate	2-4-13 [April 2, 1913]
Intended Voyage	Foreign

MASTER AND OFFICERS

Master	Edward John Smith
First Mate	Henry Tingle Wilde
Second Mate	Wm McMaster Murdoch
First Engineer	Joseph Bell
Second Engineer	William Edward Farquharson

LIFE-SAVING APPLIANCES
Description of Boats and Rafts
BOATS, SECTION A.

No.:   14
Cubic contents in feet.: 9,172
No. of persons they will accommodate 910
Materials: Wood
Number under davits: 14
Are they so placed as to be readily got into the water?: Yes
Are they provided with the equipments required by the rules: Yes

11

M23780
REPORT OF SURVEY
OF
AN EMIGRANT SHIP

Note.—Cancel the portions of this form that do not apply.

BOARD OF TRADE RECEIVED 13 APR 1912 MARINE SHIP

BOARD OF TRADE, SURVEYORS OFFICE No 403 11 APR 1912 QUEENSTOWN

SURVEYORS ... 1912

Name and official number.	Port of registry.	Tonnage.		Single, twin, triple or quadruple screw. Registered horse-power.	Where and when built.	
		Gross.	Net.			
"Titanic" 131.428	Liverpool	46328	21831 44/100	Triple Screw	Belfast 1912	Belfast 6-3-12

Date of expiration of passenger certificate.	Mean draught of water and freeboard.	Name and address of owner or agent.	Intended voyage.
2-4-13	34' 0" 31' 4	Oceanic Steam Navigation Co Ltd 30 James Street Liverpool	Foreign

MASTER AND OFFICERS.

Rank.	Name in full.	Number of certificate.	Grade.
Master	Edward John Smith	14102	Ex Master
First Mate ...	Wm McMaster Murdoch	025 450	Ex Master
	Henry Tingle Wilde	027371	Ex Master
Second Mate ...	Chas. Herbert Lightoller	05 706	Ex Master
First Engineer...	Joseph Bell	19224	1st Class
Second Engineer ...	Wm Edward Farquharson	12883	1st Class

LIFE-SAVING APPLIANCES.

Description of boats and rafts.	No.	Cubic contents in feet.	No. of persons they will accommodate.	Materials.	Number under davits.	Are they so placed as to be readily got into the water ?	Are they provided with the equipments required by the rules ?
Boats, Section A.	14	9172	910	Wood	14	Yes	Yes
Boats, " B.	✓						
Boats, " C.	✓						
Boats, " D.	2	647	80	Wood	2	Yes	Yes
Boats, { Engelhardt collapsible } E.	4	—	187	Wood with canvas lifeboats.	—	Yes	Yes.
Life Rafts	✓						

Number of life belts.	Number of life buoys.	Is the ship supplied with all the life-saving appliances required by the rules ?
3560	48	Yes

(822s) (61352) Wt.27577/G.148. 1000 11-10 W B & L

BOATS, SECTION D.

No.: 2
Cubic contents in feet.: 648
No. of persons they will accommodate: 80
Materials: Wood
Number under davits: 2
Are they so placed as to be readily got into the water?: Yes
Are they provided with the equipments required by the rules?: Yes

BOATS, ENGLEHARDT COLLAPSIBLE

No.: 4
No. of persons they will accommodate: 188
Materials: Wood and canvas
Are they so placed as to be readily got into the water?: Yes
Are they provided with the equipments required by the rules?: Yes
Number of life belts: 3,560
Number of life buoys: 48
Is the ship supplied with all the life-saving appliances required by the rules?: Yes

EQUIPMENT

No. of compasses on board: 4
Date of last adjustment: April 2, 1912
Number of chronometers: 2
No. and description of fire pumps: 3 steam pumps
Description and state of distilling apparatus: New and in good condition
No. of gallons of pure cold water that it is capable of producing in 24 hours: 14,000
Quantity of fresh water in double bottom in gallons: 1,800

SPACE AVAILABLE FOR PASSENGERS

<u>On Saloon Deck:</u>
  Total square feet: 1,732
  Total number of adults: 115
  Number of beds fitted: 50
<u>On Upper Deck:</u>
  Total square feet: 7,306
  Total number of adults: 485
  Number of beds fitted: 272

On Main Deck:
  Total square feet: 9,861
  Total number of adults: 655
  Number of beds fitted: 466
On Lower Deck:
  Total square feet: 8,093
  Total number of adults: 480
  Number of beds fitted: 346

Reports by Board of Trade Officers

NOTE.—No Officer may certify to anything which he has not personally seen and examined, and then only if he is satisfied that it complies fully with the regulations. All words that do not apply should be struck out.

REPORTS

1. A passenger certificate is in force for this vessel, and no damage to the hull or engines has been reported since its issue. I am satisfied that the hull, boilers and machinery are in good condition and fit for the voyage.
2. I have examined the distilling apparatus, which is in good working order and capable of producing **14000** gallons of cold water every 24 hours, and the engineers are competent to manage and repair it.
3. The fresh water on board is certified to amount to **206800** gallons, and is contained in **7** tanks.
4. The coal on board is certified to amount to **5892** tons, which is sufficient to take the ship to her next coaling port.
5. I have inspected the boats and their equipments, and have seen **16** swung out and lowered into the water. The lifebelts are in order and are conveniently placed. The distress signals and their magazine, and the other equipments, comply with the regulations and are to my satisfaction.
6. The various steerage compartments comply with the regulations as regards light, air and ventilation, and measurement for the numbers for which they are fitted. No cargo is stowed so as to affect the health or comfort of the steerage passengers.
7. I have inspected the provisions which are sufficient for **1150** adults; and the quality of the provisions and

water for the passengers and crew is entirely to my
satisfaction.

8. I have inspected the medical stores, and they comply
both as to quality and quantity with the regulations.

9. I have inspected the crew and steerage passengers, and
none of them appear to be by reason of bodily or
mental disease unfit to proceed or likely to endanger
the health or safety of the other persons on board.

10. I was on board this ship immediately before she
sailed. I saw **two** boats swung out and lowered into the
water. From the foregoing reports of inspection, and
from what I saw myself, I was satisfied that the ship
was in all respects fit for the intended voyage,
and that the requirements under the Merchant Shipping
Acts have been complied with.

> [Reports to be made when passengers
> are embarked at a port of call.]

I have inspected the steerage passengers, stores, medicines,
etc., embarked here, and am satisfied that the
regulations are complied with. (Queenstown, 11-4-12)

I have satisfied myself that everything on board this
vessel is in order, and have issued the necessary
certificate for clearance.

Forwarded to the Board of Trade

> Signature: William Tillar
> Date: 12th April 1912

The Assistant Secretary,
Marine Department, Board of Trade.

For some, the *Titanic* is a tale of hubris, of thinking that
technology could master nature. For others, it represented
the end of the class system. All of those people in steerage
were too poor to afford a stateroom and, because of that,
too poor to live. They died because they had a touching
faith in the ship's builders, the owners—in an elite that
failed them utterly, if only by not providing enough
lifeboats. World War I, a bit more than two years later,
offered further proof that Europe's ruling class was
composed, mainly, of imbeciles. It went over the top,
leading a generation to slaughter.

—Richard Cohen, the *New York Post,* December 24, 1997

THE *TITANIC* TIME LINE

A Year-by-Year, Day-by-Day, Minute-by-Minute
Account of the *Titanic* Tragedy and Its
Aftermath, 1850–2002

> *O Lord, methought what pain it was to drown:*
> *What dreadful noise of waters in my ears!*
> *What sights of ugly death within my eyes!*
> *Methought I saw a thousand fearful wrecks;*
> *A thousand men that fishes gnawed upon;*
> *Wedges of gold, great anchors, heaps of pearl,*
> *Inestimable stones, unvalued jewels,*
> *All scattered in the bottom of the sea.*
> *Some lay in dead men's skulls, and in those holes*
> *Where eyes did once inhabit, there were crept*
> *As 'twere in scorn of eyes, reflecting gems*
> *That wooed the slimy bottom of the deep,*
> *And mocked the dead bones that lay scattered by.*
> —William Shakespeare, *Richard III*, Act I, scene IV

1850

January 27   Edward John Smith, the ultimately doomed commander
of the R.M.S. *Titanic,* was born on Well Street in England in Hanley,
Staffordshire, Stoke-on-Trent.

1867

Shipping magnate Thomas Ismay (J. Bruce Ismay's father) acquires the White Star Line. J. Bruce Ismay is born.

1869

Edward J. Smith, nineteen, began his seafaring career as an apprentice on a clipper ship.

1874

Thomas Ismay orders a pair of new five-thousand-ton ships from Harland and Wolff, shipbuilders. These two steamers, the *Brittanic* and the *Germanic,* will both be capable of crossing the Atlantic at the previously unattained speed of 19 knots.

1880

At the age of thirty, Smith joined the White Star Line as fourth officer on the *Celtic.*

1887

Having attained the rank of captain, Smith took command of the White Star steamship *Republic.*

1898

Morgan Robertson's seemingly prophetic novella *Futility* was published. In this tale, the world's largest steamship—the *Titan*—hits an iceberg and sinks on its third voyage. *Futility* was reissued in 1912 as *The Wreck of the Titan* shortly after the *Titanic* sank. *(See the complete reprinting of* The Wreck of the Titan *in chapter 26.)*

1902

December   A deal between International Mercantile Marine (IMM—a trust owned by American financier J. Pierpont Morgan) and the White Star steamship line was finalized, giving IMM ownership of the steamship line for a total price equaling ten times the White Star Line's earnings for the year 1900, its most prosperous year. As part of the deal, Bruce Ismay, son of deceased White Star founder Thomas Ismay, would remain the White Star Line's managing director and chairman.

1907

Spring   Capt. Edward Smith commanded the *Adriatic* on her maiden voyage. After arriving safely in New York, Captain Smith told the assembled press, "When anyone asks me how I can best describe my experiences of nearly forty years at sea, I merely say, 'uneventful.' I have never been in an accident of any sort worth speaking about. I never saw a wreck and have never been wrecked, nor was I ever in any predicament that threatened to end in disaster of any sort . . . I cannot imagine any condition which would cause a ship to founder. I cannot conceive of any vital disaster happening to this vessel. Modern shipbuilding has gone beyond that."

April 30   At a dinner meeting at the Downshire House in London, J. Bruce Ismay and Lord James Pirrie (a partner in the shipbuilding firm of Harland and Wolff), agreed to build two giant ocean liners, the *Olympic* and the *Titanic*. Each ship would be at least 50 percent larger than the then-reigning *Lusitania*, which boasted thirty thousand gross tons and a length of 790 feet. The two men immediately realized that it would be necessary to build a special shipyard capable of handling the construction of the two biggest ships in the world. No site existed that could handle such a job. Following this meeting, Pirrie's staff immediately began working on a design for the two monster ships, and Harland and Wolff began converting three berths at their Belfast shipyard into two enormous slips where the *Olympic* and the *Titanic* would be constructed. They also had to build a 220-foot Arrol gantry above the slips for this unprecedented construction project. This gantry consisted of three rows of towers spaced 121 feet apart. Each of the three rows had eleven towers spaced 80 feet apart. The gantry construction consisted of one central revolving crane, ten walking cranes, and six traveling cranes. Four elevators and inclined walkways provided access to the gantry complex. The total area of the Arrol gantry was over 840 feet long and 270 feet wide. The height of the structure was 228 feet and weighed six thousand tons.

July 1   An order was officially placed with Harland and Wolff for the construction of the *Olympic* and the *Titanic*. The *Olympic* was given the shipyard number 400; *Titanic*, 401.

1908

December 16   The first keel plate for the *Olympic* was laid in Belfast.

1909

March 31   The first keel plate for the *Titanic* was laid in Belfast.
November 20   The framing of the *Olympic* was completed.

1910

April   Interior work on the beams, deck plating, and shell plating of the *Olympic* was completed and by April 1910, the *Titanic* had been fully framed.
October 19   The plating of the *Titanic* was completed. Hydraulic riveting was used to give the best quality plating for the ship. (See chapter 25 for a discussion of whether or not the *Titanic*'s rivets were fatally flawed.)
October 20   The *Olympic* was launched in a sixty-two-second "voyage." The lord lieutenant of Ireland, Lord Pirrie, and J. Bruce Ismay were present.

1911

April 1   The *Olympic* was taken to the graving dock for her final fitting out.
May 29   The *Olympic* headed out for two days of sea trials on Belfast Lough. She was accompanied by the White Star tenders *Nomadic* and *Traffic,* and she reportedly exceeded her design speed of 21 knots by three-quarters of a knot. Her test results were not made public, but her speed was reported by the engineering press.
May 31   The *Olympic* sailed on her maiden voyage; her ultimate destination was New York. J. Bruce Ismay sailed on *Olympic* in order to evaluate her performance and presentation.

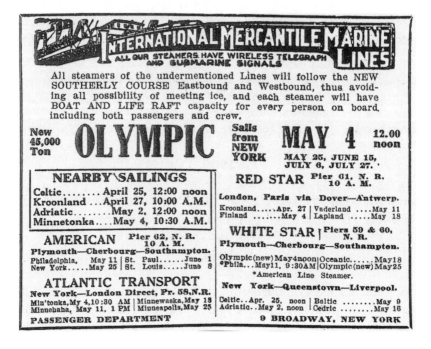

May 31, 12:13 P.M.   The *Titanic* was officially launched from Harland and Wolff Slip No. 3. Its launch also lasted sixty-two seconds and was witnessed by more than one hundred thousand people. Twenty-three tons of tallow, train oil, and soft soap were used to lubricate her way down the slip. Eighty tons of cable and three anchors on each side controlled her speed. Five tugs then towed the *Titanic* to a deepwater berth for her fitting out.

One eyewitness to the *Titanic*'s debut remarked that her rudder was "as big as an elm tree." He also noted that her propellers were "as big as windmills," and, in an interesting choice of words, this witness to history said that, regarding the *Titanic*, "Everything was on a nightmare scale."

June   Capt. Edward Smith, sixty-one, was appointed master (commander) of the *Olympic* for its maiden voyage.

June 2   The *Olympic* arrived in Southampton after a stop in Liverpool.

June 14   The *Olympic* departed Southampton for New York. She averaged 21.17 knots on her journey and 22.32 knots on her return.

September 20   The *Olympic,* on her fifth voyage and under the command of Capt. Edward Smith (who, of course, would later perish on

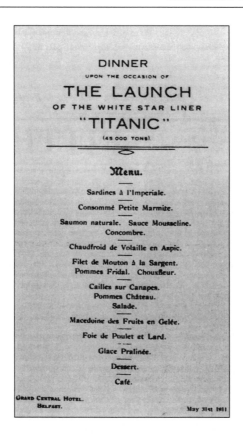

DINNER

UPON THE OCCASION OF

THE LAUNCH

OF THE WHITE STAR LINER

"TITANIC"

(45 000 TONS)

Menu.

Sardines à l'Imperiale.

Consommé Petite Marmite.

Saumon naturale. Sauce Mousseline.
Concombre.

Chaudfroid de Volaille en Aspic.

Filet de Mouton à la Sargent.
Pommes Fridal. Chouxfleur.

Cailles sur Canapes.
Pommes Château.
Salade.

Macedoine des Fruits en Gelée.

Foie de Poulet et Lard.

Glace Pralinée.

Dessert.

Café.

GRAND CENTRAL HOTEL.
BELFAST.   May 31st 1911

the *Titanic*), collided with the H.M.S. *Hawke* while leaving Southampton. The *Hawke's* bows were badly damaged and the *Olympic's* hull sustained a forty-foot gash. The *Olympic's* passengers disembarked at Cowes, and the ship returned to Southampton for inspection and repairs. An official inquiry found the *Olympic*—and thus Captain Smith—to blame. The *Olympic* was dry-docked on October 6, 1911, and many workers from the *Titanic* project were transferred to the *Olympic* for the six-week repair job. (See chapter 24, "Was the *Titanic* Really the *Olympic?*" for details on the "*Titanic* was a ringer" myth that evolved after this collision.)

1912

January Sixteen wooden lifeboats and four collapsible Englehardt boats were fitted onboard the *Titanic*.

February 24   The *Olympic* lost a propeller blade while crossing the Atlantic and immediately returned once again to Belfast for repairs. The *Titanic,* nearing completion, had to vacate her graving dock because it was the only berth large enough to handle the *Olympic*'s repairs.

March 6   The *Olympic*'s propeller blade was replaced.

March 31   The outfitting of the *Titanic* was completed.

Saturday, April 1   Scheduled sea trials for the *Titanic* were postponed due to strong northwest winds.

Sunday, April 2, 6:00 A.M.   Five tugs towed the *Titanic* down Victoria Channel to Belfast Lough for sea trials. The trials included maneuvering the ship at different speeds, evaluating the performance of the helm, and performing an emergency stop. The *Titanic* traveled less than a half mile at 20 knots before coming to an emergency stop.

Sunday, April 2, 7:00 P.M.   The *Titanic* returned to Belfast Lough from her sea trials. The Harland and Wolff observers disembarked and the *Titanic* was awarded her passenger certificate.

Sunday, April 2, 8:00 P.M.   The *Titanic* departed Belfast under the command of Capt. Edward J. Smith and proceeded to Southampton. At the time he took command of the *Titanic,* Captain Smith, known as the Millionaire's Captain, had logged two million miles aboard White Star ships.

Monday, April 3, Evening   The *Titanic* arrived at Southampton and docked at Berth 44.

Tuesday, April 4   Workers began preparing to load the *Titanic* with cargo and supplies for her maiden voyage, scheduled for six days hence.

Good Friday, April 5   Loading and preparations for the receiving of passengers continued on the *Titanic*. Photographs of the *Titanic* in her berth were taken, and hundreds came to the docks to see her. The public was not allowed onboard.

Saturday, April 6   The British coal strike was settled. The shortage of coal had necessitated the *Titanic* to be loaded with 4,427 tons of coal taken from five other IMM steamships—the *Oceanic, Majestic, Philadelphia, St. Louis, St. Paul,* and *New York*—that were then docked at Southampton, as well as with leftover coal from the *Olympic*. (The *Titanic* had arrived at Southampton with 1,880 tons of her own coal onboard.) Also, the majority of the *Titanic*'s crew was recruited on this Saturday, and cargo began to arrive at the docks. The majority of the *Titanic*'s crew were drawn from the British Seafarer's Union and the National Sailors and Firemen's Union.

Easter Sunday, April 7   No work was performed on the *Titanic*, and she remained quietly in Berth 44, awaiting her destiny.

Monday, April 8   Foodstuffs were loaded on to the *Titanic*. The *Titanic*'s builder, Thomas Andrews, oversaw all activity and remained onboard until 6:30 P.M., after which he returned to his office. Earlier, Andrews had remarked that the *Titanic* was "as nearly perfect as human brains can make her."

Tuesday, April 9   The *Titanic*'s final day in Southampton. One of the few photographs of Captain Smith on the bridge of the *Titanic* was taken on this day by a London photographer. All the officers spent the night onboard and kept regular watches. No passengers had yet been allowed onboard.

Wednesday, April 10 SAILING DAY, 7:30 A.M.   Captain Smith boarded the *Titanic* and received the sailing report from Chief Officer Henry Wilde. Shortly thereafter, J. Bruce Ismay also boarded the *Titanic* and began touring the ship.

Wednesday, April 10, 9:30 A.M. to 11:30 A.M.   Three boat-trains from Waterloo Station near London arrived at the *Titanic* carrying first-, second-, and third-class passengers.

Wednesday, April 10, 10:00 A.M.   Second-class passenger and survivor Lawrence Beesley (who would later author a book about the sinking) boarded the *Titanic*.

Wednesday, April 10, 12:00 Noon   The *Titanic*'s mighty triple-toned steam whistle blew three times and the great vessel cast off and was towed from the Southampton dock by the tugs *Hector, Hercules, Neptune, Ajax, Albert Edward,* and *Vulcan*. The movement of the water displaced by the *Titanic* caused the six mooring ropes of the nearby liner *New York*, then tied up at Berth 38, to snap with "a series of reports like those of a revolver." As the *Titanic* moved past the *New York*, the force of the water drawn behind her caused the stern of the *New York* to arc out toward the *Titanic*. The quick actions of Captain Gale, commander of the tug *Vulcan*, as well as an immediate "full astern" order given by *Titanic* pilot George Bowyer, and an order by Captain Smith to lower the starboard anchor to just above the water-line, all combined to avert a potentially disastrous collision between the two massive liners.

This near-collision—which Captain Gale would later describe as "a narrow squeak"—delayed the *Titanic*'s departure by over an hour, and at the time, many looked to this event as an inauspicious portent of bad luck. Second-class passenger Thomas Brown remarked to his daughter Edith, "That's a bad omen," and *Titanic* bedroom steward George Beedman later said, "As we left today, the American boat *New York* broke her moorings and drifted right across our bows, missed the *Oceanic* by about a foot. We had to reverse engines sharp and one of our tugs got her under control before any damage was done."

The *Titanic*'s suction was indeed powerful. Southampton authorities would later learn that a sunken barge had been dragged eight hundred yards across the harbor bottom as the gargantuan *Titanic* moved toward the open sea.

Wednesday, April 10, 6:35 P.M.   After an eighty-mile trip across the English Channel, the *Titanic* arrived at Cherbourg, France. The trip had been uneventful except for a fire that erupted during the crossing in a starboard coal bunker in Boiler Room No. 5. Between eight and ten men were assigned to keep the burning coal hosed down on each watch.

After dropping anchor in Cherbourg Harbor, 274 passengers, (142 first class, 30 second class, and 102 third class) including Col. and Mrs. John Jacob Astor (five months pregnant), American mining magnate Benjamin Guggenheim, and the "unsinkable" Molly Brown, were ferried to the *Titanic* by two White Star vessels, the *Nomadic* and the *Traffic*. Second-class passengers who boarded at Cherbourg included American illustrator Samuel Ward Stanton. Third-class passengers boarding were of Croatian, Armenian, Syrian, and other Middle Eastern nationalities. Fifteen first-class and seven second-class passengers disembarked at Cherbourg. These passengers had paid £1.50 and £1, respectively, for their cross-channel excursion.

Wednesday, April 10, 8:10 P.M.   The *Titanic* departed from Cherbourg, bound for Queenstown (now Cobh), Ireland.

During the brief trip, Thomas Andrews and a nine-man crew from Harland and Wolff worked with the *Titanic*'s engineering crew to assure that all of the ship's systems were working properly. As the *Titanic* traveled to Ireland, Andrews supervised a successful emergency test (complete with jarring alarm bells clanging) of the watertight doors.

Thursday, April 11, 11:30 A.M.   After an uneventful fourteen-hour journey down the English Channel and into St. George's Channel, the *Titanic* dropped anchor in Queenstown Harbor off the coast of Queenstown, Ireland. (Queenstown did not have a dock large enough to accommodate the biggest ship in the world, so the *Titanic* had to moor itself two miles off of Roche's Point.)

Ferried out to the *Titanic* by the tenders *America* and *Ireland* were 113 third-class passengers, 7 second-class passengers, and 1,385 sacks of mail. Seven passengers disembarked, including Francis Browne, thirty-two, a Jesuit student priest and avid photographer. Browne took the last surviving photographs aboard the *Titanic,* including the only known photograph of the *Titanic* wireless room. In this oddly foreboding black-and-white photo, Marconi operator and *Titanic* survivor Harold Bride is seen from behind. He is wearing headphones, and is seated in front of the wireless. Brown also took the last known photograph of Captain Smith standing on the starboard wing of the bridge and looking down *Titanic*'s side.

During the Queenstown stop, a fireman named John Coffey deserted the *Titanic* by hiding in a pile of mailbags being transported to shore. Coffey was from Queenstown and apparently signed on to the *Titanic* in Southampton specifically for a free ride home.

One odd story told about the *Titanic*'s Queenstown stop involved the ship's fourth funnel—a nonfunctioning funnel used only as a vent for the kitchen. As passengers were awaiting *Titanic*'s departure, many of them saw a soot-blackened face peering out of the fourth funnel, looking down upon the ship. A stoker had climbed the ladder inside the funnel, and when he reached the top, he peered down onto the mingling passengers. The effect of a black face staring out of the giant funnel was disturbing to many onboard, and some saw it as an ominous symbolic harbinger.

Prior to leaving Queenstown, the *Titanic* raised the American flag above her deck, signifying her next port of call, New York Harbor; New York, New York, U.S.A.

Thursday, April 11, 1:30 P.M.   The *Titanic* raised her starboard anchor for the final time and departed Queenstown Harbor for New York. Passenger Eugene Daly, who had boarded the *Titanic* at Queenstown, played "Erin's Lament" on his bagpipes as the *Titanic* slowly moved away from the Irish coast. From noon on this day until noon Friday, *Titanic* would steam 484 miles (Lawrence Beesley said 386 miles in his book), 26 miles more than the *Olympic* on her maiden voyage.

Friday, April 12, 12:00 P.M.   Between noon Friday and noon Saturday, April 13, *Titanic* covered 519 miles with twenty-four of her twenty-nine boilers in use.

Saturday, April 13, 10:30 A.M.   Captain Smith began his daily inspection.

Saturday, April 13, 12:00 p.m.   Between noon Saturday and noon Sunday, the *Titanic* covered 546 miles.

Saturday, April 13, 1:00 P.M.   The chief engineer reported that a coal fire that had broken out in Coal Bunker No. 10 was extinguished. (There seems to be disagreement over which bunker the fire broke out in. Some sources state the fire broke out in Coal Bunker No. 6.)

Sunday, April 14, 9:00 A.M.   The *Titanic* received a message from the *Caronia*: "Captain, *Titanic*—west-bound steamers report bergs, growlers, and field ice in 42° N. from 49° to 51° W, 12th April. Compliments—Barr." (A *growler* is a term used to describe an iceberg of small mass. Captain Smith acknowledged receipt of this message.)

Sunday, April 14, 1:42 P.M.   The *Titanic* received a message from the *Baltic*: "Captain Smith, *Titanic*—Have had moderate, variable winds and clear, fine weather since leaving. Greek steamer *Athenai* reports passing icebergs and large quantities of field ice to-day in lat. 41° 51' N., long. 49° 52' W. Last night we spoke to German oiltank steamer *Deutschland*, Stettin to Philadelphia, not under control, short of coal, lat. 40° 42' N., long. 55° 11' W. Wishes to be reported to New York and other steamers. Wish you and the *Titanic* all success. —Commander." (Captain Smith acknowledged receipt of this message.)

Sunday, April 14, 1:45 P.M.   The Hydrographic Office in Washington, D.C. received a message from the German steamer *Amerika*: "*Amerika* passed two large icebergs in 41° 27' N., 50° 8' W., on the 14th April." (This message was sent on to the *Titanic* from Washington but was not received by Harold Bride, the Marconi operator who survived the sinking. The consensus is that the message was received by Marconi Operator Phillips (who perished) and put aside until the

Titanic was within sending distance of Cape Race (at around 8:00 or 8:30 P.M. that evening), and the message was never seen by any of the *Titanic*'s officers.)

Sunday, April 14, 7:30 P.M.   On the *Titanic*, Harold Bride picked up a message from the *Californian* to the *Antillian:* "To Captain, *Antillian*, 6:30 P.M. apparent ship's time; lat. 42° 3′ N., long. 49° 9′ W. Three large bergs five miles to southward of us. Regards. —Lord." (Harold Bride testified that he delivered this message to the bridge but did not remember to what officer he handed it.)

Sunday, April 14, 9:40 P.M.   The *Titanic* received a message from the *Mesaba:* "From *Mesaba* to *Titanic* and all east-bound ships. Ice report in lat. 42° N. to 41° 25′ N., long. 49° to long. 50° 30′ W. Saw much heavy pack ice and great number large icebergs. Also field ice. Weather good, clear." (It seems that this message was put aside so that Phillips and Bride could continue sending passengers' messages, most of which were unimportant greetings intended to impress their friends in the states. The telegrams were, after all, being sent from the celebrated *Titanic!* It was never brought to the bridge nor seen by Captain Smith or any other of *Titanic*'s officers. This is especially tragic, since this message clearly indicates the presence of dangerous ice in the *Titanic*'s immediate vicinity.)

Sunday, April 14, 10:00 P.M.   First Officer William Murdoch relieved Second Officer Charles Lightoller on the bridge of the *Titanic*. Lookouts Lee and Fleet relieved lookouts Archie Jewell and George Symons in the *Titanic*'s crow's nest.

Sunday, April 14, 11:05 P.M.   *Californian* wireless operator Cyril Evans sent a message to the *Titanic*, saying, "Say, old man, we are stopped and surrounded by ice." He received the reply, "Shut up, shut up, I am busy; I am working Cape Race" from the *Titanic* wireless operator Jack Phillips. (Cape Race, Newfoundland, was a wireless station that received and passed along messages to other stations from ships at sea.)

THE LAST ACT

Sunday, April 14, 11:40 P.M.   From the crow's nest, Frederick Fleet saw an iceberg looming directly ahead in *Titanic*'s path. (Fleet and Symons, the other *Titanic* lookout that night, were watching the sea without the benefit of binoculars. The binoculars were actually onboard, but in a last-minute reshuffling of officers and their duties, the glasses were stashed in a locker in the cabin of David Blair, who had originally been assigned second officer. Blair had been replaced by Lightoller, and at the last minute, in the confusion, the whereabouts of the binoculars were not made known to Lightoller. They are probably still in Blair's locker, at the bottom of the Atlantic.) Fleet rang a sixteen-inch brass bell three times and picked up the telephone that connected to the bridge. When Sixth Officer James Moody answered, Fleet shouted into the phone, "Iceberg, right ahead!" Moody replied, "Thank you," and relayed the order to First Officer Murdoch, who ordered "hard a-starboard," which would cause the ship's bow to swing to port. Murdoch also ordered the engine room, "Stop. Full speed astern." He then sounded a bell alarm for ten seconds, warning those below that the watertight compartment doors were about to be closed. Murdoch then pulled the switch slamming the doors shut.

Sunday, April 14, 11:40:40 P.M.   The *Titanic* collided with the iceberg.

Monday, April 15, 12:05 A.M.   Captain Smith ordered the *Titanic*'s lifeboats uncovered and the crew and passengers assembled.

Monday, April 15, 12:10 A.M.   The *Titanic*'s position was estimated by Fourth Officer Boxhall to be 41° 46′ N, 50° 14′ W.

Monday, April 15, 12:15 A.M.   The *Titanic* sent out her first distress call, a C.Q.D., and it was picked up by the *La Provence* and the *Mount Temple*.

Monday, April 15, 12:45 A.M.   The *Titanic*'s first distress rocket was fired. The first lifeboat, no. 7, was lowered from the starboard side into the sea. (See chapter 5, "The Lifeboats: A Complete Accounting" for the British Board of Trade's schedule of lifeboat departures from the foundering *Titanic*.)

Monday, April 15, 1:40 A.M.   The *Titanic*'s last distress rocket was fired.

Monday, April 15, 2:05 A.M.   The *Titanic*'s lifeboat Englehardt D was lowered. (Collapsible D was the last lifeboat to actually be lowered into the water. Collapsibles A and B would float off the *Titanic* shortly thereafter.)

Monday, April 15, 2:15 A.M.   The *Titanic*'s last wireless distress call was transmitted.

Monday, April 15, 2:18 A.M.   The *Titanic*'s lights failed. People in the lifeboats heard enormous crashing as things in the ship—from grand pianos to engines—broke free and plunged forward toward the now fully-submerged bow.

Monday, April 15, 2:20 A.M.   The *Titanic*'s stern reared up out of the ocean, poised upright for a moment or two, and then the ship plunged downward, splitting in two, plunging two-and-a-half miles to the bottom of the sea. Over 1,500 souls still onboard or in the surrounding waters were lost. Close to eight hundred survivors watched the nightmarish tragedy from the lifeboats.

Monday, April 15, 3:30 A.M.   The *Titanic* survivors, adrift in the lifeboats, first saw the *Carpathia*'s rockets.

Monday, April 15, 4:10 A.M.   The *Carpathia* arrived at the site of the *Titanic*'s foundering and began taking on her survivors. The *Titanic* Lifeboat No. 2 was the first to be picked up. The rescue operation would continue for four hours.

Monday, April 15, 8:10 A.M.   Lifeboat No. 12, the last one afloat, was picked up by the crew of the *Carpathia*.

Monday, April 15, 8:30 A.M.   The *Californian* arrived at the site and pulled up alongside the *Carpathia*.

Monday, April 15, 8:50 A.M.   After asking Captain Lord of the *Californian* to remain at the site and search for any remaining survivors, Captain Rostron set sail for New York with the R.M.S. *Titanic*'s only survivors.

LLOYD'S OF LONDON'S ORIGINAL JOURNAL ENTRY RECORDING THE LOSS OF THE *TITANIC*

Tuesday, 16th April

Titanic: British Mail

Southampton for New York

foundered April 15 about 2:20 A.M.

in lat 41–16 North long 50–14 West

after collision with ice

Reported by wireless from Olympic to the

Cape Race wireless station.

Further reports state that loss of life is very

serious.

Tuesday, April 16   Advertisements touting the *Titanic*'s luxuries continued to appear in newspapers and magazines around the world.

Tuesday, April 16   A tragically erroneous (and somewhat arrogant) editorial appeared in the *Wall Street Journal* which read, in part, "The gravity of the damage done to the *Titanic* is apparent, but the important point is that she did not sink . . . Mankind is at once the weakest and most formidable creature on earth. His brain has in it the spirit of the Divine, and he overcomes natural obstacles by thought, which is incomparably the greatest force in the Universe."

Wednesday, April 17   U.S. Senator William Alden Smith, the Republican senator from Michigan, took the floor of the Senate and proposed a special investigation into the sinking of the *Titanic*. His resolution was unanimously approved, and a panel was authorized to "investigate the causes leading to the wreck of the White Star liner *Titanic*, with its attendant loss of life so shocking to the civilized world."

Thursday, April 18   Wasting no time, the White Star Line officially announced that the steamship *Majestic* would take the place of the *Titanic* for its Southampton-to-New York service. The *Majestic* was one of the first modern ocean liners. It was launched by the White

Star Line in 1889, along with the similarly-designed *Teutonic* (which was smaller, of course, than the *Titanic*). Ironically, Captain Smith had commanded the *Majestic* in 1901.

Thursday, April 18, 9:25 P.M.   The *Carpathia* arrived in New York and docked at Pier 54, North River, with the *Titanic*'s survivors. More than ten thousand people lined the docks awaiting *Carpathia*'s arrival.

Friday, April 19, 10:30 A.M.   The opening session of the U.S. Senate subcommittee hearing into the *Titanic* disaster took place at the Waldorf-Astoria Hotel in New York City. White Star managing director J. Bruce Ismay was the first witness before the committee, and Senator Smith's first (rather long-winded) question to Ismay was, "Will you kindly tell the committee the circumstances surrounding your voyage, and, as succinctly as possible, beginning with your going aboard the vessel at Liverpool, your place on the ship on the voyage, together with any circumstances you feel would be helpful to us in this inquiry?"

Saturday, April 20   Eleanor Smith, the widow of *Titanic* Capt. Edward Smith, attended a memorial service for the *Titanic* victims at St. Mary's Church in Southampton, England.

Saturday, April 20, 12:00 P.M.   This was to be the *Titanic*'s scheduled departure date and time from New York for her return trip to Southampton and other ports of call. The *Titanic* was scheduled to leave from North River Pier 59 at noon and was advertised as the "Latest, Largest, and Finest Steamer Afloat." The third-class rate to Plymouth, Southampton, London, Liverpool, and Glasgow was $36.25; to Gothenburg, Malmö, Christiania, Copenhagen, and Esbjerg was $41.50; to Stockholm, Abo, Hangö, and Helsingfors was $44.50; and to Hamburg, Bremen, Antwerp, Amsterdam, Rotterdam, Havre, and Cherbourg was $45.00. Passage was also available to Turin and Naples, Italy ($48 and $52.50, respectively); Piraeus ($55); and Beyrouth ($61).

Saturday, April 20, 8:00 P.M.   The cable ship *Mackay-Bennett* arrived at the site of the *Titanic*'s foundering to begin the grim job of retrieving bodies that had not been recovered by the *Californian*. The *Mackay-Bennett* carried forty embalmers and one hundred coffins, and on the first day, fifty-one bodies were recovered. Thirty bodies that were mutilated beyond recognition (probably due to pressure below the surface and/or being battered by passing ships) were buried at sea on Sunday. A total of 328 bodies of *Titanic* passengers were ultimately recovered. Of these, 128 were completely unidentifiable and 119 of them were buried at sea. One of the bodies recovered and returned to port was that of millionaire John Jacob Astor. Shortly after her arrival at the scene, the *Mackay-Bennett* sent the following wireless message: "Bodies are numerous in latitude 41.35 north, longitude 48.37 west, extending many miles both east and west. Mailships should give this region a wide berth. The medical opinion is that death has been instantaneous in all the cases, owing to the pressure when the bodies were drawn down in the vortex. . . . We brought away all the embalming fluid in Halifax, which is enough for 70. With a week's fine weather we think we should pretty well clear up the relics of the disaster. In my opinion the majority of the bodies will never come to the surface."

Later testimony from survivors about countless victims screaming for help in the water after the *Titanic* sank proved that the captain's theory that the people in the water died "instantaneously" was erroneous. One of the bodies found and identified was that of the *Titanic*'s bandleader Wallace Hartley, who was recovered with his music case strapped to his body. (According to British news reports, Hartley's music case was returned to the White Star Line.)

This same day, the North German liner *Bremen* passed by the site of the *Titanic*'s sinking. One woman passenger later described the scene: "It was a beautiful afternoon and the sun glistening on the big iceberg was a wonderful picture." As they neared the site of the sinking, "a feeling of awe and sadness crept over every one, and the ship proceeded in absolute silence. [We] distinctly saw a number of bodies so clearly that we could make out what they were wearing, and whether they were men or women. We saw one woman in her nightdress with a baby clasped closely to her breast. There was another woman, fully dressed, with her arms right around the body of a shaggy dog that looked like a St. Bernard. The bodies of three men, all in a group, all clinging to one steamer chair floated close by, and just beyond them were a dozen bodies of men, all in life preservers, clinging together as though in the last desperate struggle for life . . . We could see the white life preservers of many more dotting the sea . . . The scene moved everyone on board to the point of tears."

FROM *MACKAY-BENNETT* ENGINEER
FREDERICK HAMILTON'S JOURNAL

The tolling of the bell summoned all hands to the forecastle where thirty bodies are to be committed to the deep, each carefully weighted and carefully sewed up in canvas. It is a weird scene, this gathering. The crescent moon is shedding a faint light on us, as the ship lays wallowing on the great rollers. The funeral service is conducted by the Reverend Canon Hind; for nearly an hour the words "For as much as it hath pleased . . . we therefore commit his body to the deep" are repeated and at each interval comes, splash! as the weighted body plunges into the sea, there to sink to a depth of about two miles. Splash, splash, splash.

Tuesday, April 23   The British lord chancellor appointed a wreck commissioner under the Merchant Shipping Act to helm the investigation into the *Titanic* disaster.

Wednesday, April 24   *Titanic*'s sister ship, the *Olympic,* was scheduled to sail from Southampton to New York. At the direction of White Star Managing Director J. Bruce Ismay, the *Olympic* carried enough lifeboats to seat every passenger sailing on the triple-screw liner. However, close to two hundred crewmen refused to sail on the *Olympic* because of their dissatisfaction with the collapsible boats provided by the White Star Line. The voyage was ultimately canceled due to what the White Star Line described as the "crew's mutinous behaviour." The fifty-three deserters were arrested when they returned to shore in a tug and were charged with unlawfully disobeying the commands of the captain.

Wednesday, April 24   The North German liner *Bremen,* upon her arrival in New York, reported having seen seven icebergs in the vicinity where the *Titanic* sank. Officers of the Bremen also reported seeing hundreds of bodies floating in the water around the post where the ship sank. All of the bodies were wearing life belts and some were clasping the bodies of children. Others still held on to deck chairs and other objects. One cluster was estimated at consisting of around two hundred corpses.

Friday, April 26   The British home secretary appoints five assessors for a *Titanic* inquiry.

Friday, April 26   The British paper the *Daily Sketch* published on its front page a photograph of the iceberg believed to be the one with which the *Titanic* collided. The photograph had been taken at 7:00 A.M. on the morning of the disaster by chief officer Nielson, of the Russian liner *Birma*. The fatal iceberg was 140 feet high, 200 feet long, and was estimated to extend 980 feet below the surface. The *Daily Sketch* also published a second photo alleging to show a break in the berg that was believed to have been caused by the *Titanic*.

Sunday, April 28   Some of the *Titanic* survivors not needed for the U.S. Senate hearing returned to England.

Tuesday, April 30   The British Board of Trade requested a formal investigation into the sinking of the *Titanic*.

Thursday, May 2   The British Board of Trade's inquiry into the loss of the Titanic began in the Scottish Hall, Buckingham Gate, Westminster, England. (The U.S. investigation into the Titanic disaster had begun on April 19. Until the conclusion of the U.S. hearing on May 25, the two investigations were conducted concurrently. The British inquiry would conclude on July 3.)

Monday, May 7   A wax effigy of *Titanic* Capt. Edward Smith was put on display at Madame Tussaud's Wax Museum in London. Ten years later, this wax model of Smith was destroyed in a fire at the museum. Over the next few days, an advertisement for the museum ran in British papers. One in the *Daily Sketch* read: "MADAME TUSSAUD's EXHIBITION. THE LOSS OF THE TITANIC. Lifelike portrait model of the late CAPTAIN EDWARD J. SMITH. Realistic Tableau representing CHARLES DICKENS in his STUDY at GADS HILL. Free Cinematograph performances."

Friday, May 10   J. Bruce Ismay arrived at Queenstown onboard the *Adriatic* and was met by his wife. The Ismays immediately left for Liverpool, and when they arrived, on Saturday, May 11, they were met with huge crowds warmly cheering his return.

Monday, May 13   The last lifeboat belonging to the *Titanic* was found adrift in the Atlantic by the liner *Oceanic*, nearly a month after the great ship met her demise. Three bodies in the boat were buried at sea.

Tuesday, May 14 J. Bruce Ismay announced the establishment of an endowment fund of £20,000 for the benefit of disabled seamen and their survivors.

Saturday, May 18 More than thirty thousand mourners attended the burial of *Titanic*'s bandmaster Wallace Hartley in his hometown of Colne, Lancashire, England.

Saturday, May 25 The U.S. Senate subcommittee hearing into the *Titanic* disaster concluded in New York.

Tuesday, May 28 The U.S. Senate subcommittee hearing into the *Titanic* disaster issued its final report. (See chapter 9 for details on the subcommittee's findings.)

Wednesday, July 3 The British Board of Trade inquiry into the loss of the *Titanic* was concluded. (See chapter 8 for details on the Board of Trade's findings.)

1913

Spring By this time, the White Star liner *Olympic,* one of the *Titanic*'s sister ships, was back in commercial service, having been refitted to make it a safer vessel after the *Titanic* disaster. Harland and Wolff extended her double bottom up the sides of the ship to give her a "double skin," and also extended the interior bulkheads all the way up so that water could not spill over into adjoining compartments, as happened on the *Titanic.* Also, enough lifeboats for everyone onboard were added.

April As a direct result of the sinking of the *Titanic,* the North Atlantic nations created the International Ice Patrol (IIP) to monitor icebergs on the open seas. The IIP is run by the U.S. Coast Guard, and today it monitors icebergs from planes in flight.

1914

February 26 The *Titanic*'s second sister ship, the R.M.S. *Britannic,* was launched. She boasted improvements (similar to those made to the *Olympic*) made as a result of the *Titanic* tragedy.

1915

September The *Olympic* was commissioned as a naval transport, and for the next five years ferried soldiers to the front. She would ultimately survive four torpedo attacks and earn the nickname Old Reliable.

1916

November 21   During World War I, the *Brittanic* was sunk in the Kea Channel in the Aegean. She was either torpedoed or struck a mine and sunk within an hour. Of the 1,100 souls on board, only thirty died. The *Britannic* was located and explored in 1976 by Jacques Cousteau. Today she lies in 350 feet of water and is the largest intact ocean liner on the sea bottom.

1935

March   After decades of proud service, the *Olympic* made her final voyage to New York. She was then sold, stripped of her fittings, and scrapped.

1955

November   Walter Lord's history of the *Titanic* disaster, *A Night to Remember,* was first published. It would go on to become the "Bible" of *Titanic* historians and—after the December 1997 release of *Titanic,* James Cameron's epic film about the tragedy—it would again top the bestseller lists.

1985

September 1, 1:05 A.M.   During a joint French-American scientific expedition led by Dr. Robert Ballard of the Woods Hole (Massachusetts) Oceanographic Institute, the wreck of the *Titanic* was discovered two-and-a-half miles below the surface of the Atlantic, in the vicinity of where she foundered. The world's attention is instantaneously riveted to the North Atlantic, and a new period of *Titanic* fever begins, which, at the end of the twentieth century, shows no signs of abating. Dr. Ballard stated that he would keep the precise location of the wreck a secret to prevent scavengers from desecrating the site.

1986

September   Dr. Ballard returned to the site of the *Titanic* and toured and photographed the wreck.

1987

August   A Connecticut investors consortium that would grow to become RMS Titanic, Inc., funded an IFREMER (Institute for Research and Exploration of the Sea, the French oceanographic institute that codiscovered the *Titanic* in 1985) expedition to the site of the *Titanic,* during which they brought up 1,800 items from the wreck, which they then used to claim, through maritime law, "salvor-in-possession" rights to the wreck and everything around it. This status was granted by U.S. courts, and RMS Titanic has since made a total of five expeditions to the site and brought up close to five thousand objects from the wreck. RMS Titanic holds the exclusive right to remove artifacts from the *Titanic* and make money by displaying them or photos or film footage of them, but they are not allowed to sell the actual artifacts.

1995

Spring   James Cameron first pitches *Titanic* to Twentieth Century–Fox chairman Peter Chernin and a roomful of studio bigwigs. They were underwhelmed with the idea of a three-hour romantic epic from the maker of *Terminator 2* and *True Lies,* but agreed to give Cameron approximately $2 million to fund a deep-sea dive to the site of the *Titanic.*

September 8   Cameron and a Russian submersible team make their first dive (of an eventual dozen) in *Mir 1* to the side of the *Titanic.*

1996

May   James Cameron is given a green light by Twentieth Century–Fox to proceed with production of *Titanic.*

August   RMS Titanic failed to successfully raise a piece of the *Titanic*'s hull. (See the chapter, "The 'Big Piece' Debacle," and the Epilogue.)

1997

January 20   Edith Haisman, the oldest survivor of the *Titanic* disaster, died in Southampton, England, at the age of one hundred.

February 14   Eva Hart, a *Titanic* survivor who was seven years old when she was rescued from the great liner, died at the age of ninety-one.

July 2   *Titanic*'s original release date. (Cameron didn't meet it.)

December 19   James Cameron's film, *Titanic,* opened in the United States to excellent reviews and extraordinary business. It would go on to become the highest-grossing film of all time and the winner of eleven Academy Awards.

December 22   Alexander Lindsay, an independent documentary film-maker, filed a $4 million lawsuit against RMS Titanic in Manhattan Federal Court. Lindsay claimed that RMS Titanic was negotiating to sell four thousand coins and pieces of paper currency found in a suitcase recovered during a salvage operation filmed by Lindsay.

1998

Monday, March 2   The following news release ran on the P.R. Newswire (see entry for Tuesday, June 23, 1998):

Operation Titanic:
For First Time Ever, Non-Scientists Can Join Dive Expedition to Titanic's Final Resting Place in Inaugural Program of Deep Ocean Expeditions, Ltd.

For the first time since the R.M.S. *Titanic* sank off Newfoundland on the night of April 14, 1912, non-scientists will be able to dive to its resting place at over 12,000 feet as members of a working expedition employing the deep ocean submersibles MIR I and MIR II used in James Cameron's Hollywood blockbuster.

These first-ever expeditions will begin on August 2, 1998, for a maximum of 60 persons booked on a first-come, first-served basis. Participants will be organized into five expedition groups of 12 persons each. Each group's dive schedule will be completed in four to six days depending on weather and sea conditions and the dive site will be restricted to one group at a time. The expeditionary program—including transportation to and from the dive site (368 miles off the coast of Newfoundland), comfortable accommodations and meals aboard the MIR mother ship, and a guaranteed dive to the *Titanic*—is offered exclusively by the U.K.-based Deep Ocean Expeditions, Ltd.

Deep Ocean Expeditions, Ltd., is directed by Mike McDowell, founder of the pioneering adventure tour operator Quark Expeditions of Darien, Connecticut.

Until now only an elite group of scientists and expedition crew members have gained firsthand knowledge of the *Titanic*. Now, for the first time, ordinary people will be able to witness the awesome sight of the *Titanic* up close and personal.

Capable of diving to the ocean floor where the *Titanic* lies, the MIRs are in a unique class of deep diving submarines known as submersibles. The two MIRs are among only five non-military submersibles in the world capable of safely diving to the *Titanic*'s 12,000-foot depth. They are designed for use by three persons and will be operated with an expert pilot and two passengers. As atmospheric pressure inside the MIR is always one atmosphere, there is no need for decompression or recompression. Outside viewing is through window ports, allowing passengers to observe the *Titanic* sitting at her last resting place.

To support the deep dive operations of the MIRs, Deep Ocean Expeditions will use the scientific support vessel *Akademik Keldysh* as the "mother ship." Passengers will be part of a working expedition and should not expect a "love boat" experience. While the *Keldysh* is large and spacious, it was designed as a scientific research vessel. Compared to most scientific vessels, accommodations are of a high standard.

Deep dives to the *Titanic* (at 12,460 feet) will take place on a daily basis, assuming favorable weather and sea conditions.

Prices:

The cost of "Operation Titanic" is $32,000–$33,000 per participant. The cost to non-diving spouses, companions, family members, or friends is $1,750 each (subject to availability).

For further information or to reserve space for "Operation Titanic" in 1998, contact Deep Ocean Expeditions, Ltd., through its U.S. sales agent: Quark Expeditions toll-free at 800-356-5699 or 203-656-0499. Bookings can also be made through Zegrahms Deep Sea Voyages toll-free at 888-772-2366 or 206-285-3743; or by contacting your professional travel agent.

Saturday, March 7   *Titanic* survivor Eleanor Johnson Shuman, of Elgin, Illinois, died at the age of 87.

Monday, April 6   A Swiss-U.S. partnership announced it would build a $500 million, full-size replica of the *Titanic* that will be ready for the ninetieth anniversary of the ship's sinking. The plan was for the oil-fueled steamer to make a Southampton, England–New York round trip in April 2002.

Wednesday, April 6   A South African–based company announced plans to build a replica of the *Titanic* by the end of 1999, well ahead of a competing Swiss–U.S. partnership

Wednesday, April 15   The eighty-sixth anniversary of the day the *Titanic* sank. As it has done every year since its establishment in 1913, the International Ice Patrol laid a wreath in the North Atlantic at the precise spot where the *Titanic* plunged beneath the waves.

Other commemorations of the disaster included a memorial service in Belfast by the Ulster *Titanic* Society, and a wreath-laying ceremony at the *Titanic* Memorial Lighthouse at the South Street Seaport Museum in New York City.

The New York ceremony was attended by family members of some of the *Titanic*'s victims and the cast of the Broadway musical *Titanic*, who sang "Amazing Grace" during the service.

Present at the New York ceremony was Jacqueline Astor Drexel, granddaughter of millionaire John Jacob Astor, who went down with the *Titanic*. "I think my grandfather is considered a hero because he put a woman's hat on a twelve-year-old boy," she told the *New York Post*. "That hat turned him into a girl and he was able to get into a lifeboat."

Also present at the ceremony was Kevin Biddlecombe, the great-grandson of *Titanic* fireman Reginald Charles Biddlecomble. "My great-grandfather had a chance to get off the ship but he chose to stay onboard," he told the *Post*. "You feel sad at losing a relative, but you're also proud he's part of history."

Tuesday, June 23   Virginia Judge J. Calvitt Clarke Jr. issued an injunction barring Deep Ocean Expeditions Ltd. from coming within several miles of the *Titanic* wreck or taking photographs or videotape of it without permission of George Tulloch's company, RMS Titanic Inc.

(See the Monday, March 2, 1998 press release announcing the expedition.)

Thursday, July 30   An international team of scientists, oceanographers, historians, and documentary film producers departed from Boston on a new expedition—known as "*Titanic* '98"—to explore the wreck site of the submerged R.M.S. *Titanic*. A joint project between the RMS Titanic and the Discovery channel, the expedition broadcast live footage of the wreck. (See the Epilogue for complete details.)

1999

Wednesday, December 29   According to plans announced in April 1998, the South African–built *Titanic* replica will launch today.

2002

Wednesday, April 10   The $500 million replica of the *Titanic*, built by a Swiss-U.S. partnership called White Star Ltd. is scheduled to launch from Southampton.

3

LAST MEALS

Dining on the *Titanic*

On the night of the wreck our dinner tables were a
picture! The huge bunches of grapes which topped the
fruit baskets on every table were thrilling . . . I stayed at
table from soup to nuts.

—second-class passenger Kate Buss

If you were traveling on the *Titanic*, which class of passage do you think
you would have been able to afford? Would you go for a first-class ticket
at a high of $4,350 (over $100,000 in 1997 dollars), a third-class ticket
at a low of $36.25 ($700 today), or a second-class ticket somewhere in
between?

Accommodations aboard the *Titanic* reflected the price of the passage,
and yet, everything on the *Titanic* was, in a sense, first class. Third-class
steerage passengers were reportedly amazed by the comfortable surround-
ings and excellent meals even they were entitled to. In the 1997 film
Titanic, director James Cameron has Leonardo DiCaprio's character, Jack,
acknowledge *Titanic*'s superb accommodations; this was in the exchange
between Rose's mother and Jack, which takes place at the first-class dinner
Jack was invited to as "payment" for rescuing Rose. In an attempt to
embarrass him, Ruth asks Jack what he thinks of the accommodations in
"steerage" (which she says with barely-concealed disdain). Jack responds
graciously that they're the nicest he's ever seen: "Hardly any rats."

This chapter reproduces the menus for all three classes of *Titanic*'s
passengers. For many onboard, a dish from one of these menus was the
last meal they would ever enjoy.

The *Titanic* 1st Class Breakfast Menu From April 11, 1912

BAKED APPLES	FRESH FRUIT	STEWED PRUNES
QUAKER OATS	BOILED HOMINY	PUFFED RICE

FRESH HERRING

FINDON HADDOCK   SMOKED SALMON

GRILLED MUTTON KIDNEYS & BACON

GRILLED HAM   GRILLED SAUSAGE

LAMB COLLOPS   VEGETABLE STEW

FRIED, SHIRRED, POACHED & BOILED EGGS

PLAIN & TOMATO OMELETTES TO ORDER

SIRLOIN STEAK & MUTTON CHOPS TO ORDER

MASHED, SAUTÉ & JACKET POTATOES

COLD MEAT

VIENNA & GRAHAM ROLLS

SODA & SULTAN SCONES   CORN BREAD

BUCKWHEAT CAKES

BLACK CURRANT CONSERVE   NARBONNE HONEY

OXFORD MARMALADE

WATERCRESS

THE *TITANIC* 1ST CLASS LUNCHEON MENU FROM APRIL 14, 1912

LUNCHEON

CONSOMMÉ FERMIER   COCKIE LEEKIE

FILLETS OF BRILL

EGG A L'ARGENTEUIL

CHICKEN A LA MARYLAND

CORNED BEEF, VEGETABLES, DUMPLINGS

From the Grill

GRILLED MUTTON CHOPS

MASHED, FRIED & BAKED JACKET POTATOES

CUSTARD PUDDING

APPLE MERINGUE   PASTRY

BUFFET

SALMON MAYONNAISE   POTTED SHRIMPS

NORWEGIAN ANCHOVIES   SOUSED HERRINGS

PLAIN & SMOKED SARDINES

ROAST BEEF

ROUND OF SPICED BEEF

VEAL & HAM PIE

VIRGINIA & CUMBERLAND HAM

BOLOGNA SAUSAGE   BRAWN

GALANTINE OF CHICKEN

CORNED OX TONGUE

LETTUCE   BEETROOT   TOMATOES

CHEESE

CHESHIRE, STILTON, GORGONZOLA, EDAM

CAMAMEBERT, ROQUEFORT, ST. IVEL,

CHEDDAR

ICED DRAUGHT MUNICH LAGER BEER 3D & 6D A TANKARD

The *Titanic* 1st Class Dinner Menu From April 14, 1912

HORS D'OEUVRE VARIÈS

OYSTERS

CONSOMMÉ OLGA   CREAM OF BARLEY

SALMON, MOUSSELINE SAUCE, CUCUMBER

FILET MIGNONS LILI

SAUTÉ OF CHICKEN, LYONNAISE

VEGETABLE MARROW FARCIE

LAMB, MINT SAUCE

ROAST DUCKLING, APPLE SAUCE

SIRLOIN OF BEEF   CHATEAU POTATOES

GREEN PEAS   CREAMED CARROTS

BOILED RICE

PARMENTIER & BOILED NEW POTATOES

PUNCH ROMAINE

ROAST SQUAB & CRESS

COLD ASPARAGUS VINAIGRETTE

PÂTÉ DE FOIE GRAS

CELERY

WALDORF PUDDING

PEACHES IN CHARTREUSE JELLY

CHOCOLATE & VANILLA ECLAIRS

FRENCH ICE CREAM

THE *TITANIC* 2ND CLASS BREAKFAST MENU FROM APRIL 11, 1912

❖

FRUIT

ROLLED OATS   BOILED HOMINY

FRESH FISH

YARMOUTH BLOATERS

GRILLED OX KIDNEYS & BACON

AMERICAN DRY HASH AU GRATIN

GRILLED SAUSAGE, MASHED POTATOES

GRILLED HAM & FRIED EGGS

FRIED POTATOES

VIENNA & GRAHAM ROLLS

SODA SCONES

BUCKWHEAT CAKES, MAPLE SYRUP

CONSERVE   MARMALADE

TEA   COFFEE

WATERCRESS

❖

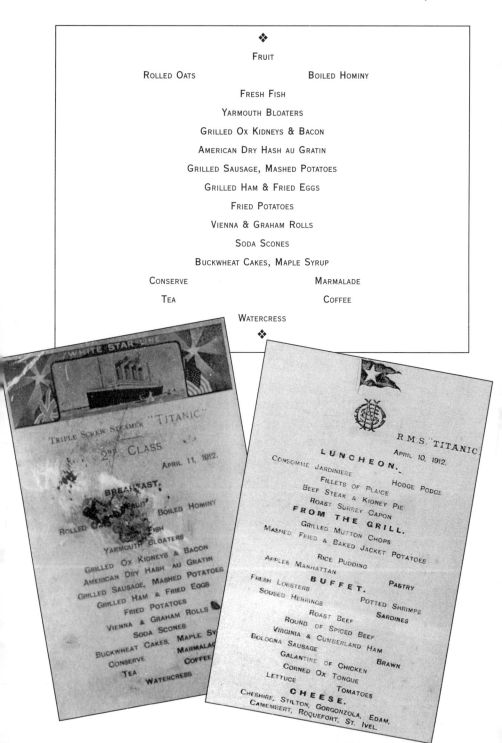

THE *TITANIC* 2ND CLASS DINNER MENU FROM APRIL 14, 1912

CONSOMME TAPIOCA

BAKED HADDOCK, SHARP SAUCE

CURRIED CHICKEN & RICE

SPRING LAMB, MINT SAUCE

ROAST TURKEY, CRANBERRY SAUCE

GREEN PEAS   PUREE TURNIPS

BOILED RICE

BOILED & ROAST POTATOES

PLUM PUDDING

WINE JELLY   COCOANUT SANDWICH

AMERICAN ICE CREAM

NUTS ASSORTED

FRESH FRUIT

CHEESE BISCUITS

COFFEE

WHITE STAR LINE
Specimen Third Class Bill of Fare
Subject to Alteration as Circumstances Require

	Sunday	Monday	Tuesday	Wednesday	Thursday	Friday	Saturday
Breakfast	Quaker Oats and Milk Smoked Herrings and Jacket Potatoes Boiled Eggs Fresh Bread and Butter Marmalade, Swedish Bread Tea and Coffee	Oatmeal Porridge and Milk Irish Stew Broiled Sausages Fresh Bread and Butter Marmalade, Swedish Bread Tea and Coffee	Oatmeal Porridge and Milk Ling Fish, Egg Sauce Fried Tripe and Onions Jacket Potatoes Fresh Bread and Butter Marmalade, Swedish Bread Tea and Coffee	Quaker Oats and Milk Smoked Herrings Beefsteak and Onions Jacket Potatoes Fresh Bread and Butter Marmalade, Swedish Bread Tea and Coffee	Oatmeal Porridge and Milk Liver and Bacon Irish Stew Fresh Bread and Butter Marmalade, Swedish Bread Tea and Coffee	Quaker Oats and Milk Smoked Herrings Jacket Potatoes Curried Beef and Rice Fresh Bread and Butter Fresh Bread and Butter Bread Tea and Coffee	Oatmeal Porridge and Milk Fried Tripe and Onions Fresh Bread and Butter Marmalade, Swedish Bread Tea and Coffee
Dinner	Vegetable Soup Roast Pork, Sage and Onions Green Peas Boiled Potatoes Cabin Biscuits, Fresh Bread Plum Pudding, Sweet Sauce Oranges Ragout of Beef, Pota- toes and Pickles Apricots	Barley Broth Beefsteak and Kidney Pie Carrots and Turnips Boiled Potatoes Cabin Biscuits, Fresh Bread Stewed Apples and Rice	Pea Soup Fricassee Rabbit and bacon Lima Beans, Boiled Po- tatoes Cabin Biscuits, Fresh Bread Semolina Pudding Apples	Rice Soup Corned Beef and Cab- bage Boiled Potatoes Cabin Biscuits, Fresh Bread Peaches and Rice	Vegetable Soup Boiled Mutton and Caper Sauce Green Peas, Boiled Po- tatoes Cabin Biscuits, Fresh Bread Plum Pudding, Sweet Sauce	Pea Soup Ling Fish, Egg Sauce Cold Beef and Pickles Cabbage, Boiled Po- toes Cabin Biscuits, Fresh Bread Cerealine Pudding Oranges	Soup and Brown Gravy Boiled Po- tatoes Cabin Biscuits, Fresh Bread Rabbit Pie Baked Potatoes Fresh Bread and Butter Rhubarb and Ginger Jam Swedish Bread. Tea
Tea	Fresh Bread and Butter Currant Buns Tea	Curried Mutton and Rice Cheese and Pickles Fresh Bread and Butter Damson Jam Swedish Bread Tea	Haricot Mutton Pickles Prunes and Rice Fresh Bread and Butter Swedish Bread Tea	Brawn Cheese and Pickles Fresh Bread and Butter Rhubarb Jam Currant Buns Tea	Sausage and Mashed Potatoes Dry Hash Apples and Rice Fresh Bread and Butter Swedish Bread Tea	Cod Fish Cakes Cheese and Pickles Fresh Bread and Butter Plum and Apple Jam Swedish Bread Tea	

Fresh Fish served as substitute for Salt Fish as opportunity offers

SUPPER—Every Day.—Cabin Biscuits and Cheese.   Gruel, Coffee.

Kosher Meat Supplied and Cooked for Jewish Passengers as desired

A TYPICAL WHITE STAR LINE 3RD CLASS BILL OF FARE

Subject to Alteration as Circumstances Require

	Breakfast	Dinner	Tea
SUNDAY	Quaker Oats and Milk Smoked Herrings and Jacket Potatoes Boiled Eggs Fresh Bread and Butter Marmalade, Swedish Bread Tea and Coffee	Vegetable Soup Roast Pork, Sage, and Onions Green Peas Boiled Potatoes Cabin Biscuits, Fresh Bread Plum Pudding, Sweet Sauce Oranges	Ragout of Beef, Potatoes, and Pickles Apricots Fresh Bread and Butter Currant Buns Tea
MONDAY	Oatmeal Porridge and Milk Irish Stew Broiled Sausages Fresh Bread and Butter Marmalade, Swedish Bread Tea and Coffee	Barley Broth Beefsteak and Kidney Pie Carrots and Turnips Boiled Potatoes Cabin Biscuits, Fresh Bread Stewed Apples and Rice	Curried Mutton and Rice Cheese and Pickles Fresh Bread and Butter Damson Jam Swedish Bread Tea
TUESDAY	Oatmeal Porridge and Milk Ling Fish, Egg Sauce Fried Tripe and Onions Jacket Potatoes Fresh Bread and Butter Marmalade, Swedish Bread Tea and Coffee	Pea Soup Fricasee Rabbit and Bacon Lima Beans, Boiled Potatoes Cabin Biscuits, Fresh Bread Semolina Pudding Apples	Haricot Mutton Pickles Prunes and Rice Fresh Bread and Butter Swedish Bread Tea

	Breakfast	Dinner	Tea
WEDNESDAY	Quaker Oats and Milk Smoked Herrings Beefsteak and Onions Jacket Potatoes Fresh Bread and Butter Marmalade, Swedish Bread Tea and Coffee	Rice Soup Corned Beef and Cabbage Boiled Potatoes Cabin Biscuits, Fresh Bread Peaches and Rice	Brawn Cheese and Pickles Fresh Bread and Butter Rhubarb Jam Currant Buns Tea
THURSDAY	Oatmeal Porridge and Milk Liver and Bacon Irish Stew Fresh Bread and Butter Marmalade, Swedish Bread Tea and Coffee	Vegetable Soup Boiled Mutton and Caper Sauce Green Peas, Boiled Potatoes Cabin Biscuits, Fresh Bread Plum Pudding, Sweet Sauce	Sausage and Mashed Potatoes Dry Hash Apples and Rice Fresh Bread and Butter Swedish Bread Tea
FRIDAY	Quaker Oats and Milk Smoked Herrings Jacket Potatoes Curried Beef and Rice Fresh Bread and Butter Marmalade, Swedish Bread Tea and Coffee	Pea Soup Ling Fish, Egg Salad Cold Beef and Pickles Cabbage, Boiled Potatoes Cabin Biscuits, Fresh Bread Cerealine Pudding Oranges	Cod Fish Cakes Cheese and Pickles Fresh Bread and Butter Plum and Apple Jam Swedish Bread Tea
SATURDAY	Oatmeal Porridge and Milk Vegetable Stew Fried Tripe and Onions Fresh Bread and Butter Marmalade, Swedish Bread Tea and Coffee	Bouillon Soup Roast Beef and Brown Gravy Green Beans, Boiled Potatoes Cabin Biscuits, Fresh Bread Prunes and Rice	Rabbit Pie Baked Potatoes Fresh Bread and Butter Rhubarb and Ginger Jam Swedish Bread Tea

SUPPER—Every Day—Cabin Biscuits and Cheese. Gruel, Coffee.
Fresh Fish served as substitute for Salt Fish as opportunity offers.
Kosher Meat Supplied and Cooked for Jewish Passengers as desired.

The Complete *Titanic* Foodstuffs Inventory

> The food was superb: caviar, lobster, quail from Egypt,
> plover's eggs, and hothouse grapes and fresh peaches. The
> night was cold and clear, the sea like glass.
>
> —first-class passenger Mahala Douglas

R.M.S *Titanic* carried food for a multitude, and the meals served aboard
the ship were one of her most memorable attractions. In many cases,
Titanic's second-class meals were equivalent to what other ships served
to their first-class passengers.

This is a listing of the foodstuffs the *Titanic* carried with her: As you'll
see, in order to prepare and serve close to 6,500 meals a day, *Titanic*'s
pre-sailing "shopping list" was, indeed, quite impressive. (See the section
on the *Titanic*'s first-, second-, and third-class menus.)

Meat, Poultry, and Fish

Fresh meat	75,000 lbs.	Poultry and game	25,000 lbs.
Fresh fish	11,000 lbs.	Sausages	2,500 lbs.
Salt and dried fish	4,000 lbs.	Sweetbreads	1,000
Bacon and ham	7,500 lbs.		

Dairy

Fresh eggs	40,000	Fresh cream	1,200 qts.
Ice cream	1,750 qts.	Condensed milk	600 gallons
Fresh milk	1,500 gallons	Fresh butter	6,000 lbs.

Beverages

Coffee	2,200 lbs.	Wines	1,500 bottles
Tea	800 lbs.	Spirits	850 bottles
Beer and stout	20,000 bottles	Mineral waters	15,000 bottles

Fruits and Vegetables

Oranges	36,000	Tomatoes	2 ¾ tons
Lemons	16,000	Fresh asparagus	800 bundles
Grapes	1,000 lbs.	Fresh green peas	2,250 lbs.
Grapefruit	50 boxes	Onions	3,500 lbs.
Lettuce	7,000 heads	Potatoes	40 tons

Dry Goods

Rice, dried beans, etc.	10,000 lbs.	Flour	200 barrels
Cereals	10,000 lbs.		

Sugar and Preserves

Sugar	10,000 lbs.	Jams and marmalade	1,120 lbs.

THE COMPLETE *TITANIC* TABLEWARE AND LINENS INVENTORY

Tableware

Asparagus tongs	400	Dinner plates	12,000
Beef tea cups	3,000	Dinner spoons	5,000
Beef tea dishes	3,000	Egg spoons	2,000
Breakfast cups	4,500	Entrée dishes	400
Breakfast plates	2,500	Finger bowls	1,000
Breakfast saucers	4,500	Fish forks	1,500
Butter dishes	400	Fish knives	1,500
Butter knives	400	Flower vases	500
Celery glasses	300	Fruit dishes	400
Champagne glasses	1,500	Fruit forks	1,500
Claret jugs	300	Fruit knives	1,500
Cocktail glasses	1,500	Grape scissors	100
Coffee cups	1,500	Ice cream plates	5,500
Coffeepots	1,200	Liqueur glasses	1,200
Coffee saucers	1,500	Meat dishes	400
Cream jugs	1,000	Mustard spoons	1,500
Crystal dishes	1,500	Nut crackers	300
Cut glass tumblers	8,000	Oyster forks	1,000
Dessert plates	2,000	Pie dishes	1,200
Dessert spoons	3,000	Pudding dishes	1,200
Dinner forks	8,000	Salad bowls	500

Salt shakers	2,000	Tea saucers	3,000
Salt spoons	1,500	Teapots	1,200
Soufflé dishes	1,500	Teaspoons	6,000
Soup plates	4,500	Toast racks	400
Sugar basins	400	Vegetable dishes	400
Sugar tongs	400	Water bottles	2,500
Table and dessert knives	8,000	Wine glasses	2,000
Tea cups	3,000		

Linens

Aprons	4,000	Glass cloths	2,000
Bath towels	7,500	Lavatory towels	8,000
Bed covers	3,600	Miscellaneous items	40,000
Blankets	7,500	Pantry towels	6,500
Cooks' cloths	3,500	Pillow slips	15,000
Counterpanes [Bedspreads]	3,000	Roller towels	3,500
Double sheets	3,000	Single sheets	15,000
Eiderdown quilts	800	Table napkins	45,000
Fine towels	7,500	Tablecloths	6,000

CALLING FOR HELP

The Complete Transcripts of the Seventy *Titanic* Marconigrams as Reported in the July 30, 1912, British Board of Trade Inquiry's "Report on the Loss of the *Titanic*"

This chapter consists of the complete replies to questions 18a through 18g of the British Board of Trade Inquiry's "Report on the Loss of the *Titanic*." It is a complete accounting of the seventy *Titanic*-related Marconigrams sent the night the *Titanic* foundered as outlined in the report. (See chapter 8 for a look at questions 1 through 17, and 19 through 26, as reported in the lord chancellor's report.)

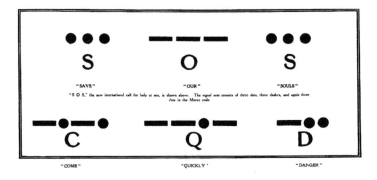

18. (a) What messages for assistance were sent by the "Titanic" after the casualty and, at what times respectively? (b) What messages were received by her in response, and at what times respectively? (c) By what vessels were the messages that were sent by the "Titanic" received, and from what vessels did she receive answers? (d) What vessels other than the "Titanic" sent or received messages at or shortly after the casualty in connection with such casualty? (e) What were the vessels that sent or received such messages? (f) Were any vessels prevented from going to the assistance of the "Titanic" or her boats owing to messages received from the "Titanic" or owing to any erroneous messages being sent or received? (g) In regard to such erroneous messages, from what vessels were they sent and by what vessels were they received and at what times respectively?

    (a) (b) (c) (d) and (e) are answered together.
    (f) Several vessels did not go owing to their distance.
    (g) There were no erroneous messages.

New York Time.	"Titanic" Time (Approx.)		Communications.
10-25 p.m.	12-15 a.m.	...	"La Provence" receives "Titanic" distress signals.
10-25 p.m.	12-15 a.m.	...	"Mount Temple" heard "Titanic" sending C.Q.D. Says require assistance. Gives position. Cannot hear me. Advise my Captain his position 41.46 N. 50.24 W.
10-25 p.m.	12-15 a.m.	...	Cape Race hears "Titanic" giving position on C.Q.D. 41.44 N. 50.24 W.
10-28 p.m.	12-18 a.m.	...	"Ypiranga" hears C.Q.D. from "Titanic." "Titanic" gives C.Q.D. here. Position 41.44 N., 50.24 W. Require assistance (calls about 10 times).
10-35 p.m.	12-25 a.m.	...	C.Q.D. call received from "Titanic" by "Carpathia." "Titanic" said "Come at once. We have struck a berg. It's a C.Q.D. O.M. Position 41.46 N. 50.14 W."
10-35 p.m.	12-25 a.m.	...	Cape Race hears M.G.Y. ("Titanic") give corrected position 41.46 N. 50.14 W. Calling him, no answer.

New York Time.	"Titanic" Time (Approx.)		Communications.
10·36 p.m.	12·26 a.m.	...	M.G.Y. ("Titanic") says C.Q.D. Here corrected position 41.46 N., 50.14 W. Require immediate assistance. We have collision with iceberg. Sinking. Can nothing hear for noise of steam. Sent about 15 to 20 times to "Ypiranga."
10·37 p.m.	12.27 a.m.	...	"Titanic" sends following: "I require assistance immediately. Struck by iceberg in 41.46 N. 50.14 W."
10·40 p.m.	12·30 a.m.	...	"Titanic" gives his position to "Frankfurt," and says, "Tell your Captain to come to our help. We are on the ice."
10·40 p.m.	12·30 a.m.	...	"Caronia" sent C.Q. message to M.B.C. "Baltic" and C.Q.D.: M.G.Y. ("Titanic") struck iceberg, require immediate assistance.
10·40 p.m.			"Mount Temple" hears M.G.Y. ("Titanic") still calling C.Q.D. Our Captain reverses ship. We are about 50 miles off.
10·46 p.m.	12·26 a.m.	...	D.K.F. ("Prinz Friedrich Wilhelm") calls M.G.Y. ("Titanic") and gives position at 12 a.m. 39.47 N. 50.10 W. M.G.Y. ("Titanic") says, "Are you coming to our?" D.F.T. ("Frankfurt") says, "What is the matter with u?" M.G.Y. ("Titanic") "We have collision with iceberg. Sinking. Please tell Captain to come." D.F.T. ("Frankfurt") says, "O.K. will tell?"
10·48 p.m.	12·38 a.m.	...	"Mount Temple" hears "Frankfurt" give M.G.Y. ("Titanic") his position 39.47 N. 52.10 W.
10·55 p.m.	12·45 a.m.	...	"Titanic" calls "Olympic" S.O.S.
11· 0 p.m.	12·50 a.m.	...	"Titanic" calls C.Q.D. and says, "I require immediate assistance. Position 41.46 N. 50.14 W." Received by "Celtic."
11· 3 p.m.	12·53 a.m.	...	"Caronia" to M.B.C. ("Baltic") and S.O.S., "M.G.Y. ("Titanic") C.Q.D. in 41.46 N., 50.14 W. Wants immediate assistance."
11·10 p.m.	1·0 a.m.	...	M.G.Y. gives distress signal. D.D.C. replies. M.G.Y.'s position 41.46 N., 50.14 W. Assistance from D.D.C. not necessary as M.K.C. shortly afterwards answers distress call.
11·10 p.m.	1·0 a.m.	...	"Titanic" replies to "Olympic" and gives his position as 41.46 N., 50.14 W., and says, "We have struck an iceberg."
11·12 p.m.	1·2 a.m.	...	"Titanic" calls "Asian" and said, "Want immediate assistance." "Asian" answered at once and received "Titanic's" position as 41.46 N., 50.14 W., which he immediately takes to the bridge. Captain instructs operator to have "Titanic's" position repeated.
11·12 p.m.	1·2 a.m.	...	"Virginian" calls "Titanic" but gets no response. Cape Race tells "Virginian" to report to his Captain the "Titanic" has struck iceberg and requires immediate assistance.
11·20 p.m.	1·10 a.m.	...	"Titanic" to M.K.C. ("Olympic"), "We are in collision with berg. Sinking Head down. 41.46 N., 50.14 W. Come soon as possible."
11·20 p.m.	1·10 a.m.	...	"Titanic" to M.K.C. ("Olympic"), Captain says, "Get your boats ready. What is your position?"
11·25 p.m.	1·15 a.m.	...	"Baltic" to "Caronia," "Please tell 'Titanic' we are making towards her."
11·30 p.m.	1·20 a.m.	...	"Virginian" hears M.C.E. (Cape Race) inform M.G.Y. ("Titanic") "that we are going to his assistance. Our position 170 miles N. of 'Titanic.'"

New York Time.	"Titanic" Time (Approx.)		Communications.
11-35 p.m.	1-25 a.m.	...	"Caronia" tells "Titanic," "'Baltic' coming to your assistance."
11-35 p.m.	1-25 a.m.	...	"Olympic" sends position to "Titanic" 4-24 a.m. G.M.T. 40.52 N., 61.18 W. "Are you steering southerly to meet us?" "Titanic" replies, "We are putting the women off in the boats."
11-35 p.m.	1-25 a.m.	...	"Titanic" and "Olympic" work together.
11-37 p.m.	1-27 a.m.	...	M.G.Y. ("Titanic") says, "We are putting the women off in the boats."
11-40 p.m.	1-30 a.m.	...	"Titanic" tells "Olympic," "We are putting passengers off in small boats."
11-45 p.m.	1-35 a.m.	...	"Olympic" asks "Titanic" what weather he had. "Titanic" replies, "Clear and calm."
11-45 p.m.	1-35 a.m.	...	"Baltic" hears "Titanic" say "Engine room getting flooded."
11-45 p.m.	1-35 a.m.	...	"Mount Temple" hears D.F.T. ("Frankfurt") ask "are there any boats around you already?" No reply.
11-47 p.m.	1-37 a.m.	...	"Baltic" tells "Titanic," "We are rushing to you."
11-50 p.m.	1-40 a.m.	...	"Olympic" to "Titanic," "Am lighting up all possible boilers as fast as can."
11-50 p.m.	1-40 a.m.	...	Cape Race says to "Virginian": "Please tell your Captain this: "The 'Olympic' is making all speed for 'Titanic,' but his ('Olympic's') position is 40.32 N., 61.18 W. You are much nearer to 'Titanic.' The 'Titanic' is already putting women off in the boats, and he says the weather there is calm and clear. The 'Olympic' is the only ship we have heard say, "Going to the assistance of the 'Titanic.' The others must be a long way from the 'Titanic.'"
11-55 p.m.	1-45 a.m.	...	Last signals heard from "Titanic" by "Carpathia," "Engine-room full up to boilers."
11-55 p.m.	1-45 a.m.	...	"Mount Temple" hears D.F.T. ("Frankfurt") calling M.G.Y. ("Titanic"). No reply.
11-57 p.m.	1-47 a.m.	...	"Caronia" hears M.G.Y. ("Titanic") though signals unreadable still.
11-58 p.m.	1-48 a.m.	...	"Asian" heard "Titanic" call S.O.S. "Asian" answers "Titanic" but receives no answer.
Midnight.	1-50 a.m.	...	"Caronia" hears "Frankfurt" working to "Titanic." "Frankfurt" according to position 172 miles from M.G.Y. ("Titanic") at time first S.O.S. sent out.
12-5 a.m.	1-55 a.m.	...	Cape Race says to "Virginian" "we have not heard 'Titanic' for about half an hour. His power may be gone."
12-10 a.m.	2-0 a.m.	...	"Virginian" hears "Titanic" calling very faintly, his power being greatly reduced.
12-20 a.m.	2-10 a.m.	...	"Virginian" hears 2 v's signalled faintly in spark similar to "Titanic's" probably adjusting spark.
12-27 a.m.	2-17 a.m.	...	"Virginian" hears "Titanic" call C.Q., but unable to read him. "Titanic's" signals end very abruptly as power suddenly switched off. His spark rather blurred or ragged. Called M.G.Y. ("Titanic") and suggested he should try emergency set, but heard no response.
12-30 a.m.	2-20 a.m.	...	"Olympic," his sigs. strong, asked him if he had heard anything about M.G.Y. ("Titanic") he says, No. Keeping strict watch, but hear nothing more from M.G.Y. ("Titanic"). No reply from him.

New York Time.		Communications.
12-52 a.m.		This was the official time the "Titanic" foundered in 41.46 N., 50.14 W. as given by the "Carpathia" in message to the "Olympic"; about 2-20 a.m.
1-15 a.m.	...	"Virginian" exchanges signals "Baltic." He tries send us M.S.G. for M.G.Y. ("Titanic"), but his signals died utterly away.
1-25 a.m.	...	Mount Temple hears M.P.A. ("Carpathia") send, "If you are there we are firing rockets."
1-35 a.m.	...	"Baltic" sent 1 M.S.G. to "Virginian" for "Titanic."
1-40 a.m.	...	M.P.A. ("Carpathia") calling M.G.Y. ("Titanic").
1-58 a.m.	...	S.B.A. ("Birma") thinks he hears "Titanic" so sends, "Steaming full speed for you. Shall arrive you 6-0 in morning. Hope you are safe. We are only 50 miles now."
2-0 a.m. ...	...	M.P.A. ("Carpathia") calling M.G.Y. ("Titanic").
2-0 a.m. ...	...	Have not heard "Titanic" since 11-50 p.m. Received from "Ypiranga."
2-28 a.m.	...	"La Provence" to "Celtic," "Nobody has heard the "Titanic" for about 2 hours."
3-24 a.m.	...	S.B.A. ("Birma") says we are 30 miles S.W. off "Titanic."
3-35 a.m....	...	"Celtic" sends message to "Caronia" for the "Titanic." "Caronia" after trying for two hours to get through to the "Titanic" tells the "Celtic" impossible to clear his message to "Titanic." "Celtic" then cancels message.
3-45 a.m....	...	"Californian" exchanges signals with M.L.Q. (Mount Temple). He gave position of "Titanic."
4-10 a.m...	...	"Californian" receives M.S.G. from M.G.N ("Virginian").
5-5 a.m. ...	...	"Baltic" signals M.P.A. ("Carpathia").
5-40 a.m....	...	"Parisian" hears weak signals from M.P.A. ("Carpathia") or some station saying "Titanic" struck iceberg. "Carpathia" has passengers from lifeboats.
5-40 a.m....	...	"Olympic Tr Asian," with German oil tank in tow for "Halifax" asked what news of M.G.Y. ("Titanic"). Sends service later saying heard M.G.Y. ("Titanic") v. faint wkg. C. Race up to 10.0 p.m., local time. Finished calling S.O.S. midnight.
6-5 a.m. ...	...	"Parisian" exchanges TRs "Virginian" O.K. nil. Informed Captain Haines what I heard passing between ships regarding "Titanic," and he decided not to return as M.P.A. ("Carpathia") was there, and "Californian" was 50 miles astern of us but requested me to stand by in case required.
6-45 a.m....	...	Mount Temple hears M.P.A. ("Carpathia") report rescued 20 boat loads.
7-7 a.m. ...	...	"Baltic" sends following to "Carpathia": "Can I be of any assistance to you as regards taking some of the passengers from you? Will be in position about 4-30. Let me know if you alter your position."
7-10 a.m....	...	"Baltic" in communication with M.P.A. ("Carpathia"). Exchanged traffic re passengers, and get instructions to proceed to Liverpool.
7-15 a.m....	...	"Baltic" turns round for Liverpool, having steamed 134 miles W. towards "Titanic."
7-40 a.m....	...	Mount Temple hears M.P.A. ("Carpathia") call C.Q. and say. no need to std. bi him. Advise my Captain, who has been cruising round the icefield with no result. Ship reversed.
7-45 a.m....	...	"Olympic" sent M.S.G. to Owners, New York via Sable Island, saying, "Have not communicated with 'Titanic' since midnight."
7-55 a.m....	...	"Carpathia" replies to "Baltic," "Am proceeding to Halifax or New York full speed. You had better proceed to Liverpool. Have about 800 passengers on board."
8-0 a.m....	...	"Carpathia" to "Virginian": "We are leaving here with all on board about 800 passengers. Please return to your Northern course."

Note: C.Q.D. was the distress signal used before S.O.S. became widely accepted as an international call for aid. *CQ* stood for "all stations attend"; *D* stood for "distress." Also, note the times at which the Marconigrams were sent and the length of time between individual messages. The continual sending and receiving of Morse code messages effectively illustrates the often crazed environment of a wireless room of a distressed ship at sea and attests to the pressure under which wireless operators ceaselessly worked.

THE THIRTY-SIX SHIPS AT SEA ON THE NORTH ATLANTIC THE NIGHT THE *TITANIC* FOUNDERED

Note: Ships in **bold italic** were owned by the *Titanic*'s owner, the International Mercantile Marine Co.

	Ship	Gross Register Tons	Length	Owner	Country of Registry
1.	*Almerian*	2,948	351.5	Leyland	Great Britian
2.	*Amerika*	22,622	669	Hamburg-Amerika	Germany
3.	*Antillian*	5,608	421	Leyland	Great Britain
4.	*Asian*	5,614	421	Leyland	Great Britain
5.	*Athinia*	6,742	420	Hellenic Trans-Atlantic Steam Navigation	Greece
6.	*Baltic*	23,876	709	White Star	Great Britain
7.	*Birma*	4,859	390	Rotterdamsche Lloyd	Holland
8.	*Bruce*	1,553	250.5	Reid Newfoundland	Great Britain
9.	*Californian*	6,223	447.5	Leyland	Great Britain
10.	*Campanello*	9,291	470	H. W. Harding	Great Britain
11.	*Caronia*	19,687	650	Cunard	Great Britain
12.	*Carpathia*	13,603	540	Cunard	Great Britain
13.	*Celtic*	20,904	681	White Star	Great Britain
14.	*Deutschland*	3,710	339	Deutsch-Amerika Petroleum	Germany
15.	*Dora*[1]	2,662	291	H. Schuld	Germany
16.	*Dorothy Baird*[2]	241	118.5	James Baird	Great Britain
17.	*Etonian*	6,438	475.5	Wilson and Furness-Leyland	Great Britain
18.	*Frankfurt*	7,431	?	Norddeutscher Lloyd	Great Britain
19.	*La Provence*	13,753	602	Compagnie General Transatlantique	France

20.	*Memphian*	6,305	400	Leyland	Great Britain
21.	*Mesaba*	6,833	482	Atlantic Transport	Great Britain
22.	*Mount Temple*	8,790	485	Canadian Pacific Railway	Great Britain
23.	*Olympic*	45,323	882.5	White Star	Great Britain
24.	*Parisian*	5,395	441	Allan	Great Britain
25.	*Paula*	2,748	283	Deutsch-Amerika Petroleum	Germany
26.	*Pisa*	4,959	390	Hamburg-Amerika	Germany
27.	*Premier*	374	155	Merritt and Chapman	Great Britain
28.	*President Lincoln*	18,168	599	Hamburg-Amerika	Germany
29.	*Prinz Friedrich Wilhelm*	17,082	455	Norddeutscher Lloyd	Germany
30.	*Rappahannock*	3,884	370	Furness Withy	Great Britain
31.	*Samson*	506	148	Saefaenger Co.	Norway
32.	*Saturnia*	8,611	456	Saturnia Steam Ship Co.[3]	Great Britain
33.	*Traufenfels*	4,699	390	Duetsche Dampfschiffahrt	Germany
34.	*Victorian*	10,635	520	Allan	Great Britain
35.	*Virginian*	10,757	520	Allan	Great Britain
36.	*Ypiranga*	8,103	448	Hamburg-Amerika	Germany

[1]At the time of the *Titanic*'s maiden voyage there were at least a dozen registered small vessels named *Dora*. Over the years, the 291-foot German Schuld vessel *Dora* has been accepted as the vessel on the North Atlantic the night the *Titanic* hit the iceberg.

[2]The Dorothy Baird was a three-masted sailing ship, not a steamship.

[3]The Saturnia Steam Ship Co. was a legal entity created by the Donaldson Brothers of Great Britain.

Also, on Friday, May 3, 1912, the British newspaper The *Daily Sketch* reported that the captain of the British steamer *Kura,* upon arriving in Algiers and learning of the sinking of the *Titanic,* sent a telegram to the Paris paper *Le Journal* in which he said he remembers having glimpsed a large liner through the fog the night the *Titanic* foundered, but that the dense mist prevented him from ascertaining if there was anything wrong with the ship. He also reported having heard the voices of passengers. Not suspecting anything amiss, he concentrated on avoiding the icebergs in the area and continued on his way to Algiers. (Since the *Kura* captain's mention of fog the night the *Titanic* sank is inconsistent with all other reports that the sky was perfectly clear, and because he claimed hearing voices of the passengers, his story must be questioned and even, unfortunately, suspected of being completely fabricated.)

The *Carpathia's* Captain Rostron's Preparations for Receiving the *Titanic* Survivors

> When day broke, I saw the ice I had steamed through during the night. I shuddered, and could only think that some other hand than mine was on that helm during the night.
>
> —Capt. Arthur Rostron of the *Carpathia* to Captain Barr of the *Caronia,* years after his rescue of the *Titanic* survivors

The code of conduct of commanders of ships at sea embodies a standard of behavior and selflessness that is incredibly impressive. To the captain, safeguarding his passengers, crew, and ship come *above everything else,* and all orders given are to serve that tenet—*with no exceptions.*

When Harold Cottam, the *Carpathia's* wireless operator, brought Captain Rostron a message reporting that the new White Star liner *Titanic* had struck an iceberg and was requesting assistance, the captain immediately ordered his ship turned around. His leisurely cruise to the Mediterranean (which had been booked by, among others, honeymooners) was over.

R.M.S. *Titanic* was fifty-eight miles to the northwest of the *Carpathia,* and *Carpathia's* maximum speed was 14 knots. Captain Rostron estimated that he could make the trip in about four hours, but ended up making it in only three and a half, traveling at an astonishing 17½ knots—a speed *Carpathia* would never again achieve.

During the United States Senate hearing into the *Titanic* disaster, Captain Rostron was asked to write out the orders he gave to prepare for *Titanic's* survivors.

The following list (meticulously conceived and remembered) is what Captain Rostron detailed for the Senate subcommittee.

1. English doctor, with assistants, to remain in first-class dining room.
2. Italian doctor, with assistants, to remain in second-class dining room.
3. Hungarian doctor, with assistants, to remain in third-class dining room.

4. Each doctor to have supplies of restoratives, stimulants, and everything to hand for immediate needs of probable wounded or sick.

5. Purser, with assistant purser and chief steward, to receive the passengers, etc., at different gangways, controlling our own stewards in assisting *Titanic* passengers to the dining rooms, etc.; also to get Christian and surnames of all survivors as soon as possible to send by wireless.

6. Inspector, steerage stewards, and master at arms to control our own steerage passengers and keep them out of the third-class dining hall, and also to keep them out of the way and off the deck to prevent confusion.

7. Chief steward: That all hands would be called and to have coffee, etc., ready to serve out to all our crew.

8. Have coffee, tea, soup, etc., in each saloon, blankets in saloons, at the gangways, and some for the boats.

9. To see all rescued cared for and immediate wants attended to.

10. My cabin and all officers' cabins to be given up. Smoke rooms, library, etc., dining rooms, would be utilized to accommodate the survivors.

11. All spare berths in steerage to be utilized for *Titanic*'s passengers, and get all our own steerage passengers grouped together.

12. Stewards to be placed in each alleyway to reassure our own passengers, should they inquire about noise in getting our boats out, etc., or the working of engines.

13. To all I strictly enjoin the necessity for order, discipline, and quietness to avoid all confusion.

14. Chief and first officers: All the hands to be called; get coffee, etc. Prepare and swing out all boats.

15. All gangway doors to be opened.

16. Electric sprays in each gangway and over side.

17. A block with line rove hooked in each gangway.

18. A chair sling at each gangway, for getting up sick or wounded.

19. Boatswains' chairs. Pilot ladders and canvas ash bags to be at each gangway, the canvas ash bags for children.

20. Cargo falls with both ends clear; bowlines in the ends, and bights secured along ship's sides, for boat ropes or to help the people up.

21. Heaving lines distributed along the ship's side, and gaskets handy near gangways for lashing people in chairs, etc.

22. Forward derricks; topped and rigged, and steam on winches; also told off officers for different stations and for certain eventualities.

23. Ordered company's rockets to be fired at 2:45 A.M. and every quarter of an hour after to reassure *Titanic*.

24. As each official saw everything in readiness, he reported to me personally on the bridge that all my orders were carried out, enumerating the same, and that everything was in readiness.

Captain Rostron also ordered his crew to have oil ready in case the sea was choppy around where the *Titanic* foundered. If necessary, the oil could have been poured down *Carpathia*'s sinks and toilets to calm the water immediately surrounding the ship.

In addition to these more than two dozen specific preparatory orders, Captain Rostron also realized that he needed to intensify his lookout or there was a good chance that his ship would suffer the same fate as the *Titanic*. With all the free-floating ice in the area, *Carpathia* could easily hit an iceberg. Rostron added a man to the crow's nest, stationed two men on the bow of the ship, and placed a man on each wing of the bridge—including assigning his second officer, James Bisset, to stand sentinel on the starboard bridge wing. The captain selected men with excellent eyesight and also personally served as a lookout from his vantage point on the bridge.

According to reports, Captain Rostron then prayed silently as the *Carpathia* steamed toward the grave of the *Titanic*. As soon as the *Carpathia* arrived on the scene, her crew began bringing *Titanic*'s passengers aboard, taking their names and class and attending to their needs. Many of the *Carpathia*'s first-class passengers gave up their quarters to the *Titanic* passengers who seemed most in need. Captain Rostron gave up his quarters to Mrs. Astor, Mrs. Widener, and Mrs. Thayer. The last *Titanic* passenger was aboard by 8:30 A.M., and by this time the *Californian* was also on site.

Before leaving the area, Captain Rostron convened a memorial service for the *Titanic*'s victims as *Carpathia* passed over the spot where the *Titanic* went down.

The *Carpathia* was on its way to Europe when it picked up our distress call and came to our rescue, so it was [partly] full of its own passengers. Therefore the 705 extra survivors had no place to sit except in the dining saloons and [on] the decks. The children sat on the floor. I remember we children ate sugar lumps off the dining room table. At night our family slept in the officers' quarters, which were in the bottom of the ship. I didn't like that at all. It scared me to be way down there. There was really nothing to do. Everybody just sat around talking, telling about their experience, and crying. The *Carpathia* passengers were wonderful. They couldn't do enough for us. One lady gave Mother a dress. We wore our coats over our night clothes.

> —Ruth Becker, *Titanic* survivor, twelve years old when the *Titanic* sank

The whole thing was absolutely providential. I will tell you this, that the wireless operator was in his cabin, at the time, not on official business at all, but just simply listening as he was undressing. He was unlacing his boots at the time. He had this apparatus on his ear, and the message came. That was the whole thing. In ten minutes maybe he would have been in bed, and we would not have heard the message.

> —Captain Rostron to the U.S. Senate subcommittee at the *Titanic* hearing

THE LIFEBOATS

The Truth Will Never Be Known

The sound of people drowning is something I cannot
describe to you. And neither can anyone else. It is the
most dreadful sound. And there is a dreadful silence that
follows it.

—Eva Hart, *Titanic* survivor

The title of this chapter refers specifically to the many conflicting reports
about *Titanic*'s lifeboats: when each was launched; who occupied them;
how many survivors were on each; when they were picked up; what happened to them after the rescue; and other unanswered questions. The
British Board of Trade Inquiry tried to answer some of these queries, and
the chart that follows is the result. But some of the facts detailed in the
chart conflict with what was testified to at the U.S. Senate subcommittee hearing, and also with Col. Archibald Gracie's accounting of the
lifeboats in his book, *The Truth About the Titanic* (1913).

The reality is that there *is* no knowable truth when it comes to
Titanic's twenty lifeboats, simply because the confusion, panic, and multiple observers that night contributed to an inevitable distortion of the
actual events that took place between the time the first boat was lowered
(Lifeboat 7 at 12:45 A.M.) until the last lifeboat (Lifeboat 12) was loaded
aboard the *Carpathia* at 8:10 A.M.

There are dozens of books in print about the *Titanic*, and many of them offer details about the lifeboats. Very few of these accounts, however, agree with any of the others. So be it.

We *do* know some things for certain about the lifeboats, though, such as the fact that Fifth Officer Lowe was in charge of Lifeboat 14 and was the only one to go back to look for survivors who might still be alive as they floated in the cold dark sea. We also know that Marconi operator Harold Bride survived atop Collapsible Boat B after it floated off the ship as she foundered. But these stories have been told many, many times and need not be repeated here. Readers interested in these episodes can consult the aforementioned book by Colonel Gracie, or Don Lynch's authoritative *Titanic: An Illustrated History* (1992).

For background, here is the British Board of Trade Inquiry's final findings regarding the lifeboats, followed by a look at some of the contradictory numbers regarding occupants and survivors:

Launch Order	Boat No.	Port or Starboard?	Time	No. of passengers
1	7	Starboard	12:45 A.M.	27
2	5	Starboard	12:55 A.M.	41
3	6	Port	12:55 A.M.	28
4	3	Starboard	1:00 A.M.	50
5	1	Starboard	1:10 A.M.	12
6	8	Port	1:10 A.M.	39
7	10	Port	1:20 A.M.	55
8	9	Starboard	1:20 A.M.	56
9	12	Port	1:25 A.M.	42
10	11	Starboard	1:25 A.M.	70
11	14	Port	1:30 A.M.	63
12	16	Port	1:35 A.M.	56
13	13	Starboard	1:35 A.M.	64
14	15	Starboard	1:35 A.M.	70
15	Englehardt C	Starboard	1:40 A.M.	71
16	2	Port	1:45 A.M.	26
17	4	Port	1:55 A.M.	40
18	Englehardt D	Port	2:05 A.M.	44
19	Englehardt B	Port (floated off)	2:15 A.M.	
20	Englehardt A	Starboard (floated off)	2:15 A.M.	

Total put into the lifeboats according to the British
Board of Trade Inquiry: **854**

The final survivor count was much different, however. In fact, there were *several* reported figures, as shown here (in descending order):

- The number the British Board of Trade Inquiry initially reported as being loaded into the lifeboats: **854**
- The number reported on the official White Star Line list of survivors on April 20, 1912:   **757**
- The final figure reported by the British Board of Trade Inquiry as being saved: **711**
- The number reported by the U.S. Senate *Titanic* Subcommittee: **706**
- The number of *Titanic* survivors *Carpathia* Captain Rostron reported picking up from the lifeboats: **705**
- The number the British Board of Trade Inquiry initially reported (April 25, 1912) as being saved: **703**

Following are two sections that detail the gear that was recovered from *Titanic*'s lifeboats after the rescue, and also the original cost of these items, *and* their salvage value after they were involved in a sinking.

THE CONTENTS OF THE *TITANIC*'S LIFEBOATS
AFTER THE RESCUE

For a short time another *Titanic* lifeboat was towed by ours. My life belt was wet and uncomfortable and I threw it overboard. Fortunately there was no further need of it for the use intended. I regret I did not preserve it as a relic.

—Col. Archibald Gracie, *The Truth About the* Titanic

This is a complete inventory of everything that was found in the thirteen *Titanic* lifeboats after they were unloaded from the *Carpathia* in New York. This listing is from the original four-page schedule prepared on White Star Line stationery on November 27, 1912, by representatives of the C. M. Lane Lifeboat Co. of Brooklyn, New York.

You will note that for each boat, a list of items missing is also included in the inventory schedule. Souvenir hunters descended upon the *Titanic*'s lifeboats as soon as they arrived in New York, and many items were taken off the boats without the White Star Line's permission. It is also quite likely that passengers from both the *Titanic* and the *Carpathia* availed themselves of a souvenir or two from the thirteen *Titanic* lifeboats during the return trip to New York.

Mere days after the sinking, the *Titanic* was already becoming the stuff of legend.

BOAT NO. 1:

5 Oars
1 Fender
1 Catch Anchor
Mast Sail and Rigging
1 Rudder
1 Water Keg
7 Thole Pins

2 Numbers
2 Liverpool Plates
2 Boat Painters

MISSING:

2 Numbers
4 Flags
1 Draft Plate

BOAT NO. 2:

1 Number
1 Sail Cover
8 Life Belts
1 Catch Anchor
1 Dipper
3 Oars
1 Stretcher
1 Water Keg
2 Boat Painters

MISSING:

3 Numbers
4 Flags
2 Names
1 Draft Plate
2 Liverpool Name Plates
No Thole Pins
No Draft Plate

BOAT NO. 3:

Mast Sail and Rigging
8 Oars
1 Boat Hook
1 Rudder
2 Water Kegs
1 Catch Anchor
4 Foot Stretchers
9 Oar Pins
21 Life Belts
1 Wrench
1 Provision Tank
2 Boat Painters

MISSING:

4 Numbers
4 Flags
1 Draft Plate

BOAT NO. 5:

Mast Sail and Rigging
1 Draft Plate
1 Number
1 Rudder
8 Oars
1 Boat Hook
1 Sail Cover
2 Water Kegs
13 Life Belts
1 Catch Anchor
5 Foot Stretchers
1 Provision Tank
27 Oar Pins

MISSING:

4 Flags
3 Numbers
2 Names

BOAT NO. 6:

1 Draft Plate
1 Name
2 Liverpool Plates
1 Boat Hook
1 Catch Anchor
13 Life Belts
2 Water Kegs
5 Oars
1 Rudder
4 Stretchers
4 Flags
4 Numbers
29 Thole Pins
1 Provision Tank
2 Boat Painters

MISSING:

1 Name

BOAT NO. 7:

1 Mast Sail & Rigging
1 Rudder
1 Oil Can
10 Oars
2 Boat Hooks
2 Water Kegs
2 Dippers
19 Life Belts
1 Catch Anchor
21 Thole Pins
4 Foot Stretchers
1 Wrench
1 Draft Plate
3 Numbers
3 Flags
2 Liverpool Name Plates
1 Provision Tank
1 Boat Painter

MISSING:

2 Names
1 Flag
1 Number

BOAT NO. 8:

2 Masts, One Sail and Rigging
2 Liverpool Plates
1 Draft Plate
1 Flag
9 Oars
1 Boat Hook
1 Rudder
2 Water Kegs
1 Dipper
27 Life Belts
1 Catch Anchor
2 Foot Stretchers
21 Thole Pins

1 Lamp
1 Provision Tank
1 Boat Painter

MISSING:

4 Numbers
2 Names
3 Flags

BOAT NO. 9:

1 Mast Sail and Rigging
2 Liverpool Name Plates
11 Oars
2 Boat Hooks
1 Catch Anchor
1 Rudder
5 Stretchers
16 Thole Pins
2 Dippers
2 Water Kegs
29 Life Belts
1 Wrench
1 Provision Tank

MISSING:

2 Names
4 Numbers
4 Flags
1 Draft Plate

BOAT NO. 10:

1 Mast Sail & Rigging
4 Numbers
1 Flag
1 Liverpool Plate
1 Draft Plate
25 Thole Pins
2 Catch Anchors
2 Water Kegs

10 Oars
2 Boat Hooks
1 Rudder
39 Life Belts
6 Foot Stretchers
1 Dipper
1 Provision Tank

MISSING:

3 Flags
1 Liverpool Plate
2 Names

BOAT NO. 11:

1 Mast Sail & Rigging
2 Liverpool Plates
4 Numbers
4 Oars
1 Wrench
2 Water Kegs
32 Life Belts
1 Oil Can
1 Catch Anchor
4 Stretchers
28 Thole Pins
1 Draft Plate
2 Flags
1 Provision Tank
2 Boat Painters

MISSING:

2 Names
2 Flags

BOAT NO. 12:

1 Mast Sail & Rigging
4 Numbers
4 Flags
2 Liverpool Name Plates
1 Draft Plate

23 Thole Pins
1 Catch Anchor
2 Water Kegs
2 Boat Hooks
7 Oars
1 Rudder
1 Dipper
1 Wrench
4 Stretchers
36 Life Belts
1 Provision Tank

MISSING:

2 Names

BOAT NO. 13:

1 Mast Sail & Rigging
4 Numbers
1 Oil Can
1 Rudder
2 Boat Hooks
10 Oars
2 Water Kegs
5 Foot Stretchers
12 Life Belts
1 Catch Anchor
1 Dipper
21 Thole Pins
1 Provision Tank
1 Boat Painter

MISSING:

2 Names
2 Liverpool Plates
4 Flags
1 Draft Plate

BOAT NO. 16:

3 Numbers
1 Mast Sail & Rigging

1 Liverpool Plate
1 Rudder
2 Dippers
15 Thole Pins
2 Water Kegs
10 Oars

2 Boat Hooks
5 Foot Stretchers
1 Wrench
27 Life Belts
1 Provision Tank

ONE COLLAPSIBLE BOAT: S.S. "OCEANIC" [Collapsible A][1]
(NO GEAR)

[1]Note: Because the *Carpathia* only had enough room for fourteen of *Titanic*'s lifeboats, boats 4, 14, 15, and collapsibles A, B, and C were abandoned at sea. On May 13, 1912, Collapsible A was later found adrift with three bodies aboard by the crew of the S.S. *Oceanic* and picked up and returned to New York to join the other *Titanic* lifeboats.

THE C. M. LANE LIFE BOAT CO.'S APPRAISAL
OF THE GEAR RECOVERED FROM THE *TITANIC*'S LIFEBOATS

Tragedy aside, insurance claims became an important element of the post-*Titanic* era, and everyone from survivors to the White Star Line filed claims to collect on their losses. This chart details the postsinking appraised values of the items recovered on the *Titanic*'s lifeboats.

December 18, 1912

	Cost New	Present Value
Oars	1.33 ea.	0.70 ea.
Fender	0.40 ea.	no value
Catch Anchor	3.25 ea.	1.75 ea.
Life Belts	1.00 ea.	.50 ea.
Mast	5.00 ea.	2.85 ea.
Sail	6.30 ea.	4.00 ea.
Yard & Rigging	2.75 ea.	1.50 ea.
Rudder	2.50 ea.	belonged to boats
Water Kegs	2.65 ea.	1.50 ea.
Thole Pins	.34 ea.	belonged to boats
Painters	1.75 ea.	.80 ea.
Sail Covers	.50 ea.	no value
Dippers (bailers)	.50 ea.	.15 ea.
Stretchers	.40 ea.	belonged to boats
Boat Hooks	.75 ea.	.50 ea.
Wrench	.25 ea.	belonged to tanks
Provision Tanks	5.00 ea.	2.50 ea.
Oil Cans	.16 ea.	.16 ea.
Draft Plates	1.15 ea.	belonged to boats
Numbers	.15 ea.	.03 ea.
Flags	1.50 ea.	.12 ea.
Liverpool Plates	1.00 ea.	.18 ea.

6

A *TITANIC* WHO'S WHO

Profiles of *Titanic* Notables, Past and Present

> "Isn't that an iceberg on the horizon, Captain?"
> "Yes, Madam."
> "What if we get in a collision with it?"
> "The iceberg, Madam, will move right along as though
> nothing had happened."
>
> —from *The People, Yes* by Carl Sandburg

The unknown, the famous, the poor, and the wealthy: All were aboard the *Titanic* on her maiden voyage. This chapter looks at some of the memorable people who unknowingly stepped into history the moment they boarded the great liner, as well as those who have made the *Titanic* legend a part of their personal and/or professional lives.

Abbott, Rosa The only *Titanic* passenger who actually went down with the ship and survived. Rosa was a third-class passenger who was on the stern when the ship went under. She was swept off and when she surfaced, she was able to make it to Collapsible A. Rosa remarried in 1914 and moved to Florida, but her whereabouts after 1928 are unknown. (See **William F. Hoyt**, who was also pulled under, but did not survive.)

Andrews, Thomas The managing director of Harland and Wolff and the head of the company's design department. Andrews, perhaps more

73

than any other man, was responsible for the final construction of the *Titanic*.

Andrews was Lord Pirrie's nephew and was a tireless worker who often arrived at the shipyard at four in the morning to begin his workday. Andrews went along on the *Titanic*'s maiden voyage (in First-Class Cabin A36, between the First-Class Smoke Room and the First-Class Lounge) to make a final inspection and note any changes necessary. It wasn't long after departing Southampton that Andrews decided to convert part of the A Deck reading and writing room into more first-class staterooms.

Andrews's secretary once wrote of her boss, "He would [obsess over the placement of] racks, tables, chairs, berth ladders, [and] electric fans, saying that [unless] he saw everything right he could not be satisfied. He was always busy, taking the owners around the ship, interviewing engineers, officials, managers, agents, subcontractors, discussing with principals the plans of new ships, and superintending generally the work of completion."

On the eve of sailing day, Andrews wrote a note to his wife in which he told her, "The *Titanic* is now about complete and will I think do the old Firm credit to morrow when we sail."

On Sunday evening, April 14, 1912, Andrews was so engrossed in studying the *Titanic*'s plans that he did not take notice of the ship's collision with the iceberg. He was subsequently summoned to the bridge and, after a short tour of the ship with Captain Smith, came to the conclusion that the *Titanic* was doomed and that she would sink within two hours at most. He was not far off.

In the time remaining before the ship foundered, Andrews worked diligently to load as many people into lifeboats as possible. He also moved through the ship, opening stateroom doors and instructing people to get into the boats. "Ladies, you must get in at once!" he shouted to one group of hesitant passengers. "There is not a minute to lose! You cannot pick and choose your boat. Don't hesitate. Get in, Get in!"

Even with such stalwart and heroic behavior to his credit, there can be no doubt that Thomas Andrews was operating in a state of utterly devastating shock. The unthinkable had become Thomas Andrews's final reality.

Andrews was last seen by Steward John Stewart in the First-Class

Smoking Room adjacent to his cabin. He was standing dazed in the middle of the room with his arms crossed, staring at a painting called *The Approach to Plymouth Harbor,* which hung above a fireplace. His life belt lay on a card table. Stewart reportedly said to Andrews, "Aren't you even going to try for it, Mr. Andrews?" Andrews did not reply, and that was the last anyone saw of Thomas Andrews, the builder of the *Titanic.* His body was never found.

Asplund, Lillian Gertrude   As of spring 1998, Lillian Asplund was one of the six remaining living *Titanic* survivors. Lillian was born on October 21, 1906, and was five-and-a-half years old when the *Titanic* sailed. She was a third-class passenger and was rescued in Lifeboat 4. She resides in Massachusetts.

Astor, Col. John Jacob   Astor was a real estate millionaire who was traveling on the *Titanic* with his pregnant, eighteen-year-old wife. Astor went down with the *Titanic,* and when his body was found it was covered in soot. Apparently, he had been crushed by the falling forward funnel. His wife Madeline survived. Regarding the accumulation of wealth, Astor had once remarked that "a man who has a million dollars is almost as well off as if he were wealthy." Astor was eulogized as a hero for going down with the ship—after seeing to his pregnant wife's safety.

Astor, Madeline   Colonel Astor's widow. After her husband's death aboard the *Titanic,* Mrs. Astor inherited a $5 million trust fund and the use of his residences on the condition that she never remarry. She eventually relinquished her inheritance in order to marry—and divorce—twice more. She died in Palm Beach, Florida, in 1940 at the age of forty-seven. Some histories report that she committed suicide.

Baclini, Eugenie   The first *Titanic* survivor to die. Lebanese immigrant Baclini was three years old when she was rescued from the *Titanic.* She died the following August from meningitis.

Ballard, Dr. Robert D.   The great nephew of Bat Masterson and the man who found the wreck of *Titanic* in 1986. (See Part IV.)

Beesley, Lawrence   Second-class passenger and *Titanic* survivor who went on to write a bestselling account of the sinking called *The Loss of the S.S. Titanic, Its Story and Its Lessons.* Beesley had been on his way to the United States for a vacation when the *Titanic* sank, and he began jotting down details of that night while still on the *Carpathia* after being rescued.

Boxhall, Joseph   *Titanic*'s fourth officer and the crewman who calculated her position on the night of the collision, wired it to the *Carpathia,* and later testified about having seen a ship in the distance that did not respond to their requests for assistance.

From Boxhall's testimony, it was determined that he had seen the *Californian* and that his calculations fixing their relative positions had been correct. At the U.S. Senate hearing, he told Senator Smith, "When you take stars you always endeavor . . . to take a set of stars. You take two stars for latitude, and two for longtitude, one star north and one star south, one star east and one star west. If you find a big difference between eastern and western stars, you know there is a mistake somewhere. But, as it happened, I think I worked out three stars for latitude and I think I worked out three stars for longtitude [and] they all agreed."

Boxhall, who was twenty-eight at the time of the sinking, ultimately attained a command position with the British Royal Navy but never achieved the rank of captain. He retired from maritime duty in 1940 at the age of fifty-six and, in 1958, at the age of seventy-four, he served as technical adviser on the film adaptation of Walter Lord's bestselling book, *A Night to Remember.*

Boxhall died in 1967 at the age of eighty-three. His ashes were scattered over the site of the *Titanic*'s sinking, near the location—41° 46', 50° 14'—that he was certain he had calculated correctly that terrible night (he did).

Bride, Harold   The only one of the two *Titanic* Marconi operators who made it into one of the lifeboats and survived. Bride told his story to the *New York Times* from the *Carpathia* after being rescued. (See Harold Bride's account of the *Titanic* disaster in chapter 11.)

Brown, Molly   Mrs. J. J. Brown, the nouveau riche Denver mining queen who took charge of Lifeboat 6 and threatened to throw Quartermaster Hitchens overboard when he refused to allow Molly and the other women in the boat to row back to the site of *Titanic*'s sinking to look for survivors in the water. Molly's fearless courage soon became the stuff of legend, and it wasn't long before the sobriquet Unsinkable became attached to her name. In 1932, twenty years after surviving the *Titanic*, Molly Brown died in New York of a stroke at the age of sixty-five. After her death, she became the subject of a hit

Broadway musical and film called—what else?—*The Unsinkable Molly Brown.*

Butt, Maj. Archibald W.   Military aide to President William Howard Taft who was returning to the United States on the *Titanic* after an extended diplomatic and recuperative stay in Italy. Butt was last seen standing quietly on the *Titanic*'s deck at about 2:00 A.M. on the morning of April 15, and he was later remembered for dying bravely and stoically, like the soldier that he was. In a letter sent to his sister-in-law just before the *Titanic* sailed, the major wrote, "If the old ship goes down, you'll find my affairs in shipshape condition."

To some, Colonel Butt quickly became a figure of legend, an almost mythical hero who died saving others. One survivor, first-class passenger Mrs. Dan Marvin, told the media that she saw Colonel Butt on the deck "with an iron bar in his hand beating back the frenzied crowd who were attempting to overcrowd the lifeboats." This version of the last moments before the colonel's demise was more than likely apocryphal, since no one else seemed to recall a scene such as Mrs. Marvin described. Perhaps the most heartfelt assessment of the good colonel, however, may have been the one proferred by an elderly black man who worked at the White House and who had frequent opportunity to come in contact with Colonel Butt. "There goes the man," he once remarked, "that's the highest with the mighty and the lowest with the lowly of any man in the city."

Cameron, James   The writer and director of the $200 million 1997 film *Titanic* that went on to gross well over $1 billion worldwide and become the most successful movie of all time. *Titanic* won eleven Academy Awards in March 1998, including a Best Director Oscar for Cameron.

Cussler, Clive   Author of *Raise the Titanic!*, the 1976 novel that imagined a feverish battle between the United States and Russia to raise the great liner and recover her secret cargo. In 1980, the book was made into a terrible movie that prompted the movie critic for the British newspaper the *Guardian* to write, "the longer it all goes on, the more one hopes that, if they ever do raise the *Titanic,* they'll leave the film overboard to replace it."

Dawson, James   A *Titanic* crew member—a trimmer— who worked in the ship's engine room and who died when the great liner went down.

Dawson's grave is in the Fairview cemetery in Halifax, marked simply "J. Dawson." After James Cameron's *Titanic* was released in 1997, Dawson's grave became a sacred place for teenage girls who believed erroneously that the fictional character of Jack Dawson in the movie (played, of course, by heartthrob Leonardo DiCaprio) was based on the *Titanic* crewman. As soon as it was discovered that there had actually been a J. Dawson on the *Titanic,* his grave was covered daily with flowers, ticket stubs, and other objects of the young female pilgrims' devotion to the spirit of Jack Dawson.

(Note: Many of the 328 bodies recovered from the sea after the *Titanic* foundered were brought to Halifax, Nova Scotia, for either disposition or burial. [Of the 328 recovered, 119 were buried at sea.] After 59 of the remaining 209 bodies were claimed and transported elsewhere for burial, the 150 bodies left were buried in Halifax, divided among three cemeteries: Fairview, which was nonsectarian; Baron de Hirsch cemetery, which was Jewish; and Mount Olivet, which was Roman Catholic. All the bodies were properly embalmed and placed in pine coffins. To this day, the "Titanic" sections of these cemeteries are often frequented by visitors to Nova Scotia, and many of these curious tourists are often moved to tears by the mantralike repetition of the legend carved into each of the 150 stone markers: "Died April 15, 1912.")

Dean, Eliza Gladys Millvina As of spring 1998, Millvina Dean was one of the six living *Titanic* survivors. Millvina was born on February 2, 1912, and was ten weeks old when the *Titanic* sailed. She was a third-class passenger and was rescued in Collapsible Lifeboat C. She resides in England and is a frequent and beloved guest at *Titanic* conventions.

DiCaprio, Leonardo The young male lead of James Cameron's film, *Titanic.* DiCaprio played the fictional steerage passenger Jack Dawson.

Dodge, Dr. Washington *Titanic* survivor who wrote a widely read account of his rescue. (See chapter 15 for the complete text of Dr. Dodge's account.)

Fleet, Frederick The twenty-four-year-old *Titanic* lookout who first spotted the fatal iceberg, shouting out, "Iceberg, right ahead!" After his rescue, Fleet was very vocal about not being given binoculars for the crow's nest, and this made some of the other *Titanic* surviving officers ostracize him in later years. Fleet continued sailing until 1936, when the Great Depression shut down much of the world's sea trade. He then went to work in a Harland and Wolff shipyard until his retirement in 1955. He then sold newspapers ("just to while away the time") on a Southampton street corner until January 10, 1965, when he committed suicide by hanging himself in his garden. His wife Eva had recently died, and shortly thereafter, Eva's brother asked Fleet to move out of the house where he and Eva lived—but which the brother-in-law owned.

Futrelle, Jacques   The "American Arthur Conan Doyle." Futrelle was a popular writer of detective stories, including his well-known "Thinking Machine" tales. He perished in the *Titanic* disaster.

Gibson, Dorothy   The twenty-eight-year-old silent movie star who survived the sinking of the *Titanic* and went on to star in a silent film called *Saved From the Titanic* (a.k.a. *I Survived the Titanic*), the first movie made about the disaster. It was released on May 14, 1912, exactly one month after her rescue. In the film Gibson wore the same dress, sweater, gloves, and black pumps she had been wearing when she was pulled from Lifeboat 7, the first boat launched, making her one of the first people saved.

Saved From the Titanic was filmed aboard the *Titanic*'s sister ship, the *Olympic,* with the name of the ship on both the *Olympic* and her lifeboats erased. The movie presented footage of the *Olympic* being towed into her berth in New York as footage of the *Titanic* being towed from her berth in Southampton.

Saved From the Titanic has been lost and as of this writing no copies have surfaced. Dorothy Gibson died of a heart attack in 1946 in Paris at the age of sixty-two. (See Dorothy Gibson's first-person account of the sinking in chapter 7.)

Gracie, Col. Archibald   First-class passenger and survivor who went on to write a bestselling account of the sinking and his rescue called *The Truth About the Titanic,* which was unfortunately published posthumously. Gracie died in December 1912. (Gracie had earlier written a book of Civil War history called *The Truth About Chickamauga.*) Gracie's *Titanic* book meticulously chronicled the launching and passenger contingents of every one of the *Titanic*'s lifeboats. Gracie was the second of the *Titanic*'s survivors to die. (See **Baclini, Eugenie**, the three-year-old Lebanese immigrant who had died in August 1912 from meningitis.)

Guggenheim, Benjamin   "We're dressed in our best and are prepared to go down like gentlemen," said wealthy industrialist and father of three, Benjamin Guggenhein, as the *Titanic* sank deeper into the icy Atlantic.

Legend has it that Guggenheim and his valet smoked cigars and sipped brandy while awaiting their deaths. (Apparently the dutiful valet did not have much to say about his *own* survival wishes.)

Guggenheim is also reported as having said, "I think there is grave doubt that the men will get off. I am willing to remain and play the man's game if there are not enough boats for more than the women and children. I won't die here like a beast. Tell my wife . . . I played the game out straight and to the end. No woman shall be left aboard this ship because Ben Guggenheim is a coward."

Haisman, Edith Brown   *Titanic* survivor who died on January 23, 1997, at the age of one-hundred. Following the passing of Marjorie Robb in 1992 (at one hundred and three), Brown was known for being the oldest living *Titanic* survivor. Edith was a second-class passenger and fifteen years old when the *Titanic* sailed. At the time of her death, she resided in a nursing home in Southampton, England.

Hart, Eva   *Titanic* survivor who died on February 14, 1996, at the age of ninety-one. Eva was adamantly opposed to the recovering of artifacts from the *Titanic* wreck and often spoke out against RMS Titanic (the company granted sole salvage rights to the wreck—see Part IV) and its salvage operations.

Hartley, Wallace   Accomplished violinist and the director of the *Titanic*'s eight-man orchestra. Hartley's selfless courage and leadership inspired his fellow musicians to continue playing in an attempt to calm the panicked passengers as the *Titanic* sank. Hartley and his bandmates did not survive the sinking. Hartley had been engaged to marry and had actually considered skipping the *Titanic* voyage. He ultimately opted to go in hopes of making contacts among the well-heeled passengers that might result in future work.

The people of Hartley's hometown of Colne, Lancashire, England, erected a memorial in Hartley's honor and forty thousand mourners attended his funeral on Saturday, May 18, 1912. On Friday, May 24, 1912, a memorial concert in honor of the *Titanic* bandsmen was held at the Royal Albert Hall in London. The concert boasted the largest orchestra—over five-hundred musicians—that had ever performed in the Albert Hall. Selections performed included Chopin's *Funeral March* and the program concluded with the ten-thousand members of the audience singing in unison, "Nearer, My God to Thee," the hymn purported to be the last piece played by the band before their deaths. (See chapter 22 for details on the unresolved mystery of the band's final song and the *Titanic* orchestra's complete repertoire.)

Hitchens, Robert   *Titanic*'s quartermaster and the man who was at the wheel when the *Titanic* collided with the iceberg. Hitchens was the helmsman who physically carried out First Officer Murdoch's order, "Hard a-starboard" (which was in response to Frederick Fleet's warning of "Iceberg, right ahead!") and turned *Titanic*'s wheel in an attempt to avoid a head-on collision with the iceberg. Hitchens's action managed to turn *Titanic* 22½ degrees to port (two compass points) but did not prevent the steamer from striking the berg.

Shortly thereafter, on Second Officer Lightoller's orders, Hitchens took charge of Lifeboat 6 (on the port side) but did not do himself proud during the time the boat was in the water.

Major Arthur Peuchen of Canada also boarded Lifeboat 6, and Hitchens immediately began ordering him around in an attempt to confirm and assert his authority over the major. Peuchen then attempted to take charge, ordering Hitchens to turn over the tiller and row, but Hitchens refused.

A few minutes later, Captain Smith, shouting through a megaphone, ordered Hitchens to return for more passengers, and Hitchens, perhaps for the first time in his entire maritime career, disobeyed a direct order from his commanding officer.

"No, we are not going back to the boat," he told the boat's occupants, "It's our lives now, not theirs."

After the *Titanic* sank, the women in Lifeboat 6—which held only twenty-eight passengers in a boat designed for sixty-five—pleaded with Hitchens to go back and try to rescue some people from the water. Hitchens refused, warning them that their boat would be swarmed by the desperate people in the frigid water and that they would all die if they went back. "There's no use going back," he coldly shouted at them, " 'cause there's only a lot of stiffs there." (At the Senate hearing, Senator Smith said that Hitchens was quoted as saying, "We are to look out for ourselves now, and pay no attention to those stiffs.")

One of the women in Lifeboat 6, however, was the "unsinkable"

Molly Brown (as she would come to be known after her rescue), and Molly was a force to be reckoned with. The indomitable Mrs. Brown grabbed the tiller out of Hitchens's hand and ordered the women in the boat (many of whom were eager to find husbands and fathers among the men in the water) to start rowing. When Hitchens stood up and made a move to grab the tiller back from Molly, she warned him that she would, indeed, throw him overboard. Hitchens backed down but started whining that they were doomed and would never survive. When Molly told Hitchens to shut up, he swore at her and was chastised by a stoker for swearing at a woman. This silenced Hitchens, and he made no further attempts to command his fellow lifeboat passengers.

Hitchens testified at the U.S. Senate hearing, and the White Star Line later gave him the position of harbormaster at Cape Town, South Africa.

Two years later, Hitchens reportedly told a British seaman that the White Star Line had paid him off and given him his new job so as to keep him quiet about certain events that took place on the *Titanic*'s bridge the night she sank. What these "events" were has never been disclosed, although Hitchens's testimony before the U.S. Senate appeared forthright.

Don Lynch, in *Titanic: An Illustrated History*, wrote that "it is more likely that the White Star Line didn't know what to do with the man who had steered the *Titanic* into an iceberg. Sailors were notoriously superstitious, and Hitchens, though innocent of any responsibility for the disaster, was probably unwelcome aboard other ships."

Hoyt, William F.   The first man pulled into Lifeboat 14 by Fifth Officer Lowe when he went back looking for people he could save. Hoyt, a lace importer from New York, was a big man and it took quite an effort to pull him into the lifeboat. Hoyt had been dragged under when the *Titanic* sank below the surface, but was eventually released as the ship began to break up on its way toward the bottom. However, Hoyt had been dragged to too deep a depth to survive, and he eventually succumbed before rescuers arrived due to internal injuries caused by the pressure he had been subjected to.

Ismay, J. Bruce   The chairman of the White Star Line and the man who sketched the first plans for the *Titanic* on a dinner napkin at Lord

Pirrie's mansion in 1907. To this day, there are those who feel that Ismay, who left the *Titanic* on one of the last lifeboats, shirked his responsibilities as a gentleman and White Star executive by leaving the ship when there were still hundreds of passengers—many of them women and children—still aboard the ship. Ismay swore that there were no more passengers on the deck when he was offered a place in a lifeboat and, in 1998, Ismay's great-nephew Michael Manser told *People* magazine that his uncle acted honorably on the *Titanic*. Regarding his great-uncle's depiction in the movie *Titanic* (he is portrayed as something of a villain), Manser said it was because they had "to have a baddie in the film."

In 1934, survivor Edith Russell wrote the following in her diary:

> I went out on the boat deck and stood in a direct line of [sight] with Mr. Bruce Ismay . . . He called out, "What are you doing in this boat? I thought all women had already left!" And [then] he cried out, "If there are any women around come over to this staircase at once!" I walked over to Mr. Ismay, who pushed me swiftly down the narrow iron staircase . . . Bruce Ismay certainly saved my life, and I don't doubt that he saved many more.

(See excerpts from Ismay's testimony before the U.S. Senate in chapter 12, followed by his official statement to the British press.)

Japanese Passenger, The   This was the third person pulled into Lifeboat 14 when Fifth Officer Lowe went back to the site of the *Titanic*'s sinking looking for survivors. Because this man was lashed to a door face-down with the water lapping over him, Lowe at first thought he was dead. He said, "What's the use? He's dead, likely, and if he isn't there's others better worth saving than a Jap!" Lowe changed his mind, though, and after the man was pulled aboard the lifeboat, he quickly revived and began rowing with a passion. "By Jove, I'm ashamed of what I said about the little blighter," Lowe then exclaimed, admitting that he would have saved a man like him "six times over if I had the chance!"

Laroche, Louise   As of spring 1998, Louise Laroche was one of the six remaining living *Titanic* survivors. Louise was born on July 2, 1910, and was one year and nine months old when the *Titanic* sailed. She was a second-class passenger and was believed to have been rescued in Collapsible Lifeboat C. She resides in France.

Lightoller, Charles H.   The *Titanic*'s second officer and its senior surviving officer. Lightoller directed the loading of the lifeboats on the port side and was diligent about enforcing the "women and children only" rule of the sea. Lightoller ultimately was sucked under when the *Titanic* sank and was held against the grating of a giant funnel until a rush of expelled hot air threw him clear of the ship and saved his life. Lightoller hung onto a collapsible boat until being rescued and later went on to write an autobiography, *Titanic and Other Ships* (1935), in which he devoted six chapters to his *Titanic* ordeal.

"Lights" defended Bruce Ismay at the U.S. Senate hearing and was subsequently accused of whitewashing the actual events of that night. He later served as a commander with the British Royal Navy during World War I.

After the war, Lightoller became a successful chicken farmer but returned to the sea in World War II when he used his private yacht, the *Sundowner*, to assist in the evacuation of Dunkirk. Lightoller held Captain Smith in very high regard; but believed that Captain Lord of the *Californian* was greatly to blame for the loss of the 1,500 lives that night, and he considered the U.S. Senate hearing "nothing but a complete farce." Lightoller died on December 8, 1952, at the age of seventy-eight.

In his book, when remembering the moments shortly after the *Titanic* sank, Lightoller wrote, "To enter into a description of those heartrending, never-to-be-forgotten sounds would serve no useful purpose. I never allowed my thoughts to dwell on them, and there are some that would be alive and well to-day had they just determined to erase from their minds all memory of those ghastly moments, or at least until time had somewhat dimmed the memory of that awful tragedy."

Lord, Capt. Stanley   Commander of the *Californian*, the ship that, in the words of historian Leslie Reade, "stood still." It seems as though Captain Lord made the conscious decision to not head in the direction of the *Titanic*, thus sealing the fate of over 1,500 of her passengers and crew. To this day, the very vocal "Lordites" defend Captain Lord's actions, but history seems to be judging him much more harshly. (See Captain Lord's U.S. Senate testimony in this chapter.)

Lord, Walter   Renowned *Titanic* authority and author of the best-sellers *A Night to Remember* and *The Night Lives On.*

Lowe, Harold Godfrey   *Titanic*'s fifth officer and the crew member remembered for two dramatic acts as *Titanic* foundered.

First, Lowe was the officer who fired his pistol in the air to prevent men from crowding a lifeboat when there were still women aboard the vessel, and second, Lowe was the only lifeboat commander who went back to the site of the sinking to rescue passengers in the water. He was able to pull from the water four men, one of whom, William Hoyt, died in the lifeboat. The other three pulled from the water were Steward Jack Stewart, a Japanese passenger whose name was never learned, and Steward Alfred Phillmore.

Lowe was also somewhat outspoken and was the officer who told the U.S. Senate that an Italian man had snuck aboard a lifeboat wearing women's clothes. He ultimately apologized to the Italian government. (See below.)

Harold Lowe's Apology to the Italian Government

(presented to The Royal Ambassador of Italy, Signor Cusani, through the secretary of the legal office of the Italian Royal Embassy, Signor Guido di Vincenzo)

This is to certify that I, Harold Godfrey Lowe . . . fifth officer of the late steamship *Titanic,* in my testimony at the Senate of the United States stated that I fired shots to prevent Italian immigrants from jumping into my lifeboats.

I do hereby cancel the word "Italian" and substitute the words "immigrants belonging to the Latin Races." In fact, I do not mean to infer that they were especially Italians, because I could only judge from their general appearance and complexion, and therefore I only meant to imply that they were of the types of the Latin races. In any case, I did not intend to cast any reflections on the Italian nation.

This is the real truth, and therefore I feel honored to give out this present statement.

H. G. Lowe
Fifth Officer late "Titanic."

Washington, D. C., *April 30, 1912*

Lowe is also remembered for another of his responses to Senator Smith at the Senate hearing. When Smith asked him what an iceberg was composed of, Lowe's somewhat impudent answer was "Ice, I suppose, sir."

Lowe's heroism did not serve him well after the sinking of the *Titanic*. He was appointed third officer on the *Medic*, a minor position, and then served as a commander in the Royal Navy during World War I. Lowe then retired to his native Deganwy, Wales, although he did serve in a minor capacity during World War II. He died in May 1944 at the age of sixty-one.

Even though Lowe rarely spoke of his actions during the *Titanic* tragedy, his deeds were remembered, and, in his eulogy, he was honored as "a man who made up his mind what his duty was and did it regardless of personal consequences."

Lynch, Don   World-renowned *Titanic* authority and author of what many consider to be the definitive illustrated book about the great liner, *Titanic: An Illustrated History* (1992). Lynch is the historian for the Titanic Historical Society, and over the two decades he has spent researching the ship, has come to personally know many of the survivors. Lynch writes the "Passenger Manifest" column in each issue of the society's magazine, *The Titanic Commutator*, and was eagerly sought after as a *Titanic* authority on many TV talk shows and documentaries when James Cameron's film *Titanic* was released in December 1997.

Marconi, Guglielmo   Legendary inventor of the wireless communication system. (See Marconi's U.S. Senate testimony in chapter 11 for details on his role in the *Titanic* tragedy.)

Marschall, Ken   Marschall's biography tell us that his "paintings [of the *Titanic*] reflect many years of close study of the ship and are known for their accuracy as well as their artistry." Quite simply, Ken Marschall is the greatest *Titanic* artist to date. His paintings of the ship and the wreck boast a verisimilitude that takes us back to the great vessel in a way existing black-and-white photographs of the ship and images of the wreck simply are incapable of doing. Ken Marschall shows us the *Titanic* in all her glory—and that is how we most want to remember her.

Millet, Francis Davis   Well-known American artist of the time and painter of historical scenes who perished on the *Titanic*. One of his best-known works was "Between Two Fires." In 1998, a British painter named Douglas Edwards told the *Washington Post* that he believed he was the reincarnation of Millet, something he learned during a hypnotic past-life regression session in the mid-1980s. During this session, he told the *Post*, he kept repeating the phrase, "Black water. Don't have a chance." He also revealed that he had been afraid of water since he was a child and that even at an early age, the name *Titanic* upset him. "I know it sounds very absurd, doesn't it?" he said in the article. "After all, you can't see the air, now can you? But it is there."

Morgan, J. P.   American transportation millionaire and owner of the White Star Line, thus making him the owner of the *Titanic*. Morgan had his own first-class suite and promenade deck on the *Titanic* and was booked on her maiden voyage but canceled at the last minute. This raised suspicions for a time, and conspiracy theorists looked to Morgan's cancellation to lend credence to the rumor that the *Titanic* had been switched with the *Olympic* in order to collect the insurance money on *Titanic*'s damaged sister ship (see chapter 24).

   Morgan was at his French chateau during the period following the *Titanic*'s sinking, and when tracked down by a reporter and asked about the financial losses as a result of the loss of the great liner, said, "Oh, someone pays, but there is no such thing as money losses in existence. Think of the lives that have been mowed down and of the terrible deaths." Morgan died in 1913 at the age of seventy-six, leaving an estate valued at $100 million, far less than the world had believed he had been worth.

Navratil, Michel M.   As of spring 1998, Michel Navratil was one of the six remaining living *Titanic* survivors. Michel was born on June 12, 1908, and was three years and ten months old when the *Titanic* sailed. He was a second-class passenger and was rescued in Collapsible Lifeboat D. In 1987, he returned to the United States for a reunion of *Titanic* survivors. This was the first time he had returned to America since his arrival in New York on the *Carpathia* in 1912. A retired professor of psychology, Michel resides in France.

Pellegrino, Charles   Author of the 1988 book, *Her Name, Titanic: The Untold Story of the Sinking and Finding of the Unsinkable Ship.*

Phillimore, Harold   *Titanic* bath attendant and the fourth and final person pulled into Lifeboat 14 when Fifth Officer Lowe went back to the site of the *Titanic*'s sinking to look for survivors.

Robb, Marjorie   *Titanic* survivor who died on June 11, 1992, at the age of one-hundred-three. She was known for being the oldest living *Titanic* survivor at her passing.

Robertson, Morgan   Author of *The Wreck of the Titan, or Futility*, the 1898 novel about the steamship *Titan* that seems to have foretold the *Titanic* tragedy. (See the complete text of *The Wreck of the Titan* in chapter 26.) Robertson also wrote a story about a Japanese aerial attack on a United States base in Hawaii that started a world war—decades before Pearl Harbor.

Rostron, Capt. Arthur   Commander of the *Carpathia*, the ship that picked up all of the *Titanic*'s survivors. (See the feature earlier in this chapter on Captain Rostron's preparations for receiving the *Titanic*'s survivors.)

Rowe, George   *Titanic* quartermaster. He was the last member of the crew to learn that the *Titanic* was sinking. He survived the disaster and continued to sail with the British Mercantile Service until his retirement in 1955.

Shuman, Eleanor Johnson   *Titanic* survivor who was less than two years old when the *Titanic* went down in 1912. Mrs. Shuman was returning to the United States on the *Titanic* after visiting with her family in Europe. Mrs. Shuman's mother and brother also survived the sinking. Mrs. Shuman died in Illinois on March 7, 1998, after suddenly taking ill.

In late 1997, Mrs. Shuman saw the premiere of the movie *Titanic,* where she met director James Cameron. She told the press that Cameron had said she reminded him of his character Rose in the movie. "So when you see Rose," she later told reporters, "think of me." (See **Wood, Beatrice.**)

Mrs. Shuman also said that the movie revived memories of the sinking, even though she was still an infant when the *Titanic* foundered. "I can still see all the hands reaching up to me from below," she told the media after seeing the movie. I didn't want to go. And I remember the noise. Everybody was yelling and crying and screaming." She also said that the film's realism made it difficult for her to watch. "I did a lot of crying," she admitted.

Symons, George   One of the *Titanic*'s lookouts the night she struck the iceberg.

Smith, Capt. Edward J.   The commander of the *Titanic,* known as the Millionaire's Captain for his popularity with the wealthy transatlantic society passengers. Smith went down with his ship, and questions still linger about his judgment and decisions during the *Titanic*'s brief maiden voyage—the main one being, why, after several ice warnings from other ships, did he steer full speed ahead into an ice field at night? Smith left a wife and daughter, and after his death his wife Eleanor issued the following statement:

> To my poor fellow sufferers—
> My heart overflows with grief for you all and is laden with sorrow that you are weighed down with this terrible burden that has been thrust upon us. May God be with us and comfort us all.
>
> Yours in sympathy,
> Eleanor Smith

Captain Smith's body was never recovered, and there were several accounts of his final moments. (See chapter 23.)

Speers, Jim   The *New York Times* journalist who interviewed surviving *Titanic* Marconi wireless operator Harold Bride upon his safe arrival in New York. (See Harold Bride's account of the sinking in chapter 11.)

Stewart, John   *Titanic* steward who was the second person pulled into Lifeboat 14 when Fifth Officer Lowe went back to the site of *Titanic*'s sinking looking for survivors.

Straus, Isidor   First-class passenger and millionaire founder of the Macy's department store chain. Straus remained on the *Titanic* and was apparently last seen sitting with his wife on deck chairs awaiting the end.

Straus, Mrs. Ida   Wife of Isidor Straus. Ida chose to remain on the

> Owing to the death of
> Mr. and Mrs. Isidor Straus
> this store is
> closed to-day, Saturday.
>
> *R. H. Macy & Co.*
>
> HERALD SQUARE,
> Broadway, 34th to 35th St.,
> NEW YORK.

Titanic and die with her husband rather than get into a lifeboat without him. "We have been living together for many years," she was recalled as saying. "Where you go, I go."

Thayer, Jack   First-class passenger and *Titanic* survivor who was apparently unable to cope with his memories of the *Titanic* and committed suicide in 1945.

Tulloch, George   President of RMS Titanic, *Titanic*'s salvor in possession, the company formed to salvage items from *Titanic*'s wreck site and that is allowed to make money from photos of artifacts and exhibitions but not allowed to sell anything from the wreck.

Van Tongerloo, Winnifred Vera Quick   As of spring 1998, Winnifred Vera Quick Van Tongerloo was one of the six remaining living *Titanic* survivors. Winnifred was born on January 23, 1904, and was eight years and three months old when the *Titanic* sailed. She was a second-class passenger and was rescued in Lifeboat 11. She resides in Michigan.

West, Barbara J.   As of spring 1998, Barbara West was one of the six remaining living *Titanic* survivors. Barbara was born in May 1911, and was eleven months old when the *Titanic* sailed. She was a second-class passenger, and it is not known in which lifeboat she was rescued. Barbara resides in England, one of only two surviving British *Titanic* passengers and, throughout her life, she has steadfastly refused to discuss *Titanic* with anyone.

Winslet, Kate   The young female lead of James Cameron's 1998 blockbuster, *Titanic*. Winslet played the fictional first-class passenger Rose DeWitt Bukater Dawson.

Wood, Beatrice   The maverick potter and artist (known as the Mama of Dada) who served as James Cameron's inspiration for his character of the one-hundred-two-year-old *Titanic* survivor Rose in his block-buster movie. (Cameron revealed his inspiration in a March 1998 interview with journalist Charlie Rose.)

In 1985, Ms. Wood published her autobiography, *I Shock Myself*, which gave Cameron the idea of centering the fictional side of his *Titanic* story around the life of an aging artist (an idea which served him nicely when he also created Jack Dawson, the artist Rose met on the *Titanic*).

Beatrice Wood died in March 1998 at the age of one-hundred-five. Only days before her death, she met with director Cameron and actress Gloria Stuart, who modeled her portrayal of the elderly Rose on a combination of Kate Winslet's mannerisms and Ms. Wood's life and sensibility.

TITANIC SURVIVORS SPEAK

Recollections by Three Women Who Lived Through the *Titanic* Disaster

A few minutes later the order came to lower the lifeboats and then for the first time I realized we were in great peril.

—Dorothy Gibson

Here are the gripping accounts of three first-class women passengers (including silent film star Dorothy Gibson) who survived the *Titanic* sinking. Their stories take us back in time and allow us to experience the terrible final moments of the great ship in a way that no clinical, historical account of the events of that night can possibly do. These accounts truly tell us what it was like to be on the R.M.S. *Titanic* the early morning of April 15, 1912.

EMILY BOSIE RYERSON

First-Class Passenger

(Emily Ryerson, who lost her son and husband on the *Titanic,* later assisted Herbert Hoover during World War I working for the American Fund for the French Wounded. She remarried in 1927 and died in 1939 while vacationing in Uruguay.)

I was a passenger on the steamship *Titanic* on April 14, 1912. At the time of collision I was awake and heard the engines stop, but felt no jar.

My husband was asleep, so I rang and asked the steward, Bishop, what was the matter. He said, "There is talk of an iceberg, ma'am, and they have stopped, not to run into it." I told him to keep me informed if there were any orders. It was bitterly cold, so I put on a warm wrapper and looked out the window (we were in the large cabins on the B deck, very far aft) and saw the stars shining and a calm sea, but heard no noise. It was 12 o'clock. After about 10 minutes I went out in the corridor, and saw far off people hurrying on deck. A passenger ran by and called out, "Put on your life belts and come up on the boat deck." I said, "Where did you get those orders?" He said, "From the captain." I went back then and told Miss Bowen and my daughter, who were in the next room, to dress immediately, roused my husband and the two younger children, who were in a room on the other side, and then remembered my maid, who had a room near us. Her door was locked and I had some difficulty in waking her. By this time my husband was fully dressed, and we could hear the noise of feet tramping on the deck overhead. He was quite calm and cheerful and helped me put the life belts on the children and on my maid. I was paralyzed with fear of not all getting on deck together in time, as there were seven of us. I would not let my younger daughter dress, but she only put on a fur coat, as I did, over her nightgown. My husband cautioned us all to keep together, and we went up to A deck, where we found quite a group of people we knew. Everyone had on a life belt, and they all were very quiet and self-possessed.

We stood about there for quite a long time—fully half an hour, I should say. I know my maid ran down to the cabin and got some of my clothes. Then we were ordered to the boat deck. I only remember the second steward at the head of the stairs, who told us where to go. My chief thought and that of everyone else was, I know, not to make a fuss and to do as we were told. My husband joked with some of the women he knew, and I heard him say, "Don't you hear the band playing?" I begged him to let me stay with him, but he said, "You must obey orders. When they say, 'Women and children to the boats,' you must go when your turn comes. I'll stay with John Thayer. We will be all right. You take a boat going to New York." This referred to the belief that there was a circle of ships around waiting. The *Olympic,* the *Baltic,* were some of the names I heard. All this time we could hear the rockets going up—signals of distress. Again, we were ordered down to A deck, which was partly enclosed. We saw people getting into boats, but waited our turn. There was a rough sort of steps constructed to get up to the window. My boy, Jack, was with me. An officer at the window said, "That boy can't go." My husband stepped forward and said, "Of course, that boy goes with his mother; he is only 13." So they let him pass. They also said, "No more boys." I turned and kissed my husband,

and as we left he and the other men I knew—Mr. Thayer, Mr. Widener, and others—were all standing there together very quietly. The decks were lighted, and as you went through the window it was as if you stepped out into the dark. We were flung into the boats. There were two men—an officer inside and a sailor outside—to help us. I fell on top of the women who were already in the boat, and scrambled to the bow with my eldest daughter. Miss Bowen and my boy were in the stern and my second daughter was in the middle of the boat with my maid. Mrs. Thayer, Mrs. Widener, Mrs. Astor, and Miss Eustis were the only others I knew in our boat.

Presently an officer called out from the upper deck, "How many women are there in that boat?" Someone answered, "Twenty-four." "That's enough; lower away."

The ropes seemed to stick at one end and the boat tipped, someone called for a knife, but it was not needed until we got into the water, as it was but a short distance, and I then realized for the first time how far the ship had sunk. The deck we left was only about 20 feet from the sea. I could see all the portholes open and water washing in, and the decks still lighted. Then they called out, "How many seaman have you," and they answered one. "That is not enough," said the officer. "I will send you another," and he sent a sailor down the rope. In a few minutes after several other men [who were] not sailors came down the ropes over the davits and dropped into our boat. The order was given to pull away. Then they rowed off—the sailors, the women, anyone—but made little progress; there was a confusion of orders; we rowed toward the stern, someone shouted something about a gangway, and no one seemed to know what to do. Barrels and chairs were being thrown overboard. Then suddenly, when we still seemed very near, we saw the ship was sinking rapidly. I was in the bow of the boat with my daughter and turned to see the great ship take a plunge toward the bow, the two forward funnels seemed to lean and then she seemed to break in half as if cut with a knife, and as the bow went under the lights went out; the stern stood up for several minutes, black against the stars, and then that, too, plunged down, and there was no sound for what seemed like hours, and then began the cries for help of people drowning all around us, which seemed to go on forever. Someone called out, "Pull for your lives, or you'll be sucked under," and everyone that could rowed like mad. I could see my younger daughter and Mrs. Thayer and Mrs. Astor rowing, but there seemed to be no suction. Then we turned to pick up some of those in the water. Some of the women protested, but others persisted, and we dragged in six or seven men; the men we rescued were principally stokers, stewards, sailors, etc., and were so chilled and frozen already they could hardly move. Two of them died in the stern later and many were raving and moaning and delirious most of the time. We had no lights or compass. There were several babies in the boat, but there was no milk or water. (I believe these were all stowed away somewhere, but no one knew where, and as the bottom of the boat was full of water and the boat full of people it was very difficult to find anything.)

After the *Titanic* sank we saw no lights, and no one seemed to know what direction to take. Lowe, the officer in charge of the boat, had called out earlier for all to tie together, so we now heard his whistle, and as soon as we could make out the other boats in the dark, five of us were tied together, and we drifted about without rowing, as the sea was calm, waiting for the dawn. It was very cold, and soon a breeze sprang up, and it was hard to keep our heavy boat bow on; but as the cries died down we could see dimly what seemed to be a raft with about 20 men standing on it, back to back. It was the overturned boat; and as the sailors on our boat said we could still carry 8 or 10 more people, we called for another boat to volunteer and go to rescue them. So we two cut loose our painters and between us got all the men off. They were nearly gone and could not have held out much longer. Then, when the sun rose we saw the *Carpathia* standing about 5 miles away, and for the first time saw the icebergs all around us. The *Carpathia* steamed toward us until it was full daylight; then she stopped and began picking up boats, and we got on board about 8 o'clock. Very soon after we got on board they took a complete list of the names of all survivors. The kindness and the efficiency of all the arrangements on the *Carpathia* for our comfort can never be too highly praised. [Her affidavit for the U.S. Senate Subcommittee *Titanic* hearing]

Daisy Minahan

First-Class Passenger

(Daisy Minahan had been returning to her home in Wisconsin following a sojourn in Europe when the *Titanic* struck the iceberg. Daisy's daughter survived the sinking; Daisy's husband, Dr. Minahan, did not.)

I was asleep in stateroom C-78; I was awakened by the crying of a woman in the passageway. I roused my brother and his wife, and we began at once to dress. No one came to give us warning. We spent five minutes in dressing and went on deck to the port side. The frightful slant of the deck toward the bow of the boat gave us our first thought of danger.

An officer came and commanded all women to follow, and he led us to the boat deck on the starboard side. He told us there was no danger, but to get into a lifeboat as a precaution only. After making three attempts to get into boats, we succeeded in getting into Lifeboat No. 14. The crowd surging around the boats was getting unruly.

Officers were yelling and cursing at men to stand back and let the women get into the boats. In going from one lifeboat to another we stumbled over huge piles of bread lying on the deck.

When the lifeboat was filled there were no seamen to man it. The officer in command of No. 14 called for volunteers in the crowd who could row. Six men offered to go. At times when we were being lowered we were at an angle of 45° and expected to be thrown into the sea. As we reached the level of each deck men jumped into the boat until the officer threatened to shoot the next man who jumped. We landed in the sea and rowed to a safe distance from the sinking ship. The officer counted our number and found us to be 48. The officer commanded everyone to feel in the bottom of the boat for a light. We found none. Nor was there bread or water in the boat. The officer, whose name I learned afterwards to be Lowe, was continually making remarks such as, "A good song to sing would be, 'Throw Out the Life Line,' " and "I think the best thing for you women to do is to take a nap."

The *Titanic* was fast sinking. After she went down the cries were horrible. This was at 2:20 A.M. by a man's watch who stood next to me. At this time three other boats and ours kept together by being tied to each other. The cries continued to come over the water. Some of the women implored Officer Lowe, of No. 14, to divide his passengers among the three other boats and go back to rescue. His first answer to those requests was, "You ought to be damn glad you are here and have got your own life." After some time he was persuaded to do as he was asked. As I came up to him to be transferred to the other boat he said, "Jump, God damn you, jump." I had showed no hesitancy and was waiting only my turn. He had been so blasphemous during the two hours we were in his boat that the women at my end of the boat all thought he was under the influence of liquor. Then he took all of the men who had rowed No. 14, together with the men from the other boats, and went back to the scene of the wreck. We were left with a steward and a stoker to row our boat, which was crowded. The steward did his best, but the stoker refused at first to row, but finally helped two women, who were the only ones pulling on that side. It was just 4 o'clock when we sighted the *Carpathia,* and we were three hours getting to her. On the *Carpathia* we were treated with every kindness and given every comfort possible.

A stewardess who had been saved told me that after the *Titanic* left Southampton there were a number of carpenters working to put the doors of the air-tight compartments in working order. They had great difficulty in making them respond, and one of them remarked that they would be of little use in case of accident, because it took so long to make them work. [Her affidavit for the U.S. Senate Subcommittee *Titanic* hearing]

Daisy Minahan's personal letter to Senator William Alden Smith, written and sent after she submitted her Senate subcommittee affidavit

Dear Sir:

I have given you my observations and experiences after the disaster, but want to tell you of what occurred on Sunday night, April 14.

My brother, his wife, and myself went to the café for dinner at about 7:15 P.M. (ship's time). When we entered there was a dinner party already dining, consisting of perhaps a dozen men and three women. Capt. Smith was a guest, as also were Mr. and Mrs. Widener, Mr. and Mrs. Blair, and Maj. Butt. Capt. Smith was continuously with his party from the time we entered until between 9:25 and 9:45, when he bid the women good night and left. I know this time positively, for at 9:25 my brother suggested my going to bed. We waited for one more piece of the orchestra, and it was between 9:25 and 9:45 (the time we departed), that Capt. Smith left.

Sitting within a few feet of this party were also Sir Cosmo and Lady Duff-Gordon, a Mrs. Meyers, of New York, and Mrs. Smith, of Virginia. Mr. and Mrs. Harris also were dining in the café at the same time.

I had read testimony before your committee stating that Capt. Smith had talked to an officer on the bridge from 8:45 to 9:25. This is positively untrue, as he was having coffee with these people during this time. I was seated so close to them that I could hear bits of their conversation.

DOROTHY GIBSON

First-Class Passenger

From the *New York Morning Telegraph,* April 21, 1912

On the night of the disaster there had been a great deal of merriment on board, the prospect of reaching the American shore having the effect of making everyone happy. After a stroll about the ship in company with my mother, I was invited by several friends to take part in a game of bridge, and I joined them after my mother had retired to her room on Deck E. The salon in which I joined my friends was on Deck A, and we played until 10 p.m. We remained in the salon. About half an hour later we felt a slight jar. No one in the party thought anything of it and we continued to laugh and converse for fully fifteen minutes. Then it was that I noticed considerable nervousness on the part of the stewards and such of the officers as came within range of my vision, but nothing was said by them to give the passengers an inkling of what had happened.

Ship Was Listing

Good nights having been said, I stepped out upon deck with the intention of taking a short stroll before retiring, when I noticed that the great ship was leaning heavily on one side. I am not enough of a sailor to know whether it was port or starboard, but the fact remains she was lopsided. On my way below to Deck E I encountered a steward and asked him if there was anything wrong. He tried to push me aside, but I stood resolutely and then he snapped out "Nothing wrong!" and disappeared to the deck above.

It was at this stage of the proceedings that I became somewhat uneasy and made haste to arouse my mother. There was little or no excitement on board the ship, and in many of the salons that I passed I saw the passengers engaged in card playing and other forms of divertissement. The night was as clear as crystal. The moon was shining brilliantly and the stars twinkled without being obscured by a single cloud. Even at a glance I could see icebergs around us and the water seemed filled with the shattered remains of others.

When my mother and myself started to go to the side of the ship that was highest out of the water, we were obliged to climb a veritable hill. By this time the officers had aroused the passengers and they were besieging the bulwarks and asking more questions than any one man could answer in a week. In the meantime the big steamship kept sagging down and when I asked one of the officers what significance the water on one of the stairways carried he replied with a smile that there was no cause for alarm. "One of the compartments has been punctured," he said with a faint smile, "but the ship is sturdy enough to weather a little thing like that."

Lifeboats Are Lowered

A few minutes later the order came to lower the lifeboats and then for the first time I realized we were in great peril. I clung to my mother and pressed my way down toward the railing. We were badly jostled and pushed about, but that mattered not, so long as I found that I was being pushed nearer the lifeboats that were being lowered. My mother remained wonderfully calm throughout the ordeal and when the crew prepared to lower the first lifeboats we were among the first to enter. The designer of the steamship, who was aboard in company with Mr. Ismay of the White Star Line, ran to and fro with a face of greenish paleness and declined to answer any of the questions hurled at him from the panic-stricken passengers crowding the rail.

When our boat pulled away there were 26 persons aboard and four of those were men. No sooner had we started for the open sea than we discovered to our dismay that the lifeboat was without a plug. This was remedied by volunteer contributions from the lingerie of the women and garments from the men. Then the third officer, who was in charge of the boat, announced that he was without lights or compass. He asked for matches, and happily I was able to supply him. During the bridge game I had picked up from the table a box of French matches which one of the gentlemen had been using, and after toying with it at intervals placed it in my belt intending to preserve it as a souvenir of the trip. To what use the third officer expected putting these matches I do not know, because the morning was clear and we were able to see many miles in all directions.

Cries of Anguish

Suddenly there was a wild coming together of voices from the direction of the ship and we noticed an unusual commotion among the people huddled about the railing. Then the awful thing happened, the thing that will remain in my memory until the day I die.

The *Titanic* seemed to lurch slightly more to the side and then the fore. A minute, or probably two minutes, later she sank her nose into the ocean, swayed for a few minutes and disappeared, leaving nothing behind her on the face of the sea but a swirl of water, bobbing heads, and lifeboats that were threatened by the suction of the waters. After the vessel had disappeared, the officer in command of our boat wanted to return, saying that there was room for several more passengers and pointing out the possibility of being able to rescue some of those who might be swimming. But immediately behind us was another lifeboat carrying forty people and as no one could be seen in the water some of the passengers in the other boat were transferred to ours.

It was a sense of desolation never to be forgotten. To make matters worse, the weather became bitterly cold, and many of the women in the boat were clad in the lightest of evening gowns and some more scantily. The men behaved like heroes, except one chap, who calmly stretched himself in the forepart of the lifeboat and promptly fell asleep regardless of what might happen. There was a young Englishman who managed to wear his monocle throughout the excitement and proved himself a much better man than he looked. He divested himself of what clothing he could spare for the shelter of the women and cheered us with his drawling dialect and his words of hope.

Carpathia is Sighted

It was shortly after 5 o'clock when the frozen and benumbed sufferers in our boat were aroused into activity by the announcement that a string of black smoke on the horizon told the approach of a steamship. Up to this time we had been wondering whether the operator of the wireless on the *Titanic* had been able to send out his signal of distress. This thought bothers us greatly. To drift about aimlessly in the open sea with the assurance that the wireless had communicated with a vessel, no matter how far distant, would be a consolation, but to drift in the hope that we might encounter a vessel accidentally was different.

Warming ourselves as best we could in the cramped quarters of a lifeboat, we watched that streak of black smoke grow larger and larger, and then we were able to discern the hull of a steamship heading in our direction. But, thank God, the volume of smoke grew and one of the men, who seemed to know the way of the sea, remarked that the vessel was crowding on all steam. This, of course, cheered us, because we knew that crowding on all steam meant haste.

It seemed ages to me, but as a matter of fact it was shortly after 6 o'clock when we found ourselves alongside the *Carpathia,* with its rails swarming with kindly faces, and men and women crowding about in the anxiety to render help. Captain Rostron of the *Carpathia* had caused everything to be placed in readiness[1], and as the accommodations were limited, the passengers opened their staterooms and did everything in their power to allay our suffering. I was a guest in the room of Mr. and Mrs. James Russell Lowell, and my mother was looked after by kind people whose names I neglected to learn.

Lack of Discipline

Once aboard the *Carpathia* it became evident to me that there had been a deplorable lack of discipline on board the *Titanic*. Comparison of the two crews brought this truth home to me. In the exciting moments before the sinking of the *Titanic*, there appeared no concerted action among the officers and crew. Everything was confusion, and it was the men among the passengers who enforced the orders of Captain Smith that the women and children be the first to enter the lifeboats. As a matter of fact, Captain Smith and Mr. Ismay dined from 6 o'clock until 10, and during that time we had learned that four steamships had warned the *Titanic* of the presence of icebergs and large masses of floating ice in our course.

Many of the collapsible lifeboats collapsed in reality when the passengers attempted to enter them, and the manner in which the life buoys were distributed was slipshod in the extreme. I am thankful that my mother and

---

[1] See the section "*Carpathia*'s Captain Rostron's Preparations for Receiving the *Titanic* Survivors" in chapter 4.

myself as well as the others were rescued, and that we are back in New York, but it is my sincere wish that the officials of the White Star Line be made to answer for the negligence which caused this disaster and the pain and sorrow they have brought upon the survivors. The "unsinkable" *Titanic* might still be the monarch of the sea had ordinary precaution been used in charting her course and providing a sufficient number of lifeboats.

8

ASKING QUESTIONS

A Comprehensive Look at the British Board of Trade Inquiry's "Report on the Loss of the *Titanic*"

The inconceivable loss of the *Titanic* had potential far-reaching negative consequences for a great many people and companies, most notably the White Star Line and, by extension, the lucrative British shipping trade. In May 1912, in response to the recent U.S. Senate hearing on the disaster, the British Board of Trade (BOT) also conducted a hearing into the *Titanic* disaster, but people on both sides of the Atlantic who were hoping for conclusions that would answer the nagging questions about the number of lifeboats, Bruce Ismay's behavior, the possible neglect of the third-class passengers, the sighting of a ship that could have rescued many of the dead, and many other riddles were ultimately disappointed.

The Board of Trade's "Report on the Loss of the *Titanic*," dated July 30, 1912, absolved the White Star Line of any blame (citing their complete compliance with lifeboat regulations and other active requirements of sea-going vessels) and essentially dumped the responsibility for the 1,522 *Titanic* deaths on Capt. Walter Lord of the S.S. *Californian*, stating "[The *Californian*] could have reached the *Titanic* if she had made the attempt when she saw the first rocket. She made no attempt."

Spin control aside, however, the Board of Trade report is an enormous repository of *Titanic* information, consisting of eight fact-filled chapters.

Report on the Loss of the "Titanic" (S.S.)

THE MERCHANT SHIPPING ACTS, 1854 to 1906.

IN THE MATTER OF the Formal Investigation held at the Scottish Hall, Buckingham Gate, Westminster, on the 2nd, 3rd, 7th, 8th, 9th, 10th, 14th, 15th, 16th, 17th, 20th, 21st, 22nd, 23rd and 24th May, the 4th, 5th, 6th, 7th, 10th, 11th, 12th, 13th, 14th, 17th, 18th, 19th, 21st, 24th, 25th, 26th, 27th, 28th and 29th June, at the Caxton Hall, Caxton Street, Westminster, on the 1st and 3rd July, and at the Scottish Hall, Buckingham Gate, Westminster, on the 30th July, 1912, before the Right Honourable Lord Mersey, Wreck Commissioner, assisted by Rear Admiral the Honourable S. A. Gough-Calthorpe, C.V.O., R.N.; Captain A. W. Clarke; Commander F. C. A. Lyon, R.N.R.; Professor J. H. Biles, D.Sc., LL.D., and Mr. E. C. Chaston, R.N.R., as Assessors, into the circumstances attending the loss of the steamship "Titanic," of Liverpool, and the loss of 1,490 lives in the North Atlantic Ocean, in lat. 41° 46′ N., long. 50° 14′ W. on the 15th April last.

REPORT OF THE COURT.

The Court, having carefully enquired into the circumstances of the above mentioned shipping casualty, finds, for the reasons appearing in the Annex hereto, that the loss of the said ship was due to collision with an iceberg, brought about by the excessive speed at which the ship was being navigated.

Dated this 30th day of July, 1912.

Mersey   *Wreck Commissioner.*

We concur in the above Report.

[signatures]
Arthur Joseph Calthorpe.
[signature]
Lyon.
Biles.
Edward. C. Chaston

Assessors.

TABLE OF CONTENTS.

The report began by asking twenty-six relevant questions about the *Titanic*'s collision and foundering, and then proceeded to answer the questions through first-person testimony of survivors and others.

Chapter 7, "Finding of the Court," provides complete answers—based on the testimony of the witnesses and the court's conclusions—to these twenty-six questions, and this chapter is reprinted in its entirety here.

Knowing what we now know about the *Titanic* and the circumstances surrounding its sinking, questions 5a–d, 9a–d, 10b, 11a, 14b, 21f, and 24b are especially interesting.

1. When the *Titanic* left Queenstown on or about April 11th last: (a) What was the total number of persons employed in any capacity on board her, and what were their respective ratings? (b) What was the total number of her passengers, distinguishing sexes and classes, and discriminating between adults and children?
Answer:
(a) The total number of persons employed in any capacity on board the *Titanic* was 885.
    The respective ratings of these persons were as follows:
        Deck Department: 66
        Engine Department: 325
        Victuals Department: 494
N.B.: The eight bandsmen are not included in this number as their names appear in the 2nd Class Passenger List.
(b) The total number of passengers was 1,316.
Of these:

	Male	Female	Total
1st Class	180	145	325
2nd Class	179	106	285
3rd Class	510	196	706
			1,316

Of the above, 6 children were in the 1st Class, 24 in the 2nd Class and 70 in the 3rd Class. Total 109.

2. Before leaving Queenstown on or about 11th April last did the *Titanic* comply with the requirements of the Merchant Shipping Acts, 1894–1906, and the rules and regulations made thereunder with regard to the safety and otherwise of "passenger steamers" and emigrant ships"?
Answer:
Yes.

3. In the actual design and construction of the *Titanic,* what special pro-visions were made for the safety of the vessel and the lives of those on board in the event of collisions and other casualties?
Answer:
These have already been described.[1]

4. (a) Was the *Titanic* sufficiently and efficiently officered and manned? (b) Were the watches of the officers and crew usual and proper? (c) Was the *Titanic* supplied with proper charts?
Answer:
    (a) Yes.
    (b) Yes.
    (c) Yes.

5. (a) What was the number of boats of any kind on board the *Titanic*? (b) Were the arrangements for manning and launching the boats on board the *Titanic* in case of emergency proper and sufficient? (c) Had a boat drill been held on board, and if so, when? (d) What was the carrying capacity of the respective boats?
Answer:
    (a) 2 Emergency boats.
        14 Lifeboats.
        4 Englehardt boats.
    (b) No, but see page 38.[2]
    (c) No.
    (d) The carrying capacity of the:
        2 Emergency boats was for 80 persons.
        14 Lifeboats was for 910 persons.
        4 Englehardt boats was for 188 persons.
          or a total of 1,178 persons.

6. (a) What installations for receiving and transmitting messages by wireless telegraphy were on board the *Titanic*? (b) How many operators were employed on working such installations? (c) Were the installations in good and effective working order, and were the number of operators suffi-cient to enable messages to be received and transmitted continuously by day and night?
Answer:
    (a) Marconi 5 Kilowatt motor generator with two complete set of appa-ratus supplied from the ship's dynamos, with an independent storage

battery and coil for emergency, was fitted in a house on the Boat Deck.

(b) Two.

(c) Yes.

7. (a) At or prior to the sailing of the *Titanic* what, if any, instructions as to navigation were given to the master or known by him to apply to her voyage? (b) Were such instructions, if any, safe, proper, and adequate, having regard to the time of year and dangers likely to be encountered during the voyage?

Answer:

(a) No special instructions were given, but he had general instructions contained in the book of Rules and Regulations supplied by the Company. (See p. 24.)[3]

(b) Yes, but having regard to subsequent events they would have been better if a reference had been made to the course to be adopted in the event of reaching the region of ice.

8. (a) What was in fact the track taken by *Titanic* in crossing the Atlantic Ocean? (b) Did she keep to the track usually followed by liners on voyages from the United Kingdom to New York in the month of April? (c) Are such tracks safe tracks at that time of the year? (d) Had the master any, and, if so, what discretion as regards the track to be taken?

Answer:

(a) The Outward Southern Track from Queenstown to New York, usually followed in April by large steam vessels. (See page 24.)[4]

(b) Yes, with the exception that instead of altering her course on approaching the position 42° N. 47° W. she stood on her previous course for some 10 miles further South West, turning to S. 86° W. true at 5:50 p.m.

(c) The Outward and Homeward bound Southern tracks were decided on as the outcome of many years' experience of the normal movement of ice. They were reasonably safe tracks for the time of year, provided, of course, that great caution and vigilance when crossing the ice region were observed.

(d) Yes. Captain Smith was not fettered by any orders to remain on the track should information as to the position of ice make it in his opinion undesirable to adhere to it. The fact, however, of Lane Routes having been laid down for the common safety of all, would necessarily influence him to keep on (or very near) the accepted route, unless circumstances as indicated above should induce him to deviate largely from it.

9. (a) After leaving Queenstown on or about the 11th April last did information reach the *Titanic* by wireless messages or otherwise by signals of the existence of ice in certain latitudes? (b) If so, what were such messages or signals and when were they received, and in what position or positions was the ice reported to be and was the ice reported in or near the track actually being followed by the *Titanic*? (c) Was her course altered in consequence of receiving such information, and, if so, in what way? (d) What replies to such messages or signals did the *Titanic* send, and at what times?
Answer:
  (a) Yes.
  (b) See particulars of ice messages already set out (pp. 26–28).[5]
  (c) No. Her course was altered as hereinbefore described, but not in consequence of the information received as to ice.
  (d) The material answers were:
      At 12:55 p.m. ss. *Titanic*. "To Commander, *Baltic*. Thanks for your message and good wishes. Had fine weather since leaving. Smith."
      At 1:26 p.m. ss. *Titanic*. "To Commander, *Caronia*. Thanks for message and information. Have had variable weather throughout. Smith."

10. (a) If at the times referred to in the last preceding question or later the *Titanic* was warned of or had reason to suppose she would encounter ice, at what time might she have reasonably expected to encounter it? (b) Was a good and proper look-out for ice kept on board? (c) Were any, and, if so, what directions given to vary the speed—if so, were they carried out?
Answer:
  (a) At, or even before, 9:30 p.m. ship's time, on the night of the disaster.
  (b) No. The men in the crow's nest were warned at 9:30 p.m. to keep a sharp look-out for ice; the officer of the watch was then aware that he had reached the reported ice region, and so also was the officer who relieved him at 10 p.m. Without implying that those actually on duty were not keeping a good look-out, in view of the night being moonless, there being no wind and perhaps very little swell, and especially in view of the high speed at which the vessel was running, it is not considered that the look-out was sufficient. An extra look-out should, under the circumstances, have been placed at the stemhead, and a sharp look-out should have been kept from both sides of the bridge by an officer.
  (c) No directions were given to reduce speed.

11. (a) Were binoculars provided for and used by the look-out men? (b) Is the use of them necessary or usual in such circumstances? (c) Had the *Titanic* the means of throwing searchlights around her? (d) If so, did she make use of them to discover ice? (e) Should searchlights have been provided and used?

Answer:
  (a) No.
  (b) No.
  (c) No.
  (d) No.
  (e) No, but searchlights may at times be of service. The evidence before the Court does not allow of a more precise answer.

12. (a) What other precautions were taken by the *Titanic* in anticipation of meeting ice? (b) Were they such as are usually adopted by vessels being navigated in waters where ice may be expected to be encountered?

Answer:
  (a) Special orders were given to the men in the crow's nest to keep a sharp look-out for ice, particularly small ice and growlers. The fore scuttle hatch was closed to keep everything dark before the bridge.
  (b) Yes, though there is evidence to show that some masters would have placed a look-out at the stemhead of the ship.

13. (a) Was ice seen and reported by anybody on board the *Titanic* before the casualty occurred? (b) If so, what measures were taken by the officer on watch to avoid it? (c) Were they proper measures and were they promptly taken?

Answer:
  (a) Yes, immediately before the collision.
  (b) The helm was put hard-a-starboard and the engines were stopped and put full speed astern.
  (c) Yes.[6]

14. (a) What was the speed of the *Titanic* shortly before and at the moment of the casualty? (b) Was such speed excessive under the circumstances?

Answer:
  (a) About 22 knots.
  (b) Yes.

15. (a) What was the nature of the casualty which happened to the *Titanic* at or about 11:45 p.m. on the 14th April last? (b) In what latitude and longtitude did the casualty occur?

Answer:
> (a) A collision with an iceberg which pierced the starboard side of the vessel in several places below the water line between the fore peak tank and No. 4 boiler room.
> (b) In latitude 41° 46′ N., longtitude 50° 14′ W.

16. (a) What steps were taken immediately on the happening of the casualty? (b) How long after the casualty was its seriousness realized by those in charge of the vessel? (c) What steps were then taken? (d) What endeavors were made to save the lives of those on board, and to prevent the vessel from sinking?
Answer:
> (a) The 12 watertight doors in the engine and boiler rooms were closed from the bridge, some of the boiler fires were drawn, and the bilge pumps abaft No. 6 boiler room were started.
> (b) About 15–20 minutes.
> (c) and (d) The boats were ordered to be cleared away. The passengers were roused and orders were given to get them on deck, and lifebelts were served out. Some of the watertight doors, other than those in the engine and boiler rooms, were closed. Marconigrams were sent out asking for help. Distress signals (rockets) were fired, and attempts were made to call up by Morse a ship whose lights were seen. Eighteen of the boats were swung out and lowered, and the remaining two floated off the ship and were subsequently utilized as rafts.

17. Was proper discipline maintained onboard after the casualty occurred?
Answer:
> Yes.

18. [See chapter 4, "Calling for Help."]

19. (a) Was the apparatus for lowering the boats on the *Titanic* at the time of the casualty in good working order? (b) Were the boats swung out, filled, lowered, or otherwise put into the water and got away under proper superintendence? (c) Were the boats sent away in seaworthy condition and properly manned, equipped and provisioned? (d) Did the boats, whether those under davits or otherwise, prove to be efficient and serviceable for the purpose of saving life?
Answer:
> (a) Yes.
> (b) Yes.

(c) The fourteen lifeboats, two emergency boats, and C and D collapsible boats were sent away in a seaworthy condition, but some of them were possibly undermanned. The evidence on this point was unsatisfactory. The total number of crew taken on board the *Carpathia* exceeded the number which would be required for manning the boats. The collapsible boats A and B appear to have floated off the ship at the time she foundered. The necessary equipment and provisions for the boats were carried in the ship, but some of the boats, nevertheless, left without having their full equipment in them.

(d) Yes.

20. (a) What was the number of (a) passengers, (b) crew taken away in each boat on leaving the vessel? (b) How was this number made up, having regard to:

1. Sex.
2. Class.
3. Rating.

(c) How many were children and how many adults? (d) did each boat carry its full load and, if not, why not?

Answer:

(a) (b) (c) It is impossible exactly to say how many persons were carried in each boat or what was their sex, class and rating, as the totals given in evidence do not correspond with the numbers taken on board the *Carpathia*.

The boats eventually contained in all 712 persons made up as shown in the answer to Question 21.

(d) No.

At least 8 boats did not carry their full loads for the following reasons:

1. Many people did not realize the danger or care to leave the ship at first.
2. Some boats were ordered to be lowered with an idea of their coming round to the gangway doors to complete the loading.
3. The officers were not certain of the strength and capacity of the boats in all cases (and see p. 39).[7]

21. (a) How many persons on board the *Titanic* at the time of the casualty were ultimately rescued and by what means? (b) How many lost their lives prior to the arrival of the ss. *Carpathia* in New York? (c) What was the number of passengers, distinguishing between men and women and adults and children of the 1st, 2nd, and 3rd classes respectively who were saved? (d) What was the number of the crew, discriminating their ratings and sex, that were saved? (e) What is the proportion which each of these

numbers bears to the corresponding total number on board immediately before the casualty? (f) What reason is there for the disproportion, if any? *Answer:*

(a) 712, rescued by Carpathia from the boats.

(b) One.

(c) (d) and (e) are answered together.

The following is a list of the saved:

1st Class.

Adult Males	57, out of 175, or 32.57 per cent.
Adult Females	140, out of 144, or 97.22 per cent.
Male children	5 All saved.
Female children	1 All saved.
	203 out of 325 or 62.46 per cent.

2nd Class.

Adult Males	14, out of 168, or 8.33 per cent.
Adult Females	80, out of 93, or 86.02 per cent.
Male children	11 All saved.
Female children	13 All saved.
	118 out of 285 or 41.40 per cent.

3rd Class.

Adult Males	75, out of 462, or 16.23 per cent.
Adult Females	76, out of 165, or 46.06 per cent.
Male children	13 out of 48, or 27.08 per cent.
Female children	14 out of 31, or 45.16 per cent.
	178 out of 706, or 25.21 per cent.
Total Passengers	499 out of 1,316, or 37.94 per cent.

Crew saved.

Deck Department	43 out of 66, or 65.15 per cent.
Engine Room Department	72 out of 325, or 22.15 per cent.
Victualling Department	97 out of 494, or 19.63 per cent.
Including Women	20 out of 23, or 86.95 per cent.
	212 out of 885, or 23.95 per cent.
Total on board saved	711 out of 2,201, or 32.30 per cent.

(f) The disproportion between the numbers of the passengers saved in the first, second, and third classes is due to various causes, among which the difference in the position of their quarters and the fact that many of the third class passengers were foreigners, are perhaps the most important. Of the Irish emigrants in the third class a large proportion was saved. The disproportion was certainly not due to any discrimination by the officers or crew in assisting the passengers to the boats. The disproportion between the numbers of the passengers and crew saved is due to the fact that the crew, for the most part, all attended to their duties to the last, and until all the boats were gone.

22. What happened to the vessel from the happening of the casualty until she foundered?
Answer:
A detailed description has already been given (see pages 32–34.)[8]

23. Where and at what time did the Titanic founder?
Answer:
2:20 a.m. (ship's time) 15th April.
Latitude 41° 46′ N., longtitude 50° 14′ W.

24. (a) What was the cause of the loss of the *Titanic,* and of the loss of life which thereby ensued or occurred? (b) What vessels had the opportunity of rendering assistance to the *Titanic* and, if any, how was it that assistance did not reach the *Titanic* before the ss. *Carpathia* arrived? (c) Was the construction of the vessel and its arrangements such as to make it difficult for any class of passenger or any portion of the crew to take full advantage of any of the existing provisions for safety?
Answer:
  (a) Collision with an iceberg and the subsequent foundering of the ship.
  (b) The *Californian.* She could have reached the *Titanic* if she had made the attempt when she saw the first rocket. She made no attempt.
  (c) No.

25. When the *Titanic* left Queenstown on or about April 11th last was she properly constructed, and adequately equipped as a passenger steamer and emigrant ship for the Atlantic service?
Answer:
Yes.

26. The Court is invited to report upon the Rules and Regulations made under the Merchant Shipping Acts, 1894–1906, and the administration of those Acts and of such Rules and Regulations, so far as the consideration thereof is material to this casualty, and to make any recommendations or

suggestions that it may think fit, having regard to the circumstances of the casualty, with a view to promoting the safety of vessels and persons at sea. *Answer:*

An account of the Board of Trade's Administration has already been given and certain recommendations are subsequently made.

FOOTNOTES

[1] See chapters 4 and 7.

[2] The relevant passage referred to on page 38 of the report states: "The evidence satisfies me that the officers did their work very well and without any thought of themselves."

[3] The page referred to begins a section of the report titled "Account of the Ship's Journey Across the Atlantic, the Messages She Received and the Disaster." The relevant section is titled "The Sailing Orders" and includes the following passage:

The masters of vessels belonging to the White Star Line are not given any special "sailing orders" before the commencement of any particular voyage. It is understood, however, that the "tracks" or "lane routes" proper to the particular time of the year, and agreed upon by the great steamship companies, are to be generally adhered to. Should any master see fit during this passage to deviate from his route he has to report on and explain this deviation at the end of his voyage. When such deviations have been in the interests of safety, and not merely to shorten his passage, his action has always been approved of by the Company.

A book of "General Ship's Rules and Uniform Regulations" is also issued by the Company as a guide; there are in this book no special instructions in regard to ice, but there is a general instruction that the safety of the lives of the passengers and ship are to be the first consideration.

[4] The passage referred to is contained in a section titled "The Route Followed" and includes the following details about *Titanic's* route:

Before the *Titanic* disaster the accepted mail steamers outward track between January 15th and August 14th followed the arc of a great circle between the Fastnet Light and a point in latitude 42° N. and 47° W. (sometimes termed the "turning point"), and from thence by Rhumb Line so as to pass just south of the Nantucket Shoal light vessel, and from this point on to New York. This track, usually called the Outward Southern Track, was that followed by the *Titanic* on her journey.

[5] The *Titanic* received three ice messages sent specifically to her during her journey. *Titanic's* Marconi room also picked up one that was sent from the *Californian* to the *Antillian,* and one ice message sent to the Hydrographic Office in Washington, D.C. which was then passed on to the *Titanic.* (See "The *Titanic* Time Line" for the texts of these messages.)

[6] Here are excerpts from Captain Lightoller's testimony before the British Board of Trade Inquiry regarding the actions of *Titanic's* officers (Thomas Scanlon represented the National Sailors' and Firemen's Union):

Thomas Scanlon: This night you have described as being a particularly bad night for seeing icebergs. Is not that so?

Second Officer Charles Lightoller: I do not think I mentioned that word "bad," did I?

TS: Although there were abnormal difficulties you took no extra precautions whatever.

CL: Have I said so?

TS: In view of the abnormal conditions and of the fact that you were nearing ice at ten o'clock, was there not a very obvious reason for going slower?

CL: Well, I can only quote you my experience throughout the last twenty-four years, that I have been crossing the Atlantic most of the time, that I have never seen the speed reduced.

TS: Is it not quite clear that the most obvious way to avoid it is by slackening speed?

CL: Not necessarily the most obvious.

TS: Well, is it one way?

CL: It is one way. Naturally, if you stop the ship you will not collide with anything.

TS: What I want to suggest to you is that it was recklessness, utter recklessness, in view of the conditions which you have described as abnormal, and in view of the knowledge you had from various sources that ice was in your immediate vicinity, to proceed at 21½ knots?

CL: Then all I can say is that recklessness applies to practically every commander and every ship crossing the Atlantic Ocean.

TS: I am not disputing that with you, but can you describe it yourself as other than recklessness?

CL: Yes.

TS: Is it careful navigation in your view?

CL: It is ordinary navigation, which embodies careful navigation.

[7] The page referred to is part of chapter 4, "Account of the Saving and Rescue of Those Who Survived." Page 39 is in the section titled "The Boats" and it provides a very detailed accounting of the use (and misuse) of the *Titanic*'s twenty lifeboats. Page 39 recounts testimony in which many survivors said that people were hesitant to get into the boats when asked to and that the consensus among the passengers seemed to be that it was probably safer onboard the gargantuan *Titanic* than adrift in a tiny boat in the middle of the frigid Atlantic in the middle of the night. "Many people thought that the risk in the ship was less than the risk in the boats," the report said. Also, "It is said further that the officers engaged in putting the people into the boats feared that the boats might buckle if they were filled; but this proved to be an unfounded apprehension, for one or more boats were completely filled and then successfully lowered to the water."

[8] Pages 32 through 34 comprise the first sections of chapter 3 of the report.

Chapter 3 is titled "Description of the Damage to the Ship and of Its Gradual and Final Effect, With Observations Thereon" and begins simply, "The damage done to the ship was as follows," and then recounts the foundering of *Titanic* in five sections: Extent of the Damage; Time in Which the Damage was Done; The Flooding in First 10 Minutes; Gradual Effect of the Damage; and Final Effect of the Damage.

The "Extent of the Damage" section reported:

The collision with the iceberg, which took place at 11:40 p.m., caused damage to the bottom of the starboard side of the vessel at about 10 feet above the level of the keel, but there was no damage above this height. There was damage in: The fore peak, No. 1 hold, No. 2 hold, No. 3 hold, No. 6 boiler room, No. 5 boiler room. The damage extended over a length of about 300 feet.

The "Time in Which the Damage was Done" section reported, "As the ship was moving at over 20 knots, she would have passed through 300 ft. in less than ten seconds, so that the damage was done in about this time."

The next section, "The Flooding in First Ten Minutes," meticulously recounts the early minutes of the disaster, noting that in the first ten minutes after the collision, there was seven feet of water in the No. 1 hold and that in the No. 3 hold, the mail room was almost immediately filled with water.

The next section, "Gradual Effect of the Damage," states, "It will thus be seen that all the six compartments forward of No. 4 boiler room were open to the sea by damage which existed at about ten feet above the keel. At ten minutes after the collision the water seems to have risen to about fourteen feet above the keel in all these compartments except No. 5 boiler room." This section then carefully accounts for the flooding through one hour and forty minutes after the collision.

The fifth section of this accounting—"Final Effect of the Damage"—notes that "The later stages of the sinking cannot be stated with any precision, owing to a confusion of the times which was natural under the circumstances." This accounts for the inaccuracy of the following passages [emphasis added]:

When the last boat, lowered from davits (D), left the ship, A deck was under water, and water came up the stairway under the Boat deck almost immediately afterwards. After this the other port collapsible (B), which had been stowed on the officers' house, was uncovered, the lashings cut adrift, and she was swung round over the edge of the coamings of the deckhouse on to the Boat deck.

Very shortly afterwards the vessel, *according to Mr. Lightoller's account,* seemed to take a dive, and he just walked into the water. When he came to the surface all the funnels were above the water.

Her stern was gradually rising out of the water, and the propellers were clear of the water. *The ship did not break in two, and she did eventually attain the perpendicular, when the second funnel from aft about reached the water.* There were no lights burning then, though they kept alight practically until the last.

Before reaching the perpendicular when at an angle of 50 or 60 degrees, there was a rumbling sound which may be attributed to the boilers leaving their beds and crashing down on to or through the bulkheads. She became more perpendicular and finally absolutely perpendicular, when she went slowly down.

After sinking as far as the after part of the Boat deck she went down more quickly. The ship disappeared at 2:20 a.m.

TELEGRAMS OF CONDOLENCE

The King's Telegram to President Taft:

The Queen and I are anxious to assure you
and the American nation of the great sorrow
which we experience at the terrible loss of
life that has occurred among the American
citizens and my own subjects by the
foundering of the Titanic. Our two countries
are so intimately allied by ties of
friendship and brotherhood that any
misfortune which affects the one must
necessarily affect the other, and on the
present heartrending occasion they are both
equal sufferers.

George R. and I

Apl. 17, 1912

Taft's Response to the King's Telegram:

His Majesty
    George V
        Sandringham. (England.)

In presence of the appalling disaster to the
TITANIC, the people of the two countries are
brought into community of grief through
their common bereavement. The American
people share in the sorrow of their kinsmen
beyond the sea. On behalf of my countrymen I
thank you for your sympathetic message.

Wm. H. Taft

MESSAGE FROM THE KING.

SYMPATHY WITH THE BEREAVED.

TELEGRAM TO WHITE STAR LINE.

The White Star Line have received the following telegram from the King and Queen :—

Sandringham,
Tuesday, 6.30 p.m.

The Managing Director,
White Star Line,
Liverpool,

The Queen and I are horrified at the appalling disaster which has happened to the Titanic and at the terrible loss of life.

We deeply sympathise with the bereaved relatives, and feel for them in their great sorrow with all our hearts.

GEORGE R.I.

Telegrams of condolence were also sent to King George by the following world leaders:

- The duke of Connaught, the governor-general of Canada
- The Russian minister of trade
- General Botha of South Africa
- Mr. Foster, the acting premier of Canada
- The lord mayor of Sydney, Australia
- Lord Islington, the governor of New Zealand

- Signor Nathan, the mayor of Rome, Italy
- The Danish Foreign Parliament
- The Swedish Foreign Parliament
- The Belgian Foreign Parliament
- The Hungarian Foreign Parliament
- Kaiser Wilhelm II of Germany

THE AFTERMATH OF SORROW : How the Tragedy Came Home to Many a Householder in Southampton.

The Last Pilgrimage

The Twenty-Eight Most Important Findings From the Final Report of the U. S. Senate Subcommittee *Titanic* Hearing

No untoward incident marred the trip . . .

—from the "Weather Conditions During Voyage" finding by the Senate Subcommittee

The U.S. Senate Subcommittee *Titanic* Hearing was ridiculed in England for the obvious dearth of "seafaring" knowledge on the part of the subcommittee's lead questioner, Senator William Alden Smith. (One of the most glaring examples of Smith's cluelessness was his inquiring of Harold Lowe as to what an iceberg was made of. "Ice," Lowe responded.)

Smith's cluelessness notwithstanding, though, these hearings were most assuredly *not* the whitewash that the British Board of Trade Inquiry became, and its findings were of importance and value.

This chapter looks at the Senate's twenty-eight most important findings and should provide a general overview of the subcommittee's conclusions. Following this chapter are explicit testimony transcripts from the hearing that will offer much information on the disaster and the roles its many participants played.

'TITANIC" DISASTER

HEARING

BEFORE A

SUBCOMMITTEE OF THE COMMITTEE ON COMMERCE UNITED STATES SENATE

SIXTY-SECOND CONGRESS

SECOND SESSION

PURSUANT TO

S. RES. 283

DIRECTING THE COMMITTEE ON COMMERCE TO INVES-
TIGATE THE CAUSES LEADING TO THE WRECK
OF THE WHITE STAR LINER "TITANIC"

PART 15

DIGEST OF TESTIMONY

Printed for the use of the Committee on Commerce

WASHINGTON
GOVERNMENT PRINTING OFFICE
1912

General Particulars of Steamship *Titanic*

The *Titanic* was built by Harland and Wolff, of Belfast, Ireland. No restriction as to limit of cost was placed upon the builders. She was launched May 31, 1911. She was a vessel of 46,328 tons register; her length was 882.6 feet, and her breadth was 92.6 feet. Her boat deck and bridge were 70 feet above the water line. She was, according to the testimony of President Ismay, "especially constructed to float with her two largest watertight compartments full of water."

The vessel, fully equipped, cost £1,500,000 sterling, or about $7,500,000.

At the time of the accident the vessel carried insurance of £1,000,000 sterling or about $5,000,000, the remaining risk being carried by the company's insurance fund.

The *Titanic* was a duplicate of the *Olympic,* which is owned by the same company, with the single exception of her passenger accommodations, and was built to accommodate 2,599 passengers, with additional accommodations for officers and crew numbering 903 persons.

Only Two Lifeboats Lowered

Many of the crew did not join the ship until a few hours before sailing, and the only drill while the vessel lay at Southampton or on the voyage consisted in lowering two lifeboats on the starboard side into the water, which boats were again hoisted to the boat deck within a half hour. No boat list designating the stations of members of the crew was posted until several days after sailing from Southampton, boatmen being left in ignorance of their proper stations until the following Friday morning.

Summary of Passengers and Survivors

Including the crew, the *Titanic* sailed with 2,223 persons aboard, of whom 1,517 were lost and 706 were saved. It will be noted in this connection that 60 per cent of the first-class passengers were saved, 42 per cent of the second-class passengers were saved, 25 per cent of the third-class passengers were saved, and 24 per cent of the crew were saved.

Weather Conditions During Voyage

During the entire voyage the weather was clear, with the single exception of a 10 minute period of fog, and the sea was calm throughout the voyage, with sunshine the whole of each day and bright starlight every night. No untoward incident marred the trip. Greetings were frequently exchanged with passing vessels by appropriate signals.

Ice Warnings

On the third day out ice warnings were received by the wireless operators on the *Titanic,* and the testimony is conclusive that at least three of these warnings came direct to the commander of the *Titanic* on the day of the accident, the first about noon, from the *Baltic* of the White Star Line. It will be noted that this message places icebergs within 5 miles of the track which the *Titanic* was following, and near the place where the accident occurred.

Ice Both to Northward and Southward Steamship *Titanic's* Track

This enables the committee to say that the ice positions so definitely reported to the *Titanic* just preceding the accident located ice on both sides of the track or lane which the *Titanic* was following, and in her immediate vicinity. No general discussion took place among the officers; no conference was called to consider these warnings; no heed was given to them. The speed was not relaxed, the lookout was not increased, and the only vigilance displayed by the officer of the watch was by instructions to the lookouts to keep "a sharp lookout for ice." It should be said, however, that the testimony shows that Capt. Smith remarked to Officer Lightoller, who was the officer doing duty on the bridge until 10 o'clock ship's time, or 8:27 o'clock New York time, "If it was in a slight degree hazy there would be no doubt we should have to go very slowly" and "If in the slightest degree doubtful, let me know." The evidence is that it was exceptionally clear. There was no haze, and the ship's speed was not reduced.

Speed

The speed of the *Titanic* was gradually increased after leaving Queenstown. The first day's run was 464 miles, the second day's run was 519 miles, the third day's run was 546 miles. Just prior to the collision the ship was making her maximum speed of the voyage—not less than 21 knots, or 24½ miles per hour.

The Collision

At 11:46 P.M. ship's time, or 10:13 P.M. New York time, Sunday evening, April 14, the lookout signaled the bridge and telephoned the officer of the watch, "Iceberg right ahead." The officer of the watch, Mr. Murdoch, immediately ordered the quartermaster at the wheel to put the helm "hard astarboard," and reversed the engines; but while the sixth officer standing behind the quartermaster at the wheel reported to officer Murdoch "The helm is hard astarboard," the *Titanic* struck the ice. The impact, while not violent enough to disturb the passengers or crew, or to arrest the ship's progress, rolled the vessel slightly and tore the steel plating above the turn of the bilge.

First Damage Reported

The testimony shows that coincident with the collision, air was heard whistling or hissing from the overflow pipe to the forepeak tank, indicating the escape of air from that tank because of the inrush of water. Practically at once, the forepeak tank, No. 1 hold, No. 2 hold, No. 3 hold, and the forward boiler room, filled with water, the presence of which was immediately reported from the mail room and the racquet court and trunk room in No. 3 hold, and also from the firemen's quarters in No. 1 hold. Leading Fireman Barret saw the water rushing into the forward fireroom from a tear about two feet above the stokehold plates and about twenty feet below the water line, which tear extended two feet into the coal bunker at the forward end of the second fireroom.

Serious Nature of Damage Realized

The reports received by the captain after various inspections of the ship must have acquainted him promptly with the serious condition, and when interrogated by President Ismay, he so expressed himself. It is believed, also, that this serious condition was promptly realized by the chief engineer and by the builders' representative, Mr. Andrews, none of whom survived.

Flooding of the Vessel

Under this added weight of water the bow of the ship sank deeper and deeper into the water, and through the open hatch leading from the mail room, and through other openings, water promptly overflowed E deck, below which, deck the third, fourth, fifth, sixth, seventh, and eighth transverse bulkheads ended, and thus flooded the compartments abaft No. 3 hold.

Water-tight Compartments

The *Titanic* was fitted with 15 transverse water-tight bulkheads. Only 1, the first bulkhead from forward, extended to the uppermost continuous deck, C; bulkheads Nos. 2, 10, 11, 12, 13, 14, and 15 extended to the second continuous deck, D; and bulkheads Nos. 3, 4, 5, 6, 7, 8, and 9 extended only to the third continuous deck, E. The openings through deck E were not designed for water-tight closing, as the evidence shows that flooding over deck E contributed largely to the sinking of the vessel. The bulkheads above described divided the ship into 16 main water-tight compartments, and the ship was so arranged that any 2 main compartments might be flooded without it in any way involving the safety of the ship. As before stated, the testimony shows that the 5 extreme forward compartments were flooded practically immediately, and under such circumstances, by reason of the nonwater-tight character of the deck at which the transverse bulkheads ended, the supposedly water-tight compartments were NOT water-tight, and the sinking of the vessel followed.

Distress Calls Sent Out

No general alarm was sounded, no whistle blown, and no systematic warning was given the passengers. Within 15 or 20 minutes the captain visited the wireless room and instructed the operator to get assistance, sending out the universal distress call, C. Q. D.

Steamship Light Seen From Steamship *Titanic*

Sixteen witnesses from the *Titanic*, including officers and experienced seamen, and passengers of sound judgment, testified to seeing the light of a ship in the distance, and some of the lifeboats were directed to pull for that light, to leave the passengers and to return to the side of the *Titanic*. The *Titanic* fired distress rockets and attempted to signal by electric lamp and Morse code to this vessel. At about the same time the officers of the *Californian* admit seeing rockets in the general direction of the *Titanic* and say that they immediately displayed a powerful Morse lamp, which could be easily seen a distance of 10 miles, while several of the crew of the *Californian* testify that the side lights of a large vessel going full speed were plainly visible from the lower deck of the *Californian* at 11:30 P.M., ship's time, just before the accident. There is no evidence that any rockets were fired by any vessel between the *Titanic* and the *Californian*, although every eye on the *Titanic* was searching the horizon for possible assistance.

The Steamship *Californian*'s Responsibility

The committee is forced to the inevitable conclusion that the *Californian,* controlled by the same company, was nearer the *Titanic* than the 19 miles reported by her captain, and that her officers and crew saw the distress signals of the *Titanic* and failed to respond to them in accordance with the dictates of humanity, international usage, and the requirements of law. The only reply to the distress signals was a counter signal from a large white light which was flashed for nearly two hours from the mast of the *Californian.* In our opinion such conduct, whether arising from indifference or gross carelessness, is most reprehensible, and places upon the commander of the *Californian* a grave responsibility. The wireless operator of the *Californian* was not aroused until 3:30 A.M., New York time, on the morning of the 15th, after considerable conversation between officers and members of the crew had taken place aboard that ship regarding these distress signals or rockets, and was directed by the chief officer to see if there was anything the matter, as a ship had been firing rockets during the night. The inquiry thus set on foot immediately disclosed the fact that the *Titanic* had sunk. Had assistance been promptly proffered, or had the wireless operator of the *Californian* remained a few minutes longer at his post on Sunday evening, that ship might have had the proud distinction of rescuing the lives of the passengers and crew of the *Titanic*.

Steamship *Titanic*'s Lifeboats Cleared Away

When Captain Smith received the reports as to the water entering the ship, he promptly gave the order to clear away the lifeboats, and later orders were given to put women and children into the boats. During this time distress rockets were fired at frequent intervals.

The lack of preparation at this time was most noticeable. There was no system adopted for loading the boats; there was great indecision as to the deck from which boats were to be loaded; there was wide diversity of opinion as to the number of the crew necessary to man each boat; there was no direction whatever as to the number of passengers to be carried by each boat, and no uniformity in loading them. On one side only women and children were put in the boats, while on the other side there was almost an equal proportion of men and women put into the boats, the women and children being given the preference in all cases. The failure to utilize all lifeboats in their recognized capacity for safety unquestionably resulted in the needless sacrifice of several hundred lives which might otherwise have been saved.

Capacity of Lifeboats Not Utilized

The vessel was provided with lifeboats . . . for 1,176 persons, while but 706 were saved. Only a few of the ship's lifeboats were fully loaded, while others were but partially filled. Some were loaded at the boat deck, and some at the A deck, and there were successfully lowered to the water. The twentieth boat was washed overboard when the forward part of the ship was submerged, and in its overturned condition served as a life raft for about 30 people, including Second Officer Lightoller, Wireless Operators Bride and Phillips (the latter dying before rescue), passengers Col. Gracie and Mr. Jack Thayer, and others of the crew, who climbed upon it from the water at about the time the ship disappeared.

Lifeboat Devices

Had the sea been rough it is questionable whether any of the lifeboats of the *Titanic* would have reached the water without being damaged or destroyed. The point of suspension of the *Titanic*'s boats was about 70 feet above the level of the sea. Had the ship been rolling heavily the lifeboats as they were lowered would have swung out from the side of the ship as it rolled toward them and on the return roll would have swung back and crashed against its side. It is evident from the testimony that as the list of the *Titanic* became noticeable the lifeboats scraped against the side as they were being lowered. Every effort should be made to improve boat-handling devices, and to improve the control of boats while being lowered.

Conflict in Lifeboat Reports

In the reports of the survivors there are marked differences of opinions as to the number carried by each lifeboat. In lifeboat No. 1, for instance, one survivor reports 10 in all. The seaman in charge reports 7 of the crew and 14 to 20 passengers. The officer who loaded this boat estimated that from 3 to 5 women and 22 men were aboard. Accepting the minimum report as made by any one survivor in every boat, the total far exceeds the number picked up by the *Carpathia*.

No Distinction Between Passengers

The testimony is definite that, except in isolated instances, there was no panic. In loading boats no distinction was made between first-, second-, and third-class passengers, although the proportion of lost is larger among third-class passengers than in either of the other classes. Women and children, without discrimination, were given preference.

Your committee believes that under proper discipline the survivors could have been concentrated into fewer boats after reaching the water, and we think that it would have been possible to have saved many lives had those in charge of boats thus released returned promptly to the scene of the disaster.

Conduct on Lifeboats

After lowering, several of the boats rowed many hours in [the] direction of the lights supposed to have been displayed by the *Californian*. Other boats lay on their oars in the vicinity of the sinking ship, a few survivors being rescued from the water. After distributing his passengers among the four other boats which he had herded together, and after the cries of distress had died away, Fifth Officer Lowe, in boat No. 14, went to the scene of the wreck and rescued four living passengers from the water, one of whom afterwards died in the lifeboat, but was identified. Officer Lowe then set sail in boat No. 14, took in tow one collapsible boat, and proceeded to the rescue of passengers on another collapsible lifeboat.

The men who had taken refuge on the overturned collapsible lifeboat were rescued, including Second Officer Lightoller and passengers Gracie and Thayer, and Wireless Operators Bride and Phillips, by lifeboats No. 4 and No. 12, before the arrival of the *Carpathia*. The fourth collapsible lifeboat was rowed to the side of the Carpathia, and contained 28 women and children, mostly third-class passengers, 3 firemen, 1 steward, 4 Filipinos, President Ismay, and Mr. Carter, of Philadelphia, and was in charge of Quartermaster Rowe.

Ship Sinking

The ship went down gradually by the bow, assuming an almost perpendicular position just before sinking at 12:47 A.M., New York time, April 15. There have been many conflicting statements as to whether the ship broke in two, but the preponderance of evidence is to the effect that she assumed an almost end-on position and sank intact.

No Suction

The committee deems it of sufficient importance to call attention to the fact that as the ship disappeared under the water there was no apparent suction or unusual disturbance of the surface of the water. Testimony is abundant that while she was going down there was not sufficient suction to be manifest to any of the witnesses who were in the water or on the overturned collapsible boat or on the floating debris, or to the occupants of the lifeboats in the vicinity of the vessel, or to prevent those in the water, whether equipped with life belts or not, from easily swimming away from the ship's side while she was sinking.

Captain Rostron

The committee invites your attention to the course followed by Captain Rostron, commanding the *Carpathia*. Immediately upon the receipt of the wireless call of distress, Captain Rostron gave the order to turn the ship around and set a definite course toward the *Titanic* and instructed the chief engineer to call another watch of stokers and make all possible speed to that ship.

Realizing the possible presence of ice, because of the collision, Captain Rostron doubled his lookouts and exerted extra vigilance, putting an extra lookout on duty forward and having another officer on the bridge. The captain immediately instructed the first officer to "prepare all our lifeboats and have them all ready for turning outboard."

The committee deems the course followed by Captain Rostron of the *Carpathia* as deserving of the highest praise and worthy of special recognition.

On the Scene of the Wreck

The first boat was picked up at 4:10 A.M. Monday, and the last of the survivors was on board by 8:30 A.M., after which Captain Rostron made arrangements "to hold service, a short prayer of thankfulness for those rescued, and a short burial service for those who were lost."

Upon the arrival of the *Californian* upon the scene, about 8 o'clock in the morning, the captain of the *Carpathia* communicated with her commander, stating that all of the passengers had been rescued from the boats but that he thought one was still unaccounted for; and arrangements were made whereby the *Californian* made an exhaustive search in the vicinity for this missing boat.

Captain Rostron stated that the *Carpathia* picked up 15 lifeboats and 2 collapsible boats. Evidence was given before the committee by at least one occupant of every lifeboat, satisfying the committee that the 16 lifeboats with which the *Titanic* was equipped were all accounted for. Thirteen of these lifeboats were hoisted on board and carried to New York by the *Carpathia*.

After arranging for a thorough search of the vicinity by the *Californian*, Captain Rostron headed his vessel for New York, reporting immediately by wireless to the officials of his company in New York, as follows:

New York, latitude 41.45; longtitude 50.20 west.—Am proceeding New York unless otherwise ordered, with about 800, after having consulted with Mr. Ismay and considering the circumstances. With so much ice about, consider New York best. Large number icebergs, and 20 miles field ice with bergs amongst.

Bodies Not Visible

The committee directs attention to the fact that Captain Rostron, of the *Carpathia*, although four hours in the vicinity of the accident, saw only one body, and that Captain Lord, of the *Californian*, who remained three hours in the vicinity of the wreckage, saw none. The failure of the captain of the *Carpathia*, of the captain of the *Californian*, and of the captain of the *Mount Temple* to find bodies floating in that vicinity in the early morning of the day following can only be accounted for on the theory that those who went down with the ship either did not rise to the surface or were carried away or hidden by the extensive ice flow which during the night came down over the spot where the ship disappeared, while those bodies which have been found remote from the place where the ship went down were probably carried away from the scene by the currents or by the movement of the ice.

Information Withheld

The committee does not believe that the wireless operator on the *Carpathia* showed proper vigilance in handling the important work confided to his care after the accident. Information concerning an accident at sea had been used by a wireless operator prior to this accident for his own advantage. That such procedure had been permitted by the Marconi Co. may have had its effect on this occasion. The disposition of officials at the Marconi Co. to permit this practice and the fact of that company's representatives making the arrangements for the sale of the experiences of the operators of the *Titanic* and *Carpathia* subjects the participants to criticism, and the practice should be prohibited. The committee are pleased to note that Mr. Marconi approves of such prohibition.

Recommendations

The committee finds that this accident clearly indicates the necessity of additional legislation to secure safety of life at sea.

By statute the United States accepts reciprocally the inspection certificates of foreign countries having inspection laws approximating those of the United States. Unless there is early revision of inspection laws of foreign countries along the lines laid down hereinafter, the committee deems it proper that such reciprocal arrangements be terminated, and that no vessel shall be licensed to carry passengers from ports of the United States until all regulations and requirements of the Laws of the United States have been fully complied with.

The committee recommends that sections 4481 and 4488, Revised Statutes, be so amended as to definitely require sufficient lifeboats to accommodate every passenger and every member of the crew. That the importance of this feature is recognized by the steamship lines is indicated by the fact that on many lines steps are being taken to provide lifeboat capacity for every person on board, including crew; and the fact of such equipment is being widely advertised. The president of the International Mercantile Marine Co., Mr. Ismay, definitely stated to the committee:

> We have issued instructions that none of the ships of our lines shall leave any port carrying more passengers and crew than they have capacity for in the lifeboats.

Not less then four members of the crew, skilled in handling boats, should be assigned to every boat. All members of the crew assigned to lifeboats should be drilled in lowering and rowing the boats, not less than twice each month and the fact of such drill or practice should be noted in the log.

The committee recommends the assignment of passengers and crew to lifeboats before sailing; that occupants of certain groups of staterooms and the stewards of such groups of rooms be assigned to certain boats most conveniently located with reference to the room in question; the assignment of boats and the shortest route from stateroom to boat to be posted in every stateroom.

The committee recommends that every ocean steamship carrying 100 or more passengers be required to carry 2 electric searchlights.

The committee finds that this catastrophe makes glaringly apparent the necessity for regulation of radiotelegraphy. There must be an operator on duty at all times, day and night, to insure the immediate receipt of all distress, warning, or other important calls. Direct communication either by clear-speaking telephone, voice tube, or messenger must be provided between the wireless room and the bridge, so that the operator does not have to leave his station. There must be definite legislation to prevent interference by amateurs, and to secure secrecy of radiograms or wireless messages. There must be some source of auxiliary power, either storage battery or oil engine, to insure the operation of the wireless installation until the wireless room is submerged.

The committee recommends the early passage of S. 6412, already passed by the Senate and favorably reported by the House.

The committee recommends that the firing of rockets or candles on the high seas for any other purpose than as a signal of distress be made a misdemeanor.

The committee recommends that the following additional structural requirements be required as regards ocean-going passenger steamers the construction of which is begun after this date:

All steel ocean and coastwise seagoing ships carrying 100 or more passengers should have a water-tight skin inboard of the outside plating, extending not less than 10 per cent of the load draft above the full-load waterline, either in the form of an inner bottom or of longitudinal water-tight bulkheads, and this construction should extend from the forward collision bulkhead over not less than two-thirds of the length of the ship.

All steel ocean and coastwise seagoing ships carrying 100 or more passengers should have bulkheads so spaced that any two adjacent compartments of the ship may be flooded without destroying the flotability or stability of the ship. Water-tight transverse bulkheads should extend from

side to side of the ship, attaching to the outside shell. The transverse bulkheads forward and abaft the machinery spaces should be continued water-
tight vertically to the uppermost continuous structural deck. The uppermost
continuous structural deck should be fitted water-tight. Bulkheads within the
limits of the machinery spaces should extend not less than 25 per cent of the
draft of the ship above the load waterline and should end at a water-tight
deck. All water-tight bulkheads and decks should be proportioned to withstand, without material permanent deflection, a water pressure equal to 5 feet
more than the full height of the bulkhead. Bulkheads of novel dimensions or
scantlings should be tested by being subjected to actual water pressure.

**Upon that broken hull new vows were taken, new fealty
expressed, old love renewed, and those who had been
devoted in friendship and companions in life went
proudly and defiantly on the last life pilgrimage together.
In such a heritage we must feel ourselves more intimately
related to the sea than ever before, and henceforth it will
send back to us on its rising tide the cheering salutations
from those we have lost.**

**—Senator William Alden Smith
May 28, 1912**

THE EIGHTY-SIX WITNESSES WHO TESTIFIED AT THE U.S. SENATE SUBCOMMITTEE HEARING INTO THE *TITANIC* DISASTER

This list of U.S. Senate witnesses is notable for its diversity: The Subcommittee called everyone from steerage passengers to Marconi Wireless
executives to ship's captains and *Titanic* crew members.

1. Abelseth, Olaus (steerage passenger)
2. Adams, C. C. (testimony given in letter)
3. Andrews, Charles E. (assistant steward)
4. Archer, Ernest (able seaman)
5. Balfour, Gilbert William (inspector, the Marconi Wireless Tele-
    graph Co. of America)
6. Barrett, Frederick (leading coal fireman)

7. Binns, John R. (reporter for the *New York American*)
8. Bishop, Dickinson H. (first-class passenger)
9. Bishop, Mrs. Helen W. (first-class passenger)
10. Bottomley, John (general manager of the Marconi Wireless Telegraph Co. of America)
11. Boxhall, Joseph G. (fourth officer)
12. Brice, W. (able seaman)
13. Bride, Harold S. (wireless operator)
14. Bright, Arthur John (quartermaster)
15. Brooks, B. (testimony given in letter)
16. Buckley, Daniel (steerage passenger)
17. Buley, Edward John (able seaman)
18. Burke, William (saloon steward)
19. Campbell, Benjamin (vice president of the New York, New Haven and Hartford Rail Road Co.)
20. Chambers, Norman Campbell (first-class passenger)
21. Clench, Frederick (able seaman)
22. Collins, John (scullion or assistant cook in the first-class galley)
23. Cone, Adm. H. I. (engineer in chief, United States Navy; testimony given in memorandum)
24. Cottam, Harold Thomas (wireless operator on the *Carpathia*)
25. Crawford, Alfred (first-class bedroom steward)
26. Crosby, Catherine E. (first-class passenger; testimony given in affidavit)
27. Crowe, George Frederick (saloon steward)
28. Cunningham, Andrew (stateroom steward)
29. Dauler, Frederick (clerk for the Western Union Telegraph Co.)
30. Douglas, Mahala D. (first-class passenger; testimony given in affidavit)
31. Dunn, Edward J. (salesman)
32. Etches, Henry Samuel (bedroom steward)
33. Evans, Cyril Furmstone (wireless operator on the *Californian*)
34. Evans, Frank Oliver (able seaman)
35. Farrell, Maurice L. (managing editor of the *Wall Street Journal*; testimony given in a statement and in person)
36. Fleet, Frederick (able seaman and lookout)
37. Franklin, Philip A. S. (American vice president of the International Mercantile Marine Co., the parent company of the White Star Line)

38. Gill, Ernest (assistant engineer on the *Californian*)
39. Gracie, Col. Archibald (first-class passenger)
40. Haddock, Capt. Herbert James (commander of the R.M.S. *Olympic*)
41. Haines, Albert (boatswain's mate)
42. Harder, George A. (first-class passenger)
43. Hardy, John (chief second-class steward)
44. Hemming, Samuel S. (able seaman)
45. Hitchens, Robert (helmsman)
46. Hogg, George Alfred (lookout)
47. Hosey, James A. (testimony given in affidavit)
48. Ismay, J. Bruce (managing director of the White Star Line and president of the International Mercantile Marine Co.)
49. Jones, Thomas (able seaman)
50. Knapp, Capt. John J. (hydrographer, United States Navy, Bureau of Navigation)
51. Lightoller, Charles Herbert (second officer)
52. Lord, Captain Stanley (commander of the *Californian*; testimony given in affidavit)
53. Lowe, Harold Godfrey (fifth officer; testimony given in an affidavit and a statement)
54. McGough, James R. (able seaman; testimony given in affidavit)
55. Marconi, Guglielmo (inventor of the wireless and founder of the Marconi Wireless Telegraph Co. of America)
56. Minahan, Daisy (first-class passenger; testimony given in affidavit)
57. Moore, Ernest James (wireless operator on the R.M.S. *Olympic*)
58. Morgan, Charles H. (Deputy U.S. Marshall)
59. Olliver, Alfred (quartermaster)
60. Osman, Frank (able seaman)
61. Perkis, Walter John (quartermaster)
62. Peuchen, Maj. Arthur C. (first-class passenger)
63. Pickard, Berk (steerage passenger)
64. Pitman, Herbert John (third officer)
65. Quitzrau, Dr. F. C. (second-class *Mount Temple* passenger)
66. Ray, Frederick D. (first-class steward)
67. Rostron, Capt. Arthur Henry (commander of the *Carpathia*)
68. Rowe, George Thomas (quartermaster)

69. Ryerson, Mrs. Emily Bosie (first-class passenger)
70. Sammis, Frederick M. (general engineer of the Marconi Wireless Telegraph Co. of America)
71. Shelley, Mrs. Imanita (second-class passenger; testimony given in affidavit)
72. Shelley, William (testimony given in letter)
73. Smith, George Otis (director of the United States Geological Survey; testimony given in letter)
74. Smith, Mrs. Lucian P. (first-class passenger, testimony given in affidavit)
75. Stengel, C. E. Henry (first-class passenger)
76. Stone, Melville E. (steward)
77. Symons, George (able seaman)
78. Taylor, William Henry (fireman)
79. Ward, William (saloon steward)
80. Weikman, August H. (barber; testimony given in affidavit)
81. Wheelton, Edward (saloon steward)
82. White, Mrs. J. Stuart (first-class passenger)
83. Widener, Eleanor Elkins (first-class passenger; testimony given in affidavit)
84. Widgery, James (baths steward)
85. Wolfe, C. H. (correspondent for the *New York World*; testimony given in letter)
86. Woolner, Hugh (first-class passenger)

The U.S. Senate Subcommittee Testimony of Guglielmo Marconi

Sir:

It is an undoubted fact that nobody would have been saved from the ill-fated *Titanic* had it not been for the great invention of Signor Marconi. I would therefore suggest that one of the big liners soon to be launched should be named Marconi.

Yours, Lorenzo Salazat

—letter to the editor of Britain's *Daily Sketch*,
published on Wednesday, May 1, 1912

The passage of time always helps us see people and events in their proper light and in their proper context, and a quintessential example of this is the ridiculous and shortsighted grilling of the communications pioneer Guglielmo Marconi—one of the most influential figures in the grand panoply of human achievement—at the United States Senate hearings into the *Titanic* disaster.

Was the inventor of the inestimable wireless queried about the role of his wondrous invention in the rescue of the *Titanic* passengers who were able to be saved?

No.

Was the groundbreaking Italian genius asked for his opinions on how sea travel could be made safer with more effective use of his invention?

No.

The great Marconi was, instead, mercilessly questioned about whether or not he gave his blessing to the selling of the surviving wireless operators' stories to the newspapers.

Nonetheless, Marconi answered Senator Smith's questions with as much deference and respect as he could muster. It is also to Marconi's credit that he honestly admitted that he saw nothing wrong with the operators being paid to talk to the newspapers about their ordeal. Senator Smith tried to insinuate that Marconi urged the operators to withhold details about the disaster from the public in order to sell this information for personal gain. Marconi adamantly denied that this was the case, but, again, staunchly defended the right of the operators to be paid for their stories.

The following is a transcript of Marconi's impassioned testimony before the committee. "Bride" is Harold Bride, the surviving *Titanic* wireless operator; "Phillips" is the *Titanic* wireless operator who perished; "Bottomley" is John Bottomley, Marconi's American operations manager; "Sammis" is Frederick Sammis, Marconi's chief U.S. engineer; "Cottam" is Harold Cottam, the *Carpathia*'s wireless operator; "Mr. Ochs" is Adolph S. Ochs, the publisher of the *New York Times;* "Van Ander" is Carr Van Ander, the managing editor of the *New York Times.*

> **SENATOR SMITH:** What is the pay of a wireless operator, generally speaking, in this country?
>
> **GUGLIELMO MARCONI:** I am not aware of the exact pay in this country.
>
> **SS:** What is it in England?

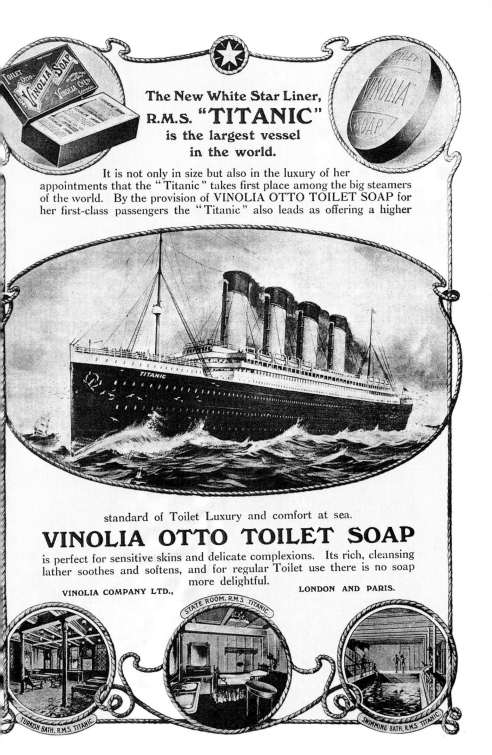

The New White Star Liner,
R.M.S. "TITANIC"
is the largest vessel
in the world.

It is not only in size but also in the luxury of her appointments that the "Titanic" takes first place among the big steamers of the world. By the provision of VINOLIA OTTO TOILET SOAP for her first-class passengers the "Titanic" also leads as offering a higher

standard of Toilet Luxury and comfort at sea.

VINOLIA OTTO TOILET SOAP

is perfect for sensitive skins and delicate complexions. Its rich, cleansing lather soothes and softens, and for regular Toilet use there is no soap more delightful.

VINOLIA COMPANY LTD.,   LONDON AND PARIS.

Titanic boasted a "higher standard" of luxury. Even its soap on board was the best. AUTHOR'S COLLECTION

The White Star Line's ad promoting *Titanic*'s sailing from New York following her maiden voyage. AUTHOR'S COLLECTION

Links from the great ship's center anchor cable—at the time, the largest links ever forged. AUTHOR'S COLLECTION

Final preparations being made for the ship's official launching.
AUTHOR'S COLLECTION

Titanic being fitted after its launch at Belfast. AUTHOR'S COLLECTION

Some of the sumptuous accommodations of the White Star sister ships *Olympic* and *Titanic*. AUTHOR'S COLLECTION

Captain Smith (front, second from right) and the officers of the ill-fated *Titanic*. AUTHOR'S COLLECTION

Left: White Star chairman J. Bruce Ismay. AUTHOR'S COLLECTION

Center: Titanic's owner, American millionaire J. P. Morgan, had booked passage on the prized ship's maiden voyage, but business affairs called him elsewhere. AUTHOR'S COLLECTION

Right: Thomas Andrews supervised every detail of the ship's construction. He did not survive. AUTHOR'S COLLECTION

surance *is wanted by* OCEANIC STEAM NAVIGATION COMPANY LIMITED *for account*

om it may concern.

loss, if any, payable to OCEANIC STEAM NAVIGATION
COMPANY, LIMITED.

$ $100,000. *on* STR. TITANIC

Valued at $5,000,000.

and to be insured at and from

the 30 day of March 1912 at 7 P.M.

until

the 30 day of March 1913 at 7 P.M.

is policy is subject to total loss or constructive total loss of the
ssel only, and to cover General Average and salvage charges if both
arges combined amount to $750,000., which amount is deductible.

emium at the rate of 2-1/10% per annum, predicated on the rate of
 for each trip, and in the event of the vessel being detained in
ct for any cause, the premium returned for such detention to be
ed on the number of trips. But in the event of the total loss of
 Steamer during the period covered by this policy, the full annual
mium of 2 1/10% to be paid by the Assured.

Detail of the White Star Line's $5,000,000 insurance policy
on *Titanic*. Because of the "total loss of the Steamer,"
the company collected. AUTHOR'S COLLECTION

The British publication *The Sphere* recreates the moment of the collision on the cover of its April 20, 1912, issue.
AUTHOR'S COLLECTION

The Sphere's artist depicts the moment when the ship slipped under the waves.
AUTHOR'S COLLECTION

GM: In England it is from, I should say, beginning at $4 a week to $10 or $12 a week, with board and lodging. Of course, you have not asked me this, but I might say it is fairly easy to get operators on those terms in England because it is a rate of pay which is considerably higher than what they get on the shore telegraphs; and, of course, the fact of going to sea is very attractive to a great number of young men.

SS: The hazard does not seem to deter them from that service.

GM: No, it does not.

SS: Was Mr. Bride, who survived the *Titanic* disaster, employed in England or America?

GM: He was employed in England.

SS: And the same is true of Mr. Phillips, who perished?

GM: The same is true of Mr. Phillips.

SS: Where were you on Sunday, April 14, last?

GM: I was in New York.

SS: Where were you when the *Carpathia* landed at the Cunard dock with the survivors of the *Titanic* wreck?

GM: I was dining with Mr. Bottomley. I had the intention of going on board the *Carpathia* as soon as she reached dock, but she happened to get in sooner than we expected. I therefore left the house where I was dining and proceeded to the dock, and we got on board.

SS: What time?

GM: At about half past 9, just when the survivors were leaving, or just when the last survivors were leaving.

SS: You got on board?

GM: I got on board.

SS: What did you do when you got on board?

GM: I went to the wireless operating room.

SS: Did you find the operator there?

GM: I found the operator there.

SS: What did you say to him?

GM: I said I was glad to see him, and congratulated him on what I had heard he had done. I inquired after his senior operator, Phillips.

SS: That is, you inquired of Bride about his senior operator, Phillips?

GM: About Phillips. The operator of the *Carpathia*, Cottam, was not there.

SS: Where was he?

GM: He had gone ashore immediately [after] the ship arrived.

SS: Did you send a wireless to the operator on the *Carpathia* and ask him to meet you and Sammis at the Strand Hotel, 502 West Fourteenth Street, saying, "Keep your mouth shut"?

GM: No, sir; I did not.

SS: If any message of that kind was sent in your name, you did not send it?

GM: I did not send it.

SS: And you know nothing of it?

GM: I know nothing of it, except some statements or rumors I have heard of it in the press.

SS: Do you know of the naval vessel *Florida*?

GM: Yes; I have heard of her.

SS: Is she equipped with wireless apparatus?

GM: Yes, sir; I think they all are.

SS: I am going to read to you the following, and ask whether you know anything about any fact or circumstance connected with it.

This is from the commanding officer of the *Florida* to the Secretary of the Navy, dated April 22, and reads as follows:

On the evening of the steamship *Carpathia*'s arrival in New York, the four following radiograms were intercepted by the chief operator, J. R. Simpson, chief electrician, United States Navy. They appear to me to be significant enough to be brought to the attention of the department:

SEAGATE TO CARPATHIA—8:12 P.M.

"Say, old man, Marconi Co. taking good care of you. Keep your mouth shut, and hold your story. It is fixed for you so you will get big money. Now, please do your best to clear."

That was 8:12 p.m. Then follows this one:

8:30 P.M.

To Marconi officer, Carpathia and Titanic

Arranged for your exclusive story for dollars in four figures, Mr. Marconi agreeing. Say nothing until you see me. Where are you now?

J. M. Sammis, Opr. C

9:00 P.M.

From <u>Seagate</u> to <u>Carpathia</u> operator: Go to
Strand Hotel, 502 West Fourteenth Street. To
meet Mr. Marconi.

C.

9:33 P.M.

From <u>Seagate</u> to <u>Carpathia</u>: A personal to
operator <u>Carpathia</u>. Meet Mr. Marconi and
Sammis at Strand Hotel, 502 West Fourteenth
Street. Keep your mouth shut.

Mr. Marconi

What can you say about that, Mr. Marconi?

GM: I do not know anything whatever about any of those messages. They are not in the phraseology which I would have approved of if I had passed them. I should, however, say that I told Mr. Sammis or Mr. Bottomley—I do not remember which—that I, as an officer of the British company, would not prohibit or prevent these operators from making anything which they reasonably could make out of selling their story of the wreck. I was anxious that, if possible, they might make some small amount of money out of the information they had.

SS: Is that a custom of your company?

GM: It is not a custom; it is a thing that is done—

SS: Is it a habit?

GM: No; it is not a habit. It is done on very special occasions.

SS: Mr. Marconi, do you wish the committee to understand that you approve that method?

GM: I was in favor of it, or at least I approved of or consented to his getting something out of this story.

SS: I know, but let me ask you this. With the right to exact compensation for an exclusive story detailing the horrors of the greatest sea disaster that ever occurred in the history of the world, do you mean that an operator under your company's direction shall have the right to prevent the public from knowing of that calamity—

GM (interrupting): No.

SS: Hold on a moment.—from knowing of that calamity except through the exclusive appropriation of the facts by the operator who is cognizant of them?

GM: I say, not at all. I gave no instructions in regard to withholding any information, and I gave no advice or instructions in regard to any exclusive story to anybody. The only thing I did say or did authorize was that if he was offered payment for a story of the disaster, he was permitted, so far as the English company went, to take that money.

SS: You have seen the rumors of this matter, have you not, in the papers?

GM: Yes.

SS: I have not seen those rumors; but after seeing those rumors did you talk with Sammis about the matter?

GM: I saw Mr. Sammis for a few moments some time ago, and I told him—I said, "You know that I did not authorize that message."

SS: When did you tell him that?

GM: I told him that since the survivors were landed. I do not remember the exact date.

SS: About what time?

GM: Three or four days ago, I should say.

SS: Have you talked with him about it since?

GM: No, sir. I should state in explanation, also, of this matter—

SS: Please do; I would like to have you [do so], in your own way. I am not seeking to embarrass you, at all. I simply feel it my duty to get the information I have asked for.

GM: What I meant and intended when I stated to the operator that he could take something for a story or for an account of the disaster was that newspapers and reporters would be so interested in what he had to say personally, in view of the fact especially that Bride had behaved in such a brave and gallant manner, that, without withholding any general information, they would be ready to pay him an amount for a story or a description which he could give to them.

SS: Have you finished?

GM: Yes, sir.

SS: Mr. Marconi, did you expect the operator to syndicate this information, or to give it exclusively to one newspaper?

GM: I did not expect him to give it exclusively.

SS: Did you expect him to put the story up to the highest bidder?

GM: No, sir.

SS: If I understand you correctly, you did not seek to control the operator, at all, in what he would say or to whom he would say it?

GM: No; I did not.

SS: Do you know what the use of the words, "Arranged for your exclusive story for dollars in four figures, Mr. Marconi agreeing. Say nothing until you see me. J. M. Sammis," would indicate? What did he mean by "four figures"?

GM: I suppose it was something over a thousand dollars; but if you will allow me to repeat again—

SS: Please do. I wish you would say anything you want to about it.

GM (continuing): For the fourth or fifth or sixth time, I say that I know nothing whatever about those messages.

SS: And you understand that I am not saying that you do.

GM: Thank you.

SS: I am simply inquiring. Do you know whether Cottam or Bride sold their story?

GM: I think they received remuneration for it, and that may be called "sold," I presume. I mean that they were paid for it.

SS: Do you know how much they got?

GM: I do not know how much Cottam got.

SS: Do you know how much Bride got?

GM: I was told that Bride got $500.

SS: From whom?

GM: From the *New York Times*.

SS: Who told you that?

GM: I think it was Mr. Bottomley.

SS: The general manager of your company?

GM: Yes. I should also say, I believe, one of the editors of the *New York Times*, either Mr. Ochs or Van Ander . . .

SS: Is any officer of the Marconi Co. interested in the *New York Times*?

GM: I do not know. I do not think so, because if anyone was I would probably hear of it in some way.

SS: Is any director of your company interested in the *New York Times*?

GM: No.

SS: Have you heard from any source any statement given as to the amount Cottam received for his story?

GM: No; I have not.

SS: Did you see his story?

GM: I saw the headlines of his story; I did not read it through.

SS: In the *New York Times*?

GM: In the *Times*.

THE U.S. SENATE SUBCOMMITTEE TESTIMONY
OF *CALIFORNIAN* CAPTAIN STANLEY LORD

If there is a single villain in the *Titanic* disaster (and, of course, there *isn't* only one single villain), it is probably Capt. Stanley Lord of the steamer *Californian*. In fact, there are today two schools of thought regarding Captain Lord's actions (or lack thereof) that tragic evening, and these two factions are called Lordites and anti-Lordites. History has a way of resolving riddles, though, and today, the alleged evidence put forth by the Lordites supposedly exonerating Captain Lord crumbles like a house of cards struck by a gust of wind.

We now know that Captain Lord was an autocratic, arrogant despot and that his own crew feared him enough that they would go out of their way to avoid conflicts with the man. After decades of research and study, most *Titanic* authorities today believe that the *Californian* was indeed the "mystery ship" seen by passengers of the *Titanic* that night; that the crew of the *Californian* did see *Titanic*'s eight distress rockets; that Captain Lord consciously refused to go to the aid of the stricken vessel; and that the *Californian*'s log may have been altered to reflect Lord's version of the story.

The debate over Captain Lord's role and culpability in the death of over 1,500 *Titanic* souls will never end. There are too many people on both sides of the Atlantic who refuse to believe that Lord was capable of such coldhearted behavior.

Captain Lord defended himself and his actions at the U.S. Senate *Titanic* Hearing, and here is the complete transcript of his testimony. You must decide for yourself if he is believable.

SENATOR SMITH: Did you attempt to communicate with the vessel *Titanic* on Sunday?
CAPTAIN LORD: Yes, sir.
SS: At what time of the day?
CL: Ten minutes to 11.
SS: A.M.?
CL: P.M.
SS: That is ship's time?
CL: At the ship's time for 47 °25′ west.
SS: That was of longtitude 47° 25′ west?
CL: Yes, sir.

SS: What was that communication?

CL: We told them we were stopped and surrounded by ice.

SS: Did the *Titanic* acknowledge that message?

CL: Yes, sir; I believe he told the operator he had read it, and told him to shut up, to stand by, or something; that he was busy.

SS: That was the *Titanic*'s reply?

CL: Yes, sir.

SS: Did you have further communication with the *Titanic*?

CL: Not at all, sir.

SS: Did the *Titanic* have further communication with you?

CL: No, sir.

SS: Do you know the *Titanic*'s position on the sea when she sank?

CL: I know the position given to me by the *Virginian* as the position where she struck an iceberg, 41° 56′ and 50° 14′.

SS: Figuring from the *Titanic's* position at the time she went down and your position at the time you sent this warning to the *Titanic,* how far were these vessels from one another?

CL: From the position we stopped in to the position at which the *Titanic* is supposed to have hit the iceberg, 19½ to 19¾ miles; south 16 west, sir, was the course.

SS: Do you know what time the *Titanic* sent out this C. Q. D. call?

CL: No, sir; I do not.

SS: Did the *Californian* receive that call?

CL: No, sir.

SS: Either from the *Titanic* or any other ship?

CL: We got it from the *Virginian*.

SS: What time did you receive it?

CL: Six o'clock, sir.

SS: A.M.?

CL: A.M., on the 15th.

SS: When you notified the *Titanic* that you were in the ice, how much ice were you in?

CL: Well, we were surrounded by a lot of loose ice, and we were about a quarter of a mile off the edge of the field.

SS: Were there any icebergs in view?

CL: No; I could not see that; not then.

SS: This ice that you were in was field ice?

CL: Field ice.

SS: And how large an area, in your judgment, would it cover?

CL: Well, my judgment was from what I saw the next day; not what I saw that night.

SS: Exactly; but how large an area would it cover the next morning?

CL: I suppose about 25 miles long and from 1 to 2 miles wide.

SS: How badly were you interfered with by the ice on Sunday evening?

CL: How were we interfered with?

SS: Yes.

CL: We stopped altogether.

SS: What did you stop for?

CL: So we would not run over the top of it.

SS: You stopped your ship so that you might avoid the ice?

CL: To avoid the ice.

SS: And did you avoid it?

CL: I did.

SS: When did you notify the *Titanic* of your condition? What was your purpose?

CL: It was just a matter of courtesy. I thought he would be a long way from where we were. I did not think he was anywhere near the ice. By rights, he ought to have been 18 or 19 miles to the southward of where I was. I never thought the ice was stretching that far down.

SS: Do you know anything regarding the *Titanic* disaster, of your own knowledge? Did you see the ship on Sunday?

CL: No, sir.

SS: Or any signals from her?

CL: Not from the *Titanic*.

SS: Was the *Titanic* beyond your range of vision?

CL: I should think so; 19$\frac{1}{2}$ or 20 miles away.

SS: How long did it take you to reach the scene of the accident, from the time you steamed up and got under way Monday morning?

CL: From the time we received the message of the *Titanic*'s position?

SS: Yes.

CL (reading): Six o'clock, proceeded slow, pushing through the thick ice. I will read this from the log book.

Six o'clock, proceeded slow, pushing through the thick ice. 6:30, clear of thickest of ice; proceeded full speed, pushing the ice. 8:30, stopped close to steamship *Carpathia*.

SS: Was the *Carpathia* at that time at the scene of the wreck?

CL: Yes, sir; she was taking the last of the people out of the boats.

SS: I would like to ask you, Captain Lord, to tell the committee what kind of watch you kept on Sunday night after the engines stopped. Did you keep an unusual lookout on duty?

CL: No, not after we stopped the engines.

SS: Did you, up to the time you stopped?

CL: Yes.

SS: Tell the committee of what that consisted.

CL: We doubled the lookout from the crew, put a man on the forecastle head—that is, right at the bow of the ship—and I was on the bridge myself with an officer, which I would not have been under ordinary circumstances.

SS: What time did you increase the watch?

CL: When it got dark that night.

SS: As soon as it got dark?

CL: About 8 o'clock. I went on the bridge at 8 o'clock.

SS: And you remained on the bridge how long?

CL: Until half past 10.

SS: And this increased watch was maintained during all that time?

CL: Until half past 10.

SS: You thought that was necessary in your situation at that time?

CL: Well, we had had a report of this ice three or four days before, so we were just taking the extra precautions.

SS: Where did you sail from on that voyage?

CL: London.

SS: Bound for Boston?

CL: Boston; yes, sir.

SS: If you had received the C. Q. D. call of distress from the *Titanic* Sunday evening after your communication with the *Titanic*, how long, under the conditions which surrounded you, would it have taken you to have reached the scene of that catastrophe?

CL: At the very least, two hours.

SS: Two hours?

CL: At the very least, the way the ice was packed around us, and it being nighttime.

SS: Do you know how long it took for the *Carpathia* to reach the scene of the accident from the time the C. Q. D. call was received by Captain Rostron?

CL: Only from what I have read in the paper.

SS: You have no knowledge of your own on that?

CL: No, sir.

SS: Captain Rostron told you nothing?

CL: Oh, no. I asked him the particulars of the accident; that was all.

SS: It took the *Carpathia* about four hours to reach the scene of *Titanic*'s accident, after they received word.

CL: So I understand.

SS: You were about 20 miles away?

CL: Nineteen and one-half to twenty miles from the position given me by the *Titanic*.

SS: At the hour the *Titanic* sank?

CL: We were 19½ to 20 miles away.

SS: And the *Carpathia* was 53 miles away?

CL: Yes, sir.

SS: How long after the *Carpathia* reached the scene of this accident did you reach the scene?

CL: Well, I don't know what time we got there.

SS: Had the lifeboats, with their passengers, been picked up and taken aboard the *Carpathia*?

CL: I think he was taking the last boat up when I got there.

SS: Did you see any of the wreckage when you got there?

CL: Yes, sir.

SS: Tell the committee what you saw?

CL: I saw several empty boats, some floating planks, a few deck chairs, and cushions; but considering the size of the disaster, there was very little wreckage. It seemed more like an old fishing boat that had sunk.

SS: Did you see any life preservers?

CL: A few life belts floating around.

SS: Did you see any persons, dead or alive?

CL: No, sir.

SS: Captain, during Sunday, when you were in the vicinity of ice, did you give any special instructions to your wireless operator?

CL: No, sir.

SS: You had but one operator, had you?

CL: That is all.

SS: And what was his name?

CL: Mr. Evans.

SS: Is he here with you?

CL: Yes, sir; this is he.

SS: Do you know whether your wireless operator was on duty Sunday night after you sent this warning message to *Titanic*?

CL: I do not think he was.

SS: You do not think he was on duty?

CL: No.

SS: Then you are unable to say whether an attempt was made to communicate with the *Californian*?

CL: No; I do not know as to that. I went past his room at about a quarter to 12, and there was no light in there.

SS: Does that indicate he was out, or asleep?

CL: That would indicate he was asleep. As a rule there is always a light in the accumulator burning when he is not asleep.

SS: Did he have any hours particularly prescribed for him by yourself or anyone else after you became aware of your proximity to ice?

CL: No.

SS: On Sunday?

CL: No.

SS: Suppose your wireless operator had been at his post in the operating room when the C. Q. D. call of distress came out from the *Titanic*, which was received by the *Carpathia* and other ships, would your ship have been apprised of the distress of the *Titanic*? I mean, have you such a wireless apparatus on that ship as would have in all probability caught this message?

CL: If the operator had been on duty?

SS: Yes.

CL: Most certainly.

SS: What has been the custom on your ship with reference to wireless service? Do you profess or undertake to have the operator on duty during the daytime or in the night?

CL: I have never interfered with them.

SS: In any way?

CL: From what I have seen of him, he is generally around until about 10 o'clock in the morning, and next day gives me reports of things that happen after midnight, very frequently.

SS: If you were to have the service of a wireless operator at a time when he might be of most service, when would it be, ordinarily, day or night?

CL: As it happens, there are so many one-operator ships around that at nighttime most of those fellows are asleep; and he would be more useful in the daytime. We would get a great deal more information in the daytime, as it happens now.

SS: But at night your passengers are also asleep?

CL: Yes, sir.

SS: Would it not be well to have your wireless operator at his post on duty at night, when other eyes are closed, in order that any possible signal of distress might not escape your attention?

CL: We have the officer on the bridge, who can see as far at night as in the daytime.

SS: But the officer on the bridge could not see the *Titanic* even with glasses, you said, that night.

CL: No.

SS: The wireless operator could have heard the call from the *Titanic* if he had been at his post of duty?

CL: Yes; he would have heard that.

SS: I simply want to ask, Captain, whether the wireless operator had any regular hours or not? If so, what were they?

CL: No; I do not think there are any regular hours. I understand they are usually around from 7 in the morning to half-past 2, and then I think they lie down, because I never, as a rule, receive any messages between half-past 2 and 4. I presume they are asleep.

SS: You think it is better to have two operators on every ship, do you, so as to have continuous service?

CL: It would be much nicer. You would never miss a message, then.

SS: Captain, did you see any distress signals on Sunday night, either rockets or the Morse signals?

CL: No, sir; I did not. The officer on watch saw some signals, but he said they were not distress signals.

SS: They were not distress signals?

CL: Not distress signals.

SS: But he reported them?

CL: To me. I think you had better let me tell you that story.

SS: I wish you would.

CL: When I came off the bridge, at half past 10, I pointed out to the officer that I thought I saw a light coming along, and it was a most peculiar light, and we had been making mistakes all along with the stars, thinking they were signals. We could not distinguish where the sky ended and where the water commenced. You understand, it was a flat calm. He said he thought it was a star, and I did not say anything more. I went down below. I was talking with the engineer about keeping the steam ready, and we saw these signals coming along, and I said, "There is a steamer coming. Let us go to the wireless and see what the news is." But on our way down I met the operator coming, and I said, "Do you know anything?" He said, "The *Titanic*." So, then, I gave him instructions to let the *Titanic* know. I said, "This is not the *Titanic*; there is no doubt about it." She came and lay, at half past 11, alongside of us until, I suppose, a quarter past 1, within 4 miles of us. We could see everything on her quite distinctly; see her lights. We signaled her, at half past 11, with the Morse lamp. She did not take the slightest notice of it. That was between half past 11 and 20 minutes to 12. We signaled her again at 10 minutes past 12, half past 12, a quarter to 1, and 1 o'clock. We have a very powerful Morse lamp. I suppose you can see that about 10 miles, and she was about 4 miles off, and she did not take the slightest notice of it. When the second officer came on the bridge, at 12 o'clock, or 10 minutes past 12, I told him to watch that steamer, which was stopped, and I pointed out the ice to him; told him we were surrounded by ice; to watch the steamer that she did not get any closer to her. At 20 minutes to 1 I whistled up the speaking tube and asked him if she was getting any nearer. He said, "No; she is not taking any notice of us." So, I said, "I will go and lie down a bit." At a quarter past 1 he said, "I think she has fired a rocket." He said,

"She did not answer the Morse lamp and she has commenced to go away from us." I said, "Call her up and let me know at once what her name is." So, he put the whistle back, and, apparently, he was calling. I could hear him ticking over my head. Then I went to sleep.

SS: You heard nothing more about it?

CL: Nothing more until about something between then and half past 4, I have a faint recollection of the apprentice opening my room door; opening it and shutting it. I said, "What is it?" He did not answer and I went to sleep again. I believe the boy came down to deliver me the message that this steamer had steamed away from us to the southwest, showing several of these flashes or white rockets; steamed away to the southwest.

The captain told me he was going to stop because of the ice, and the captain asked me if I had any boats, and I said the *Titanic.* He said, "Better advise him we are surrounded by ice and stopped." So I went to my cabin, and at 9:05 New York time I called him up. I said, "Say, old man, we are stopped and surrounded by ice." He turned around and said, "Shut up, shut up, I am busy; I am working Cape Race."

—Testimony of Cyril Evans,
wireless operator on the *Californian*

Excerpts From J. Bruce Ismay's U.S. Senate Testimony

Was White Star President J. Bruce Ismay a coward and a cad, or just a lucky male passenger who took a place in a lifeboat after seeking out women and children to rescue, but finding none? Did J. Bruce Ismay urge Captain Smith to speed recklessly through ice fields in order to break a transatlantic crossing record, or is his denial of this accusation (as his testimony below indicates) the complete truth? James Cameron painted Ismay as a villain in his film *Titanic,* and yet, Ismay has his defenders.

For conceiving the greatest ship ever built, J. Bruce Ismay deserves to be heard. This section reproduces his testimony from his two Senate appearances and, then, his statement to the media following his return to England.

History is on its way to passing judgment on Ismay: It is up to each reader to decide if Ismay's own words are convincing and whether or not his condemnation deserves reconsideration.

FROM J. BRUCE ISMAY'S FIRST APPEARANCE: DAY ONE, FRIDAY, APRIL 19, 1912

SENATOR SMITH: Will you describe what you did after the impact or collision?

J. BRUCE ISMAY: I presume the impact awakened me. I lay in bed for a moment or two afterwards, not realizing, probably, what had happened. Eventually I got up and walked along the passageway and met one of the stewards, and said, "What has happened?" He said, "I do not know, sir."

I then went back into my room, put my coat on, and went up on the bridge, where I found Capt. Smith. I asked him what had happened, and he said, "We have struck ice." I said, "Do you think the ship is seriously damaged?" He said, "I am afraid she is."

* * *

SS: You say that the trip was a voluntary trip on your part?

JBI: Absolutely.

SS: For the purpose of viewing this ship in action, or did you have some business in New York?

JBI: I had no business to bring me to New York at all. I simply came in the natural course of events, as one is apt to, in the case of a new ship, to see how she works, and with the idea of seeing how we could improve on her for the next ship which we are building.

* * *

SS: Did you have occasion to consult with the captain about the movement of the ship?

JBI: Never.

SS: Did he consult you about it?

JBI: Never. Perhaps I am wrong in saying that. I should like to say this: I do not know that it was quite a matter of consulting him about it, or of his consulting me about it, but what we had arranged to do was that we would not attempt to arrive in New York at the lightship before 5 o'clock on Wednesday morning.

SS: That was the understanding?

JBI: Yes. But that was arranged before we left Queenstown.

* * *

SS: Were you cognizant of your proximity to icebergs at all on Saturday?

JBI: On Saturday? No, sir.

SS: Do you know anything about a wireless message from the *Amerika* to the *Titanic*—

JBI: No, sir.

SS: Saying that the *Amerika* had encountered ice in that latitude?

JBI: No, sir.

* * *

SS: In the boat in which you left the ship how many men were on board?

JBI: Four.

SS: Besides yourself?

JBI: I thought you meant the crew.

SS: I did mean the crew.

JBI: There were four of the crew.

SS: What position did these men occupy?

JBI: I do not know, sir.

SS: Were any of them officers?

JBI: No.

SS: Or seamen?

JBI: I believe one was a quartermaster.

SS: One was a quartermaster?

JBI: I believe so, but I do not know.

SS: You saw three of the boats lowered yourself?

JBI: Yes.

SS: And three of them loaded?

JBI: Yes.

SS: As they were loaded, was any order given as to how they should be loaded?

JBI: No.

SS: How did it happen that the women were first put aboard these lifeboats?

JBI: The natural order would be women and children first.

SS: Was that the order?

JBI: Oh, yes.

SS: That was followed?

JBI: As far as practicable.

SS: So far as you observed?

JBI: So far as I observed.

SS: And were all the women and children accommodated in these lifeboats?

JBI: I could not tell you, sir.

SS: How many passengers were in the lifeboat in which you left the ship?

JBI: I should think about forty-five.

SS: Forty-five?

JBI: That is my recollection.

SS: Was that its full capacity?

JBI: Practically.

SS: How about the other two boats?

JBI: The other three, I should think, were fairly loaded up.

SS: The three besides the one you were in?

JBI: Yes.

SS: They were fairly well filled?

JBI: Yes.

SS: Was there any struggle or jostling?

JBI: I saw none.

SS: Or any attempt by men to get into the boats?

JBI: I saw none.

* * *

SS: What were the circumstances of your departure from the ship? I ask merely that—

JBI: The boat was there. There was a certain number of men in the boat, and the officer called out asking if there were any more women, and there was no response, and there were no passengers left on the deck.

SS: There were no passengers on the deck?

JBI: No, sir; and as the boat was in the act of being lowered away, I got into it.

SS: At that time the *Titanic* was sinking?

JBI: She was sinking.

* * *

SS: Mr. Ismay, what can you say about the sinking and disappearance of the ship? Can you describe the manner in which she went down?

JBI: I did not see her go down.

SS: You did not see her go down?

JBI: No, sir.

SS: How far were you from the ship?

JBI: I do not know how far we were away. I was sitting with my back to the ship. I was rowing all the time I was in the boat. We were pulling away.

SS: You were rowing?

JBI: Yes; I did not wish to see her go down.

SS: You did not care to see her go down?

JBI: No. I am glad I did not.

SS: When you last saw her, were there indications that she had broken in two?

JBI: No, sir.

* * *

SS: There has been some suggestion by passengers who left the ship in lifeboats, that an explosion took place after the collision. Have you any knowledge on that point?

JBI: Absolutely none.

SS: Do you think you would have known about that if it had occurred?

JBI: Yes; I should.

* * *

SS: Mr. Ismay, did you have anything to do with the selection of the men who accompanied you in the last boat?

JBI: No, sir.

* * *

SS: If she had hit the iceberg head on, in all probability she would be here now?

JBI: I say in all human probability that ship would have been afloat today.

* * *

SS: Mr. Ismay, did you in any manner attempt to influence or interfere with the wireless communication between the *Carpathia* and other stations?

JBI: No, sir. I think the captain of the *Carpathia* is here, and he will probably tell you that I was never out of my room from the time I got on board the *Carpathia* until the ship docked here last night. I never moved out of the room.

From J. Bruce Ismay's Second Appearance: Day Ten, Tuesday, April 30, 1912

SS: Who of your company directed the Harland & Wolff Co. to build the *Titanic*?

JBI: I did, sir.

SS: What did you say to them?

JBI: It is very difficult for me to say what I said. It would be in a conversation with Lord Pirrie, that we had decided to build the *Olympic* and the *Titanic*.

SS: Were both ships ordered at the same time?

JBI: Yes, sir.

SS: What did you say to them? Did you say, "We want the largest and best ship that you can build safely?"

JBI: We would naturally try to get the best ship we possibly could. We wanted the best ship crossing the North Atlantic when we built her.

SS: And when you gave the order that was your instruction?

JBI: Yes, sir.

SS: And you made no limitation as to cost?

JBI: Absolutely none.

SS: You were content that they should build that ship at whatever it cost to build it?

JBI: Yes, sir. What we wanted was the very best ship they could possibly produce.

* * *

SS: Were you in conference with the captain during this journey from Southampton?

JBI: I was never in the captain's room the whole voyage over, sir, and the captain was never in my room. I never had any conversation with the captain except casual conversation on the deck.

SS: Were you on the bridge at any time?

JBI: I was never on the bridge until after the accident.

* * *

SS: There has been considerable confusion about the cost of the *Titanic*. I will take the liberty of asking you to state it.

JBI: She cost $7,500,000, sir.

SS: And for how much was she insured?

JBI: For $5,000,000, I understand, sir.

SS: Did you have anything to do with the insurance?

JBI: No; very little. That is done in New York; that is dealt with and handled in New York.

SS: I will ask you whether you know of any attempt being made to reinsure any part of the vessel on Monday, the 14th of April?

JBI: Absolutely none, sir; and I can not imagine anybody connected with the International Mercantile Marine Co. endeavoring to do such a dishonorable thing.

SS: I do not want you to understand me to assert that it was attempted.

JBI: I know, sir; but it is such a horrible accusation to have been made.

SS: You would regard it as a very dishonorable thing to do?

JBI: It would have been taking advantage of private knowledge which was in my possession; yes, sir. Yes, sir; I should so regard it.

* * *

SS: Did you have any talk with the captain with reference to the speed of the ship?

JBI: Never, sir.

SS: Did you, at any time, urge him to greater speed?

JBI: No, sir.

SS: Do you know of any one who urged him to greater speed than he was making when the ship was making 70 revolutions?

JBI: It is really impossible to imagine such a thing on board ship.

SS: Did you, in your position of general manager of this company, undertake in any way to influence or direct the management of that ship, from the time she left Southampton until the time of the accident?

JBI: No, sir; I did not. That matter would be entirely out of my province.

* * *

SS: Had the *Titanic* carried double the number of lifeboats or treble the number of lifeboats, do you consider that there might have been an increase in the number of passengers and crew saved?

JBI: I think that is quite probable, sir.

SS: I do not want to commit you to any special course in your company, and presume I will not do so, by this inquiry; but in view of all that has occurred, are you willing to say that the proportion of lifeboats should be increased to more approximately meet such exigencies as you have just passed through?

JBI: I think, having regard to our experience, there is no question that that should be done; but I think it may be quite possible to improve on the construction of the ship.

SS: Also?

JBI: Yes, sir.

SS: Have you given any instructions to increase the lifeboat capacity of other White Star ships?

JBI: We have given instructions that no ship belonging to the I. M. M. Co. is to leave any port unless she has sufficient boats on board for the accommodation of all the passengers and the whole of the crew.

SS: Who gave those instructions?

JBI: I did, sir.

SS: When?

JBI: The day after I landed from the *Carpathia*.

* * *

SENATOR BURTON: [Did you] attempt to put any embargo on news of any kind while you were on board the *Carpathia*?

JBI: Absolutely none, sir; and I asked for no preferential treatment for any messages that I sent. I do not know that any was given.

J. BRUCE ISMAY'S OFFICIAL STATEMENT TO THE BRITISH MEDIA FOLLOWING THE U.S. SENATE HEARING

I did not suppose the question of my personal conduct was the subject of the enquiry . . .

—J. Bruce Ismay

When I appeared before the Senate Committee on Friday morning I supposed the purpose of the enquiry was to ascertain the cause of the sinking of the *Titanic* with a view to determining whether additional legislation was required to prevent the recurrence of so horrible a disaster.

I welcomed such an enquiry and appeared voluntarily without subpoena, and answered all questions put to me by the members of the Committee to the best of my ability, with complete frankness and without reserve. I did not suppose the question of my personal conduct was the subject of the enquiry, although I was ready to tell everything I did on the night of the collision. As I have been subpoenaed to attend before the Committee in Washington to-morrow I should prefer to make no public statement out of respect for the Committee, but I do not think that courtesy requires me to be silent in the face of the untrue statements made in some of the newspapers.

When I went on board the *Titanic* at Southampton on April 10 it was my intention to return by her. I had no intention of remaining in the United States at that time. I came merely to observe the new vessel as I had done in the case of other vessels of our lines. During the voyage I was a passenger and exercised no greater right or privileges than any other passenger. I was not consulted by the commander about the ship, her course, speed, navigation, or her conduct at sea. All these matters were under the exclusive control of the captain.

I saw Capt. Smith casually, as other passengers did. I was never in his room; I was never on the bridge until after the accident. I did not sit at his table in the saloon. I had not visited the engine room, nor gone through the ship, and did not go, or attempt to go, to any part of the ship to which any other first-class passenger did not have access.

It is absolutely and unqualifiedly false that I ever said that I wished that the *Titanic* should make a speed record or should increase her daily runs. I deny absolutely having said to any person that we would increase our speed in order to get out of the ice zone, or words to that effect. As I have already testified, at no time did the *Titanic* during the voyage attain her full speed. It was not expected that we would reach New York before Wednesday morning. If she had been pressed she could probably have arrived on Tuesday evening.

The statement that the White Star Line would receive an additional sum by way of bounty, or otherwise, for attaining a certain speed is absolutely untrue. The White Star Line received from the British Government a fixed compensation of £70,000 per annum for carrying mails without regard to the speed of any of its vessels, and no additional sum is paid on account of any increase in speed.

I was never consulted by Capt. Smith, nor by any other person. Nor did I ever make any suggestion whatsoever to any human being about the course of the ship. The *Titanic*, as I am informed, was on the southernmost westbound track. The transatlantic steamship tracks or lanes were designated many years ago by agreement on the part of all the important steamship lines and all the captains of the White Star Line are required to navigate their vessels as closely as possible on these tracks, subject to the following standing instructions:

"Commanders must distinctly understand that the issue of these regulations does not in any way relieve them from responsibility for the safe and efficient navigation of their respective vessels, and they are also enjoined to remember that they must run no risks that might by any possibility result in accident to their ships. It is to be hoped that they will ever bear in mind that the safety of the lives and property entrusted to their care is the ruling principle that should govern them in the navigation of their vessels, and that no supposed gain in expedition or saving of time on the voyage is to be purchased at the risk of accident. The company desires to maintain for its vessels a reputation for safety, and only looks for such speed on the various voyages as is consistent with safe and prudent navigation.

Commanders are reminded that the steamers are to a great extent uninsured, and that their own livelihood, as well as the company's success, depends upon immunity from accident. No precaution which ensures safe navigation is to be considered excessive."

The only information I ever received in the ship that other vessels had sighted ice was by a wireless message received from the *Baltic* which I have already testified to. This was handed to me by Captain Smith, without any remarks, as he was passing me on the passenger deck on the afternoon of Sunday, April 14. I read the telegram casually, and put it in my pocket. At about ten minutes past 7, while I was sitting in the smoking room, Captain Smith came in and asked me to give him the message received from the *Baltic* in order to post it for the information of the officers. I handed it to him, and nothing further was said by either of us. I did not speak to any of the other officers on the subject.

If the information I had received had aroused any

apprehension in my mind—which it did not—I should not have
ventured to make any suggestion to a commander of Captain
Smith's experience and responsibility, for the navigation
of the ship rested solely with him.

It has been stated that Captain Smith and I were having
a dinner party in one of the saloons from 7:30 to 10:30
on Sunday night, and that at the time of the collision
Captain Smith was sitting with me in the saloon. Both of
these statements are absolutely false. I did not dine with
the Captain. Nor did I see him during the evening of
April 14. The doctor dined with me in the restaurant at
7:30, and I went directly to my state-room and went to
bed at about 10:30.

I was asleep when the collision occurred. I felt a jar,
went out into the passage-way without dressing, met a
steward, asked him what was the matter, and he said he
did not know. I returned to my room. I felt the ship slow
down. I put on an overcoat over my pyjamas and went up on
the bridge deck, and on the bridge I asked Captain Smith
what was the matter, and he said we had struck ice. I
asked him whether he thought it serious, and he said he
did.

On my way to my room I met the chief engineer, and
asked him whether he though the damage serious, and he
said he thought it was.

I then returned to my room and put on a suit of
clothes. I had been in my overcoat and pyjamas up to this
time. I then went back to the boat deck and heard Captain
Smith give the order to clear the boats. I helped in this
work for nearly two hours as far as I can judge.

I worked at the starboard boats, helping women and
children into the boats and lowering them over the side. I
did nothing with regard to the boats on the port side. By
that time every wooden lifeboat on the starboard side had
been lowered away, and I found that they were engaged in
getting out the forward collapsible boat on the starboard
side. I assisted in this work, and all the women that
were on this deck were helped into the boat. They were
all, I think, third-class passengers.

As the boat was going over the side Mr. Carter, a
passenger, and myself got in. At that time there was not a
woman on the boat deck, nor any passengers of any class,

as far as we could see or hear. The boat had between 35 and 40 in it; I should think most of them women. There were, perhaps, four or five men, and it was afterwards discovered that there were four Chinamen concealed under the thwarts in the bottom of the boat. The distance that the boat had to be lowered into the water was, I should estimate, about 20 ft. Mr. Carter and I did not get into the boat until after they had begun to lower it away.

When the boat reached the water I helped to row it, pushing the oar from me as I sat. This is the explanation of the fact that my back was to the sinking steamer.

The boat would have accommodated certainly six or more passengers in addition, if there had been any on the boat deck to go.

These facts can be substantiated by Mr. W. E. Carter of Philadelphia, who got in at the same time that I did, and was rowing the boat with me. I hope I need not say that neither Mr. Carter nor myself would, for one moment, have thought of getting into the boat if there had been any women there to go in it. Nor should I have done so if I had thought that by remaining on the ship I could have been the slightest further assistance.

It is impossible for me to answer every false statement, rumour, or invention that has appeared in the newspapers. I am prepared to answer any questions that may be asked by the Committee of the Senate or any other responsible person. I shall, therefore, make no further statement of this kind, except to explain the messages that I sent from the *Carpathia*.

These messages have been completely misunderstood. An inference has been drawn from them that I was anxious to avoid the Senate Committee's inquiry, which it was intended to hold in New York. As a matter of fact, when despatching these messages I had not the slightest idea that any inquiry was contemplated, and I had no information regarding it until the arrival of the *Carpathia* at the Cunard dock in New York on Thursday night, when I was informed by Senators Smith and Newlands of the appointment of a Special Committee to hold an inquiry.

The only purpose I had in sending those messages was to express my desire to have the crew returned to their homes in England for their own benefit at the earliest possible moment, and I, also, was naturally anxious to return to my family, but I left this matter of my return entirely to our representatives in New York.

I deeply regret that I am compelled to make any personal statement when my whole thought is on the horror of the disaster. In building the *Titanic* it was the hope of my associates and myself that we had built a vessel which could not be destroyed by the perils of the sea or the dangers of navigation. The event has proved the futility of that hope. Present legal requirements have proved inadequate. They must be changed, but whether they are changed or not, this awful experience has taught the steamship owners of the world that too much reliance has been placed on watertight compartments and on wireless telegraphy, and that they must equip every vessel with lifeboats and rafts sufficient to provide for every soul on board, and sufficient men to handle them.

William E. Carter's Statement to the Press

Mr. Ismay and myself and several officers walked up and down the deck crying, "Are there any more women here?" We called for several minutes and got no answer. One of the officers then said if we wanted to, we could get into the boat if we took the place of seamen. He gave us preference because we were among the first-class passengers. Mr. Ismay called again, and after we had no reply we got into the lifeboat. We took oars and rowed with two seamen.

THE U.S. SENATE'S OFFICIAL SUMMARY
OF *TITANIC* SOULS LOST AND SAVED

The U.S. Senate subcommittee hearing into the *Titanic* disaster determined that the *Titanic* sailed with 2,223 passengers (1,324) and crew (899) aboard, of which 1,517 were lost and 706 were saved. As an appendix to its final report, the subcommittee provided specific details on the classes and sex of those lost and saved, as well as the percentage of each class and the crew who survived.

Here is a breakdown of the subcommittee's findings. (Compare these findings with those of the British Board of Trade Inquiry earlier in this chapter.)

	Onboard	
First-Class Women and Children:	156	
First-Class Men:	<u>173</u>	
Total First-Class Passengers:	329	
Second-Class Women and Children:	128	
Second-Class Men:	<u>157</u>	
Total Second-Class Passengers:	285	
Third-Class Women and Children:	224	
Third-Class Men:	<u>486</u>	
Total Third-Class Passengers:	710	
Total Passengers:	1,324	1,324
Crew Women and Children:	23	
Crew Men:	<u>876</u>	
Total Crew:	899	<u>899</u>
Total Onboard:		2,223

* * *

	Saved	
First-Class Women and Children:	145	
First-Class Men:	<u>54</u>	
Total First-Class Passengers:	199	
Second-Class Women and Children:	104	
Second-Class Men:	<u>15</u>	
Total Second-Class Passengers:	119	
Third-Class Women and Children:	105	
Third-Class Men:	<u>69</u>	
Total Third-Class Passengers:	174	
Total Passengers Saved:	492	492
Crew Women and Children:	20	
Crew Men:	<u>194</u>	
Total Crew:	214	<u>214</u>
Total Saved:		706

* * *

Lost

First-Class Women and Children:	11	
First-Class Men:	<u>119</u>	
Total First-Class Passengers:	130	
Second-Class Women and Children:	24	
Second-Class Men:	<u>142</u>	
Total Second-Class Passengers:	166	
Third-Class Women and Children:	119	
Third-Class Men:	<u>417</u>	
Total Third-Class Passengers:	536	
Total Passengers Lost:	832	832
Crew Women and Children:	3	
Crew Men:	<u>682</u>	
Total Crew:	685	<u>685</u>
Total Lost:		1,517

* * *

Percentage of First-Class Passengers Saved:	60 percent
Percentage of Second-Class Passengers Saved:	42 percent
Percentage of Third-Class Passengers Saved:	25 percent
Percentage of Crew Saved:	24 percent

PART II

On the *Titanic*: A Collection of Original 1912 Writings

THE FIRST *NEW YORK TIMES* STORY ABOUT THE *TITANIC* TRAGEDY

As It Appeared on the Front Page of the Monday, April 15, 1912 Edition

New York Times managing editor Carr Van Anda scooped the world on the *Titanic* story when he decided to, first, publish the news of the *Titanic*'s collision with the iceberg in the morning edition of the April 15, 1912, edition, and then announce in the afternoon edition—with certainty—that the ship had sunk.

Van Anda's instinct to publish was based on an unconfirmed Associated Press bulletin that had been issued because of an intercepted wireless message. His instinct proved sound, and the *New York Times* was the first newspaper in the country to break the news of the *Titanic* disaster. In 1912, the *New York Times* was not the prestigious "newspaper of record" it is today; it was just one of several daily papers competing in New York.

Van Anda's story immediately boosted the paper's reputation and was a contributing factor in transforming the paper into the highly respected institution it is today. The story instantly gave the paper clout and an esteem it has retained for more than eight decades.

Here is the complete text of Van Anda's groundbreaking story.

NEW LINER TITANIC HITS AN ICEBERG; SINKING BY THE BOW AT MIDNIGHT; WOMEN PUT OFF IN LIFE BOATS; LAST WIRELESS AT 12:27 A.M. BLURRED

Allan Liner *Virginian* Now Speeding Toward the Big Ship.

***BALTIC* TO THE RESCUE, TOO**

The *Olympic* Also Rushing To Give Aid—Other Ships Within Call.

***CARMANA* DODGED BERGS**

Reports French Liner *Niagara* Injured and Several Ships Caught.

BIG *TITANIC*'S FIRST TRIP

Bringing Many Prominent Americans, and Was Due in New York To-morrow.

MISHAP AT VERY START

Narrowly Escaped Collision with the American Liner *New York* When Leaving Port.

Special to The New York Times.

HALIFAX, N. S., April 14.—A wireless dispatch received to-night by the Allan line officials here from Capt. Gambell of the steamer *Virginian,* states that the White Star liner *Titanic* struck an iceberg off the Newfoundland Coast and flashed out wireless calls for immediate assistance.

The *Virginian* put on full speed and headed for the *Titanic*.

No particulars have been received as to the extent of the damage sustained by *Titanic*.

The *Virginian* sailed from Halifax at midnight on Saturday night, and would probably be 300 miles off this coast when she picked up the calls from the *Titanic* for assistance.

The Allan liner has only about 200 passengers on board and would have ample accommodations for a large number of persons in case a transfer from the *Titanic* was necessary. The *Virginian* is a mail steamer, and so she is not likely to take the *Titanic* in tow.

MONTREAL, April 14.—The new White Star liner *Titanic* is reported in advices received here late to-night to have struck an iceberg.

The news was received at the Allan line offices here in a wireless message from the Captain of the steamer *Virginian* of that line.

It was stated that the *Virginian* had been in wireless communication wit [sic] the *Titantic,* that she had reported being in collision with an iceberg and asked for assistance.

The *Virginian* reported that she was on her way to the *Titanic*.

The *Virginian* sailed from Halifax this morning, and at the time the wireless was sent she is reckoned to have been about abeam of Cape Race. She has 200 passengers on board, but can accommodate 900 more of the *Titanic*'s passengers should their removal be necessary.

The message from the *Virginian*'s Captain was sent by wireless to Cape Race, and thence by cable to Halifax, and then by wire to Montreal.

The Allan Line officials here expect to hear further news at any moment.

LATEST NEWS FROM THE SINKING SHIP

CAPE RACE, N. F., Sunday night, April 14.—At 10:25 o'clock to-night the White Star line steamship *Titanic* called "C. Q. D." to the Marconi wireless station here, and reported having struck an iceberg. The steamer said that immediate assistance was required.

Half an hour afterward another message came reporting that they were sinking by the head and that women were being put off in the lifeboats.

The weather was calm and clear, the *Titanic*'s wireless operator reported, and gave the position of the vessel as 41.46 north latitude and 50.14 west longtitude.

The Marconi station at Cape Race notified the Allan liner *Virginian*, the captain of which immediately advised that he was proceeding for the scene of the disaster.

The *Virginian* at midnight was about 170 miles distant from the *Titanic* and expected to reach that vessel about 10 A. M. Monday.

2 A. M., Monday.—The *Olympic* at an early hour this, Monday, morning, was in latitude 40.32 north and longtitude 61.18 west. She was in direct communication with the *Titanic,* and is now making haste toward her.

The steamship *Baltic* also reported herself as about 200 miles east of the *Titanic,* and was making all possible speed toward her.

The last signals from the *Titanic* were heard by the *Virginian* at 12:27 A. M.

The wireless operator on the *Virginian* says these signals were blurred and ended abruptly.

"THRILLING STORY BY *TITANIC*'S SURVIVING WIRELESS MAN"

by Harold Bride

As It First Appeared in the *New York Times* on Friday, April 19, 1912

(Interview conducted by Jim Speers)

> **The decks were full of scrambling men and women.**
> —Second Marconi Operator Harold Bride

This remembrance of *Titanic*'s final hours by Second Marconi Operator Harold Sydney Bride is one of the most powerful archival records of the disaster that we have. Bride was only twenty-two when he signed on to the *Titanic,* and was one of the lucky crew members to survive the sinking.

This oral history (for which Bride was paid $1,000 by the *New York Times*—although Guglielmo Marconi told the U.S. Senate he had heard that Bride received $500 for his story) was dictated by Bride to a *Times* reporter a few minutes after 9:00 P.M. on Thursday, April 18, 1912, in the Marconi room of the *Carpathia,* immediately after the *Carpathia* docked in New York. "Thrilling Story by *Titanic*'s Surviving Wireless Man" first appeared in the following day's edition and was reprinted in the Sunday, April 28, 1912, special *Titanic* edition of the *New York Times,* where it was retitled "Thrilling Tale by *Titanic*'s Surviving Wireless Man."

Bride Tells How He and Phillips Worked and How He Dealt with a Stoker Who Tried to Steal Phillips's Life Belt— Titanic's Band Played "Autumn" as She Went Down

In the first place, the public should not blame anybody because more wireless messages about the disaster to the *Titanic* did not reach shore from the *Carpathia*. I positively refused to send press dispatches because the bulk of personal messages with touching words of grief was so large. The wireless operators aboard the *Chester* got all they asked for. And they were wretched operators.

They knew American Morse, but not Continental Morse sufficiently to be worth while. They taxed our endurance to the limit.

I had to cut them out at last, they were so insufferably slow, and go ahead with our messages of grief to relatives. We sent 119 personal messages to-day, and 50 yesterday.

When I was dragged aboard the *Carpathia* I went to the hospital at first. I stayed there for ten hours. Then somebody brought word that the *Carpathia*'s wireless operator was "getting queerer" from the work.

They asked me if I could go up and help. I could not walk. Both my feet were broken or something, I don't know what. I went up on crutches with somebody helping me.

I took the key, and I never left the wireless cabin after that. Our meals were brought to us. We kept the wireless working all the time. The navy operators were a great nuisance. I advise them all to learn the Continental Morse and learn to speed up in it if they ever expect to be worth their salt. The *Chester*'s man thought he knew it, but he was as slow as Christmas coming.

We worked all the time. Nothing went wrong. Sometimes the *Carpathia* man sent, and sometimes I sent. There was a bed in the wireless cabin. I could sit on it and rest my feet while sending sometimes.

To begin at the beginning, I joined the *Titanic* at Belfast. I was born at Nunhead, England, twenty-two years ago, and joined the Marconi forces last July. I first worked on the *Hoverford*, and then on the *Lusitania*. I joined the *Titanic* at Belfast.

ASLEEP WHEN CRASH CAME

I didn't have much to do aboard the *Titanic* except to relieve Phillips from midnight until some time in the morning, when he should be through sleeping. On the night of the accident I was not sending, but was asleep. I was due to be up and relieve Phillips earlier than usual. And that reminds me—if it hadn't been for a lucky thing, we never could have sent any call for help.

The lucky thing was that the wireless broke down early enough for us to fix it before the accident. We noticed something wrong on Sunday, and Phillips and I worked seven hours to find it. We found a "secretary" burned out, at last, and repaired it just a few hours before the iceberg was struck.

Phillips said to me as he took the night shift, "You turn in, boy, and get some sleep, and go up as soon as you can and give me a chance. I'm all done for with this work of making repairs."

There were three rooms in the wireless cabin. One was a sleeping room, one was a dynamo room, and one an operating room. I took off my clothes and went to sleep in bed. Then I was conscious of waking up and hearing Phillips sending to Cape Race. I read what he was sending. It was traffic matter.

I remembered how tired he was, and I got out of bed without my clothes on to relieve him. I didn't even feel the shock. I hardly knew it had happened after the Captain had come to us. There was no jolt whatever.

I was standing by Phillips telling him to go to bed when the Captain put his head in the cabin.

"We've struck an iceberg," the Captain said, "and I'm having an inspection made to tell what it has done to us. You better get ready to send out a call for assistance. But don't send it until I tell you."

The Captain went away and in ten minutes, I should estimate the time, he came back. We could hear a terrible confusion outside, but there was not the least thing to indicate that there was any trouble. The wireless was working perfectly.

"Send in the call for assistance," ordered the Captain, barely putting his head in the door.

"What call should I send?" Phillips asked.

"The regulation international call for help. Just that."

Then the Captain was gone. Phillips began to send "C. Q. D." He flashed away at it and we joked while he did so. All of us made light of the disaster.

JOKED AT DISTRESS CALL

We joked that way while he flashed signals for about five minutes. Then the Captain came back.

"What are you sending?" he asked.

"C. Q. D.," Phillips replied.

The humor of the situation appealed to me. I cut in with a little remark that made us all laugh, including the Captain.

"Send 'S. O. S.,'" I said. "It's the new call, and it may be your last chance to send it."

Phillips with a laugh changed the signal to "S. O. S." The Captain told us we had been struck amidships, or just back of amidships. It was ten minutes, Phillips told me, after he had noticed the iceberg that the slight jolt that was the collision's only signal to us occurred. We thought we were a good distance away.

We said lots of funny things to each other in the next few minutes. We picked up first the steamship *Frankfurd*. We gave her our position and said we had struck an iceberg and needed assistance. The *Frankfurd* operator went away to tell his Captain.

He came back, and we told him we were sinking by the head. By that time we could observe a distinct list forward.

The *Carpathia* answered our signal. We told her our position and said we were sinking by the head. The operator went to tell the Captain, and in five minutes returned and told us that the Captain of the *Carpathia* was putting about and heading for us.

GREAT SCRAMBLE ON DECK

Our Captain had left us at this time and Phillips told me to run and tell him what the *Carpathia* had answered. I did so, and I went through an awful mass of people to his cabin. The decks were full of scrambling men and women. I saw no fighting, but I heard tell of it.

I came back and heard Phillips giving the *Carpathia* fuller directions. Phillips told me to put on my clothes. Until that moment I forgot that I was not dressed. I brought an overcoat to Phillips. It was very cold. I slipped the overcoat upon him while he worked.

Every few minutes Phillips would send me to the Captain with little messages. They were merely telling how the *Carpathia* was coming our way and gave her speed.

I noticed as I came back from one trip that they were putting off women and children in lifeboats, I noticed that the list forward was increasing.

Phillips told me the wireless was growing weaker. The Captain came and told us our engine rooms were taking water and that the dynamos might not last much longer. We sent that word to the *Carpathia*.

I went out on deck and looked around. The water was pretty close up to the boat deck. There was a great scramble aft, and how poor Phillips worked through it I don't know.

He was a brave man. I learned to love him that night, and I suddenly felt for him a great reverence to see him standing there sticking to his work while everybody else was raging about. I will never live to forget the work of Phillips for the last awful fifteen minutes.

I thought it was about time to look about and see if there was anything detached that would float. I remembered that every member of the crew had a special lifebelt and ought to know where it was. I remembered mine under my bunk. I went and got it. Then I thought how cold the water was.

I remembered I had some boots, and I put those on, and an extra jacket and I put that on. I saw Phillips standing out there still sending away, giving the *Carpathia* details of just how we were doing.

We picked up the *Olympic* and told her we were sinking by the head and were about all down. As Phillips was sending the message I strapped his lifebelt to his back. I had already put on his overcoat.

I wondered if I could get him into his boots. He suggested with a sort of laugh that I look out and see if all the people were off in the boats, or if any boats were left, or how things were.

I saw a collapsible boat near a funnel and went over to it. Twelve men were trying to boost it down to the boat deck. They were having an awful time. It was the last boat left. I looked at it longingly a few minutes. Then I gave them a hand, and over she went. They all started to scramble in on the boat deck, and I walked back to Phillips. I said the last raft had gone.

Then came the Captain's voice: "Men, you have done your full duty. You can do no more. Abandon your cabin. Now it's every man for himself. You look out for yourselves. I release you. That's the way of it at this kind of time. Every man for himself."

I looked out. The boat deck was awash. Phillips clung on sending and sending. He clung on for about ten minutes, or maybe fifteen minutes, after the Captain had released him. The water was then coming into our cabin.

When he worked something happened I hate to tell about. I was back in my room getting Phillips's money for him, and as I looked out the door I saw a stoker, or somebody from below decks, leaning over Phillips from behind. He was too busy to notice what the man was doing. The man was slipping the lifebelt off Phillips's back.

He was a big man, too. As you can see, I am very small. I don't know what it was I got hold of. I remembered in a flash the way Phillips had clung on—how I had to fix that lifebelt in place because he was too busy to do it.

I knew that man from below decks had his own lifebelt and should have known where to get it.

I suddenly felt a passion not to let that man die a decent sailors' death. I wished he might have stretched rope or walked a plank. I did my duty. I hope I finished him. I don't know. We left him on the cabin floor of the wireless room, and he was not moving.

BAND PLAYS IN RAGTIME

From aft came the tunes of the band. It was a ragtime tune, I don't know what. Then there was "Autumn." Phillips ran aft, and that was the last I ever saw of him alive.

I went to the place I had seen the collapsible boat on the boat deck, and to my surprise I saw the boat and the men still trying to push it off. I guess there wasn't a sailor in the crowd. They couldn't do it. I went up to them and was just lending a hand when a large wave came awash of the deck.

The big wave carried the boat off. I had hold of an oarlock, and I went off with it. The next I knew I was in the boat.

But that was not all. I was in the boat, and the boat was upside down, and I was under it. And I remember realizing that I was wet through, and that whatever happened I must not breathe, for I was under water.

I know I had to fight for it, and I did. How I got out from under the boat I do not know, but I felt a breath of air at last.

There were men all around me—hundreds of them. The sea was dotted with them, all depending on their lifebelts. I felt I simply had to get away from the ship. She was a beautiful sight then.

Smoke and sparks were rushing out of her funnel. There must have been an explosion, but we had heard none. We only saw the big stream of sparks. The ship was gradually turning on her nose—just like a duck that goes down for a dive. I had only one thing on my mind—to get away from the suction. The band was still playing. I guess all of the band went down.

They were playing "Autumn" then. I swam with all my might. I suppose I was 150 feet away when the *Titanic* on her nose, with her after-quarter sticking straight up in the air, began to settle—slowly.

PULLED INTO A BOAT

When at last the waves washed over her rudder there wasn't the least bit of suction I could feel. She must have been going just so slowly as she had been.

I forgot to mention that, besides the *Olympic* and *Carpathia,* we spoke to some German boat, I don't know which, and told them how we were. We also spoke to the *Baltic*. I remembered those things as I began to figure what ships would be coming towards us.

I felt, after a little while, like sinking. I was very cold. I saw a boat of some kind near me and put all my strength into an effort to swim to it. It was hard work. I was all done when a hand reached out from the boat and pulled me aboard. It was our same collapsible. The same crowd was on it.

There was just room for me to roll on the edge. I lay there, not caring what happened. Somebody sat on my legs. They were wedged in between slats and were being wrenched. I had not the heart left to ask the man to move. It was a terrible sight all around—men swimming and sinking.

I lay where I was, letting the man wrench my feet out of shape. Others came near. Nobody gave them a hand. The bottom-up boat already had more men than it would hold and it was sinking.

At first the larger waves splashed over my clothing. Then they began to splash over my head, and I had to breathe when I could.

As we floated around on our capsized boat, and I kept straining my eyes for a ship's lights, somebody said, "Don't the rest of you think we ought to pray?" The man who made the suggestion asked what the religion of the others was. Each man called out his religion. One was a Catholic, one a Methodist, one a Presbyterian.

It was decided the most appropriate prayer for all was the Lord's Prayer. We spoke it over in chorus with the man who first suggested that we pray as the leader.

Some splendid people saved us. They had a right-side-up boat, and it was full to its capacity. Yet they came to us and loaded us all into it. I saw some lights off in the distance and I knew a steamship was coming to our aid.

I didn't care what happened. I just lay and gasped when I could and felt the pain in my feet. At last the *Carpathia* was alongside and the people were being taken up a rope ladder. Our boat drew near and one by one the men were taken off of it.

ONE DEAD ON THE RAFT

One man was dead. I passed him and went to the ladder, although my feet pained terribly. The dead man was Phillips. He had died on the raft from exposure and cold, I guess. He had been all in from work before the wreck came. He stood his ground until the crisis had passed, and then he had collapsed, I guess.

But I hardly thought then. I didn't think much of anything. I tried the rope ladder. My feet pained terribly, but I got to the top and felt hands reaching out to me. The next I knew a woman was lean-ing over me in a cabin, and I felt her hand waving back my hair and rubbing my face.

I felt somebody at my feet and felt the warmth of a jolt of liquor. Somebody got me under the arms. Then I was hustled down below to the hospital. That was early in the day, I guess. I lay in the hospital until near night, and they told me the *Carpathia*'s wireless man was getting "queer," and would I help.

After that I never was out of the wireless room, so I don't know what happened among the passengers. I saw nothing of Mrs. Astor or any of them. I just worked wireless. The splutter never died down. I knew it soothed the hurt and felt like a tie to the world of friends and home.

How could I, then, take news queries? Sometimes I let a newspaper ask a question and get a long string of stuff asking for full particulars about everything. Whenever I started to take such a message I thought of the poor people waiting for their messages to go—hoping for answers to them.

I shut off the inquirers, and sent my personal messages. And I feel I did the white thing.

If the *Chester* had had a decent operator I could have worked with him longer, but he got terribly on my nerves with his insufferable incompetence. I was still sending my personal messages when Mr. Marconi and *The Times* reporter arrived to ask that I prepare this statement.

There were, maybe, 100 left. I would like to send them all, because I could rest easier if I knew all those messages had gone to the friends waiting for them. But an ambulance man is waiting with a stretcher, and I guess I have got to go with him. I hope my legs get better soon.

The way the band kept playing was a noble thing. I heard it first while we were still working wireless, when there was a ragtime tune for us, and the last I saw of the band, when I was floating out in the sea with my lifebelt on, it was still on deck playing "Autumn." How they ever did it I cannot imagine.

That and the way Phillips kept sending after the Captain told him his life was his own, and to look out for himself, are two things that stand out in my mind over all the rest.

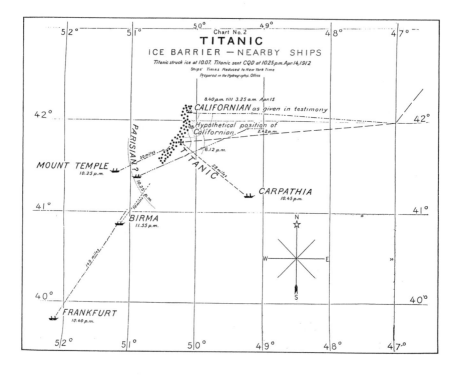

THE *TITANIC* ACCOUNTS OF DR. WASHINGTON DODGE AND MRS. DODGE

Original Articles From Three April 1912 Issues of the *San Francisco Bulletin*

These first-person accounts of the wreck of the *Titanic* and the subsequent rescue attempts are three of the most compelling and horrifying of the many stories to come out of that terrible "night to remember."

As *Titanic* foundered, Dr. Washington Dodge, a millionaire financier and the city of San Francisco's assessor, saw his wife Ruth and son Washington safely into Lifeboat 7, and then managed to make it himself into Lifeboat 13.

Lifeboat 7, with a capacity of sixty-five passengers, was launched from the starboard side of the *Titanic* at 12:45 A.M. under the command of Lookout George Hogg. Lifeboat 7 was the first boat to leave the ship and it contained only twenty-seven people, thirty-eight short of capacity.

Lifeboat 13, also with a capacity of sixty-five passengers, was launched from the starboard side of the *Titanic* at 1:40 A.M. under the command of Leading Fireman Frederick Barrett. Lifeboat 13 was the thirteenth boat to leave the ship and it contained only fifty-four people, eleven short of capacity. It arrived at the *Carpathia* at 4:45 A.M. on the morning of April 15, 1912.

Upon his arrival in New York, Dr. Dodge and his family checked into the Hotel Wolcott. Over the next few days, he talked to reporters from all over the world and the first two stories reprinted here were reported from New York. Mrs. Dodge's account was given to a reporter in San Francisco upon her and her family's return home.

These three articles are breathtaking in their verisimilitude: They manifest a sense of realism that could only have come from having lived through the experience. (Marconi operator Harold Bride's account of the wreck and his rescue—also reprinted in this section—bespeak a similar stark honesty, obviously born from surviving such a terrifying ordeal.)

Dr. and Mrs. Dodge tell some grisly stories, including firsthand accounts of seeing steerage passengers shot and their bodies falling into the water. Dr. Dodge also relates hearing Captain Smith exclaim "My God!" upon being told that the ship had an 18-degree list, and he remembers seeing disgraced White Star President J. Bruce Ismay fleeing the ship in a lifeboat.

Mrs. Dodge tells of traversing fifty-six miles of icebergs in her lifeboat, with her five-year-old son wearing nothing but a pair of pajamas and a life belt. Mrs. Dodge also tells of the conflict in her lifeboat over some passengers wanting to go back for people in the water and others threatening to overpower the crew if such an attempt was made.

These historical reports are powerful and thrilling, and yet, if they do anything, they reemphasize that even though the *Titanic* story has evolved into almost mythical status, the nightmare happened to real people—cowards and heroes among them—and the actions of both the victims and the survivors cannot help but make us wonder how we ourselves would react in such a surreal and dreadful situation.

San Francisco's Assessor Tells Story of the Wreck of the *Titanic* From Which He Escapes After Thrilling Experience

NEW YORK, April 19.—Dr. Washington Dodge of San Francisco, at the Hotel Wolcott here, gave the following account of the wreck:

"We had retired to our stateroom, and the noise of the collision was not at all alarming. We had just fallen asleep. My wife awakened me and said that something had happened to the ship. We went on deck and everything seemed quiet and orderly.

"The orchestra was playing a lively tune. They started to lower the lifeboats after a lapse of some minutes. There was little excitement."

SHIP SEEMED SAFER

"As the lifeboats were being launched, many of the first-cabin passengers expressed their preference of staying on the ship. The passengers were constantly being assured that there was no danger, but that as a matter of extra precaution the women and children should be placed in the lifeboats.

"Everything was still quiet and orderly when I placed Mrs. Dodge and the boy in the fourth or fifth boat. I believe there were 20 boats lowered away altogether. I did what I could to help in keeping order, as after the sixth or seventh boat was launched the excitement began.

"Some of the passengers fought with such desperation to get into the lifeboats that the officers shot them, and their bodies fell into the ocean.

"It was 10:30 when the collision occurred, and 1:55 o'clock when the ship went down," he said. "Major Archibald Butt stood with John Jacob Astor as the water rolled over the *Titanic.*"

CAPTAIN WAS CALM

"I saw Colonel Astor, Major Butt and Captain Smith standing together about 11:30 o'clock. There was absolutely no excitement among them. Captain Smith said there was no danger.

"The starboard side of the *Titanic* struck the big berg and the ice was piled up on the deck. None of us had the slightest realization that the ship had received its death wound.

"Mrs. [Isidor] Straus showed most admirable heroism. She refused in a very determined manner to leave her husband, although she was twice entreated to get into the boats. Straus declined with great fervor to get in the boat while any women were left.

"I wish you would say for me that Colonel Astor, Major Butt, Captain Smith and every man in the cabins acted the part of a hero in that awful night.

"As the excitement began I saw an officer of the *Titanic* shoot down two steerage passengers who were endeavoring to rush the lifeboats. I have learned since that twelve of the steerage passengers were shot altogether, one officer shooting down six. The first-cabin men and women behaved with great heroism."

OWES LIFE TO STEWARD

One of the stewards of the *Titanic,* with whom Dr. and Mrs. Dodge had crossed the Atlantic before on the *Olympic,* knew them well. He recognized

Dodge as the thirteenth boat was being filled. The steerage passengers were being shot down and some of the steerage passengers were stabbing right and left in an endeavor to reach the boat.

The thirteenth boat was filled on one side with children, fully 20 or 30 of them, and a few women. All in the boat were panic-stricken and screaming. The steward had been ordered to take charge of the thirteenth, and, seizing Dodge, pushed him into the boat, exclaiming that he needed his help in caring for his helpless charges.

Dodge said that when the boats were drawing away from the ship they could hear the orchestra playing "Lead, Kindly Light," and rockets were going up from the *Titanic* in the wonderfully clear night. "We could see from the distance that two boats were being made ready to be lowered. The panic was in the steerage, and it was that portion of the ship that the shooting was made necessary.

"I will never forget," Mrs. Dodge said, "the awful scene of the great steamer as we drew away. From the upper rails heroic husbands and fathers were waving and throwing kisses to their womenfolk in the receding lifeboats."

DR. DODGE GIVES STORY OF RESCUE

Several Boats Lowered Only Half Filled; "Tumbled In" When Told to

By Dr. Washington Dodge

NEW YORK, April 20.—At 10 P.M. Sunday while my wife and I went out for a stroll along the *Titanic*'s promenade deck we found the air icy cold—so cold, in fact, that we were driven inside although we had on heavy wraps. This change of temperature had occurred in the previous two hours. We went to bed and were awakened about 11:40 by a jar which gave me the impression that a blow on the side had moved the entire vessel laterally to a considerable angle. With only my overcoat and slippers, I went through the companion way, but, to my surprise, found no one seriously considering the shock.

"Men in evening clothes stood about chatting and laughing, and when an officer—I did not know his name—hurried by I asked, 'What is the trouble?' He replied:

"'Something [is] wrong; something is wrong with the propeller; nothing serious.'

"I went back to my stateroom, where my wife had already arisen to dress herself and I dissuaded her from dressing herself or our four-year-old [sic] son.

"A little while later, still feeling nervous, I went up to the promenade deck and there saw a great mass of ice close to the starboard rail. Going back to my cabin again, I met my bedroom steward, with whom I had crossed the ocean before, who whispered to me that 'Word has come from down below for everyone to put on life preservers.'

"I rushed back to my stateroom and told my wife the news and made her come up on deck with the baby, even half clothed. The boats on the starboard side were then suspended from the davits, but no passengers wanted to get in."

ROOM IN THE BOAT

"It was a drop of fifty feet to the surface of the sea, and, apparently everybody considered that they were safer on the 'unsinkable *Titanic*' than in a small boat whose only propelling power was four oars. The first boat was only half filled, for the simple reason that no one would get aboard.

"Personally, I waited for the lifeboat to become filled, and then saw there was plenty of room. I asked the officer at the rail, whose name I do not know, why I also could not get in, as there was plenty of room. His only reply was, 'Women and children first,' and the half-filled boat sheered off.

"Before the next boats were lowered passengers who had become excited were calmed by the utterances of the officers that the injury was trivial and that in case it proved serious at least four steamships had been summoned by wireless and would be on hand within an hour."

SAW WIFE IN BOAT

"I watched the lowering of the boat in which my wife and child were until it was safely launched on an even keel, and then I went to the starboard side of the ship, where the boats with the odd numbers from one to fifteen were being prepared for dropping over the side.

"The thing that impressed me was that there was not sufficient men to launch the boats, and, as a matter of fact, when the ship went down there was still one boat on the davits and one on the deck. The peculiar part of the whole rescue question was that the first boats had no more than thirty passengers, with four seamen to row, while the latter

boats averaged from forty to fifty, with hardly one person aboard who knew how to move an oar.

"All this time the *Titanic* had a slight list to port, but just after the collision Captain Smith, coming hurriedly up and inquiring what the list was and finding it eighteen degrees to starboard, said 'My God!'"

SAILOR OFFERS STOCKINGS

As there is always a touch of humor in the most gruesome of happenings, it is told by Mrs. Dodge that one of the sailors in the boat in which she embarked insisted on taking off his shoes and giving her his stockings, saying: "I assure you, ma'm, that they are perfectly clean. I just put them on this morning."

"I waited until what I thought was the end," continued Dr. Dodge. "I certainly saw no signs of any women or children on deck when I was told to take a seat in boat number thirteen. When lowered we nearly came abreast of the three-foot stream that the condenser pumps were still sending out from the ship's side. We cried out and the flow halted. I cannot imagine how that was done.

"Another danger to us was that the boat in which [J. Bruce] Ismay escaped was lowered, owing to the angle of the sinking ship, almost directly above us. If it had come ten feet farther both boats would have gone to the bottom, but our yells and cries stopped this catastrophe also."

"TUMBLED IN"

"When boat number [thirteen] was being lowered from the 'A' deck it stayed there for at least two minutes while the officers in charge were calling for more women and children. But as none responded the officers said (and I am sorry I do not know their names) 'some of you men tumble in,' and I 'tumbled.'

"In my boat when we found ourselves afloat we also found that the four oars were secured with strands of tarred rope. No man in the crowd had a pocket knife, but one had sufficient strength in his fingers to tear open one of the strands. That was the only way in which we got our boat far enough away from the *Titanic*'s side to escape the volume of the condenser pumps.

"Here is another thing that I want to emphasize; only one of all the boats set adrift from the vessel's side had a lantern. We had to follow the only boat that had one, and if it had not been for that solitary lantern possibly many of the other boats might have drifted away and gone down.

"To show how lightly even the executive officers of the ship took the matter of the collision is proven by the fact that the officer in charge of the boat in which my wife was saved refused to let his men row more than half a mile from the *Titanic* because that he would soon have orders to come back.

"We saw the sinking of the vessel. The lights continued burning all along its starboard side until the moment of its downward plunge. After that a series of terrific explosions occurred, I suppose either from the boilers or weakened bulkheads.

"And then we just rowed about until dawn when we caught sight of the port light of the *Carpathia,* and knew that we were saved."

BOATS WITHOUT PASSENGERS

"One curious point I noticed is that the first two boats launched held only their crews. Half an hour later I was told by an officer that they were launched in that shape to stand by in case of accident to her small boats.

"But there were no accidents and practically nothing for these boats to do, so many valuable lives were lost.

"If a sea had been running I do not see how many of the small boats would have lived. For instance, on my boat there were neither one officer or a seaman. The only men at the oars were stewards, who could no more than row than I could serve a dinner.

"While order prevailed until the last lifeboat had been lowered, hell prevailed when the officers, who had kept the steerage passengers below, with their revolvers pointed at them to prevent them from making their way to the upper deck."

STEERAGE PASSENGER SHOT

"When the steerage passengers came up many of them had knives, revolvers and clubs and sought to fight their way to the two unlaunched, collapsible boats. Many of these were shot by the officers.

"Only one of the rafts floated, and even that did not float above the water's edge. From 40 to 50 persons who had jumped overboard clambered aboard it and stood upon it, locked arm and arm together until it was submerged to a depth of at least 18 inches. They all tried to hold together, but when the *Carpathia*'s boat reached them there were only 16 left.

"The most horrible part of the story is that statement that several persons in the lifeboats saw, when the *Titanic* took her final plunge, that her four great smoke-stacks sucked up and carried down in their giant maws dozens of the third class passengers, then huddled together on the forward upper deck."

DR. DODGE'S WIFE TELLS STORY OF *TITANIC* WRECK

Reaches Home with Husband and Son
After Terrible Experience at Sea

SAN FRANCISCO, APRIL 30.—Seated in the library of her home on Washington street, amid a profusion of flowers sent by friends to express their welcome home, Mrs. Washington Dodge again told the story of her experiences on the night the ill-fated *Titanic* went down.

Dr. and Mrs. Dodge and their 5-year-old son, Washington Dodge Jr., arrived in the city yesterday afternoon, little the worse for their experience. The parents' one anxiety is for the boy, who is seriously ill from the effects of the exposure to the ice-chilled air on the night of the disaster.

"Was it cold?" said Mrs. Dodge. "You can imagine how cold it was when I tell you that we passed fifty-six miles of icebergs after we got on the *Carpathia*. The baby had nothing on but his pajamas and a life preserver.

"I think it is foolish to speak of the heroism displayed. There was none that I witnessed. It was merely a matter of waiting your turn for a lifeboat, and there was no keen anxiety to enter the boats because everybody had such confidence in that wretched ship. The officers told us that they had wireless communication with seven vessels, which were on the way to relieve us, and the men believed themselves as safe on board as in the boats. It seemed the vaguest possibility that the ship might sink before one of the seven vessels arrived.

"Of course, I left the *Titanic* before it began to settle into the water. The steerage passengers had not come on deck. In fact, there were few on the deck from which we left and more men than women."

TOOK SECOND BOAT

"It happened this way. There seems to have been an order issued that all women should congregate on the port side of the vessel. The vessel was injured on the starboard side, and even when I left the ship there was a slight list to starboard. We did not hear this order. I was in my stateroom, had retired again after the accident when the doctor came saying he had met our steward and had been told to get into a life preserver. I slipped on my fur coat over my night robe and preserver, put on my shoes without stockings; I did not stop to button them.

"We had made a practice of sitting on the starboard side of the deck, the gymnasium was there, and naturally when we went above we turned to starboard. They were lowering boats. I entered the second boat with my baby. This boat had an officer in command, and enough officers to man the oars. Several women entered with me and as we commenced to lower the boat the women's husbands jumped in with them. I called to the doctor to come, but he refused because there were still a few women on deck. Every woman in that second boat, with the exception of myself, had her husband with her."

BOATS HALF FILLED

"I supposed all the women were congregated on the port side because it would naturally be the highest side, and the safest because [it would be] the last to go down. We had no idea then that there would not be enough boats to go around. In fact, the first boats were only half filled.

"There must have been some confusion in orders, else I do not see why some of the women were not sent from port to starboard to enter those boats being lowered there. My husband got into the thirteenth boat. At that time there were no woman on the starboard side. There was not one woman in the boat he entered, and no member of the crew.

"Bruce Ismay entered the fifteenth boat from starboard. It was being lowered at the same time, and the doctor says he remembers this because there was some fear that the boats might swing into each other as they were lowered down the side of the vessel."

CRYING OF THE DOOMED

"The most terrible part of the experience was that awful crying after the ship went down. We were a mile away, but we heard it—oh, how we heard it. It seemed to last about an hour, although it may have been only a short time, for some say a man could not have lived in that water over fifteen minutes. At last it died down.

"Our officer and the members of the crew wanted to go back and pick up those whom they could, but the women in the boat would not let them. They told them if they attempted to turn back their husbands would take the oars from them, and the other men outnumbered the crew. I told them I could not see how they could forbid turning back in the face of those awful cries. I will remember it until I die, as it is. I told them: 'How do I know, you have your husbands with you,

but my husband may be one of those who are crying.'

"They argued that if we got back where the people were struggling, some of the steerage passengers, crazed with fear and the cold, might capsize the boat struggling to get it, or might force the officers to overload so we would all go down."

WOMEN HYSTERICAL

"After the crying died down, two or three of the women became hysterical— about what I don't know; they were missing none of their people. I was trying to keep [my] baby from realization of what was happening, but when these women shrieked he would begin crying and asking, 'Where's papa?'

"Finally I did what everyone thinks a strange thing. I changed lifeboats in mid-ocean. We overtook the first boat. It was hardly half filled. They offered to take any of us aboard, and to get away from the hysteria of the others I changed."

ON THE CARPATHIA

"The most pathetic thing was the scene on board the *Carpathia* during the rescue. As each boat drew up the survivors would peer over, straining to see the face of someone they had left behind. They were the young brides— everybody on board, of course, had known they were brides, and they had watched them laughing and promenading with their husbands.

"The moans of anxiety and disappointment as each boat failed to bring up those that they were looking for were awful and finally that awful despair which fell over everyone when we knew there were no more boats to pick up.

"Still they would not give up hope.

" 'Are you missing anyone?' the passengers would ask each other, never 'Have you lost anyone?'"

KINDNESS OF PASSENGERS

"Too much cannot be said of the kindness of the *Carpathia*'s passengers.

They gave up staterooms, they took the very clothing off their bodies for us. I left the *Carpathia* wearing garments given me by a women whose name I do not know and will never know."

She exhibited the bloomer trousers she had cut for Baby Dodge from a blanket given her by a sailor.

"I am sorry that I knew the names of so few passengers. There were two men aboard particularly, who every day used to come on the sun deck to play with the baby, and we often fell into conversation. Those men were not among the survivors. I do wish I had known their names that I might tell their wives some of the beautiful things they had said to me of their home life, casually, in these conversations."

DIAGRAM IV.—THE LOWERING OF THE BOATS.

13

A Front Page Editorial From the *New York Evening Journal*

Tuesday, April 16, 1912

Within twenty-four hours, the truth about the shortage of lifeboats on the *Titanic* had been learned and blame was already being assigned. This passionate and angry editorial appeared on the front page of New York's popular *Evening Journal* the day after the *Titanic* sank. In this essay, the *Evening Journal* not only holds the White Star Line to blame for the terrible loss of life, but also blames every other steamship company that was allowing its ships to sail without adequate lifeboats for all its passengers and crew.

This editorial was the beginning of a loud outcry that would result in more lifeboats and safer ships, but for the 1,500 who died on the *Titanic,* these safety measures were too little, too late.

The *Titanic* Crime

The judgment of the world upon the shortsightedness, the moral manners, the criminal carelessness of the White Star Company in its failure to provide lifeboats sufficient to transport its passengers from a sinking ship, should be crushing and exemplary.

In a calm sea, a gigantic steamship, freighted with thousands of lives, sinks slowly down. There is time and opportunity to carry off from the ship as many people as the lifeboats will hold. BUT THE LIFEBOATS WILL HOLD ONLY A FEW MORE THAN A QUARTER OF THE NUMBER OF MEN, WOMEN AND CHILDREN WHO HAVE COMMITTED THEMSELVES TO THE CARE OF THIS STEAMSHIP COMPANY!

What a satire on modern civilization! What irony of mechanical progress! From the four quarters of the horizon the ships of many destinations turn in their courses and rush in response to the whisper of the miraculous "wireless" to save the people on the stricken *Titanic*. But it is impossible to save them. No means have been provided for keeping the people afloat for a single precious hour.

This *Titanic* was the last cry and the faultless reach in the science and art of shipbuilding. It was supposed to be irreproachable and incomparable. It was equipped with all the luxuries and sumptuosities of modern travel. BUT THE PRIME NECESSARY OF LIFE WAS LACKING. No means were provided whereby the 2,200 people might survive for a few hours an accident such as that which actually took place—an accident of the commonest and least avoidable kind.

The dispatches say that all the lifeboats of the *Titanic* were fully accounted for; that the means of escape that were provided were used to the fullest capacity. All was done successfully that the management of the company could have hoped for in such an emergency. THE AWFUL WASTE OF LIFE WAS A PART OF THE PROGRAMME THAT MUST HAVE BEEN CALCULATED AND FORESEEN AS THE CONCOMITANT OF SUCH AN ACCIDENT.

The company simply took the risk. They staked the lives of passengers and crew on the chance that that kind of an accident would not happen.

The Bureau of Inspection of Steam Vessels at this port gives statistics concerning the life-saving apparatus of the *Olympic*, the sister ship of the *Titanic*—almost identical with the *Titanic* in capacity and equipment. It appears from these figures that the theory of the company was that lifeboat accommodation should be provided for one person in three of those on board. It appears that in actual fact lifeboat accommodation WAS provided for about one in six of the number that MIGHT HAVE BEEN on board the *Titanic* and for about one in four of those who actually were on board the *Titanic*.

The White Star Company may have such consolation as they can get from the fact that OTHER STEAMSHIP COMPANIES ARE EQUALLY GUILTY. It seems indeed to be the settled custom of reckless parsimony in the transatlantic passenger service to provide life-saving apparatus for only a minor fraction of the people who commit themselves to the mercies of the steamship corporations.

It is a shallow fiction to say that—as is often said in extenuation of this great wrong—it is mechanically impracticable for a big liner to carry lifeboats enough in a manner convenient for speedy launching. The truth is, of course, simply that the inventive ingenuity of marine architects has not been applied to this problem. A thousand varieties of portable and collapsible lifeboats could easily be devised if the steamship companies were willing to pay for them.

It is a kind of gambler's spirit that rules in this matter. The steamship companies, in their hurry for the last increment of dividends, lie under the illusion that the inevitable disaster will always strike elsewhere than upon their own greed and folly.

They stake the lives of travellers on their own anticipated luck. They invest money readily enough in every refinement of cookery, in every device of obvious elegance and ease. THESE INVESTMENTS PAY QUICK DIVIDENDS IN THE SHAPE OF EXTRAVAGANT PASSENGER FARES. But it is supposed that passengers will not notice the lack of the absolute NECESSARIES OF LIFE.

Henceforth the *Evening Journal* is determined that people who cross the Atlantic from New York SHALL NOTICE THIS LACK.

There must be a reform in this matter. And it must be immediate. Americans should refuse hereafter to take passage on ships that contain only facilities for death and destruction—in case of contact with an iceberg.

This newspaper has called attention to the standing outrage several times during the last few years—but never with so tragic a text to enforce this lesson.

The reform should be enforced by law—under the severest penalties.

As matters stand, the great lines that come into this port carry the British flag, are subject only to the regulations of the British Board of Trade in regard to their life-saving equipment.

The awful event of yesterday proves that the British Board of Trade does not know its business.

It becomes necessary for the law of the United States to intervene for the protection of the people of the United States that sail the seas.

THE FEDERAL AUTHORITIES SHOULD WITHOUT LOSS OF TIME IMPOSE NEW REGULATIONS UPON BRITISH SHIPS AND ALL OTHER SHIPS ENTERING AMERICAN PORTS—REGULATIONS THAT WOULD MAKE THE LIFE-SAVING EQUIPMENT OF EVERY SHIP SUIT THE NUMBERS OF THE PASSENGERS AND CREW.

This is not a thing to discuss and dispute about—and forget. It is a thing to DO RIGHT NOW, WHILE THE SHADOW OF THIS TERRIFIC WARNING LIES OVER ALL THE LAND.

NO SEA-GOING VESSEL SHOULD BE PERMITTED TO CLEAR FROM AN AMERICAN PORT WITHOUT BEING PROVIDED WITH LIFE-SAVING APPLIANCES OF SUCH A CHARACTER THAT ALL THE SHIP'S COMPANY MIGHT HOPE TO LIVE AFLOAT FOR DAYS EVEN IF THE SHIP WENT DOWN—AS THE *TITANIC* DID—IN A QUIET SEA.

14

Two Articles From the April 1912 *Scientific American*

This comprehensive and authoritative article about the sinking of the *Titanic* looks at the disaster from an almost purely scientific view and comes to some well-founded conclusions (too much speed, not enough lifeboats, etc.), all of which would be confirmed over the coming months and years as the many investigations into the *Titanic* disaster were carried out. What is so impressive about this article, though, is that it appeared a mere *two weeks* after the *Titanic* went down.

WRECK OF THE WHITE STAR LINER *TITANIC*

How the World's Greatest Steamship Went Down With 1,600 Souls

—from *Scientific American,* Saturday, April 27, 1912

In the long list of maritime disasters there is none to compare with that which, on Sunday, April 14th, overwhelmed the latest and most magnificent of the ocean liners on her maiden voyage across the Western Ocean. Look at the disaster from whatever point we may, it stands out stupefying in its horror and prodigious in its many-sided significance.

Titanic the Last Word in Naval Architecture.

The *Titanic* stood for the "last word" in naval architecture. Not only did she carry to a far greater degree than any other ship the assurance of safety which we have come to associate with more size; not only did she embody every safeguard against accident known to the naval architect; not only was

189

there wrought into her structure of greater proportionate mass of steel than had been put into any, even of the recent giant liners; but she was built at the foremost shipyard of Great Britain, and by a company whose vessels are credited with being the most strongly and carefully constructed of any afloat.

Unusual Strength of Construction.

To begin with, the floor of the ship was of exceptional strength and stiffness. Keel, keelson, longtitudinals and inner and outer bottoms were of a weight, size and thickness exceeding those of any previous ship. The floor was carried well up into the sides of the vessel, and in addition to the conventional framing, the hull was stiffened by deep web frames—girders of great strength—spaced at frequent and regular intervals throughout the whole length of the vessel. Tying the ship's sides together were the deck beams, 10 inches in depth, covered, floor above floor, with unbroken decks of steel. Additional strength was afforded by the stout longtitudinal bulkheads of the coal bunkers, which extended in the wake of the boiler rooms, and, incidentally, by their watertight construction, served, or rather, in view of the loss of the ship, we should say were intended to serve, to prevent water, which might enter through a rupture in the ship's outer shell, from finding its way into the boiler rooms.

Watertight Compartments and Pumps.

As a further protection against sinking, the *Titanic* was divided by 15 transverse bulkheads into 16 separate watertight compartments; and they were so proportioned that any two of them might have been flooded without endangering the flotation of the ship.

Furthermore, all the multitudinous compartments of the cellular double bottom, and all the 16 main compartments of the ship, were connected through an elaborate system of piping, with a series of powerful pumps, whose joint capacity would suffice to greatly delay the rise of water in the holds, due to any of the ordinary accidents of the sea involving a rupture of the hull of the ship.

Size as an Element of Safety.

Finally there was the security against foundering due to vast size, a safeguard which might reasonably be considered the most effective of all. For it is certain that with a given amount of damage to the hull, the flooding of one compartment will affect the stability of a ship in the inverse ratio of her size—or, should the water-tight doors fail to close, the ship will stay afloat for a length of time approximately proportional to her size.

And so, for many and good reasons, the ship's company who set sail from Southampton on the first and last voyage of the world's greatest vessel believed that she was unsinkable.

And unsinkable she was by any of the seemingly possible accidents of wind and weather or deep-sea collision. She could have taken the blow of a colliding ship on bow, quarter or abeam and remained afloat, or even made her way to port. Bow on, and *under the half speed called for by careful seamanship,* she could probably have come without fatal injury through the ordeal of head-on collision with an iceberg.

The One Fatal Peril.

But there was just one peril of the deep against which this mighty ship was as helpless as the smallest of coasting steamers—the long glancing blow below the waterline, due to the projecting shelf of an iceberg. It was this that sent the *Titanic* to the bottom in the brief space of 2½ hours, and it was her very size and the fatal speed at which she was driven, which made the blow so terrible.

The Climax of Seventy-five Years Development.

The *Titanic,* with the sister vessel *Olympic,* set the latest mark in the growth of the modern ocean liner toward the ship [of] one thousand feet in length. The *Britannia* of 1840 was 207 feet long; the *Scotia* of 1862 was 379 feet and the *Bothnia* of 1874, 420 feet long. The *Servia* in 1881 was the first ship to exceed 500 feet with her length of 515 feet. In 1803 the *Campania* carried the length to 625 feet; and the first liner to pass 700 feet was the *Oceanic,* whose length on deck was 704 feet. The *Mauritania* was 10 feet short of 800 feet; and then with an addition of nearly 100 feet the *Olympic* and *Titanic* carried the over-all length to 882½ feet; the tonnage to 46,000 and the displacement to 60,000. The indicated horse-power of the *Titanic* was 50,000, developed in two reciprocating engines driving two wing propellers and a single turbine driving a central propeller. The ship had accommodations for a whole townful of people (3,356, as a matter of fact), of whom 750 could be accommodated in the first class, 550 in the second, and 1,200 in the third. The balance of the company was made up of 63 officers and sailors, 322 engineers, firemen, oilers, and 471 stewards, waiters, etc.

Warned of the Iceberg Peril.

When the *Titanic* left Southampton on her fatal voyage she had on board a total of 2,340 passengers and crew. The voyage was uneventful until Sunday, April 14th, when the wireless operator received and acknowledged a message from the *Amerika,* warning her of the existence of a large field of ice into which her course would lead her toward the close of the day.

Full Speed Through the Ice Field.

The *Titanic* had been running at a steady speed of nearly 22 knots, having covered 545 miles during the day ending at noon April 14th; yet, in spite of the grave danger presented by the ice field ahead, she seems to have maintained during Sunday night a speed of not less than 21 knots. This is made clear by the testimony of Mr. Ismay, of the White Star Line, who stated at the Senate investigation that the revolutions were 72 as against the 78 revolutions which gave her full speed. She could make about 22½ knots at full speed, and 72 revolutions would correspond to about 21 knots.

The Captain Takes a Chance.

How such an experienced commander as Captain Smith should have driven his ship at high speed, and in the night, when he knew he was in the proximity of heavy ice fields is a mystery, which may never be cleared up. The night, it is true, was clear and starlit, and the sea perfectly smooth. Probably the fact that conditions were favorable for a good lookout, coupled with the desire to maintain a high average speed on the maiden trip of the vessel, decided the captain to "take a chance." Whatever the motive, it seems to be well established that the ship was not slowed down; and to this fact and no other must the loss of the *Titanic* be set down.

Had the "Titanic" been running under a slow bell, she would probably have been afloat to-day.

The Fatal Blow.

There were the usual lookout men at the bow and in the crow's nest, and officers on the bridge were straining their eyes for indications of the dreaded ice, when the cry suddenly rang out from the crow's nest, "Berg ahead," and an iceberg loomed up in the ship's path, distant only a quarter of a mile. The first officer gave the order "Starboard your helm." The great ship answered smartly and swung swiftly to port. But it was too late. The vessel took the blow of a deadly, underwater, projecting shelf of ice, on her starboard bow near the bridge, and before she swung clear, the mighty ram of the iceberg had torn its way through plating and frames as far aft as amidships, opening up compartment after compartment to the sea.

Thus, at one blow, were all the safety appliances of this magnificent ship set at naught! Of what avail was it to close water-tight doors, or set going the powerful pumps, when nearly half the length of the ship was open to the inpouring water. It must have taken but a few minutes' inspection to show the officers of the ship that she was doomed.

Half Speed Would Have Saved the Ship.

And yet that underwater blow, deadly in its nature, would scarcely have been fatal had the ship been put, as she should have been, under half speed. For then *the force of the reactive blow would have been reduced to one-fourth.* The energy of a moving mass increases as the *square* of the velocity. The 60,000 ton *Titanic,* at 21 knots, represented an energy of 1,161,000 foot-tons. At 10 knots, her energy would have been reduced to 290,250 foot-tons. Think of it, that giant vessel rushing on through the ice-infested waters, was capable of striking a blow equal to the combined broadsides of the twenty 12-inch guns of the "Delaware" and "North Dakota," each of whose guns develops 50,000 foot-tons at the muzzle!

Work of One Million Foot-tons of Energy.

Little wonder is it that the ripping up of the frail ¾-inch or ⅞-inch side plating and the 10-inch frames of the *Titanic* had little retarding effect upon the onward rush of the ship. So slight, in proportion to the enormous total energy of the vessel, was the energy absorbed in tearing open the hull or the bottom, or both, that the passengers were scarcely disturbed by the shock.

Newton's first law of motion "will be served."

But had the speed been only one-half and the energy one-fourth as great, the ship might well have been deflected from the iceberg before more than two or three of her compartments had been ripped open; and with the water confined to these, the powerful pumps could have kept the vessel afloat for many hours, and surely until a fleet of rescuing ships had taken every soul from the stricken vessel.

There is remarkable unanimity of testimony on the part of the survivors as to the slight nature of the shock; and this, coupled with the universal confidence in the unsinkability of the vessel, and the perfect quiet of both sea and ship, contributed no doubt to the marvellous absence of panic among the passengers.

The Call for Help.

The wireless again, as in the case of the *Republic,* proved its inestimable value. The collision occurred at 11:40 Sunday night in latitude 41.16 north, longtitude 50.14 west. The call for help was heard by several ships, the nearest of which was the *Carpathia,* which caught the message at 12:35 A. M. Monday, when she was 58 miles distant from the *Titanic.* Setting an extra watch the captain crowded on all speed, reaching the scene of the disaster by 4 A.M.

The Mockery of the Boats.

Meanwhile, with the ship sinking swiftly beneath them, there remained as a last hope for that hapless multitude the boats. The boats! Twenty in all, with a maximum accommodation of say 1,000 for 2,340 human beings!

A Blot on the British Board of Trade.

For years the British Board of Trade, renowned the world over for the jealous care with which it safeguards the life of the individual, has been guilty of the amazing anomaly of permitting the passenger ships of the vast British merchant marine to put to sea carrying boat accommodation for only one out of every three persons on board. The penalty for such unspeakable folly, we had almost said criminal and brutal negligence, may have been long delayed; but it was to come this night in a wholesale flinging away of human life, which has left a blot upon this institution which can never be effaced! Had the regulations called for the boat accommodations demanded by the German or our own government, every soul on board the *Titanic* could have been transferred and picked up by the rescuing ship.

Sun Parlors Versus Safety.

We can conceive of no other motive than that of commercial expediency, the desire to reserve valuable space for restaurants, sun parlors or other superfluous but attractive features of the advertising pamphlet and the placard, for this criminal reduction of the last recourse of the shipwrecked to so small a measure.

No practical steamship man can claim that the provision of boat accommodation for the full complement of a ship like the *Titanic* was impracticable. The removal of deckhouse structures from the boat deck of the ship, and the surrender of this deck to its proper uses, would give ample storage room for the sixty boats, more or less, which would be necessary.

Plans for a Full Complement of Boats.

We present on the front page a study of this problem, in which the number of boats on the *Titanic* has been raised from 20 to 56 and the accommodation from about 1,000 to about 3,100. The boats are carried continuously along the whole length of the boat-deck rails, and between each pair of smokestacks two lines of four boats each are stowed athwartship. The chocks in which these boats rest are provided with gun-metal wheels, which run in transverse gunmetal tracks, countersunk on the deck. As soon as the boat at the rail is loaded and lowered, the next boat inboard is wheeled to the davits and loaded, ready to be picked up and swung outboard as soon as the tackle has been cast loose from the boat that has been lowered. This method has the great advantage that if the ship has a heavy list, practically the whole of the boats can be transferred to the low side of the ship.

Is a Man Worth More Than a Sheep?

"But," says the shipping man, "all this means heavy top weights, the loss of valuable space, and heavy costs for installation and maintenance;" to which we reply, in the words of a certain venerable book, *"By how much, then, is the life of a man worth more than that of a sheep?"*

Light Out of Darkness.

Never, surely, in all the annals of human heroism, was there written a chapter at once so harrowing and inspiring as that which was gathered by the press from the pitiful remnant of that night of sacrificial horror. We turn from its heartrending story with a new sense of the God-like within us, and an exultant faith in the eternal uplift of the human race.

How the Great Ship Went Down.

Piecing together what the survivors witnessed from the boats, it is easy to understand the successive events of the ship's final plunge. The filling of the forward compartments brought her down by the head, and, gradually, to an almost vertical position. Here she hung awhile, stern high in air, like a huge, weighted spar buoy. As she swung to the perpendicular, her heavy engines and boilers, tearing loose from their foundations, crashed forward (downward); and, the water pressure increasing as she sank, burst in the so far intact after compartments. It was the muffled roar of this "death rattle" of the dying ship that caused some survivors to tell of bursting boilers and a hull broken apart. The shell of the ship, except for the injuries received in the collision, went to the bottom intact. When the after compartments finally gave way, the stricken vessel, weighted with the mass of engine and boiler-room wreckage at her forward end, sank, to bury herself, bows down, in this soft ooze of the Atlantic bottom, two miles below. There, for aught we know, she may at this moment be standing, with several hundred feet of her rising sheer above the ocean floor, a sublime memorial shaft to the sixteen hundred hapless souls who perished in this unspeakable tragedy!

A Tribute to the Engineers of the *Titanic*

—from *Scientific American,* April 27, 1912

> But this courage is required of every engineer and it is not called by that name: it is called "duty." To stand by his engines to the last possible moment is his duty. There could be no better example of the supremest courage being but duty well done than to remember the engineers of the *Titanic* still at work as she heeled over and flung them with their engines down the length of the ship. The simple statement that the lights kept on to the last is really their epitaph . . .
>
> —Lawrence Beesley, *The Loss of the S.S. Titanic*

We can only imagine the furious panic that would have occurred had the *Titanic's* lights not stayed on until she went down at 2:20 A.M. on Monday, April 15, 1912. The great ship was afloat on a jet black sea in moonless, pitch darkness and yet was an oasis of light amid the blackness. For almost three hours, from the time *Titanic* collided with the iceberg until her stern reared up and then plunged to the bottom, all her lights blazed, thanks to the dedicated and selfless engineering crew, all of whom never left their posts.

The editors and staff of the respected journal *Scientific American* knew that the *Titanic's* engineers were heroes of the noblest breed, and yet none of these men were even acknowledged by the survivors in the days immediately following the sinking.

The following editorial was *Scientific American's* attempt to honor the memory of the *Titanic's* brave engineering crew and to right what they (correctly) saw as a grave injustice.

> There is a world of heroic and tragic significance in the fact that the survivors' stories of the last hours of the *Titanic* make no reference whatever to the thirty-five officers of the engineer force. Of the officers of the deck there is frequent mention and many of them are among the survivors. This is natural and proper, for they were standing at their posts of duty. We read

also of farewells between them and other officers whose duties were concerned with the welfare of the *Titanic*'s passengers; but in all the records of those final eventful hours there is not a mention of any one of the band of men whose duties called for their presence far down in the deepest recesses of the ship.

In the roll of the saved there is not the name of a single certified engineer. Why this literal silence of the grave? There can be but one answer. Every man of the engineer watch stuck to his post to the very last and went down with the ship. Furthermore, this devotion to duty leads us to believe that such engineers as were not on watch may have voluntarily gone below to render what assistance they could in the sudden and frightful emergency.

This heroic devotion on the part of a little recognized body of professional men, the importance of whose duties on board ship is overlooked by the average trans-Atlantic passenger, will make an even greater impression upon our minds if we remember that they, above everybody else on that ship, must have known that she had received her death wound and that the hour of her sinking might be delayed, but not by any possibility averted. While those above deck, conscious of the enormous magnitude of the *Titanic* were exclaiming, "You cannot sink her," these men standing on the double bottom of the ship may possibly have seen the submerged edge of the iceberg come ripping through the sides of the ship, opening up boiler room after boiler room to the savage inrush of the water!

The bunkers, we learn, were arranged transversely to the ship. Hence if the bilges of side plating were ruptured, the inrush of water must have occurred before the very eyes of the engineers; and to the seafaring man there is no sight before which his courage will quail so quickly as this. Nevertheless, there is every reason to believe that not a man flinched from his trial. Steam was maintained in such boiler rooms as were not invaded by the water; the powerful bilge pumps were kept going to the very last minute; and the electric lighting plant was watched over, evidently with most careful solicitude. It is certain the pumps alone must have very materially delayed the sinking of the ship; and the value, in that hour of terrible stress, of the work done by the electrical engineers in keeping the lights going until the last trace of the ship had disappeared, is impossible to over-estimate.

15

"ALL SAVED"

The Front Page of the April 15, 1912, *New York Evening Sun*

TWA Flight 800 was probably not shot out of the sky by a missile, and Princess Diana was definitely not murdered by the paparazzi. And yet in the 1990s a wide range of news outlets all reported these incidents as fact.

This is nothing new. Rushing to judgment has become the standard course of action for the media and there are a plethora of reasons for such journalistic recklessness: the proliferation of instantaneous media (CNN, the Internet, and others); the increased competition among news sources for the viewers', readers', and listeners' attention; and an overall decline in professional standards. But, again, as these front page articles from the April 15, 1912, *New York Evening Sun* prove, this is nothing new.

The *Titanic* was believed to be utterly unsinkable (see Captain Jameson's remarks in the second article), and thus we cannot help but wonder if that belief made *Evening Sun* journalists more willing to believe the erroneous reports they ended up publishing on the front page?

BASEBALL
FINAL EDITION
Min. 40   TEMPERATURE.   Min. of

The Evening Sun.

BASEBALL
FINAL EDITION
Probable showers tonight and Tuesday;
raw; warmer; N. to E. winds.

VOL. XXVI. NO. 25.   NEW YORK, MONDAY, APRIL 15, 1912.—Copyright, 1912, by The Sun Printing and Publishing Association.   PRICE ONE CENT.

ALL SAVED FROM TITANIC AFTER COLLISION

RESCUE BY CARPATHIA AND PARISIAN; LINER IS BEING TOWED TO HALIFAX AFTER SMASHING INTO AN ICEBERG

Baltic, Virginian, Olympic and Other Ships Summoned by Urgent Wireless Calls.

BIGGEST OF LINERS IN CRASH

She Carried Over 1,400 Passengers, Many of Prominence---Message from Olympic Telling of Rescue.

HEADS FOR HALIFAX.

Titanic Reported Afloat Limping Toward Shore.

Montreal, April 15.—At 4:30 o'clock an unofficial despatch reached Montreal from Halifax, stating that the Titanic was still afloat and was making her way slowly toward Halifax.

Agents of the Allan line at Halifax have no news from the Virginian. Advices from the steamer Parisian from Glasgow states that she was 120 miles

MARCONI'S COMMENT.

Wireless Inventor Talks About Talking to Titanic.

Guglielmo Marconi, the inventor of the wireless telegraph, who is in this country at the present time, was found at the offices of the Marconi Wireless Company of America this morning, where he had gone to attend a directors' meeting. When asked about the delays in the transmission of wireless telegrams from the Titanic to-day he said that the delay was in no way due to the breaking of the

MERKLE QUITS.

Giants' First Baseman Jules Haldani Brigade.

Boston, April 15.—It developed here to-day that Fred Merkle, first baseman of the Giants, is a holdout. Merkle was present at the Grand Central Station in New York when John J. McGraw and the squad left for this city at midnight and refused to join the squad. Merkle is said to want considerably more money than McGraw is willing to give him. When the team pulled out

GIANTS DROP GAME AT HUB

Boston Braves Win From McGrawites.

MATTY MAKES HIS DEBUT

Snodgrass Plays First in Place of Merkle.

THE TITANIC UNDER WAY.

CANSO, N. S., April 15— The White Star liner *Titanic,* having transferred her passengers to the *Parisian* and *Carpathia,* was at 2 o'clock this afternoon being towed to Halifax by the *Virginian* of the Allan line.

The *Virginian* passed a line to the *Titanic* as soon as the passengers had been transferred, and the latest word received by wireless was that there was no doubt that the new White Star liner would reach port.

Agents of the White Star line at Halifax have been ordered to have wrecking tugs sent out to aid the *Virginian* with her tow into port.

OLYMPIC SENDS FIRST WORD OF RESCUE

The first definite news received direct by the White Star line officers here about the accident to the *Titanic* came at 11:05 o'clock.

The message read:

"*Parisian* and *Carpathia* in attendance on *Titanic. Carpathia* has taken twenty boatloads of passengers. *Baltic* approaching. *Olympic* 260 away."

CAPT. HADDOCK

It was later reported that the *Virginian* had arrived at the scene, had passed a line to the *Titanic* and would tow her to Halifax.

A special train has been made up by the New York, New Haven & Hartford Railroad and is ready to leave New York for Halifax to take on the passengers who will have been landed from the *Titanic* when the train arrives there. The route will be over the Boston & Maine, Maine Central, Canadian Pacific and Inter-Colonial railroads. The train will accommodate 710 passengers and will be made up of sleepers, dining cars and day coaches.

The *Baltic* of the White Star line has reported that it has taken aboard twenty boatloads of passengers from the *Titanic.* These may be brought direct to this port.

The immigration bureau of the Canadian Department of Commerce has sent inspectors to Halifax who will inspect the baggage of the passengers landed there, and will in every way facilitate the rapid removal of passengers to their final destination.

The *Parisian* is an Allan liner. She was bound from Boston to Glasgow. The *Carpathia* is a Cunarder bound from New York. The *Virginian* is an Allan liner. She was eastbound from Halifax. The *Baltic* is a White Star ship. She was bound from New York for Liverpool and at midnight yesterday was reported 355 miles south of Cape Race. The *Baltic* was the ship that brought in the rescued passengers from the sinking steamship *Republic* in January, 1909. At that time the *Baltic,* summoned by the far-reaching wireless, started for the *Republic,* which had been rammed by the *Florida,* the morning of the disaster, Jan. 23. She reached the two disabled ships that evening and found that the passengers and crew had been taken from the sinking *Republic* aboard the *Florida,* which was badly damaged. The passengers and crew of the *Republic* and the passengers of the *Florida,* 1,650 persons in all, were transferred at sea to the *Baltic* and she brought them in to New York.

The *Olympic,* also a White Star line ship, was outward bound from there.

The White Star steamship *Titanic,* the biggest ship in the world, on her maiden voyage from Southampton to this port, with over 2,200 souls on board, including many passengers of national and international prominence, struck an iceberg off the Grand Banks of Newfoundland early this morning.

The collision occurred in about lat. 41.46 north and long. 50.14 west, about 1,200 miles east of Sandy Hook and about 900 miles southeast of Halifax.

The *Titanic* sent her wireless signals of distress flashing all over the ocean, and steamships from all directions headed to her rescue.

ANXIOUS INQUIRERS AT LOCAL OFFICE

White Star Folk Beseiged by Friends of Passengers

Throughout the morning the White Star offices here were beseiged by friends of passengers on the big liner who wanted definite information. The telephones were kept busy with inquiries. To all the White Star officers extended assurances that the vessel was afloat and that the passengers were not in danger.

The *Titanic* was scheduled to sail from New York on her return trip on next Saturday, and so great was the request for tickets that 600 bookings had been made in the first cabin. These will all be transferred to other ships, and probably the *Cedric,* which is due to sail on Thursday, will delay her departure until Saturday.

Two messages were sent out this morning by the White Star line officers here. The first was addressed to Capt. Smith and read as follows:

"8:41, via Cape Sable.—Anxiously awaiting information and probable disposition of passengers. Franklin."

P. A. S. Franklin is the New York representative of the White Star line.

A further message was sent to the Marconi wireless station at Camperdown, N. S. It read:

"8:46—Get us quick information condition *Titanic.* Answer this office. Imodram."

Imodram is the local office's code signature.

Among those who visited the White Star offices at 9 Broadway was J. P. Morgan Jr., who had an interview with P. A. S. Franklin, vice-president of the White Star line. Asked if the Morgans named on the passenger list were his relatives, Mr. Morgan said they were not. He seemed confident, after talking with Mr. Franklin, that the passengers would get off the ship safely. Others who were noticed in the throng were J. Bradley Martin, Former United States Senator Clark of Montana, W. H. Force, father of Mrs. John Jacob Astor, and Col. Astor's secretary.

Capt. Jameson of the American liner *St. Paul* told the newspaper men that it would be practically impossible for the *Titanic* to sink because her fifteen bulkheads would keep her afloat indefinitely.

HEADS FOR HALIFAX

Titanic Reported Afloat Limping Toward Shore

MONTREAL, April 15—At 8:30 o'clock an unofficial despatch reached Montreal from Halifax, stating that the *Titanic* was still afloat and was making her way slowly toward Halifax.

Agents of the Allan line at Halifax have no news from

the *Virginian.* A wireless from the steamer *Parisian* from Glasgow states that she was 330 miles from Sable Island at 8 o'clock last night, but contains no mention of the *Virginian.*

At 8 o'clock this morning no further word had been received concerning the White Star liner *Titanic.*

The last direct word received was that which was conveyed through the *Virginian* at 12:27 A.M. This stated that the distressed steamship was still calling for relief. The last message was badly blurred and was cut off with great suddenness.

Marine men express no undue alarm over this fact, as any one of a dozen causes might arise to cut off communication. The Allan Line headquarters in this city are without additional information and from *Halifax* comes the report that they have nothing new there.

It may be noon today, or even later, before the actual fate of the liner is definitely ascertained.

CUTTERS TOO FAR OFF

Revenue Speeders Unable to Help the *Titanic*

WASHINGTON, April 15— At service headquarters here today it was planned to rush revenue cutters to the aid of the disabled liner *Titanic.* As soon as wireless communication could be established with the cutter *Gresham,* the fastest boat in the service and now believed to be near Boston, it was said that that vessel would probably be ordered full speed to succor the giant steamship. It seemed likely also that the revenue cutter *Androscoggin,* now off the Maine coast, would be sent to the vessel.

Later in the morning, following an interchange of wireless messages with revenue cutters off the New England coast, the service headquarters announced that it would not send aid to the *Titanic.*

TWO 1912 ARTICLES FROM
ENGINEERING NEWS

Night perfectly clear starlight, no wind, sea calm.
—from the White Star Line's official statement
about the *Titanic* disaster

These articles from *Engineering News* offer an overview of the *Titanic* disaster, the effect of the sinking on transatlantic steamship routes, and a discussion of the two official hearings about the disaster, one held on either side of the Atlantic.

The first article contains one of the earliest mentions of what was originally believed to be an anecdotal anomaly, but that we now know to be true: that the *Titanic* broke in two before she sank.

The second article makes the important point that the majority of *Titanic*'s victims were American, while the responsibility for their lives was completely British. As the writer astutely analyzes the two hearings, he comes to the somewhat accusatory conclusion that one was "an avenging body"; the other, a "vindicating" one.

April 25, 1912

The Wreck of the *Titanic:* Its Effect on Transatlantic Steamship Routes

One immediate result of the sinking of the White Star liner *Titanic,* after collision with an iceberg on Apr. 14, has been the adoption of new routes for transatlantic steamships some 200 miles south of the former summer routes.

The official statement of the disaster given out Apr. 21 by the White Star Line is as follows:

> *Titanic* followed strictly southernmost track westbound, changing course at corner 47 meridian, 42 latitude, thence south 86° west. True, all officers watch perished, except Fourth Officer Boxhall, who was working observations in chart-room and making rounds. Night perfectly clear starlight, no wind, sea calm. Had encountered no lee previously. Proceeding with vigilant lookout full speed, but reduced consumption, probably 21 to 22 knots. Engineers all perished. 11:45 p.m., Apr. 14, ship sighted low lying berg direct ahead. First Officer starboard-helm reversed full speed, and closed all compartments. Struck berg bluff starboard bow. Slight jar, but grinding sound, evidently opening several compartments starboard side. Boats cleared, filled with women and children, lowered and sent off under responsible persons. Ship sank bow first 2:20 a.m. All boats away except one collapsible. *Carpathia* rescued 4 a.m. Discipline perfect.

The time of the accident was given in our issue of Apr. 18 as 10:25 p.m. This, however, was the time when the first news of the wreck was received at the Cape Race wireless station. The difference in time between this station and the place of the wreck accounts for the discrepancy. It appears then that the vessel went down about 2½ hours after the collision.

From the accounts of survivors, as published in the daily press, it is fairly well established that the ship sank bow first and slowly to the very last. The inclination of the deck toward the bow gradually increased and the stern rose from the water, several observers who left the ship near the last noticing that the propellers were visible. Nothing like a rapid plunge seems to have occurred until only a portion of the hull, at the stern, remained above water. The "suction" of the sinking ship was much less than was expected.

The lighting system, according to the stories of survivors again, remained in operation practically until the ship went down, and this was a most important factor in aiding the work of loading and launching the lifeboats. An explosion of considerable violence is mentioned in the stories of a number of the survivors, some of them even believing that the vessel was broken in two near the middle just before she sank.

The steamships *Carpathia, Virginian, Californian, Frankfurt, Birma, Baltic* and *Olympic* were informed of the disaster by wireless and started toward the sinking *Titanic.* The *Carpathia* was the first to reach the scene, at about 4 a.m., and picked up the survivors from the *Titanic*'s lifeboats. A statement issued by the North German Lloyd S. S. Co., Apr. 21, gives the time of arrival of the *Frankfurt* at the scene of the disaster as 10:50 a.m., and adds that she found there the steamers *Birma, Virginian* and *Carpathia.*

The number of lifeboats carried by the *Titanic,* according to the testimony of Fourth Officer Boxhall before the Senate investigating committee, was 14. In addition there were two "sea boats" and four collapsible boats. The capacity of the lifeboats was 60 passengers each and the other boats could carry about 25 or 30. Thus the total capacity of all boats was about 1000.

The survivors, all of whom were brought to New York on the *Carpathia,* numbered 705. The number of lives lost, including those who died from exposure in the lifeboats, was 1442. Of those saved, 210 were members of the crew and 846 of the dead were passengers. This is according to figures given out to the press Apr. 19 and 20 by W. W. Jeffries, General Passenger agent of the White Star Line.

The New Routes

The position of the *Titanic* as given in her calls for assistance by wireless, was lat. 41° 46′, long. 50° 14′. This was about 14′, or about 16 miles, south of the regular westbound summer route. The early reports that the *Titanic* was using the shorter route—the northern or winter route—were plainly erroneous.

The general position of the group of icebergs upon one of which the liner was wrecked is indicated on our chart. The iceberg symbols on the chart mark positions at which icebergs were sighted by different vessels in the few days immediately preceding and following the wreck. For the sake of clearness, only a few of the numerous reports received at the New York office of the U. S. Hydrographic Bureau are marked on the chart.

The course of the group of bergs to the southward under the influence of the Labrador current can be traced by means of the pilot charts issued monthly by the Hydrographic Office. The Labrador current curves around the coast of Newfoundland and is believed to pass below the Gulf Stream. The ice brought down by the current from the north is picked up by the Gulf Stream and carried slowly eastward, being at the same time rapidly melted as a general rule by the warmer water. The speed of the Gulf Stream in this vicinity is only 15 or 20 miles per day. Slight variations in the flow of the two currents or a difference in the character of the ice itself may account for the further progress of the ice to the southward in some years.

The progress of the ice southward was indicated in another way by the nature of the ice reports received at the Hydrographic Office from steamships sailing over the regular summer routes, which are used from mid-January to the middle of August. Field ice was reported as early as Mar. 29 and 30, some steamers finding it advisable to take a more southerly course to pass around it. Beginning with Apr. 3, bergs of considerable height were reported in increasing numbers, and from Apr. 10 to 20 as many as 30 or 40 separate reports of icebergs came in. Typical reports for this period stated that "a large number," "two hundred" and "several hundred bergs" were sighted.

The ice this year is further south than it has been during a long period of years, and on Apr. 16 the transatlantic lines announced an agreement "in consequence of the reports as to ice in the Atlantic" to shift the established routes so as to bring them 60 or 70 miles farther south in the vicinity where icebergs are met. Three days later, on Apr. 19, an agreement was effected between the steamship lines and the U. S. Hydrographic Office moving the routes some 100 miles farther south still to the position indicated on the chart reproduced herewith. The chart shows also the former routes, which were established in 1898. The new routes are about 175 miles longer than the former summer routes.

We are indebted to Lieut. John Grady, U. S. N., in charge of the New York branch of the Hydrographic Office for assistance in preparing the chart [that showed the ships' positions that night].

August 15, 1912

The British and the American *Titanic* Investigations

We give in another portion of this issue an abstract of the final report of the British official commission appointed to investigate the loss of the steamship *Titanic,* and append thereto the recommendations of the U. S. Senatorial Committee, which reported on the same subject some two months ago. Strangely enough, and contrary to the general expectation, the two reports are essentially the same in effect, though differences in national temperament lent a somewhat different hue to the conduct of the two inquiries and to the manner of expressing the opinions of those who had them in charge.

The American investigation was in charge of politicians, though statesmen may possibly be the more respectful term. For the most part, the investigators were lawyers, and outwardly at least they did not deign to call into consultation any expert on marine matters. The inquiry was started when the horror of the disaster was fresh in the minds of everyone and assumed at times more of the character of the much-despised coroner's inquest than a dignified, sober investigation. Ignorant questions and spectacular oratory played a very important part in the investigation proper and the public soon came to discredit the committee and its possible findings even before the findings were brought in.

The British Commission, in contrast, was made up of a Commissioner who had long experience in maritime affairs and five assistants who were either members of the navy, the naval reserves or experts on naval design. The inquiry was held after the first wave of horror of the accident had passed and was conducted under the most dignified conditions. In addition to the expert character of the court itself, a great effort was made to bring before it a number of engineers and seamen who were expert in the design and operation of ocean-going vessels.

Finally the one great moral difference in the two commissions lay in the fact that the greater percentage of those lost were Americans, while the laws and individuals responsible for the catastrophe were for the most part British. Though none of the gentlemen concerned would probably admit it, the one was an avenging body; the other a vindicating.

In spite of these great differences in make-up, procedure and intent, the final recommendations of the two commissions—and we wish to emphasize the word "recommendations"—were about the same. Place them side by side, Senator Smith's commission recommends life-boats for the whole complement of the ship, frequent life-boat drills, a wireless man always on duty, a double skin for the hull, longitudinal bulkheads and watertight decks. So does Lord Mersey's court. With the difference that the American commission, ignorant of all things marine but cocksure in its judgment, recommends that these provisions be incorporated in law; the British court, while possessing no little technical ability, refuses to accept final responsibility for its opinions, but urges their study upon the properly qualified Board of Trade before final legal measures are adopted. In only one minor detail is there a difference; the American committee recommends the compulsory use of searchlights, presumably to detect icebergs; the British court, on testimony of experts, rejects them as of no value for that service. On the other hand, the English court emphasizes the lack of sufficient lookouts on the *Titanic,* which is not made a point of comment in the American report.

So much for the technical features of the reports. As regards the construction of the ship, and the circumstances of the accident, the two reports agree as to details, though the British report is the more concise of the two in this regard. Finally, in the matter of assigning responsibility for the disaster, there is a marked dissimilarity. The American commission, after an investigation conducted somewhat on the principle of the French courts, that everyone is guilty until proved innocent, avoided all reference to the question of responsibility in its report, and contented itself with a brief reference to the negligence of the captain of the *Californian* and severe condemnation of the wireless transmission of news *subsequent* to the sinking of the vessel. The British court, taking care of its own, spread an enveloping coat of whitewash over all the persons concerned in the loss of the ship (except the unfortunate master of the *Californian*), and rebuked the Board of Trade somewhat mildly for its true British conservation in not revising its rule in 18 years, and transatlantic seaman in general for certain time-worn customs that would seem to be the better for reform. In fact, the result of the reams of testimony on both sides of the ocean simmers down to the ancient verdict, "Nobody's to blame, but don't do it again."

It may be remarked that the final report of the U. S. Senate Committee is much more moderate than the utterances of its chairman, Senator Smith, either during the hearings or in the speech printed as an appendix to the original report. It is fair to assume that this moderation is due to the other members of the Committee.

It now remains to be seen to what degree the concurrent judgment of a body of American lawyers and a body of English marine experts, based in each case on comparatively brief investigations of one marine disaster, will be confirmed by the technical experts of the British Board of Trade in application to the vast numbers of vessels sailing under the British flag.

THE MECHANISM BY WHICH THE BOATS WERE LOWERED.

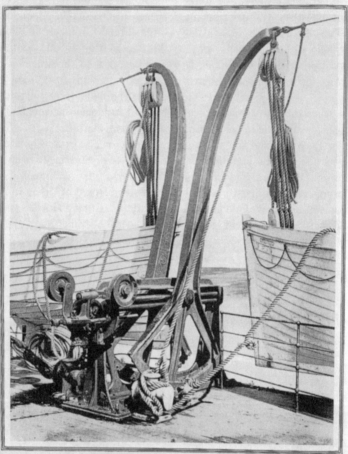

A PAIR OF THE WELIN DAVITS ON BOARD THE "TITANIC"

R. Welch, Belfast

The Welin davit, which was fitted to the "Titanic," and is also found on a large number of the latest type of passenger liners, is the important invention of Mr. Axel Welin. The davit is carried over the side by turning the geared worm, seen in the centre of the picture. The bottom of the quadrant is a cog which, working on a long lever, forms a double action, thus throwing the davit outwards to its extreme limit in a matter of moments. The coil-rope davit has to be completely turned in two operations which take a considerable amount of time.

17

A Selection of Articles From the April 16, 1912, *Boston Daily Globe*

Reading these articles publishing the news of the *Titanic* tragedy *as it happened,* one cannot help but be transported back to a time when communication was *a chore* and receiving accurate news was almost magical. Let's face it: we are jaded. We now live in a world of instantaneous communication and we have come to take for granted such incredible conveniences as next-day delivery halfway across the world for twelve bucks or so, and e-mail to anywhere on earth all day long.

In 1912 there were no satellite-delivered transcontinental telephone calls; nor were there airplanes delivering mail to Europe and back. Thus, the nightmare of the sinking of a great liner like the *Titanic* was made even more dramatic by the waiting for accurate news and the horrible anticipation of awaiting official lists of survivors.

These *Boston Daily Globe* newspaper articles are endlessly fascinating. Hindsight renders pathetic White Star Line Vice President Franklin's public assurance that the *Titanic* had "sufficient lifeboats to take all the passengers away from the *Titanic*." And the arrogance of the times and the ceaseless faith in "Man the Builder's ability to best Nature" is also evident in the April 16th story from London.

Captain Sealby's astute appraisal of what actually happened to the *Titanic* is evidence of the wisdom that twenty-five years on the sea could bestow, and the articles about the loss of 7 million pieces of mail illustrate just how important transatlantic sea travel was in 1912.

The Bosto

VOL LXXXI--NO 107.   BOSTON. TUESDAY MO

TITANIC SII

Carpathia Picks Up 675
York---Survivors Mo

POLICE ORDER
DORR'S ARREST

Lynn Chief Accuses Him of the Murder of George E. Marsh.

Suspect Said to Have Left Boston Thursday Night--Auto Found Here.

LYNN, April 15—Though facts were added to facts today with dramatic swiftness, the mystery of the murder of George E. Marsh, the soap manufacturer who was found shot through the heart on the West Lynn marsh Friday morning, is even more baffling tonight than it has been at any time.

Mr Marsh's cane and an automo-

bile cap identified as belonging to William A. Dorr, were found on the boulevard within a few yards of where Marsh's body lay, and the man who found them insists that he picked them up not later than 4:30 p m on Thursday.

If he is given credence, the aged man was murdered in broad day-

Continued on the Second Page.

aily Globe.

16. 1912—TWENTY PAGES.

COPYRIGHT, 1912, BY
THE GLOBE NEWSPAPER CO.

PRICE TWO CENTS.

S, 1500 DIE

of 2200---Races for New Women and Children.

CAPT. E. J. SMITH
Photo by
Bach Bros.

Giant Steamer Goes Down Before Help Arrives.

Virginian or Parisian May Have Some Survivors

White Star Officials Admit "Horrible Loss of Life".

Greatest Sea Tragedy in History Off Newfoundland Coast.

The Morning Edition

The White Star Line steamer *Titanic,* the largest vessel in the world, sank at 2:20 yesterday morning at almost the exact spot at which she crashed into an iceberg less than four hours before she went to the bottom.

Out of about 2200 souls on board the steamer but 675 are known to have been saved. These, according to wireless dispatches, are on board the Cunard Liner *Carpathia* bound for New York.

This is believed to mean almost beyond doubt that more than 1500 people went down with the mammoth liner.

The only hope that more than 675 of the 1300 passengers and crew of 860 survive lies in the chance that the Allan liners *Virginian* or *Parisian,* which are known to have been in the vicinity of the *Titanic,* reached the scene in time to make some rescues.

The *Carpathia* is expected to reach New York Friday morning with the refugees.

Meager reports available indicate that when the *Carpathia* reached the scene of the disaster the *Titanic* was already beneath the waves and that the rescued were picked up from lifeboats and rafts as had been successfully cleared away on the *Titanic* before she went down.

Greatest of Sea Tragedies

NEW YORK, APRIL 15—More than 1500 persons, it is feared, sank to their death early this morning, when within four hours after she crashed into an iceberg

the mammoth White Star Line steamer *Titanic,* bound from Liverpool to New York on her maiden voyage, went to the bottom off the Newfoundland Banks.

Of the nearly 2200 persons on board the giant liner, some of them of world-wide prominence, only 675 are known to have been saved.

Accepting the early estimates of the fatality list as accurate, the disaster is the greatest in the modern marine history of the world.

Nearest approaching it in magnitude were the loss of the steamer *Atlantic* in 1873, when 574 lives were lost, and that of *La Bourgogne* in 1898, with a list of fatalities of 571.

Should it prove that other liners, notably the Allan Liners *Parisian* and *Virginian,* known to have been in the vicinity of the *Titanic* early yesterday, picked up others of her passengers, the extent of the calamity may fortunately be greatly reduced. This hope still remains.

HOPES DASHED BY NEWS

News of the sinking of [the] liner and the consequent loss of life reached New York early tonight with a much greater shock because hope had been buoyed up all day by reports that the steamship, although badly damaged, was not in a sinking condition and that all her passengers had been safely taken off.

The messages were mostly unofficial, however, and none came direct from the liner, so that a lurking fear remained of possible bad tidings to come.

Shortly after 7 o'clock tonight there came flashing over the wires from Cape Race, within 400 miles of which, in the treacherous region of the Newfoundland Banks, the huge liner struck the berg, that at 2:20 o'clock Monday morning, 3 hours and 55 minutes after receiving her death blow, the *Titanic* sank.

CARPATHIA PICKS UP SURVIVORS

The news came from the steamer *Carpathia* and it was relayed by the White Star Liner *Olympic,* and it revealed that by the time the *Carpathia,* outward bound from New York, and racing for the *Titanic* on a wireless call, reached the scene, the ill-starred vessel had disappeared.

Left on the surface, however, were lifeboats from the *Titanic,* and in them, as appears from the meager reports received up to a late hour, were some 675 survivors of the disaster.

These, according to advices, the *Carpathia* picked up and is now bringing them to New York.

For the rest, the scene as the *Carpathia* came was one of desolation. All that remained of the $10,000,000 floating palace, on which nearly 1400 passengers were luxuriously traveling to this side of the Atlantic, were bits of wreckage.

The biggest ship in the world had gone down, snuffing out in her downward plunge, it appeared, hundreds of human lives.

ONLY WOMEN AND CHILDREN?

A significant line in the dispatch from Cape Race was the statement that of those saved by the *Carpathia,* nearly all were women and children.

Should no other vessel have picked up any other passengers of the sinking steamer it may mean that few of the men on board were saved, for the proportion of women and children among the passengers was large.

This would almost certainly mean the loss of practically the entire crew of 860.

In the two saloons were 230 women and children, but it is not known how many there were among the 740 third class passengers.

In the first saloon there were 128 women and 15 children and in the second 79 women and 8 children.

CARRIED NOTABLE PEOPLE

Notable persons, travelers on the *Titanic,* whose fate was in doubt in the lack of definite advices as to the identity of the survivors, were Mr. and Mrs. John Jacob Astor; Maj. Archibald Butt, aid to President Taft; Charles M. Hayes, president of the Grand Trunk Pacific of Canada, his wife and daughter; W. T. Stead; Benjamin Guggenheim; F. D. Miller, the artist; and J. C. Widener of Philadelphia; Mr. and Mrs. Isidor Straus; J. B. Thayer, vice president of the Pennsylvania Railroad; J. Bruce Ismay; Henry B. Harris, the theatrical manager, and Mrs. Harris; and Col. Washington Roebling, builder of the Brooklyn Bridge.

RAY OF HOPE FROM SABLE ISLAND

A ray of hope appeared shortly before 11 o'clock tonight in a message to New York from the operator at the Marconi wireless station at Sable Island, near the scene of the disaster.

To an inquiry regarding the delivery

of wireless messages to the passengers of the *Titanic* he replied that it was difficult to deliver them "as the passengers are believed to be dispersed among several vessels."

Even this faint indication that other vessels than the *Carpathia* had picked up survivors was eagerly seized upon by thousands of friends of those who set sail on her for this country.

SEEK LIST OF RESCUED

The White Star Line officers endeavored vainly from 8 o'clock until 11 o'clock to get further word from the *Olympic* about the *Titanic.* Vice Pres. Franklin said at 11 o'clock they were still hopeful of getting another message tonight.

The company was also trying to get into wireless communication with the *Carpathia* and filed a message asking that if possible the entire list of the names of the 675 survivors said to be on board the *Carpathia* be sent by wireless.

Such a list, Vice Pres. Franklin believes, is of the utmost importance, for hope was waning among the White Star Line officials tonight that any others than these 657 persons had survived.

LITTLE HOPE IN ALLAN LINES

Amid confusion at the offices the situation was studied as calmly as possible. Mr. Franklin figured that notwithstanding his fervent hope to the contrary, the Allan Line steamers *Virginian* and [*Parisian*] could hardly have reached the scene of the disaster in time to have been of assistance.

When the *Virginian* first reported her receipt of the startling signal "S. O. S.," late last night, she said she was not likely to be able to reach the *Titanic* before 10 o'clock today. This would have been nearly eight hours after the *Titanic* sank.

It was equally doubtful that the *Parisian* could have reached the scene in time.

OLYMPIC STILL FAR AWAY

There was discussion as to whether all the male passengers had sacrificed opportunity to save themselves by giving women and children the first chance at the boats.

"There is no rule of the sea," said Mr. Franklin, "which requires such a sacrifice. It is a rule of courtesy on land, as well as sea, that gallant men have often observed in time of disaster."

It was generally true, he added, that men made this vital sacrifice at sea to the women of the steerage as well as those of wealthier class in the first and second saloons.

The White Star Line officers reckoned from their data that the *Olympic* was 40 miles from the scene of *Titanic*'s loss when she sent the news of it at 7 o'clock tonight.

At that hour the *Carpathia* was estimated at 1080 miles east of Sandy Hook.

RICH AND POOR IN TEARS

By midnight Bowling Green, in front of the White Star Line offices, was the parking place of a large number of automobiles of prominent residents of the city who had driven down town for the first-hand information.

Wealth rubbed elbows with poverty and democracy in the crowd which beseiged the steamship line officials, and both classes were in deep grief.

There were many instances of fashionably gowned women going into hysterics when the hopeful reports of the afternoon were blasted by the news that only 675 persons had probably been saved.

BROADWAY IN GLOOM

Vincent Astor, only son of Col. John Jacob Astor, accompanied by A. J. Biddle of Philadelphia and Col.

Astor's secretary, were among the crowd at the offices, and left with tears in their eyes after a 15-minute talk with Vice Pres. Franklin.

Relatives of Isidor Strauss and of a number of other prominent passengers had similar talks with Mr. Franklin and came away equally dejected.

Police reserves were called to several sections of the city tonight to govern the crowds which congregated around newspaper bulletin boards for news of the *Titanic*.

The disaster stunned the gay Broadway district, for many of those who poured out of the theatres had friends on the steamer. The newspaper district was crowded till long after midnight.

ADMITS LIVES LOST

Vice President Franklin Can Account For Only 675 of 2200 on *Titanic*

NEW YORK, APRIL 15—Vice Pres. Franklin of the White Star Line, at 8:40, conceded that there had been "a horrible loss of life" in the *Titanic* disaster. He said that he had no information to disprove the Associated Press report from Cape Race to the effect that only 675 of the 2330 passengers and crew had been rescued.

He said that the monetary loss could not be estimated tonight, although he intimated that it would run into millions.

"We can replace the money," he added, "but not the lives."

"As far as we know," Mr. Franklin

continued, "it has been rumored from Halifax that three steamers have passengers on board, namely: The *Virginian,* the *Carpathia* and *Parisian*. Now, we have heard from Capt. Haddock that the *Titanic* sank at 2:20 this morning. We have also learned from him that the *Carpathia* had 675 survivors on board.

"It is very difficult to learn if the *Virginian* and the *Parisian* have any survivors on board. We have asked Capt. Haddock and our agent at Halifax to ascertain if there are any passengers aboard the two steamships.

"We very much fear, however, that

there has been a great loss of life, but it is impossible for us to give further particulars until we have heard from the *Parisian* and *Virginian*. We have no information that there are any passengers aboard these two steamships."

Mr. Franklin said there were sufficient lifeboats to take all the passengers away from the *Titanic*. He said

he was confident today, when he made the statement that "the *Titanic* was unsinkable," that the steamship was safe and that there would be no loss of life.

The first definite news received came in the message from Capt. Haddock, he said, and was given to the press at once.

LONDON IN IGNORANCE

Papers Went to Press Thinking *Titanic* Passengers All Saved—Much Excitement at Lloyd's

LONDON, APRIL 16—Some of the London newspapers went to press this morning in the belief that all aboard the *Titanic* were safe and that the vessel was proceeding for Halifax. These in editorials congratulate all concerned that man's inventive genius has reduced the perils of a sea voyage to a minimum.

Later dispatches recording the sinking of the *Titanic* with loss of life appear only in the very latest editions, and the terrible extent of the disaster will not become known to the British public generally until much later in the day.

All news on the subject still comes exclusively from New York. No wireless communication appears to have been established with this side. A dispatch just received from Liverpool says that the White Star officials have received

information from the *Olympic* of the sinking of the *Titanic* and of the saving of many of the passengers and crew.

All day the White Star offices were beseiged with an anxious crowd of relatives and friends of the passengers.

Exciting scenes were witnessed at Lloyd's yesterday. Insurance losses in the last six months have been unparalleled in the history of Lloyd's in liners of the biggest class. Since the *Olympic*'s collision with the *Hawke* both the *Delhi* and *Oceana* have been wrecked.

When business opened there was a rush to reinsure and 50 percent was charged, and this rapidly rose to 60, but later dropped to 25 on the news that the *Titanic* was being towed to Halifax.

It is understood that there was no specie aboard the liner, but large insurances had been written on diamonds and other valuables in her cargo.

WHITE STAR LINE.

Rev. J Stuart Holden

YOUR ATTENTION IS SPECIALLY DIRECTED TO THE CONDITIONS OF
TRANSPORTATION IN THE ENCLOSED CONTRACT.

THE COMPANY'S LIABILITY FOR BAGGAGE IS STRICTLY LIMITED, BUT
PASSENGERS CAN PROTECT THEMSELVES BY INSURANCE.

irst Class Passenger Ticket per Steamship *Titanic*

SAILING FROM

10/4 191 2

The only known surviving ticket from the *Titanic*. Its holder, the Rev.
J. Stuart Holden, canceled his plans at the last moment because his
wife took ill. AUTHOR'S COLLECTION

Sailing off into its last sunset. PHOTOFEST

Form No. 19.

Signal Letters (if any) H V M P

Transcript of Register for Transmission to Registrar-General of Shipping and Seamen.

Official Number	Name of Ship	No., Date, and Port of Registry
131,428	*Titanic*	24 / 1912 *Liverpool*

No., Date, and Port of previous Registry (if any)   *new vessel*

Whether British or Foreign Built	Whether a Sailing or Steam Ship; and if a Steam Ship, how propelled	Where Built	When Built	Name and Address of Builders
British	*Steamship Triple screw.*	*Belfast*	*1912*	*Harland and Wolff Ld, Belfast.*

		Feet	Tenths
Number of Decks *first & two partial*	Length from fore part of stem, under the bowsprit, to the aft side of the head of the stern post	852	5
Number of Masts ... *two*	Length at quarter of depth from top of weather deck at side amidships to bottom of keel	849	2
Rigged ... ... *Schooner*	Main breadth to outside of plank *plating*	92	5
Stern ... ... *Elliptical*	Depth in hold from tonnage deck to ceiling *ceiling* at midships ...	31	6
Build ... ... *clincher*	Depth in hold from upper deck to ceiling at midships, in the case of three decks and upwards	59	8.8
Galleries	Depth from top of beam amidships to top of keel	64	9.1
Head	Depth from top of deck at side amidships to bottom of keel	65	3.3
Framework and description of *steel* vessel ... ... *steel*	Round of beam		2.5
Number of Bulkheads ... ... *fifteen*	Length of engine room, if any		
Number of water ballast tanks, *seventeen* and their capacity in tons ... *5726 Tons*			

PARTICULARS OF DISPLACEMENT.

Total to quarter the depth from weather deck at side amidships to bottom of keel ... *77,780* Tons.   Ditto per inch immersion at same depth ... *150* Tons.

PARTICULARS OF PROPELLING ENGINES, &c. (if any).

No. of sets of Engines	Description of Engines	Whether British or Foreign made	When made	Name and address of makers	No. and Diameter of Cylinders in each set.	Length of Stroke.	No. of Cylinders in each set.	N.H.P. I.H.P. Speed of Ship.
propeting and turbine	*Four cylinder triple expansion inverted vertical direct acting surface condensing*	*British*	*1912*	*Harland & Wolff Ld Belfast*	*1—54* *2—97"*	*75*	*one*	*6906* *150,000*
No. of Shafts. *Three*	Particulars of Boilers, Number *24* D.E. and *5* S.E. Iron or Steel *Steel* Loaded Pressure *215 Lbs.*	*British*	*1912*					*21 knots*

PARTICULARS OF TONNAGE.

[in red handwriting across the form:] Registry closed 31st May 1912. Vessel wrecked in the Atlantic Ocean 14th April 1912. Certificate... with the

A close-up of *Titanic*'s Transcript of Register. Note what has been scrawled in red: "Registry closed 31st May 1912. Vessel wrecked in Atlantic Ocean 14th April 1912. Certificate of Registry lost with the vessel." AUTHOR'S COLLECTION

First class cabin window

The starboard bow of
the wreck, above where
the iceberg was struck.
EMORY KRISTOF/ NATIONAL
GEOGRAPHIC IMAGE
COLLECTION

The *Titanic*'s bow,
in the eerie glow of
two Russian submarines.
EMORY KRISTOF/
NATIONAL GEOGRAPHIC
IMAGE COLLECTION

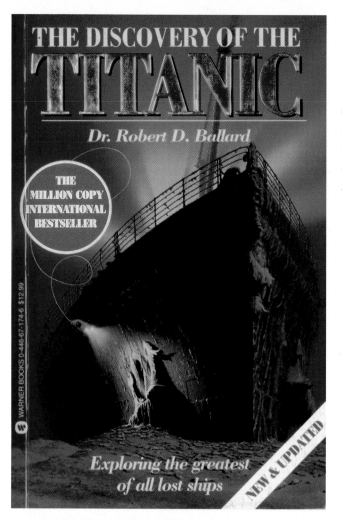

The cover of Robert Ballard's bestselling account of his discovery of the wreck.
AUTHOR'S COLLECTION

Survivors Bertram Dean and Eva Hart examine ship mementos at Merseyside Maritime Museum in Liverpool, including Captain Smith dress sword (far right).
BRUCE DALE/ NATIONAL GEOGRAPHIC IMAGE COLLECTION

Rose (Kate Winslet) contemplating a leap from *Titanic*'s stern. PHOTOFEST

Love grows between Jack (Leonardo DiCaprio) and Rose. PHOTOFEST

Passengers being lowered in lifeboats from a badly wounded *Titanic*.
PHOTOFEST

The young lovers try to race past *Titanic*'s grand staircase as the waters rise. PHOTOFEST

An example of the media frenzy that surrounded the most successful film of all time. AUTHOR'S COLLECTION

The J. Peterman Company capitalizing on the success of Cameron's *Titanic* in order to sell their "faux" jewelry.
AUTHOR'S COLLECTION

"Heart of the Ocean"™ Necklace.

75 carats.
The Hope Diamond is only 45.

Exact replica of astonishing he
pendant necklace worn by Rose De
(as portrayed by Kate Winslet), and
movie "Titanic."

Length: 18 inches. Comprised
diamonds linked together in precio
rhodium-plate settings.

Fairly enormous heart-shaped
diamond solitaire, encircled by a si
diamonds, is detachable, enabling necklace to be worn a
solitaire, when mood so dictates.

"Heart of the Ocean" Necklace (Nº. HRT10322). Note
replica with a certificate from Twentieth Century Fox. Hing
box. Price: $198. (The original necklace: $3+ million.)

Deferred Billing. No payment 'til June 1, 1998 if you

 The J. Peterman Compa

☎ 1-800-231-7341

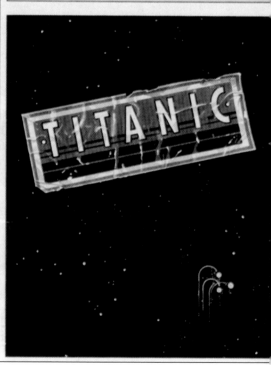

PLAYBILL®

LUNT-FONTANNE THEATRE

TITANIC

The *Titanic* continues to thrill audiences on Broadway.
AUTHOR'S COLLECTION

PRESIDENT TAFT ANXIOUS

Sought News of His Aide, Maj. Archibald W. Butt, USA, Passenger on *Titanic*

WASHINGTON, APRIL 16—President Taft was greatly anxious tonight for news of his aide, Maj. Archibald W. Butt, one of the four Washington persons on the *Titanic*. The President had frequent inquiries made of the newspaper offices and steamship agency.

No word had been received at a late hour at the homes of Col. Archibald Gracie or Clarence Moore, two other Washingtonians aboard.

INSURED FOR $5,000,000

Titanic Loss Will Be Much More Than This— Diamonds on Board Worth As Much

NEW YORK, APRIL 15—The *Titanic* was insured at Lloyd's for $5,000,000, according to advices from London tonight, and it was said here that the International Mercantile Marine Company also carried a surplus fund for insurance, which could be applied to the loss.

The cost of building the great liner has been estimated at $10,000,000, although Vice President Franklin of the White Star Line insisted tonight that her value was not more than $8,000,000.

The total monetary loss caused by the sinking of the ship, however, will run into many millions more, but the total amount cannot even be conjectured. It is generally understood that the vessel had aboard diamonds of great value and estimated as highly as $5,000,000, and also a large amount of bonds.

The *Titanic* carried 3423 bags of mail of unknown value, which it is hardly likely was saved.

The Boston Daily Globe.

VOL LXXXI—NO 107.   BOSTON, TUESDAY EVENING, APRIL 16, 1912—TWENTY PAGES.   PRICE TWO CENTS.

EVENING EDITION—7:30 O'CLOCK

ALL DROWNED BUT 868

About 1232 Lost Lives in the Titanic's Plunge, Greatest Sea Disaster for Years.

EXCITING EVENTS BEFORE TITANIC'S FINAL PLUNGE

Virginian and Parisian Found None Alive.

Women and Children Safe But Few Notable Men.

Carpathia Has Survivors— On Way to New York.

Only Partial List of Them Received Owing to Interruption.

AMATEURS INTERFERE

Difficult for Wireless Stations Here to Get Names of Survivors on the *Carpathia*

Interference on the part of amateur wireless operators made it difficult for the Boston stations to get the list of names being sent out by the *Carpathia* correctly.

In several instances the names as picked up have no counterpart in the list of passengers as given out by the White Star Line officials, and in other cases the operators were not able to get last names.

CAPT. INMAN SEALBY'S VIEWS

Commander of Ill-Fated *Republic* Believes the Side Was Torn out of the *Titanic*

ANN ARBOR, MICH. APRIL 16—Capt. Inman Sealby, in charge of the ill-fated *Republic* at the time she sank, now a senior law student in the University of Michigan, is most interested in the news of the sinking of the *Titanic*. He expressed no surprise that a collision with an iceberg would cause such a vessel, supposed to be absolutely safe, to sink.

Capt. Sealby has had 25 years' experience on the Atlantic and knows the grave danger of icebergs. He called attention to the fact that the *Titanic* struck the berg on the eve of the day when the trans-Atlantic liners change from the north to the south track because of danger from ice.

His opinion is that the *Titanic* did not strike the berg head on, as that would have only damaged her bow and could hardly have caused her to sink. He figures from his experience that a glancing blow was struck and that the berg scraped down one side, tearing holes through a large number of bulkheads. The *Republic* and the *Titanic* were both White Star liners.

SUGGEST SUCTION AS CAUSE

Experts in London Discuss Possibility—Sir William White Thinking Liner Simply Struck an Iceberg

LONDON, APRIL 16—Interviews are published here with experts relative to the possible cause of the disaster. Considerable attention is called to the question whether it was possible that suction could have had anything to do with it, and it is pointed out that this question came up in the inquiry into the *Olympic-Hawke* collision.

Sir Ernest H. Shackleton points out that the scene of the *Titanic* disaster was 14 miles south of the supposed possible range of ice fields.

Sir William White, the famous naval constructor, considers that there can be no question of suction in the case of the *Titanic*, because suction, he says, depends upon relative speeds, and an iceberg is almost stationary. He thinks that the *Titanic* simply struck an iceberg.

HAD HEAVY LOT OF MAIL

With the *Titanic* Went Down 3500 Sacks Full, in All About 7,000,000 Pieces of Matter

NEW YORK, APRIL 16—Postmaster Edward M. Morgan stated today that the White Star liner *Titanic* had on board 3500 sacks of mail. It is not possible, he said, that the mail was saved, because during the few hours that the vessel floated after running into the iceberg, there must have been an exciting scramble among those on board the disabled liner to launch and man the lifeboats.

As the standard ocean mail bag holds about 2000 letters, it is estimated that in all about 7,000,000 pieces of mail matter have been lost.

18

THE "UNSINKABLE" MOLLY BROWN'S *TITANIC* INSURANCE CLAIM

```
CONSULATE OF THE UNITED STATES :
EMPIRE OF GERMANY             :  ss.:
STATE OF PRUSSIA              :
CITY OF WEISBADEN             :
```

MARGARET BROWN being duly sworn, says: I am the claimant, in the above entitled claim; the above claim is true to my own knowledge except as to the matters therein stated to be alleged upon information and belief and as to those matters I believe it to be true.

```
sworn to before me this
31st day of December 1912        Margaret Brown

                                 John B. Brewer
                                 Consular Agent of the
                                 United States of America
```

SCHEDULE A.

Street furs	$ 300.00
Ermine Collarette	75.00
Ermine Opera Cape	500.00
Brussels Lace Gown	375.00
Persian Over dress	175.00
6 Dinner Gowns ($75 each)	450.00
Green Lace Gown	175.00
1 Sealskin Jacket	700.00
4 Gowns ($200 each)	800.00

```
1 necklace                                          20000.00
Odd laces                                             200.00
1 Pearl Brooch                                        150.00
14 hats                                               225.00
6 lace shirtwaists                                     75.00
6 Embroidered waists, lace                            140.00
Silk hosiery                                           75.00
Lingerie                                              300.00
Souveniers (Egypt)                                    500.00
3 crates ancient models for Denver Museum             500.00
2 Japanese Kimonos                                     50.00
1 Black Satin Gown                                    150.00
1 blue and white serge gown                            75.00
3 satin evening gowns                                 450.00
1 Irish lace gown                                     150.00
3 dozen gloves                                         50.00
1 hat                                                  35.00
6 shoes (10 Each)                                      60.00
4 tailored gowns and 2 coats                          500.00
3 shoes                                                36.00
1 evening wrap                                        150.00
4 Evening slippers                                     16.00
Brown velvet gown                                     200.00
Brown velvet coat                                     100.00
2 black gowns                                         150.00
                                                  $27887.00
```

19

JOSEPH CONRAD ON THE SINKING
OF THE *TITANIC*

Not everyone living in 1912 treated the *Titanic* disaster with solemnity or perceived it as a subject unsuitable for any sentiment other than sanctimonious regret marked by tearful mourning.

The legendary British writer Joseph Conrad—author of such classics as *Lord Jim* (1900), *Heart of Darkness* (1902), *Nostromo* (1904), and *The Secret Agent* (1907)—was fifty-five in 1912 when the *Titanic* sank and by this time was famed around the world for his gripping tales of dangerous adventures at sea. He must have felt obligated (or at least justified) in weighing in on the disaster that was making headlines around the world, and so he did with the following essay.

In "Some Reflections," Conrad pulls no punches. (Conrad bluntly warns that his gloves are off by describing his "reflections" as "seamanlike and otherwise" in the very title of his essay.)

Conrad tears into the *Titanic*'s owners and builders; the wealthy swells who lined up for tickets for her maiden voyage, the British Board of Trade; American railroads; and especially the senators who made up the United States Senate subcommittee hearing into the disaster.

Regardless of his point of view, though, this essay is fascinating reading and truly illustrates just how passionate and animated the dialogue about the sinking of the *Titanic* was back in 1912 on both sides of the Atlantic.

We are honored to reprint this important essay in *The Complete Titanic*. (This piece originally appeared in the May 1912 issue of the *English Review*.)

Some Reflections, Seamanlike And Otherwise, On The Loss Of The *Titanic*

by Joseph Conrad

It is with a certain bitterness that one must admit to oneself that the late S.S. *Titanic* had a "good press." It is perhaps because I have no great practice of daily newspapers (I have never seen so many of them together lying about my room) that the white spaces and the big lettering of the headlines have an incongruously festive air to my eyes, a disagreeable effect of a feverish exploitation of a sensational God-send. And if ever a loss at sea fell under the definition, in the terms of a bill of lading, of Act of God, this one does, in its magnitude, suddenness and severity; and in the chastening influence it should have on the self-confidence of mankind.

I say this with all the seriousness the occasion demands, though I have neither the competence nor the wish to take a theological view of this great misfortune, sending so many souls to their last account. It is but a natural REFLECTION. Another one flowing also from the phraseology of bills of lading (a bill of lading is a shipping document limiting in certain of its clauses the liability of the carrier) is that the "King's Enemies" of a more or less overt sort are not altogether sorry that this fatal mishap should strike the prestige of the greatest Merchant Service of the world. I believe that not a thousand miles from these shores certain public prints have betrayed in gothic letters their satisfaction—to speak plainly—by rather ill-natured comments.

In what light one is to look at the action of the American Senate is more difficult to say. From a certain point of view the sight of the august senators of a great Power rushing to New York and beginning to bully and badger the luckless "Yamsi"—on the very quay-side so to speak—seems to furnish the Shakespearean touch of the comic to the real tragedy of the fatuous drowning of all these people who to the last moment put their trust in mere bigness, in the reckless affirmations of commercial men and mere technicians and in the irresponsible paragraphs of the newspapers booming these ships! Yes, a grim touch of comedy. One asks oneself what these men are after, with this very provincial display of authority. I beg my friends in the United States pardon for calling these zealous senators men. I don't wish to be disrespectful. They may be of the stature of demi-gods for all I know, but at that great distance from the shores of effete Europe and in the presence of so many guileless dead, their size seems diminished from this side. What are they after? What is there for them to find out? We know what had happened. The ship scraped her side against a piece of ice, and sank after floating for two hours and a half, taking a lot of people down with her. What more can they find out from the unfair badgering of the unhappy "Yamsi," or the ruffianly abuse of the same?

"Yamsi," I should explain, is a mere code address, and I use it here symbolically. I have seen commerce pretty close. I know what it is worth, and I have no particular regard for commercial magnates, but one must protest against these Bumble-like proceedings. Is it indignation at the loss of so many lives which is at work here? Well, the American railroads kill very many people during one single year, I dare say. Then why don't these dignitaries come down on the presidents of their own railroads, of which one can't say whether they are mere means of transportation or a sort of gambling game for the use of American plutocrats. Is it only an ardent and, upon the whole, praiseworthy desire for information? But the reports of the inquiry tell us that the august senators, though raising a lot of questions testifying to the complete innocence and even blankness of their minds, are unable to understand what the second officer is saying to them. We are so informed by the press from the other side. Even such a simple expression as that one of the look-out men was stationed in the "eyes of the ship" was too much for the senators of the land of graphic expression. What it must have been in the more recondite matters I won't even try to think, because I have no mind for smiles just now. They were greatly exercised about the sound of explosions heard when half the ship was under water already. Was there one? Were there two? They seemed to be smelling a rat there! Has not some charitable soul told them (what even schoolboys who read sea stories know) that when a ship sinks from a leak like this, a deck or two is always blown up; and that when a steamship goes down by the head, the boilers may, and often do break adrift with a sound which resembles the sound of an explosion? And they may, indeed, explode, for all I know. In the only case I have seen of a steamship sinking there was such a sound, but I didn't dive down after her to investigate. She was not of 45,000 tons and declared unsinkable, but the sight was impressive enough. I shall never forget the muffled, mysterious detonation, the sudden agitation of the sea round the slowly raised stern, and to this day I have in my eye the propeller, seen perfectly still in its frame against a clear evening sky.

But perhaps the second officer has explained to them by this time this and a few other little facts. Though why an officer of the British merchant service should answer the questions of any king, emperor, autocrat, or senator of any foreign power (as to an event in which a British ship alone was concerned, and which did not even take place in the territorial waters of that power) passes my understanding. The only authority he is bound to answer is the Board of Trade. But with what face the Board of Trade, which, having made the regulations for 10,000 ton ships, put its dear old bald head under its wing for ten years, took it out only to shelve an important report, and with a dreary murmur, "Unsinkable," put it back again, in the hope of not being disturbed for another ten years, with what face it will be putting questions to that man who has done his duty, as to the facts of this disaster and as to his professional conduct in it—well, I don't know! I have the greatest respect for our established authorities. I am a disciplined man, and I have a natural indulgence for the weaknesses of human institutions; but I will own that at times I have regretted their—how shall I say it?—their imponderability. A Board of Trade—what is it? A Board of . . . I believe the Speaker of the Irish Parliament is one of the members of it. A ghost. Less than that; as yet a mere memory. An office with adequate and no doubt comfortable furniture and a lot of perfectly irresponsible gentlemen who exist packed in its equable atmosphere softly, as if in a lot of cotton-wool, and with no care in the world; for there can be no care without personal responsibility—such, for instance, as the seamen have—those seamen from whose mouths this irresponsible institution can take away the bread—as a disciplinary measure. Yes—it's all that. And what more? The name of a politician—a party man! Less than nothing; a mere void without as much as a shadow of responsibility cast into it from that light in which move the masses of men who work, who deal in things and face the realities—not the words—of this life.

Years ago I remember overhearing two genuine shellbacks of the old type commenting on a ship's officer, who, if not exactly incompetent, did not commend himself to their severe judgment of accomplished sailor-men. Said one, resuming and concluding the discussion in a funnily judicial tone:

"The Board of Trade must have been drunk when they gave him his certificate."

I confess that this notion of the Board of Trade as an entity having a brain which could be overcome by the fumes of strong liquor charmed me exceedingly. For then it would have been unlike the limited companies of which some exasperated wit has once said that they had no souls to be saved and no bodies to be kicked, and thus were free in this world and the next from all the effective sanctions of conscientious conduct. But, unfortunately, the picturesque pronouncement overheard by me was only a characteristic sally of an annoyed sailor. The Board of Trade is composed of bloodless departments. It has no limbs and no physiognomy, or else at the forthcoming inquiry it might have paid to the victims of the *Titanic* disaster the small tribute of a blush. I ask myself whether the Marine Department of the Board of Trade did really believe, when they decided to shelve the report on equipment for a time, that a ship of 45,000 tons, that ANY ship, could be made practically indestructible by means of watertight bulkheads? It seems incredible to anybody who had ever reflected upon the properties of material, such as wood or steel. You can't, let builders say what they like, make a ship of such dimensions as strong proportionately as a much smaller one. The shocks our old whalers had to stand amongst the heavy floes in Baffin's Bay were perfectly staggering, notwithstanding the most skillful handling, and yet they lasted for years. The *Titanic,* if one may believe the last reports, has only scraped against a piece of ice which, I suspect, was not an enormously bulky and comparatively easily seen berg, but the low edge of a floe—and sank. Leisurely enough, God knows—and here the advantage of bulkheads comes in—for time is a great friend, a good helper—though in this lamentable case these bulkheads served only to prolong the agony of the passengers who could not be saved. But she sank, causing, apart from the sorrow and the pity of the loss of so many lives, a sort of surprised consternation that such a thing should have happened at all. Why? You build a 45,000 ton hotel of thin steel plates to secure the patronage of, say, a couple of thousand rich people (for if it had been for the emigrant trade alone, there would have been no such exaggeration of mere size), you decorate it in the style of the Pharaohs or in the Louis Quinze style—I don't know which—and to please the aforesaid fatuous handful of individuals, who have more money than they know what to do with, and to the applause of two continents, you launch that mass with two thousand people on board at twenty-one knots across the sea—a perfect exhibition of the modern blind trust in mere material and appliances. And then this happens. General uproar. The blind trust in material and appliances has received a terrible shock. I will say nothing of the credulity which accepts any statement which specialists, technicians and office-people are pleased to make, whether for purposes of gain or glory. You stand there astonished and hurt in your profoundest sensibilities. But what else under the circumstances could you expect?

For my part I could much sooner believe in an unsinkable ship of 3,000 tons than in one of 40,000 tons. It is one of those things that stand to reason. You can't increase the thickness of scantling and plates indefinitely. And the mere weight of this bigness is an added disadvantage. In reading the reports, the first reflection which occurs to one is that, if that luckless ship had been a couple of hundred feet shorter, she would have probably gone clear of the danger. But then, perhaps, she could not have had a swimming bath and a French cafe. That, of course, is a serious consideration. I am well aware that those responsible for her short and fatal existence ask us in desolate accents to believe that if she had hit end on she would have survived. Which, by a sort of coy implication, seems to mean that it was all the fault of the officer of the watch (he is dead now) for trying to avoid the obstacle. We shall have presently, in deference to commercial and industrial interests, a new kind of seamanship. A very new and "progressive" kind. If you see anything in the way, by no means try to avoid it; smash at it full tilt. And then—and then only you shall see the triumph of material, of clever contrivances, of the whole box of engineering tricks in fact, and cover with glory a commercial concern of the most unmitigated sort, a great Trust, and a great ship-building yard, justly famed for the super-excellence of its material and workmanship. Unsinkable! See? I told you she was unsinkable, if only handled in accordance with the new seamanship. Everything's in that. And, doubtless, the Board of Trade, if properly approached, would consent to give the needed instructions to its examiners of Masters and Mates. Behold the examination-room of the future. Enter to the grizzled examiner a young man of modest aspect: "Are you well up in modern seamanship?" "I hope so, sir." "H'm, let's see. You are at night on the bridge in charge of a 150,000 tons ship, with a motor track, organ-loft, etc., etc., with a full cargo of passengers, a full crew of 1,500 cafe waiters, two sailors and a boy, three collapsible boats as per Board of Trade regulations, and going at your three-quarter speed of, say, about forty knots. You perceive suddenly right ahead, and close to, something that looks like a large ice-floe. What would you do?" "Put the helm amidships." "Very well. Why?" "In order to hit end on." "On what grounds should you endeavour to hit end on?" "Because we are taught by our builders and masters that the heavier the smash, the smaller the damage, and because the requirements of material should be attended to."

And so on and so on. The new seamanship: when in doubt try to ram fairly—whatever's before you. Very simple. If only the *Titanic* had rammed that piece of ice (which was not a monstrous berg) fairly, every puffing paragraph would have been vindicated in the eyes of the credulous public which pays. But would it have been? Well, I doubt it. I am well aware that in the eighties the steamship *Arizona*, one of the "greyhounds of the ocean" in the jargon of that day, did run bows on against a very unmistakable iceberg, and managed to get into port on her collision bulkhead. But the *Arizona* was not, if I remember rightly, 5,000 tons register, let alone 45,000, and she was not going at twenty knots per hour. I can't be perfectly certain at this distance of time, but her sea-speed could not have been more than fourteen at the outside. Both these facts made for safety. And, even if she had been engined to go twenty knots, there would not have been behind that speed the enormous mass, so difficult to check in its impetus, the terrific weight of which is bound to do damage to itself or others at the slightest contact.

I assure you it is not for the vain pleasure of talking about my own poor experiences, but only to illustrate my point, that I will relate here a very unsensational little incident I witnessed now rather more than twenty years ago in Sydney, N.S.W. Ships were beginning then to grow bigger year after year, though, of course, the present dimensions were not even dreamt of. I was standing on the Circular Quay with a Sydney pilot watching a big mail steamship of one of our best-known companies being brought alongside. We admired her lines, her noble appearance, and were impressed by her size as well, though her length, I imagine, was hardly half that of the *Titanic*.

She came into the Cove (as that part of the harbour is called), of course very slowly, and at some hundred feet or so short of the quay she lost her way. That quay was then a wooden one, a fine structure of mighty piles and stringers bearing a roadway—a thing of great strength. The ship, as I have said before, stopped moving when some hundred feet from it. Then her engines were rung on slow ahead, and immediately rung off again. The propeller made just about five turns, I should say. She began to move, stealing on, so to speak, without a ripple; coming alongside with the utmost gentleness. I went on looking her over, very much interested, but the man with me, the pilot, muttered under his breath: "Too much, too much." His exercised judgment had warned him of what I did not even suspect. But I believe that neither of us was exactly prepared for what happened. There was a faint concussion of the ground under our feet, a groaning of piles, a snapping of great iron bolts, and with a sound of ripping and splintering, as when a tree is blown down by the wind, a great strong piece of wood, a baulk of squared timber, was displaced several feet as if by enchantment. I looked at my companion in amazement. "I could not have believed it," I declared. "No," he said. "You would not have thought she would have cracked an egg—eh?"

I certainly wouldn't have thought that. He shook his head, and added: "Ah! These great, big things, they want some handling."

Some months afterwards I was back in Sydney. The same pilot brought me in from sea. And I found the same steamship, or else another as like her as two peas, lying at anchor not far from us. The pilot told me she had arrived the day before, and that he was to take her alongside tomorrow. I reminded him jocularly of the damage to the quay. "Oh!" he said, "we are not allowed now to bring them in under their own steam. We are using tugs."

A very wise regulation. And this is my point—that size is to a certain extent an element of weakness. The bigger the ship, the more delicately she must be handled. Here is a contact which, in the pilot's own words, you wouldn't think could have cracked an egg; with the astonishing result of something like eighty feet of good strong wooden quay shaken loose, iron bolts snapped, a baulk of stout timber splintered. Now, suppose that quay had been of granite (as surely it is now)—or, instead of the quay, if there had been, say, a North Atlantic fog there, with a full-grown iceberg in it awaiting the gentle contact of a ship groping its way along blindfold? Something would have been hurt, but it would not have been the iceberg.

Apparently, there is a point in development when it ceases to be a true progress—in trade, in games, in the marvellous handiwork of men, and even in their demands and desires and aspirations of the moral and mental kind. There is a point when progress, to remain a real advance, must change slightly the direction of its line. But this is a wide question. What I wanted to point out here is—that the old *Arizona,* the marvel of her day, was proportionately stronger, handier, better equipped, than this triumph of modern naval architecture, the loss of which, in common parlance, will remain the sensation of this year. The clatter of the presses has been worthy of the tonnage, of the preliminary paeans of triumph round that vanished hull, of the reckless statements, and elaborate descriptions of its ornate splendour. A great babble of news (and what sort of news too, good heavens!) and eager comment has arisen around this catastrophe, though it seems to me that a less strident note would have been more becoming in the presence of so many victims left struggling on the sea, of lives miserably thrown away for nothing, or worse than nothing: for false standards of achievement, to satisfy a vulgar demand of a few moneyed people for a banal hotel luxury—the only one they can understand—and because the big ship pays, in one way or another: in money or in advertising value.

It is in more ways than one a very ugly business, and a mere scrape along the ship's side, so slight that, if reports are to be believed, it did not interrupt a card party in the gorgeously fitted (but in chaste style) smoking-room—or was it in the delightful French cafe?—is enough to bring on the exposure. All the people on board existed under a sense of false security. How false, it has been sufficiently demonstrated. And the fact which seems undoubted, that some of them actually were reluctant to enter the boats when told to do so, shows the strength of that falsehood. Incidentally, it shows also the sort of discipline on board these ships, the sort of hold kept on the passengers in the face of the unforgiving sea. These people seemed to imagine it an optional matter: whereas the order to leave the ship should be an order of the sternest character, to be obeyed unquestioningly and promptly by every one on board, with men to enforce it at once, and to carry it out methodically and swiftly. And it is no use to say it cannot be done, for it can. It has been done. The only requisite is manageableness of the ship herself and of the numbers she carries on board. That is the great thing which makes for safety. A commander should be able to hold his ship and everything on board of her in the hollow of his hand, as it were. But with the modern foolish trust in material, and with those floating hotels, this has become impossible. A man may do his best, but he cannot succeed in a task which from greed, or more likely from sheer stupidity, has been made too great for anybody's strength.

The readers of *The English Review,* who cast a friendly eye nearly six years ago on my *Reminiscences,* and know how much the merchant service, ships and men, has been to me, will understand my indignation that those men of whom (speaking in no sentimental phrase, but in the very truth of feeling) I can't even now think otherwise than as brothers, have been put by their commercial employers in the impossibility to perform efficiently their plain duty; and this from motives which I shall not enumerate here, but whose intrinsic unworthiness is plainly revealed by the greatness, the miserable greatness, of that disaster. Some of them have perished. To die for commerce is hard enough, but to go under that sea we have been trained to combat, with a sense of failure in the supreme duty of one's calling is indeed a bitter fate. Thus they are gone, and the responsibility remains with the living who will have no difficulty in replacing them by others, just as good, at the same wages. It was their bitter fate. But I, who can look at some arduous years when their duty was my duty too, and their feelings were my feelings, can remember some of us who once upon a time were more fortunate.

It is of them that I would talk a little, for my own comfort partly, and also because I am sticking all the time to my subject to illustrate my point, the point of manageableness which I have raised just now. Since the memory of the lucky *Arizona* has been evoked by others than myself, and made use of by me for my own purpose, let me call up the ghost of another ship of that distant day whose less lucky destiny inculcates another lesson making for my argument. The *Douro,* a ship belonging to the Royal Mail Steam Packet Company, was rather less than one-tenth the measurement of the *Titanic*. Yet, strange as it may appear to the ineffable hotel exquisites who form the bulk of the first-class Cross-Atlantic Passengers, people of position and wealth and refinement did not consider it an intolerable hardship to travel in her, even all the way from South America; this being the service she was engaged upon. Of her speed I know nothing, but it must have been the average of the period, and the decorations of her saloons were, I dare say, quite up to the mark; but I doubt if her birth had been boastfully paragraphed all round the Press, because that was not the fashion of the time. She was not a mass of material gorgeously furnished and upholstered. She was a ship. And she was not, in the apt words of an article by Commander C. Crutchley, R.N.R., which I have just read, "run by a sort of hotel syndicate composed of the Chief Engineer, the Purser, and the Captain," as these monstrous Atlantic ferries are. She was really commanded, manned, and equipped as a ship meant to keep the sea: a ship first and last in the fullest meaning of the term, as the fact I am going to relate will show.

She was off the Spanish coast, homeward bound, and fairly full, just like the *Titanic*; and further, the proportion of her crew to her passengers, I remember quite well, was very much the same. The exact number of souls on board I have forgotten. It might have been nearly three hundred, certainly not more. The night was moonlit, but hazy, the weather fine with a heavy swell running from the westward, which means that she must have been rolling a great deal, and in that respect the conditions for her were worse than in the case of the *Titanic.* Some time either just before or just after midnight, to the best of my recollection, she was run into amidships and at right angles by a large steamer which after the blow backed out, and, herself apparently damaged, remained motionless at some distance.

My recollection is that the *Douro* remained afloat after the collision for fifteen minutes or thereabouts. It might have been twenty, but certainly something under the half-hour. In that time the boats were lowered, all the passengers put into them, and the lot shoved off. There was no time to do anything more. All the crew of the *Douro* went down with her, literally without a murmur. When she went she plunged bodily down like a stone. The only members of the ship's company who survived were the third officer, who was from the first ordered to take charge of the boats, and the seamen told off to man them, two in each. Nobody else was picked up. A quartermaster, one of the saved in the way of duty, with whom I talked a month or so afterwards, told me that they pulled up to the spot, but could neither see a head nor hear the faintest cry.

But I have forgotten. A passenger was drowned. She was a lady's maid who, frenzied with terror, refused to leave the ship. One of the boats waited nearby till the chief officer, finding himself absolutely unable to tear the girl away from the rail to which she clung with a frantic grasp, ordered the boat away out of danger. My quartermaster told me that he spoke over to them in his ordinary voice, and this was the last sound heard before the ship sank. The rest is silence. I daresay there was the usual official inquiry, but who cared for it? That sort of thing speaks for itself with no uncertain voice; though the papers, I remember, gave the event no space to speak of: no large headlines—no headlines at all. You see it was not the fashion at the time. A seaman-like piece of work, of which one cherishes the old memory at this juncture more than ever before. She was a ship commanded, manned, equipped—not a sort of marine Ritz, proclaimed unsinkable and sent adrift with its casual population upon the sea, without enough boats, without enough seamen (but with a Parisian cafe and four hundred of poor devils of waiters) to meet dangers which, let the engineers say what they like, lurk always amongst the waves; sent with a blind trust in mere material, light-heartedly, to a most miserable, most fatuous disaster.

And there are, too, many ugly developments about this tragedy. The rush of the senatorial inquiry before the poor wretches escaped from the jaws of death had time to draw breath, the vituperative abuse of a man no more guilty than others in this matter, and the suspicion of this aimless fuss being a political move to get home on the M. T. Company, into which, in common parlance, the United States Government has got its knife, I don't pretend to understand why, though with the rest of the world I am aware of the fact. Perhaps there may be an excellent and worthy reason for it; but I venture to suggest that to take advantage of so many pitiful corpses, is not pretty. And the exploiting of the mere sensation on the other side is not pretty in its wealth of heartless inventions. Neither is the welter of Marconi lies which has not been sent vibrating without some reason, for which it would be nauseous to inquire too closely. And the calumnious, baseless, gratuitous, circumstantial lie charging poor Captain Smith with desertion of his post by means of suicide is the vilest and most ugly thing of all in this outburst of journalistic enterprise, without feeling, without honour, without decency.

But all this has its moral. And that other sinking which I have related here and to the memory of which a seaman turns with relief and thankfulness has its moral too. Yes, material may fail, and men, too, may fail sometimes; but more often men, when they are given the chance, will prove themselves truer than steel, that wonderful thin steel from which the sides and the bulkheads of our modern sea-leviathans are made.

R.M.S. TITANIC IN MID-OCEAN

PART III

Mysteries of the *Titanic*: A Century of Secrets

Students of the *Titanic* tragedy will be aware, whether they believe in them or not, that there were a number of premonitions and coincidences of a psychic nature surrounding the sinking of the ship . . .

—*Daily Sketch,* April 16, 1912

[A] horoscope cast for a 31 May 1911 birth (*Titanic*'s launch date) at 12:15 P.M. on latitude 54° 36′ N, longitude 5° 56′ W, (the coordinates of Belfast) predicted, among other things, danger on or near water, accidents in travel and sorrow and loss through relatives.

—from *Titanic: Destination Disaster*

Mrs. Shrubsall, the wife of a draughtsman, is said to have dreamt last Sunday night that the *Titanic* was sinking. She woke her husband, to tell him her dream, but he dismissed it as a fancy, saying that no doubt the fact that she had relatives on board had made her anxious. Mrs. Shrubsall's sister, a member of the staff of the vessel, is among the drowned.

—from the Monday, April 22, 1912 *Daily Sketch*

Shortly before nine o'clock last evening the entire electricity supply of Liverpool failed suddenly. The streets were plunged into darkness, electric cars came to a sudden standstill, and all social life was held up. It was fully three-quarters of an hour before normal conditions were restored.

—from the Tuesday, April 16, 1912, British newspaper, the *Daily Sketch,* a periodical which often reported on news from Liverpool, the British city that was *Titanic*'s port of registration

236

All unthinkable disasters attract all manner of speculation as to whether or not the tragedy had been foretold and whether or not it could have been prevented. For instance, did Nostradamus accurately predict John F. Kennedy's assassination and, if so, should precautions have been taken? And was the sinking of the *Titanic* predicted fourteen years before the great liner set out on her maiden voyage, and, if so, should she have not even been built? As the previous epigraphs dramatically illustrate, there were people who simply did not "feel right" about the *Titanic*, and astrology seemed to bear their fears out.

Other than alleged precognitive warnings about the ship itself and her ultimate fate, the events of that "night to remember" also pose questions that have yet to be completely answered (if they ever will be). How did Captain Smith die? Did First Officer William Murdoch shoot himself in the head? What was the mystery ship the survivors saw? What was the band's last song? Did the White Star Line try to pass off the *Olympic* as the *Titanic* for insurance purposes? Were the *Titanic*'s three million rivets fatally flawed?

These are the questions that have fascinated *Titanic* buffs for decades. In this section, we will look at a few of the many mysteries surrounding the *Titanic* and her sinking.

20

WERE SHOTS FIRED ON THE *TITANIC*, AND DID FIRST OFFICER WILLIAM MURDOCH COMMIT SUICIDE?

Were shots fired on the *Titanic* as she sank? In a word, yes. There are simply too many credible accounts of shots being fired to dismiss the story as apocryphal.

Fifth Officer Harold Lowe is the crew member most often named as the shooter (although surviving passenger Jack Thayer also recalled seeing Chief Purser Herbert McElroy fire his revolver in the air to prevent people from rushing one of the lifeboats). Even though Lowe tried to prevent passengers from getting into an overcrowded lifeboat (thereby sealing their fate) he was also hailed after his rescue for being the only *Titanic* officer to go back to the site to pick up four men from the water. Some survivors also claimed to have seen First Officer William Murdoch shoot two passengers and then kill himself. (See his entry.)

Here is a sampling of some of the firsthand accounts of guns being fired on the *Titanic* as she sank.

Abraham Hyman, third-class passenger   "When [some of the steerage passengers] got on deck, they found a rope drawn closer to their quarters than usual, and this made some of them think there was danger. One or two of the women began to cry, and a panic began to spread. An officer came forward, stood close to the rope and waved the people back . . . The officer who was standing at the rope had a pistol in his hand, and he ordered everybody to keep back.

First, one woman screamed and then another, and then one man (I think he was an Italian) pushed toward the boat and the officer fired at him."

Jules Sop, Belgian, third-class passenger   Sop reported being threatened with death twice by officers with revolvers; first on the boat deck and then in the water when he tried to get into a lifeboat.

George Rheims, first-class passenger   Rheims wrote a private letter dated April 19, 1912, to his wife in which he stated that he personally saw an officer shoot a passenger who was trying to force his way into a lifeboat. His account read: "When the last boat was leaving, I saw an officer fire a shot and kill a man who was trying to climb into it. As there remained nothing more for him to do, the officer told us, 'Gentlemen, each man for himself. Good-bye.' He gave a military salute and then fired a bullet into his head. That's what I call a man!!"

Eugene Daly, third-class passenger   Daly wrote a private letter to his sister in which he reported seeing an officer shoot two men who were trying to get into a lifeboat. After awakening and praying with two female passengers, Daly wrote, "We afterwards went to the second cabin deck, and the two girls and myself got into a boat. An officer called on me to go back, but I would not stir. They then got hold of me and pulled me out.

"At the first cabin, when a boat was being lowered, an officer pointed a revolver and said if any man tried to get in he would shoot him on the spot. I saw the officer shoot two men dead because they tried to get into the boat. Afterwards there was another shot, and I saw the officer himself lying on the deck. They told me he shot himself, but I did not see him.

"I was up to my knees in water at the time. Everyone was rushing around and there were no more boats. I then dived overboard and got in a boat."

Frederick Scott, greaser   Scott saw Fifth Officer Lowe fire his revolver and shout, "If any man jumps in the boat I'll shoot him like a dog."

Harold Lowe, Fifth Officer   When asked during the British inquiry into the *Titanic* disaster why he fired his revolver, Lowe replied, "Because while I was at the boat deck two men jumped into my boat. I chased one out and to avoid another occurrence of that sort I fired my revolver as I was going past each deck. The boat had about sixty-four persons in it and would not stand a sudden jerk."

Frederick Clench, able seaman   When Clench was asked by Senator
Bourne at the U.S. Senate hearing if he heard any shooting from his
lifeboat, he responded, "Yes, sir; Mr. Lowe was in number fourteen
boat, and he sings out, 'Anybody attempting to get into these boats
while we are lowering them, I will shoot them,' and he shot three
shots." When asked if he saw Lowe actually shoot anyone, Clench
replied, "He shot straight down in the water."

DID FIRST OFFICER MURDOCH COMMIT SUICIDE?

On December 12, 1997, one week before the movie *Titanic* opened in
the United States, someone posted the following on one of the Internet
Titanic newsgroups: "I will say this though. If the movie has Murdoch
committing suicide I'll scream." Another message poster immediately
responded to this threat with just two words: "Start screaming." Thus,
the debate raged on.

The question of First Officer William Murdoch's reported suicide has
never been definitively answered, but there has been so much written
about the alleged incident that a review of the various accounts can help
us draw our own conclusions.

According to the depiction of Murdoch and his actions in James
Cameron's film *Titanic*—the most recent rendering of this story—the
First Officer, in his final hours, accepted bribes for places on lifeboats,
shot two panicked third-class passengers attempting to get into an
already overcrowded lifeboat, and ultimately committed suicide by shooting himself in the head.

This is not, however, the version of Murdoch's story that his family
and townsfolk believe. In fact, the residents of Dalbeattie, Scotland, Murdoch's hometown, believe that William Murdoch's actions during
Titanic's final hours were heroic and selfless, and that he dutifully went
down with the ship instead of gutlessly killing himself as the situation on
the sinking ship began to fall apart.

At an April 15, 1998, ceremony in Dalbeattie commemorating the
eighty-sixth anniversary of the sinking, Scottish-born Twentieth
Century–Fox executive Scott Neeson tried to paint a prettier picture than
the film might suggest. "[*Titanic*]," Neeson told the media, "never
intended to portray him as a coward. I believe he was portrayed as a hero

in the film. In the film and in real life, he is saving an enormous number of lives."

Neeson, in an attempt to mollify the offended supporters of Murdoch's memory, gave Dalbeattie High School a check for $8,000 and an inscribed silver tray. He also officially apologized to Dalbeattie and Murdoch's family on behalf of Twentieth Century–Fox for causing them all "so much distress."

Considering the portrayal of Murdoch in the film and the film's enormous success, this apology (and the size of the check) does seem a bit like insincere spin control by the studio, especially considering that Neeson then said the studio would neither change the depiction of Murdoch for the forthcoming *Titanic* video, nor add a note in the credits at the end of the film in an attempt to restore his good name.

Linda Kirkwood, head of Dalbeattie High School, praised the studio's donation but said it did not make up for Murdoch's memory being "besmirched." She also said that "People in Dalbeattie and the rest of Britain know he was a hero, but filmgoers all over the world will see him portrayed as a coward."

William Murdoch's nephew, Scott Murdoch, eighty, was more magnanimous about the incident. Saying he was "very pleased" that the studio had issued an apology, he noted that "It was important to clear the name of my uncle. I don't think I can forget, but today certainly makes it easier to forgive."

So what exactly happened to First Officer William Murdoch, and how did he actually behave during *Titanic*'s final moments?

Several survivors reported seeing Murdoch assigning passengers to lifeboats and helping with their loading and launching. *Titanic* expert Walter Lord, in his book *The Night Lives On,* his sequel to *A Night to Remember,* noted that when last seen, just as Second Officer Lightoller jumped into the sea, William Murdoch was still on deck, working at trying to launch a collapsible lifeboat. If Murdoch had considered suicide, Lord wrote, it was understandable. He was, after all, the officer who had been in charge of the bridge at the time of the collision with the iceberg and had been the one to give "the orders that failed to save the ship." And yet, surviving *Titanic* officers who knew Murdoch well all agreed that he would not be the type to kill himself.

Thomas Whitely, one of *Titanic*'s saloon stewards, said that he watched Murdoch "shoot one man . . . and then shoot himself." Whitely's testimony is unclear, however, because he also said, "I did not see this, but three others did," and it is not clear if he's talking about Murdoch shooting a man or shooting himself.

Third-class passenger Carl Jensen said that he "glanced toward the bridge and saw the chief officer place a revolver in his mouth and shoot himself. His body toppled overboard."

The question of whether or not Murdoch killed himself arose almost immediately after the sinking. In a story that ran in the Friday, April 19, 1912, edition of Britain's *Daily Sketch* newspaper, the subject of Murdoch's and Captain Smith's ultimate outcomes was already being discussed:

> The reports that Captain Smith committed suicide are quite discredited by the overwhelming volume of evidence volunteered by the survivors, while the alternative suggestion that it was the first officer, Mr. Murdoch, who shot himself on the bridge is disproved in an equally emphatic manner by the quartermaster at the wheel, Robert Hitchens, who declares that Mr. Murdoch was in charge of the vessel at the time of the accident and that he acted in the coolest possible manner, closing the watertight doors and stopping the engines.

Ten days later, in the *Daily Sketch*'s April 30, 1912, edition, survivor Charles Williams was quoted as saying, "[The Captain] did ask what had become of First Officer Murdoch. We told him Murdoch had blown his brains out with a revolver."

There is, in the end, no definitive answer to the question of whether or not First Officer William Murdoch killed himself as the *Titanic* sank beneath the waves. What is clear, though, is that *someone* killed himself on *Titanic*'s deck. Again, there are just too many detailed accounts from credible witnesses to dismiss the story as fiction. Apology notwithstanding, though, Cameron's film will serve to "carve in stone" the version of the story that has Murdoch blowing his brains out.

As with many elements of the *Titanic* tale, much of what we believe is what we personally *want* to believe. Murdoch's loved ones want to believe he died a hero. Cameron and other *Titanic* historians want to believe he killed himself. There are no final answers, and perhaps this unavoidable uncertainty is part of what has kept the *Titanic* legend alive for almost nine decades.

21

SHOULD THE *TITANIC*'S WATERTIGHT DOORS HAVE REMAINED OPEN?

In April 1998, WPIX-TV (Channel 11) in New York broadcast a new *Titanic* documentary called *Titanic: Secrets Revealed*. It was hosted by Bernard Hill, the dignified British actor who had played Capt. Edward Smith in James Cameron's *Titanic,* and the two-hour special used interviews, re-creations, and computer simulations to explore some of the more tenacious "secrets" surrounding the sinking of the great liner.

Overall, this documentary would not have been of enormous interest to *Titanic* buffs who possessed even a perfunctory knowledge of the facts and rumors that have surfaced over the years. Frankly, much of what *Titanic: Secrets Revealed* "revealed" had been explored earlier and more comprehensively in other documentaries about the *Titanic*. (This production seems to have been, in part, an RMS Titanic public relations piece—at one point Bernard Hill goes out of his way to tell viewers that RMS Titanic is "preserving the memory of the *Titanic* with dignity and respect.")

But *Titanic: Secrets Revealed* did provide new information in one critical area: The question of whether or not *Titanic*'s sixteen watertight doors should have remained open. Could Captain Smith have bought *Titanic* time and kept her afloat long enough for everyone to be rescued if he had ordered the watertight compartment doors opened after they had been automatically closed?

If *Titanic* had been allowed to fill with water evenly, would she have remained on the surface long enough for the *Carpathia* and the *Californian* to transfer all of *Titanic*'s passengers and crew to their decks?

The producers of *Titanic: Secrets Revealed* commissioned a scientific experiment to answer this important question.

With the assistance of naval architect Arthur Sanderford and technical consultant Bill Sauder, a transparent Lucite model of the *Titanic* was built precisely to scale. The great liner's size, weight, and buoyancy—as well as all of her watertight compartments—were carefully duplicated to scale. The plan was to sink *Titanic* in a tank, meticulously duplicating first, the conditions under which she foundered on the morning of April 15, 1912; and then sinking her with all of her sixteen watertight compartment doors open.

The team first allowed boiler rooms 5 and 6 to fill with water just as they did that night. The watertight compartment doors were all quickly closed after striking the iceberg, and the water filled the bow and sank *Titanic* in just over two hours, exactly as it happened in 1912.

For years, *Titanic* theorists have speculated that the ship could have remained afloat a full *two hours longer* if the doors had remained open.

Is this theory correct? And, if so, is it provable?

The experiment moved to its next phase. This time, the team started the clock (i.e., struck the iceberg) at 11:40 P.M., Sunday, April 14, 1912, and began filling the *Titanic* model with water, only this time they left all of her watertight doors open.

By 11:50 P.M. water was pouring into the six watertight compartments opened by the iceberg, only now the water was flowing the entire length of the ship instead of pooling in just the six front compartments in the bow. At 12:20 A.M., the first lifeboat was launched and water continued to pour into the *Titanic* at the rate of 350 tons per minute. The ship sank more evenly as the water filled the hull along the entire length of the keel.

At 12:40 the *Carpathia* received *Titanic*'s distress signal and began steaming towards her. She was fifty-eight miles away. By now, there were over twenty-thousand tons of water flooding the *Titanic*—but, remarkably, she was still level.

Around 12:50, the icy water of the Atlantic flooded *Titanic*'s last boiler and killed all power on the ship. The *Titanic* was now dark, a full ninety minutes earlier than she was in 1912. Hundreds and hundreds of *Titanic*'s passengers and crew are now trapped below decks in the frigid cold, and in pitch darkness.

By 1:30 A.M., fourteen of *Titanic*'s lifeboats were away and her bow remained above water, but the *Carpathia* was still forty miles away. At 1:40, the *Titanic,* now filled with close to forty-thousand tons of water, begins to roll over. The remaining lifeboats cannot be launched, and by 1:45 the ship is terribly unstable.

According to technical consultant Bill Sauder, "A heavy list makes it very difficult to launch lifeboats, so instead of the relatively calm sinking that we saw actually happen in 1912, we would have wound up with a ship in the dark for over an hour with a heavy list, panic; possibly stampedes on the lifeboats. It would have been a catastrophe."

At 1:47, the *Titanic* rolls completely over on her side and capsizes, sinking a full *thirty-three minutes earlier* than she did in 1912. Her heavy list would have prevented the loading of the remaining lifeboats and many more people would have died. At this time, the *Carpathia* was still over thirty miles away.

"If Smith had left the watertight doors opened," Sauder concluded, "contrary to his instructions, contrary to his training, the loss of life would have been catastrophic." This experiment therefore showed that "nothing within the captain's power could have saved the ship."

22

THE BAND'S FINAL SONG

> The ship was gradually turning on her nose—just like a
> duck that goes down for a dive. I had only one thing on
> my mind—to get away from the suction. The band was
> still playing. I guess all of the band went down. They
> were playing "Autumn" then.
>
> —*Titanic*'s Marconi Operator Harold Bride

What final song did the stalwart *Titanic* orchestra play before the band members put down their instruments and prepared themselves for their inevitable death? No one knows for sure, but there are three main contenders for the band's last song. They are the hymn "Nearer, My God to Thee," the popular song of the time, "Autumn," and the traditional waltz by Archibald Joyce, "Songe d'Automne."

In the accompanying section listing the complete repertoire of the orchestra you will see that "Nearer, My God to Thee" and "Autumn" are not specifically listed; but "Songe d'Automne" is (at number 114 on the playlist). However, you will notice that items 96 and 100 on the orchestra's list of music are, respectively, "Popular Songs" and "National Anthems, Hymns, etc. of all Nations," and these categories would almost certainly include "Nearer, My God to Thee" and "Autumn."

Throughout the years, "Nearer, My God to Thee" has become ensconced in the *Titanic* legend as the band's final song. Many survivors are on record as recalling hearing the song being played as the lifeboats were being loaded and the ship continued to sink. One 1912 newspaper account even stated that some of the lifeboat passengers were actually

Nearer, My God, to Thee

Nearer, my God, to thee,
Nearer to thee!
Even though it be a cross
That raiseth me;
Still all my song shall be—
Nearer, my God, to thee,
Nearer to thee!

Though, like the wanderer,
The sun gone down,
Darkness be over me,
My rest a stone;
Yet in my dreams I'd be
Nearer, my God, to thee,
Nearer to thee!

There let the way appear
Steps unto heaven;
All that thou sendest me
Is mercy given;
Angels to beckon me
Nearer, my God, to thee,
Nearer to thee!

Then with my waking thoughts,
Bright with thy praise,
Out of my stony griefs
Bethel I'll raise;
So by my woes to be
Nearer, my God, to thee,
Nearer to thee!

Or if on joyful wing,
Cleaving the sky,
Sun, moon, and stars forgot,
Upward I fly;
Still all my song shall be—
Nearer, my God, to thee,
Nearer to thee.

humming along with the band as they played the popular hymn.

But Harold Bride, *Titanic*'s only surviving Marconi operator (a job requiring accuracy and attention to detail), remembered hearing "Autumn," yet he did not specify if it was the Joyce waltz, which appears on the orchestra's playlist, or the popular song "Autumn," which does (by name, that is).

There is no doubt that "Nearer, My God to Thee" was immediately embraced as the band's final song. An April 22, 1912, article in the British paper, the *Daily Sketch,* revealed that Wallace Hartley, the band's leader, had once told a fellow musician that if he was ever onboard a sinking liner, he would get his men together and play music as the ship sank. When asked what he would play, Hartley replied, "Well, I don't think I could do better than play 'Oh God Our Help in Ages Past' or 'Nearer, My God to Thee.' They are both favorite hymns of mine, and they would be very suitable to the occasion." These words from the dead seem to confirm that what many of the survivors remembered hearing the band play was, indeed, exactly what Wallace Hartley had his band perform.

One early mention of "Nearer, My God to Thee" being played came from Edward Wheelton, one of *Titanic*'s saloon stewards, whose account of the *Titanic*'s final moments appeared in the Saturday, April 20, 1912, *Daily Sketch:*

> As the boats were being lowered the orchestra was playing operatic selections and some of the latest popular melodies from Europe and America.
>
> It was only just before the liner made her final plunge that the character of the programme was changed, and then they struck up "Nearer, My God to Thee."

In early May, the crew of the *Mackay-Bennett,* the ship sent to the site of the *Titanic*'s sinking to search for bodies still afloat, found and identified bandmaster Wallace Hartley's body. On Friday, May 17, 1912, Hartley's body was returned to Liverpool on the liner *Arabic* and claimed by his father. Hartley's coffin was driven by hearse to his hometown of Colne, where his funeral would take place the following day.

The following account from the Monday, May 20, 1912, *Daily Sketch* details Hartley's funeral and again asserted the "Nearer, My God to Thee" story:

> In keeping with the heroism of the man who led the *Titanic*'s band as they stood on the deck of the doomed liner calmly playing "Nearer, My God to Thee," while the last of the lifeboats pulled away from the sinking ship were the striking scenes witnessed Saturday when the remains of Mr. Wallace Hartley were laid to rest in the cemetery of his native town of Colne, Lancashire.
>
> The Bethel Choir and the Colne Orchestral Society played "Nearer, My God to Thee" as Hartley's remains were interred.

It is extremely likely (in fact, considering the number of eyewitness accounts, almost a certainty) that Hartley and company did, indeed, play "Nearer, My God to Thee" (and probably one or both of the "Autumn" songs) as they serenaded the anxious passengers attempting to fill the *Titanic*'s lifeboats. But was it the absolute last song the band played? Unfortunately, this is impossible to know, but what we can be sure of is that the beloved hymn was without a doubt one of the last songs the band played, but that the truth of the *final* song is lost for all time.

Note: See Walter Lord's *The Night Lives On* for a complete discussion of the many and varied views of hymnologists regarding the different melodies of "Autumn" and some of the other songs rumored to have been played by the *Titanic* main orchestra on the night of the sinking.

THE COMPLETE REPERTOIRE OF THE *TITANIC* ORCHESTRA

It was quite a responsibility being the sole source of musical entertainment on a gigantic liner like the *Titanic,* and the eight members of *Titanic*'s main orchestra performed admirably.

This section is the complete repertoire of music the *Titanic*'s band could play on demand. Their playlist included everything from operatic and classical pieces for accompanying dining, to ragtime and waltzes for postprandial dancing. This listing, however, is probably not the only music they played. Survivors have mentioned hearing songs that are not on this list, and considering the vast range of musical expertise the members of the orchestra possessed, it is likely that this official repertoire was probably just a starting point for their performances. (For instance, Edwina Troutt remembered hearing Edward Elgar's *Pomp and Circumstance* performed by the musicians, and yet there is nothing specifically by Elgar on this list.)

Rounding out the orchestra's selection list was a wide assortment of national anthems, sacred hymns, and popular songs of the day.

THE MEMBERS OF THE *TITANIC* MAIN ORCHESTRA

Wallace Henry Hartley
Bandmaster

W. Theodore Brailey
Pianist

Roger Bricoux
Cellist

John Fred Clarke
Bass Violist

John Law Hume
First Violinist

George Krins
Violist

Percy C. Taylor
Cellist

John Wesley Woodward
Cellist

THE BAND'S REPERTOIRE

OVERTURES

1. Il Barbiere di Siviglia..Rossini
2. Zampa..Herold
3. Semiramide..Rossini

4. La Gazza Ladra ....Rossini
5. Muta di Portici ....Auber
6. Italiana in Algieri ....Rossini
7. Tancredi ....Rossini
8. Guglielmo Tell ....Rossini
9. Morning, Noon and Night in Vienna ....Suppè
10. Pique Dame ....Suppè
11. Poet and Peasant ....Suppè
12. Raymond ....A. Thomas
13. Martha ....Flotow
14. Agnes...F. Paer
15. The Bohemian Girl..Balfe

Operatic Selections, etc.

16. The Quaker Girl...Monckton
17. The Girl in the Train ....Leo Fall
18. Samson and Delilah ....St. Saëns
19. Madame Sherry...K. Hoschna
20. Cadix ....Valverde
21. Aïda ....Verdi
22. Thaïs...Massenet
23. The Chocolate Soldier ....O. Straus
24. Cavalleria Rusticana ....Mascagni
25. Mignon ....Thomas
26. Un Ballo in Maschera ....Verdi
27. Pagliacci..Leoncavallo
28. Orphee Aux Enfers...Offenbach
29. Madam Butterfly ....Puccini
30. The Dollar Princess ....Leo Fall
31. A Waltz Dream...O. Straus
32. Miss Hook of Holland ....Rubens
33. The Merry Widow..Lehar
34. Our Miss Gibbs..Monckton
35. The Arcadians ....Monckton
36. The Belle of Brittany ....Talbot
37. Havana ....Stuart
38. Dear Little Denmark ....Rubens
39. The Fair Co-ed..Luder
40. The Grand Mogul ....Luder
41. The Gay Musician...Julian Edward
42. A Trip to Japan..Klein

43. His Honour the Mayor .... Julian Edward
44. The Red Mill .... V. Herbert
45. The Prima Donna .... V. Herbert
46. The Three Twins .... Karl Hoschna
47. The Prince of Pilsen .... Luder
48. It Happened in Nordland .... V. Herbert
49. Neptune's Daughter .... V. Herbert
50. Faust .... Gounuod
51. Carmen .... Bizet
52. Il Trovatore .... Verdi
53. Rigoletto .... Verdi
54. La Traviata .... Verdi
55. Puritani .... Bellini
56. La Sonnambula .... Bellini
57. Lucia di Lammermoor .... Donizetti
58. La Favorita .... Donizetti
59. Tosca .... Puccini
60. La Bohéme .... Puccini
61. The Mikado .... Sullivan
62. Pirates of Penzance .... Sullivan
63. Iolanthe .... Sullivan
64. A Princess of Kensington .... E. German
65. Merrie England .... E. German
66. Tom Jones .... E. German
67. Manon Lescaut .... Puccini
68. Les Contes D'Hoffman .... Offenbach
69. Mefistofele .... Boito
70. Tannhauser .... Wagner
71. Lohengrin .... Wagner
72. The Girls of Gottenburg .... Caryll and Monckton
73. Haddon Hall .... Sullivan
74. The Gondoliers .... Sullivan
75. Recollections of Gounuod .... Godfrey
76. Sullivan's Melodies .... Godfrey
77. The Maid and the Mummy .... A. Aarons
78. Love's Lottery .... Julian Edwards
79. M'lle Modisté .... Julian Edwards
80. Miss Dolly Dollars .... Julian Edwards
81. Wonderland .... Julian Edwards
82. The Princess Beggar .... A. G. Robyn
83. The Geisha .... Jones
84. San Toy .... Jones

SUITES, FANTASIAS, ETC.

85. Peer Gynt Suite ....Greig
86. Three Dances: "Henry VIII" ....E. German
87. Three Dances: "Nell Gwyn" ....E. German
88. Three Dances: "Tom Jones"...............................E. German
89. The Rose...Myddleton
90. The Thistle...Myddleton
91. The Shamrock...Myddleton
92. American National Airs ....Tobani
93. Plantation Songs ....Clutsam
94. Canadian Songs...Retford
95. Tosti's Popular Songs ....Godfrey
96. Popular Songs...S. Adams
97. Reminiscences of the Savoy...................................M. Moore
98. Reminiscences of Wales ....Godfrey
99. Reminiscences of All Nations ....Godfrey
100. National Anthems, Hymns, etc., of all Nations

WALTZES

101. Love and Life in Holland ....Joyce
102. Partners Galore..G. V.
103. The Druid's Prayer...Davson
104. Vision of Salome..Joyce
105. Remembrance..Joyce
106. Beautiful Spring ....Lincke
107. Wedding Dance ....Lincke
108. Comedie d'Amou...G. Colin
109. Valse Septembre...F. Godwin
110. Mondaine...Bosc
111. Réve d'Artiste ....Bosc
112. Swing Song ....Hollaender
113. Sphinx ....Popy
114. Songe d'Automne ....Joyce
115. La Lettre de Manon ....Giliet
116. Cecilia ....Pether
117. Apach's Dance...Offenbach
118. Verschmähte Liebe..P. Lincke
119. Lysistrata ....P. Lincke
120. Luna...P. Lincke

Nearer, my God, to Thee,
Nearer to Thee;
E'en though it be a cross
That raiseth me;
Still all my song shall be,
"Nearer, my God, to Thee,
Nearer to Thee".

23

THE RIDDLE OF CAPTAIN SMITH'S DEATH AND LAST WORDS

> Walking through six inches of water Smith goes into the
> enclosed **WHEELHOUSE** and closes the door. He is
> alone on the bridge, surrounded by the gleaming brass
> instruments. He seems to inwardly collapse. . . . He stands
> just behind the ship's wheel, squaring his shoulders as he
> gazes out into the blackness. . . . CAPTAIN SMITH,
> standing near the wheel, watches the black water climbing
> the windows of the enclosed wheelhouse. He has the
> stricken expression of a damned soul on Judgment Day.
> Water is fountaining under the doors. The windows burst
> suddenly and a wall of water edged with shards of glass
> slams Smith against the back wall. He disappears in a
> vortex of foam.
>
> —from James Cameron's *Titanic* film treatment

How did *Titanic*'s Capt. Edward J. Smith die, and what were his final
words? As you can see from the above excerpt from James Cameron's
epic 1997 film *Titanic,* many believe that the ill-fated captain walked
calmly back into the bridge wheelhouse just as the ship was going under
and was drowned when a huge flood of water came bursting through the
bridge windows.

Even though Cameron went with a completely feasible account of
Captain Smith's demise, there are a couple of other versions of the

commander's final moments. Here is a sampling of what some of the survivors recalled about the death of their captain:

Robert W. Daniel of Philadelphia, survivor   Daniel said that Captain Smith stood calmly on the bridge as it was submerged under the icy Atlantic waters: "I saw Captain Smith on the bridge. My eyes seemingly clung to him. The deck from which I had leapt was immersed. The water had risen slowly, and was now to the floor of the bridge. Then it was to Captain Smith's waist. I saw him no more. He died a hero." Daniel also said, "Captain Smith was the biggest hero I ever saw. He stood on the bridge, shouting through the megaphone, trying to make himself heard."

Dr. J. F. Kemp, a passenger on the *Carpathia*   Dr. Kemp said that Captain Smith committed suicide by shooting himself in the head. Kemp said he spoke with a young boy—a *Titanic* passenger—who claimed to have seen "Captain Smith put a pistol to his head and then fall down." Some other survivors also confirmed seeing this happen, but *Titanic* crew members passionately denied even the *possibility* of Smith killing himself instead of going down with his ship.

Harold Bride, *Titanic* Marconi operator   Bride said he saw Captain Smith dive into the ocean just as Collapsible B was levered off the roof of the officers' quarters and it fell onto the boat deck: "The last I saw of the captain, he went overboard from the bridge. He jumped overboard from the bridge when we were launching the collapsible lifeboat."

George Alfred Hogg, lookout   "I saw Captain Smith in the water alongside a raft. 'There's the skipper,' I yelled. 'Give him a hand.' They did, but he shook himself free and shouted to us, 'Goodbye boys. I'm going to follow the ship.' That was the last we saw of our skipper."

G. A. Brayton of Los Angeles, survivor   "I saw Captain Smith while I was in the water. He was standing on the deck all alone. Once he was swept down by a wave, but managed to get to his feet again. Then, as the boat sank, he was again knocked down by a wave, and then disappeared from sight."

Lawrence Beesley, survivor   "The captain stood on the bridge and continued directing his men right up to the moment when the bridge on which he stood became level with the water. He then calmly climbed over the rail and dropped into the sea.

Charles Williams, survivor   Williams said he saw Captain Smith swimming around in the icy water with an infant in his arms and wearing a life belt. He reportedly handed the infant to someone in a lifeboat but refused to get in himself. Smith then asked what had become of Murdoch and when told he had killed himself, pushed himself away from the boat, took off his life belt, and sank beneath the surface to his death. This version of the story was confirmed by a steward named John Maynard, who claimed to have personally taken the baby from Captain Smith, and by *Titanic* fireman Harry Senior, who reported having seen the captain rescue the child.

Robert Williams, *Titanic* fireman   "The captain was swimming close alongside me, and he, too, had a baby in his arms. I saw him swim to one of the boats and hand the baby to someone, and the last I saw of him he was heading back towards the ship." (Again, this was the baby that was reportedly taken by Entree Cook and Steward John Maynard.)

Edward Brown, first-class steward   "As the *Titanic*'s bridge was nearly touching the water another collapsible boat was got out. Captain Smith, megaphone in hand, passed and said, 'Well, boys, do the best for the women and children, and then look after yourselves.' Captain Smith then went on the bridge. A very short time after that the vessel sank."

Charles Lightoller, *Titanic* second officer   In his U.S. Senate testimony, Lightoller, when asked about Captain Smith, said, "I think the bridge was the last place I saw him . . . I think he was crossing the bridge." When asked what Captain Smith's last orders were, Lightoller replied, "When I asked him, 'Shall I put the women and children in the boats?' he replied, 'Yes; and lower away.' Those were the last orders he gave."

Colonel Archibald Gracie, survivor   In his account of the *Titanic* tragedy titled *The Truth About the Titanic,* Gracie asks himself the question, "Did either the Captain or the First Officer shoot himself?" He then writes, "Notwithstanding all the current rumors and newspaper statements answering this question affirmatively, I have been unable to find any passenger or member of the crew cited as authority for the statement that either Captain Smith or First Officer Murdoch did anything of the sort. On the contrary, so far as relates to Captain Smith, there are several witnesses, including Harold S. Bride, the junior Marconi operator, who saw him at the last on the bridge of his ship, and later, when sinking and struggling in the water. . . . About ten minutes before the ship sank, Captain Smith gave word for every man to look to his own safety."

Other accounts of Captain Smith's death include being crushed to death by the falling forward funnel of the starboard bridge wing, and being swept off the bridge when it lunged forward. One survivor said, "I saw him swim back onto the sinking ship. He went down with it in my sight."

Regarding Captain Smith's last words, history here is also inconclusive, yet consistent: Regardless of precisely what the doomed commander actually said, all postrescue accounts of his words emphasized Smith's heroism and self-sacrifice. He was reported to have said all, some, or none of the following:

"Be British, boys! Be British!"
"Every man for himself!"
"Goodbye, boys! I'm going to follow the ship!"
"I will follow the ship!"
"Well boys, do your best for the women and children, and look out for yourselves."
"All right, boys. Good luck and God bless you."

CONCLUSION

Regardless of how Captain Smith died, there is no doubt that he did his duty as ship's captain and went down with his ship. Based on survivors' accounts and the belief that Captain Smith would probably have done everything in his power to save as many passengers as possible, one possible scenario could be that he did, indeed, swim to one of the lifeboats with a baby in his arms and then swim back to the ship, where he returned to the wheelhouse and awaited his and his ship's destiny.

It is feasible that the majority of the accounts of the captain's final moments are true—except for the suicide story. There are not enough credible accounts of the captain shooting himself for it to be considered seriously, and yet there are repeated accounts of both the "swimming with the baby" story and of seeing the captain on the bridge just before the ship went under.

We can only imagine Captain Smith's profound embarrassment and the overwhelming feeling that he had let down his passengers, his crew, and his ship as the *Titanic* foundered. Captain Smith was where the buck stopped. When the R.M.S. *Titanic* left Southampton under Captain Smith's command, *he* was the one ultimately responsible for over 2,200 lives and a $10 million vessel.

Captain Smith must have gone to his death in the deepest throes of despair over his failure. In all likelihood, he probably welcomed death, since it would serve as an escape from his torment—and as what he may have considered a deserved punishment for failing to save his passengers and his ship—regardless of the actual reasons for her foundering.

> Captain "E. J." was one of the ablest skippers on the Atlantic, and accusations of recklessness, carelessness, not taking due precautions, or driving his ship at too high a speed, were absolutely, and utterly unfounded; but the armchair complaint is a very common disease, and generally accepted as one of the necessary evils from which the seafarer is condemned to suffer.
>
> —Second Officer Charles Lightoller

24

WAS THE *TITANIC* REALLY
THE *OLYMPIC*?

**I have done two days . . . You can hardly tell the
difference between the two boats. I have been standing
by the ship today to see she doesn't run away.**

> —Steward George Beedem, in a letter to his wife after
> being transferred from the *Olympic* to the *Titanic*

At first, this riddle sounds utterly ridiculous, and yet it dramatically
proves that today's rampant conspiracy paranoia is not a phenomenon
unique to our modern times.

As discussed in the *Titanic* time line in this volume, on September
20, 1911, the *Titanic's* sister ship, the *Olympic,* on her fifth voyage and
under the command of Capt. Edward J. Smith, collided with the H.M.S.
Hawke while leaving Southampton.

The *Hawke's* bows were badly damaged, and the *Olympic's* hull sustained a forty-foot gash. The *Olympic's* passengers were disembarked at
Cowes and the ship then returned to Southampton for inspection and
repairs. An official inquiry found the *Olympic*—and by extension, Captain
Smith (even though he was actually *not* to blame, since the pilot had
been in charge of navigation at the time of the collision)—at fault. The
Olympic was dry-docked on October 6, 1911, and many workers from
the *Titanic* project were transferred to the *Olympic* for her six-week
repair job.

According to one of the myths surrounding the *Titanic's* foundering, the White Star Line deliberately switched the *Olympic*'s nameplates with the *Titanic*'s before the *Titanic*'s maiden voyage, and then sent the damaged *Olympic* off to the North Atlantic masquerading as the brand-new *Titanic*. Once out at sea, the "*Titanic*" (really the wounded *Olympic*) would deliberately ram an iceberg and sink. The alleged reason for this suspected deception was that the White Star Line could then collect on the "*Titanic*'s" insurance and still have a brand-new ship back in Belfast waiting to be launched (under another name, of course).

Two of the reasons why some people back then believed this rumor (and today there are probably people in Southampton who *still* believe it) is that J. P. Morgan refused to board the *Titanic* on her maiden voyage. Morgan was the wealthy American financier whose company, International Mercantile Marine, owned the White Star Line. Another reason was that White Star Line president J. Bruce Ismay was somehow inexplicably saved from drowning when the *Titanic* sank, while many hundreds of others perished.

Allegedly, none other than Captain Smith himself was also in on this plan, and that is supposed to explain why he (deliberately) ignored the many ice warnings *Titanic* received in her first couple of days at sea. The reason things ultimately went wrong was because Smith did not execute the devious plan correctly and ended up crashing into the iceberg in the wrong place and at the wrong time—resulting in a real disaster instead of a faux one.

This rumor also explained why *Californian*'s Captain Lord ignored the *Titanic*'s requests for help: He, too, was in on the switch and knew that he needn't go to the aid of *Titanic*'s passengers: They would all eventually be rescued by other White Star Line ships in the area who were also in on the switch and who were thus prepared for the stranded passengers. (It seems as though everyone *but* the passengers was in on this enormous deception, doesn't it?)

Several factors contributed to the perpetuation of this rumor. The first was the fact that the *Titanic* and the *Olympic* were virtually identical and were built in Belfast at the same time, sitting right next to each other.

Granted, the two ships were almost identical, but there *were* differences—albeit minor—between them. The *Olympic* had an *open* area on the forward promenade deck while the *Titanic* had an *enclosed* front forward promenade section on the same deck below the first two funnels.

The modification installing steel-framed screens with sliding windows for *Titanic*'s A deck was ordered by J. Bruce Ismay to protect passengers from sea spray. Apparently passengers on the *Olympic*'s maiden voyage had complained about the spray, and therefore, Ismay decided to correct the problem on the *Titanic,* while not doing anything about the problem on the *Olympic.*

Also, the windows on the forward section of the *Olympic*'s B deck (which was shorter than *Titanic*'s) were *evenly* spaced, vertically aligned portholes, while on the *Titanic,* the same openings were a mix of actual windows *and* portholes and were *unevenly* spaced, supposedly to deliberately change the visual lines of the ship.

How, then, did the rumor that the *Titanic* had been a ringer, get started?

The suspicion was probably born because the *Titanic* and the *Olympic* were virtually identical sister ships and, after the sinking, many theaters, newspapers, and magazines used pictures of the *Olympic* to illustrate articles and quickly create fake posters in order to capitalize on the public's rabid demand for information about the ship and the tragedy.

Also, exactly one month after the disaster, the ten-minute silent film, *Saved From the Titanic,* was released starring *Titanic* survivor and silent movie star Dorothy Gibson.

Saved From the Titanic was filmed aboard the *Olympic,* with the *Olympic*'s name on both her hull and her lifeboats erased. The movie deliberately presented footage of the *Olympic* being towed into her berth in New York as footage of the *Titanic* being towed from her berth in Southampton. Thus, the seed was planted.

Postcard publishers were also quick to exploit the disaster by printing picture postcards showing the *Olympic* and naming it the *Titanic.* One postcard that clearly showed the *Olympic*'s open promenade deck was captioned, "The Ill-Fated White Star Liner *Titanic.*" Some publishers were really shameless: They published postcards with a watercolor painting of the *Olympic* and called it the *Titanic.* Substituting a photograph is almost understandable, but deliberately using a painting seems to be gilding the lily just a tad: Why didn't they just publish the card with a (presumably readily available) painting of the *Titanic* instead?

(A truly bizarre twist in this tale of naval misrepresentation involves an "In Memoriam" postcard published years after the *Titanic*'s sinking to commemorate the loss of the steamship *Lusitania,* which had been torpedoed by a German submarine off the coast of Ireland on May 7, 1915. The photo the publishers used to represent the *Lusitania* was an April 10, 1912, photo of the *Titanic* departing Southampton!)

The rumor that the *Olympic* was switched with the *Titanic* does have a lot going for it. Conspiracy theorists especially like a financial motive for their suspected schemes: It somehow adds credibility. After all, people will do almost anything for money, right?

The fact that the ruthless financier J. P. Morgan was the actual owner of the *Titanic* and the *Olympic* made the suspicion that he'd try a plan that would net him millions even more believable.

Collusion is always taken for granted when it comes to deconstructing these kinds of conspiracies. (A recent example of this was the jury's willingness to believe that many members of the Los Angeles Police Department had gotten together in secret and agreed to "get" O. J. Simpson.) Thus, the seductive suggestion that captains Smith and Lord, as well as shipyard workers and many other White Star employees, had all agreed to switching the ships. But the suspicion that the two ships had been clandestinely exchanged to benefit their American owner (all it supposedly would have taken was switching a few nameplates on the ships and their lifeboats) was totally disproved when the wreck of the *Titanic* was discovered by Dr. Robert Ballard in September, 1985 (and it is, indeed, the R.M.S. *Titanic* two and a half miles down).

Finding the ship led to artifacts being retrieved, expeditions being mounted—and mountains of photographic documentation being compiled. The 1990 Imax film *Titanica* shows one of *Titanic*'s port propellers. On it is stamped the number 401. Also, the *Titanic*'s stern bridge's helm indicator was recovered from the debris field, and on it was also stamped the number 401. This was concrete proof as to which ship has been resting on the ocean bottom in the frigid darkness for the past eight decades.

According to official Harland and Wolff construction records, the R.M.S. *Olympic*'s hull number was 400. And her sister ship, *Titanic*'s? 401.

25

WERE THE *TITANIC*'S RIVETS FATALLY FLAWED?

Everything that could go wrong, did.
—naval architect William H. Garzke

Were the three million rivets that held *Titanic* together metallurgically flawed—so flawed, in fact, that their composition played a major role in the great liner's demise (a source of fascination for *Titanic* fanatics who call themselves Rivet Heads)? Recent research on two retrieved rivets from *Titanic*'s hull seems to confirm that the answer to that question is a qualified yes.

For decades, it was believed that the three-hundred thousand-ton iceberg that the forty-six thousand-ton *Titanic* collided with sliced a three-hundred-foot gash in her hull, a wound so devastating that it sank the "unsinkable" ship in less than three short hours. But an August 1996 dive to the site of the wreck revealed that the damage to the *Titanic*'s side was much smaller than anyone could have ever imagined—the total area of damage was between twelve and thirteen square feet, about the total size of a human body.

Through ultrasound imaging, it was learned that six small slits in the *Titanic*'s starboard hull were what sank her, and that what ultimately sealed her fate was where these six gashes were placed: they were spaced across six of the *Titanic*'s sixteen watertight compartments, thus allowing flooding in one of the unlikeliest scenarios guaranteed to sink her. The *Titanic* had been designed to survive total flooding of three of her watertight compartments, and in some cases four, depending on which four were opened to the sea. But it was not designed to withstand the flooding of *six* compartments—an eventuality no one—not the owners, builders, crew, or passengers—even considered a remote possibility.

When the French oceanographic group IFREMER made a dive to *Titanic* in August 1996, they brought along Paul Matthias, president of the Rhode Island–based company Polaris Imaging. Matthias used a device called a sub-bottom profiler to image the wreck of the *Titanic*, hoping to identify the exact cause of her sinking. After establishing an analytic baseline with images of the port side, he then examined the starboard side, the side which had struck the iceberg. His findings were surprising.

"There's no gash," Matthias said in a postdive interview. "What we're seeing is a series of deformations in the starboard side that start and stop along the hull. They're about ten feet above the bottom of the ship. They appear to follow the hull plate."

What this ultimately meant was that instead of the *Titanic*'s hull plates being ripped open by the iceberg, as had been believed for decades, it now appeared that iron rivets holding the plates to the hull's cross beams popped open, creating splits the size of a hardcover book. These small slits, because they were about twenty feet below the waterline, would have allowed water to shoot into the watertight compartments under tremendous pressure, ultimately filling the *Titanic* with approximately thirty-nine thousand tons of water before she sank. The mystery now was: Why did the iron rivets pop?

Two wrought-iron rivets retrieved from the wreck of the *Titanic* were examined and found to contain high concentrations of slag. Slag is the glass residue left over from the smelting of metallic ores, and it is added in small quantities—usually around 2 percent—to wrought iron to give it strength. "Otherwise it would be taffy," said Paul Foecke, the metallurgist who performed the microscopic examination of the *Titanic* rivets.

Foecke discovered that the slag content of the *Titanic*'s rivets was a dangerously high 9.3 percent, a concentration that would have made the rivets extremely brittle and substantially weaker than they would have been with an appropriate level of slag. He also found that the slag streaks, which are supposed to run lengthwise along the rivet, made a sharp 90 degree turn at the head end, thereby causing further weakness in the rivet. "To have the slag turned around this way," Foecke said, "this is a major area of weakness." In a report released in early 1998 called "Metallurgy of the R.M.S. *Titanic,*" Foecke stated, "The microstructure of the rivets is the most likely candidate for becoming a quantifiable metallurgical factor in the loss of *Titanic.*"

A conclusion from this new finding could be that the structurally weak rivets allowed the hull plates to pop, and that if they were not flawed, they might have held the plates together after striking the iceberg.

After learning of Foecke's findings, William H. Garzke Jr., a naval architect who heads a team of marine forensic experts investigating the disaster, told the media, "We think they popped and allowed the plates to separate and let in the water." Garzke did admit that these findings should be considered tentative because of the small sampling (only two rivets) used for the testing.

After being queried about these new findings, Peter Harbinson, a spokesman for Harland and Wolff, *Titanic*'s builders, refused to comment specifically, saying that the subject was too old. "We don't have an archivist or anything like that," Harbinson told the press. "We don't have anybody in a position to comment."

A question that immediately arose after the slag results were made public was one of standards: Was a 9 percent slag content acceptable in 1912, based on the prevailing technologies? In an attempt to answer this question, Foecke dug up a 1906 metallurgical reference book that defined "medium quality" wrought iron as containing from 2 to 2.5 percent slag. So the 9.3 percent slag content of *Titanic*'s rivets was too high even for the standards of the time. This appears damning, and yet Foecke would not assign too much weight to the 1906 text. "As far as I can tell," he said in an interview, "there was no standard of the time," and Foecke also noted that the *Titanic*'s rivets conceivably could have been "state of the art back then."

It is quite possible that the high slag content of the two rivets tested could have been a fluke. After all, two out of three million is a minuscule test sample, and in order for results to be conclusive, many thousands more rivets would have to be tested with identical results for these findings to become *Titanic* gospel.

Defenders of Harland and Wolff's building skills and the quality of the iron used (and Paul Foecke himself is included in this group) point to *Titanic*'s sister ship the *Olympic* for refutation of the flawed rivets claim.

"[The *Olympic*] sailed for twenty-seven years," Foecke said in an interview. "It collided with two ships. It ran over and sank a submarine. It was hit by a dud torpedo. And it was called Old Reliable and was scrapped in 1936. So it's not what it's made of, and what its design is. It's also circumstance."

So what should we conclude about this theory? Undoubtedly, the high slag content of the two rivets tested is an important finding, but it cannot be considered conclusive until many, many more rivets are tested with the same results. Until that day, *Titanic* still holds on to one of her many secrets.

26

THE WRECK OF THE TITAN

A Complete Reprinting of the 1898 Novella That Seems to Have Predicted the *Titanic* Disaster

> **She was the largest craft afloat and the greatest of the works of men.**
>
> —The opening line of Morgan Robertson's novella,
> *The Wreck of the Titan*

In 1898, Morgan Robertson, a popular adventure writer of the time, published a novella called *Futility,* which was a thrilling story about the largest passenger steamship ever built striking an iceberg in the North Atlantic and sinking. The ship was called the *Titan,* and close to three-thousand souls were lost when she foundered. Fourteen years later, the *Titanic* would strike an iceberg in the North Atlantic and sink within three hours. Did Robertson predict the sinking of the *Titanic* fourteen years before the great liner's maiden voyage?

Shortly after the *Titanic* was lost, Robertson's publishers rereleased *Futility,* but this time it had a new title: *The Wreck of the Titan.* How close *were* the two ships—and their two stories?

The following table provides a side-by-side look at some of the most amazing parallels. As you read the actual novella that follows, you may even find more. Regardless of the presence—or lack thereof—of pre-cognitive ability on the part of Morgan Robertson, there is no denying that his writing *The Wreck of the Titan* is one of the stranger elements of the *Titanic* legend.

	The *Titan*	The *Titanic*
Length	800 feet	882.5 feet
Number of propellors	3	3
Watertight compartments	19	16
Watertight doors	92	12
Passenger capacity	3,000	3,000
Passengers onboard	3,000	2,200
Displacement (in tons)	45,000 (1898 edition) 70,000 (1912 edition)	66,000
Gross tonnage	45,000	46,328
Nickname	"Unsinkable"	"Unsinkable"
Horsepower	40,000 (1898 edition) 75,000 (1912 edition)	46,000
Lifeboats	24	20
Speed at time of collision	25 knots	22.5 knots
Month voyage began	April	April
Side of ship that struck iceberg	Starboard	Starboard
Time iceberg was struck	Near midnight	11:40 P.M.
Itinerary	New York to England	England to New York
Location of collision	North Atantic, a few hundred miles off the U.S. coast	North Atantic, a few hundred miles off the U.S. coast
First warning of danger	"Ice, ice ahead. Iceberg. Right under the bows."	"Iceberg! Right Ahead!"
Ship's owners	British company	British company
Ship's owners' headquarters	Liverpool	Liverpol
Ship's owners' U.S. office location	New York	New York
Deaths	2,987	1,523
Nationality of principal stock owners	American	American

THE WRECK OF THE TITAN

by
Morgan Robertson

Chapter I

She was the largest craft afloat and the greatest of the works of man. In her construction and maintenance were involved every science, profession, and trade known to civilization. On her bridge were officers, who, besides being the pick of the Royal Navy, had passed rigid examinations in all studies that pertained to the winds, tides, currents, and geography of the sea; they were not only seamen, but scientists. The same professional standard applied to the personnel of the engine-room, and the stewards' department was equal to that of a first-class hotel.

Two brass bands, two orchestras, and a theatrical company entertained the passengers during waking hours; a corps of physicians attended to the temporal, and a corps of chaplains to the spiritual, welfare of all on board, while a well-drilled fire-company soothed the fears of nervous ones and added to the general entertainment by daily practice with their apparatus.

From her lofty bridge ran hidden telegraph lines to the bow, stern engine-room, crow's-nest on the foremast, and to all parts of the ship where work was done, each wire terminating in a marked dial with a movable indicator, containing in its scope every order and answer required in handling the massive hulk, either at the dock or at sea—which eliminated, to a great extent, the hoarse, nerve-wracking shouts of officers and sailors.

From the bridge, engine-room, and a dozen places on her deck the ninety-two doors of nineteen watertight compartments could be closed in half a minute by turning a lever. These doors would also close automatically in the presence of water. With nine compartments flooded the ship would still float, and as no known accident of the sea could possibly fill this many, the steamship *Titan* was considered practically unsinkable.

Built of steel throughout, and for passenger traffic only, she carried no combustible cargo to threaten her destruction by fire; and the immunity from the demand for cargo space had enabled her designers to discard the flat, kettle-bottom of cargo boats and give her the sharp dead-rise—or slant from the keel—of a steam yacht, and this improved her behavior in a seaway. She was eight hundred feet long, of seventy thousand tons' displacement, seventy-five thousand horse-power, and on her trial trip had steamed at a rate of twenty-five knots an hour over the bottom, in the face of unconsidered winds, tides, and currents. In short, she was a floating city—containing within her steel walls all that tends to minimize the dangers and discomforts of the Atlantic voyage—all that makes life enjoyable.

Unsinkable—indestructible, she carried as few boats as would satisfy the laws.

These, twenty-four in number, were securely covered and lashed down to their chocks on the upper deck, and if launched would hold five hundred people. She carried no useless, cumbersome life-rafts; but—because the law required it—each of the three thousand berths in the passengers', officers', and crews' quarters contained a cork jacket, while about twenty circular life-buoys were strewn along the rails.

In view of her absolute superiority to other craft, a rule of navigation thoroughly believed in by some captains, but not yet openly followed, was announced by the steamship company to apply to the *Titan:* She would steam at full speed in fog, storm, and sunshine, and on the Northern Lane Route, winter and summer, for the following good and substantial reasons: First, that if another craft should strike her, the force of the impact would be distributed over a larger area if the *Titan* had full headway, and the brunt of the damage would be borne by the other. Second, that if the *Titan* was the aggressor she would certainly destroy the other craft, even at half-speed, and perhaps damage her own bows; while at full speed, she would cut her in two with no more damage to herself than a paintbrush could remedy. In either case, as the lesser of two evils, it was best that the smaller hull should suffer. A third reason was that, at full speed, she could be more easily steered out of danger, and a fourth, that in case of an end-on collision with an iceberg—the only thing afloat that she could not conquer—her bows would be crushed in but a few feet further at full than at half speed, and at the most three compartments would be flooded—which would not matter with six more to spare.

So, it was confidently expected that when her engines had limbered themselves, the steamship *Titan* would land her passengers three thousand miles away with the promptitude and regularity of a railway train. She had beaten all records on her maiden voyage, but, up to the third return trip, had not lowered the time between Sandy Hook and Daunt's Rock to the five-day limit; and it was unofficially rumored among the two thousand passengers who had embarked at New York that an effort would now be made to do so.

Chapter II

Eight tugs dragged the great mass to midstream and pointed her nose down the river; then the pilot on the bridge spoke a word or two; the first officer blew a short blast on the whistle and turned a lever; the tugs gathered in their lines and drew off; down in the bowels of the ship three small engines were started, opening the throttles of three large ones; three propellers began to revolve; and the mammoth, with a vibratory tremble running through her great frame, moved slowly to sea.

East of Sandy Hook the pilot was dropped and the real voyage begun. Fifty feet below her deck, in an inferno of noise, and heat, and light, and shadow, coal-passers wheeled the picked fuel from the bunkers to the fire-hold, where half-naked stokers, with faces like those of tortured fiends, tossed it into the eighty white-hot mouths of the furnaces. In the engine-rooms, oilers passed to and fro, in and out of the plunging, twisting, glistening steel, with oil-cans and waste, overseen by the watchful staff on duty, who listened with strained hearing for a false note in the confused jumble of sound—a clicking of steel out of tune, which would indicate a loosened key or nut. On deck, sailors set the triangular sails on the two masts, to add their propulsion to the momentum of the record-breaker, and the passengers dispersed themselves as suited their several tastes. Some were seated in steamer chairs, well wrapped—for, though it was April, the salt air was chilly—some paced the deck, acquiring their sea legs; other listened to the orchestra in the music-room, or read or wrote in the library, and a few took to their berths—seasick from the slight heave of the ship on the ground-swell.

The decks were cleared, watches set at noon, and then began the never-ending cleaning-up at which steamship sailors put in so much of their time. Headed by a six-foot boatswain, a gang came aft on the starboard side, with paint-buckets and brushes, and distributed themselves along the rail.

"Davits an' stanchions, men—never mind the rail," said the boatswain. "Ladies, better move your chairs back a little. Rowland, climb down out o' that—you'll be overboard. Take a ventilator—no, you'll spill paint—put your bucket away an' get some sandpaper from the yeoman. Work inboard till you get it out o' you."

The sailor addressed—a slight-built man of about thirty, black-bearded and bronzed to the semblance of healthy vigor, but watery-eyed and unsteady of movement—came down from the rail and shambled forward with his bucket. As he reached the group of ladies to whom the boatswain had spoken, his gaze rested on one—a sunny-haired young woman with the blue of the sea in her eyes—who had arisen at his approach. He started, turned aside as if to avoid her, and raising his hand in an embarrassed half-salute, passed on. Out of the boatswain's sight he leaned against the deck-house and panted, while he held his hand to his breast.

"What is it?" he muttered, wearily: "whisky nerves, or the dying flutter of a starved love. Five years, now—and a look from her eyes can stop the blood in my veins—can bring back all the heart-hunger and helplessness, that leads a man to insanity—or this." He looked at his trembling hand, all scarred and tar-stained, passed on forward, and returned with the sandpaper.

The young woman had been equally affected by the meeting. An expression of mingled surprise and terror had come to her pretty, but rather weak face; and without acknowledging his half-salute, she had caught up a little child from the deck behind her, and turning into the saloon door, hurried to the library, where she sank into [a] chair beside a military-looking gentleman, who glanced up from a book and remarked: "Seen the sea-serpent, Myra, or the Flying Dutchman? What's up?"

"Oh, George—no," she answered in agitated tones. "John Rowland is here—Lieutenant Rowland. I've just seen him—he is so changed—he tried to speak with me."

"Who—that troublesome flame of yours? I never met him, you know, and you haven't told me much about him. What is he—first cabin?"

"No, he seems to be a common sailor; he is working, and is dressed in old clothes—all dirty. And such a dissipated face, too. He seems to have fallen—so low. And it is all since—"

"Since you soured on him? Well, it is no fault of yours, dear. If a man has it in him he'll go to the dogs anyhow. How is his sense of injury? Has he a grievance or a grudge? You're badly upset. What did he say?"

"I don't know—he said nothing—I've always been afraid of him. I've met him three times since then, and he puts such a frightful look in his eyes—and he was so violent, and headstrong, and so terribly angry—that time. He accused me of leading him on, and playing with him; and he said something about an immutable law of chance, and a governing balance of events—that I couldn't understand, only where he said that for all the suffering we inflict on others, we receive an equal amount ourselves. Then he went away—in such a passion. I've imagined ever since that he would take some revenge—he might steal our Myra—our baby." She strained the smiling child to her breast and went on. "I liked him at first, until I found out that he was an atheist—why, George, he actually denied the existence of God—and to me, a professing Christian."

"He had a wonderful nerve," said the husband, with a smile; "didn't know you very well, I should say."

"He never seemed the same to me after that," she resumed; "I felt as though in the presence of something unclean. Yet I thought how glorious it would be if I could save him to God, and tried to convince him of the loving care of Jesus; but he only ridiculed all I hold sacred, and said, that much as he valued my good opinion, he would not be a hypocrite to gain it, and that he would be honest with himself and others, and express his honest unbelief—the idea; as though one could be honest without God's help—and then, one day, I smelled liquor on his breath—he always smelled of tobacco—and I gave him up. It was then that he—that he broke out."

"Come and show me this reprobate," said the husband, rising. They went to the door and the young woman peered out. "He is the last man down there—close to the cabin," she said as she drew in. The husband stepped out.

"What! that hang-dog ruffian, scouring the ventilator? So, that's Rowland, of the navy, is it! Well, this is a tumble. Wasn't he broken for conduct unbecoming an officer? Got roaring drunk at the President's levee, didn't he? I think I read of it."

"I know he lost his position and was terribly disgraced," answered his wife.

"Well, Myra, the poor devil is harmless now. We'll be across in a few days, and you needn't meet him on this broad deck. If he hasn't lost all sensibility, he's as embarrassed as you. Better stay in now—it's getting foggy."

Chapter III

When the watch turned out at midnight, they found a vicious half-gale blowing from the northeast, which, added to the speed of the steamship, made, so far as effects on her deck went, a fairly uncomfortable whole gale of chilly wind. The head sea, choppy as compared with her great length, dealt the *Titan* successive blows, each one attended by supplementary tremors to the continuous vibrations of the engines—each one sending a cloud of thick spray aloft that reached the crow's-nest on the foremast and battered the pilot-house windows on the bridge in a liquid bombardment that would have broken ordinary glass. A fog-bank, into which the ship had plunged in the afternoon, still enveloped her—damp and impenetrable; and into the gray, ever-receding wall ahead, with two deck officers and three lookouts straining sight and hearing to the utmost, the great racer was charging with undiminished speed.

At a quarter past twelve, two men crawled in from the darkness at the ends of the eighty-foot bridge and shouted to the first officer, who had just taken the deck, the names of the men who had relieved them. Backing up to the pilot-house, the officer repeated the names to a quartermaster within, who entered them in the log-book. Then the men vanished—to their coffee and "watch-below." In a few moments another dripping shape appeared on the bridge and reported the crow's-nest relief.

"Rowland, you say?" bawled the officer above the howling of the wind. "Is he the man who was lifted aboard, drunk, yesterday?"

"Yes, sir."

"Is he still drunk?"

"Yes, sir."

"All right—that'll do. Enter Rowland in the crow's-nest, quartermaster," said the officer; then, making a funnel of his hands, he roared out: "Crow's-nest, there."

"Sir," came the answer, shrill and clear on the gale.

"Keep your eyes open—keep a sharp lookout."

"Very good, sir."

"Been a man-o'-war's-man, I judge, by his answer. They're no good," muttered the officer. He resumed his position at the forward side of the bridge where the wooden railing afforded some shelter from the raw wind, and began the long vigil which would only end when the second officer relieved him, four hours later. Conversation—except in the line of duty—was forbidden among the bridge officers of the *Titan,* and his watchmate, the third officer, stood on the other side of the larger bridge binnacle, only leaving this position occasionally to glance in at the compass—which seemed to be his sole duty at sea. Sheltered by one of the deck-houses below, the boatswain and the watch paced back and forth, enjoying the two hours respite which steamship rules afforded, for the day's work had ended with the going down of the other watch, and at two o-clock the washing of the 'tween-deck would begin, as an opening task in the next day's labor.

By the time one bell had sounded, with its repetition from the crow's-nest, followed by a long-drawn cry—"all's well"—from the lookouts, the last of the two thousand passengers had retired, leaving the spacious cabins and steerage in possession of the watchmen; while, sound asleep in his cabin abaft the cart-room was the captain. The commander who never commanded—unless the ship was in danger; for the pilot had charge, making and leaving port, and the officers, at sea.

Two bells were struck and answered; then three, and the boatswain and his men were lighting up for a final smoke, when there rang out overhead a startling cry from the crow's-nest:

"Something ahead, sir—can't make it out."

The first officer sprang to the engine-room telegraph and grasped the lever. "Sing out what you see," he roared.

"Hard aport, sir—ship on the starboard tack—dead ahead," came the cry.

"Port your wheel—hard over," repeated the first officer to the quartermaster at the helm—who answered and obeyed. Nothing as yet could be seen from the bridge. The powerful steering-engine in the stern ground the rudder over; but before three degrees on the compass card were traversed by the lubber's-point, a seeming thickening of the darkness and fog ahead resolved itself into the square sails of a deep-laden ship, crossing the *Titan*'s bow, not half her length away.

"H—l and d——" growled the first officer. "Steady on your course, quartermaster," he shouted. "Stand from under on deck." He turned a lever which closed compartments, pushed a button marked—"Captain's Room," and crouched down, awaiting the crash.

There was hardly a crash. A slight jar shook the forward end of the *Titan* and sliding down her foretopmast-stay and rattling on deck came a shower of small spars, sails, blocks, and wire rope. Then, in the darkness to starboard and port, two darker shapes shot by—the two halves of the ship she had cut through; and from one of these shapes, where still burned a binnacle light, was heard, high above the confused murmur of shouts and shrieks, a sailorly voice:

"May the curse of God light on you and your cheese-knife, you brass-bound murderers."

The shapes were swallowed in the blackness astern; the cries were hushed by the clamor of the gale, and the steamship *Titan* swung back to her course. The first officer had not turned the lever of the engine-room telegraph.

The boatswain bounded up the steps of the bridge for instructions.

"Put men at the hatches and doors. Send every one who comes on deck to the chart-room. Tell the watchman to notice what the passengers have learned, and clear away that wreck forward as soon as possible." The voice of the officer was hoarse and strained as he gave these directions, and the "aye, aye, sir" of the boatswain was uttered in a gasp.

Chapter IV

The crow's-nest "look-out," sixty feet above the deck, had seen every detail of the horror, from the moment when the upper sails of the doomed ship had appeared to him above the fog to the time when the last tangle of wreckage was cut away by his watchmates below. When relieved at four bells, he descended with as little strength in his limbs as was compatible with safety in the rigging. At the rail, the boatswain met him.

"Report your relief, Rowland," he said, "and go into the chart-room!"

On the bridge, as he gave the name of his successor, the first officer seized his hand, pressed it, and repeated the boatswain's order. In the chart-room, he found the captain of the *Titan,* pale-faced and intense in manner, seated at a table, and, grouped around him, the whole of the watch on deck except the officers, lookouts, and quartermaster. The cabin watchmen were there, and some of the watch below, among whom were stokers and coal-passers, and also, a few of the idlers—lampmen, yeomen, and butchers, who, sleeping forward, had been awakened by the terrific blow of the great hollow knife within which they lived.

Three carpenters' mates stood by the door, with sounding-rods in their hands, which they had just shown the captain—dry. Every face, from the captain's down, wore a look of horror and expectancy. A quartermaster followed Rowland in and said:

"Engineer felt no jar in the engine-room, sir; and there's no excitement in the stokehold."

"And you watchmen report no alarm in the cabins. How about the steerage? Is that man back?" asked the captain. Another watchman appeared as he spoke.

"All asleep in the steerage, sir," he said. Then a quartermaster entered with the same report of the forecastles.

"Very well," said the captain, rising; "one by one come into my office—watchmen first, then petty officers, then the men. Quartermasters will watch the door—that no man goes out until I have seen him." He passed into another room, followed by a watchman, who presently emerged and went on deck with a more pleasant expression of face. Another entered and came out; then another, and another, until every man but Rowland had been within the sacred precincts, all to wear the same pleased, or satisfied look on reappearing. When Rowland entered, the captain, seated at a desk, motioned him to a chair, and asked his name.

"John Rowland," he answered. The captain wrote it down.

"I understand" he said, "that you were in the crow's-nest when this unfortunate collision occurred."

"Yes, sir; and I reported the ship as soon as I saw her."

"You are not here to be censured. You are aware, of course, that nothing could be done, either to avert this terrible calamity, or to save life afterward."

"Nothing at a speed of twenty-five knots an hour in a thick fog, sir." The captain glanced sharply at Rowland and frowned.

"We will not discuss the speed of the ship, my good man," he said, "or the rules of the company. You will find, when you are paid at Liverpool, a package addressed to you at the company's office containing one hundred pounds in banknotes. This, you will receive for your silence in regard to this collision—the reporting of which would embarrass the company and help no one."

"On the contrary, captain, I shall not receive it. On the contrary, sir, I shall speak of this wholesale murder at the first opportunity!"

The captain leaned back and stared at the debauched face, the trembling figure of the sailor, with which this defiant speech so little accorded. Under ordinary circumstances, he would have sent him on deck to be dealt with by the officers. But this was not an ordinary circumstance. In the watery eyes was a look of shock, and horror, and honest indignation; the accents were those of an educated man; and the consequences hanging over himself and the company for which he worked—already complicated by and involved in his efforts to avoid them—which this man might precipitate, were so extreme, that such questions as insolence and difference in rank were not to be thought of. He must meet and subdue this Tartar on common ground—as man to man.

"Are you aware, Rowland," he asked, quietly, "that you will stand alone—that you will be discredited, lose your berth, and make enemies?"

"I am aware of more than that," answered Rowland, excitedly. "I know of the power vested in you as captain. I know that you can order me into irons from this room for any offense you wish to imagine. And I know that an unwitnessed, uncorroborated entry in your official log concerning me would be evidence enough to bring me life imprisonment. But I also know something of admiralty law; that from my prison cell I can send you and your first officer to the gallows."

"You are mistaken in your conceptions of evidence. I could not cause your conviction by a logbook entry; nor could you, from a prison, injure me. What are you, may I ask—an ex-lawyer?"

"A graduate of Annapolis. Your equal in professional technic."

"And you have interest at Washington?"

"None whatever."

"And what is your object in taking this stand—which can do you no possible good, though certainly not the harm you speak of?"

"That I may do one good, strong act in my useless life—that I may help to arouse such a sentiment of anger in the two countries as will forever end this wanton destruction of life and property for the sake of speed—that will save the hundreds of fishing-craft, and others, run down yearly, to their owners, and the crews to their families."

Both men had risen and the captain was pacing the floor as Rowland, with flashing eyes and clinched fists, delivered this declaration.

"A result to be hoped for, Rowland," said the former, pausing before him, "but beyond your power or mine to accomplish. Is the amount I named large enough? Could you fill a position in my bridge?"

"I can fill a higher; and your company is not rich enough to buy me."

"You seem to be a man without ambition; but you must have wants."

"Food, clothing, shelter—and whisky," said Rowland with a bitter, self-contemptuous laugh. The captain reached down a decanter and two glasses from a swinging tray and said as he placed them before him:

"Here is one of your wants; fill up." Rowland's eyes glistened as he poured out a glassful, and the captain followed.

"I will drink with you, Rowland," he said; "here is to our better understanding." He tossed off the liquor; then Rowland, who had waited, said: "I prefer drinking alone, captain," and drank the whisky at a gulp. The captain's face flushed at the affront, but he controlled himself.

"Go on deck, now, Rowland." he said; "I will talk with you again before we reach soundings. Meanwhile, I request—not require, but request—that you hold no useless conversation with your shipmates in regard to this matter."

To this first officer, when relieved at eight bells, the captain said: "He is a broken-down wreck with a temporarily active conscience; but is not the man to buy or intimidate: he knows too much. However, we've found his weak point. If he gets snakes before we dock, his testimony is worthless. Fill him up and I'll see the surgeon, and study up on drugs."

When Rowland turned out to breakfast at seven bells that morning, he found a pint flask in the pocket of his pea-jacket, which he felt of but did not pull out in sight of his watchmates.

"Well, captain," he thought, "you are, in truth, about as puerile, insipid a scoundrel as ever escaped the law. I'll save you your drugged Dutch courage for evidence." But it was not drugged, as he learned later. It was good whisky—a leader—to warm his stomach while the captain was studying.

Chapter V

An incident occurred that morning which drew Rowland's thoughts far from the happenings of the night. A few hours of bright sunshine had brought the passengers on deck like bees from a hive, and the two broad promenades resembled, in color and life, the streets of a city. The watch was busy at the inevitable scrubbing, and Rowland, with a swab and bucket, was cleaning the white paint on the starboard taffrail, screened from view by the after deck-house, which shut off a narrow space at the stern. A little girl ran into the inclosure, laughing and screaming, and clung to his legs, while she jumped up and down in an overflow of spirits.

"I wunned 'way," she said; "I wunned 'way from mamma."

Drying his wet hands on his trousers, Rowland lifted the tot and said, tenderly: "Well, little one, you must run back to mamma. You're in bad company." The innocent eyes smiled into his own, and then—a foolish proceeding, which only bachelors are guilty of—he held her above the rail in jesting menace. "Shall I drop you over to the fishes, baby?" he asked, while his features softened to an unwonted smile. The child gave a little scream of fright, and at that instant a young woman appeared around the corner. She sprang toward Rowland like a tigress, snatched the child, stared at him for a moment with dilated eyes, and then disappeared, leaving him limp and nerveless, breathing hard.

"It is her child," he groaned. "That is the mother-look. She is married—married." He resumed his work, with a face as near the color of the paint he was scrubbing as the tanned skin of a sailor may become.

Ten minutes later, the captain, in his office, was listening to a complaint from a very excited man and woman.

"And you say, colonel," said the captain, "that this man Rowland is an old enemy?"

"He is—or was once—a rejected admirer of Mrs. Selfridge. That is all I know of him—except that he has hinted at revenge. My wife is certain of what she saw, and I think the man should be confined."

"Why, captain," said the woman, vehemently, as she hugged her child, "you should have seen him; he was just about to drop Myra over as I seized her—and he had such a frightful leer on his face, too. Oh, it was hideous. I shall not sleep another wink in this ship—I know."

"I beg you will give yourself no uneasiness, madam," said the captain, gravely. "I have already learned something of his antecedents—that he is a disgraced and broken-down naval officer; but, as he has sailed three voyages with us, I had credited his willingness to work before-the-mast to his craving for liquor, which he could not satisfy without money. However—as you think—he may be following you. Was he able to learn of your movements—that you were to take passage in this ship?"

"Why not?" exclaimed the husband; "he must know some of Mrs. Selfridge's friends."

"Yes, yes," she said, eagerly; "I have heard him spoken of, several times."

"Then it is clear," said the captain. "If you agree, madam, to testify against him in the English courts, I will immediately put him in irons for attempted murder."

"Oh, do, captain," she exclaimed. "I cannot feel safe while he is at liberty. Of course I will testify."

"Whatever you do, captain," said the husband, savagely, "rest assured that I shall put a bullet through his head if he meddles with me or mine again. Then you can put me in irons."

"I will see that he is attended to, colonel," replied the captain as he bowed them out of his office.

But, as a murder charge is not always the best way to discredit a man; and as the captain did not believe that the man who had defied him would murder a child; and as the charge would be difficult to prove in any case, and would cause him much trouble and annoyance, he did not order the arrest of John Rowland, but merely directed that, for the time, he should be kept at work by day in the 'tween-deck, out of sight of the passengers.

Rowland, surprised at the sudden transfer from the disagreeable scrubbing to a "soldier's job" of painting life-buoys in the warm 'tween-deck, was shrewd enough to know that he was being closely watched by the boatswain that morning, but not shrewd enough to affect any symptoms of intoxication or drugging, which might have satisfied his anxious superiors and brought him more whisky. As a result of his brighter eyes and steadier voice—due to the curative sea air—when he turned out for the first dog-watch on deck at four o'clock, the captain and boatswain held an interview in the chart-room, in which the former said: "Do not be alarmed. It is not poison. He is half-way into the horrors now, and this will merely bring them on. He will see snakes, ghosts, goblins, shipwrecks, fire, and all sorts of things. It works in two or three hours. Just drop it into his drinking pot while the port forecastle is empty."

There was a fight in the port forecastle—to which Rowland belonged—at supper time, which need not be described beyond mention of the fact that Rowland, who was not a participant, had his pot of tea dashed from his hand before he had taken three swallows. He procured a fresh supply and finished his supper; then, taking no part in his watchmates' open discussion of the fight, and guarded discussion of collisions, rolled into his bunk and smoked until eight-bells, when he turned out with the rest.

Chapter VI

"Rowland," said the big boatswain, as the watch mustered on deck; "take the starboard bridge lookout."

"It is not my trick, boats'n," said Rowland, in surprise.

"Orders from the bridge. Get up there."

Rowland grumbled, as sailors may when aggrieved, and obeyed. The man he relieved reported his name, and disappeared; the first officer sauntered down the bridge, uttered the official "keep a good lookout," and returned to his post; then the silence and loneliness of a night-watch at sea, intensified by the never-ceasing hum of the engines, and relieved only by the sounds of distant music and laughter from the theater, descended on the forward part of the ship. For the fresh westerly wind, coming with the *Titan,* made nearly a calm on her deck; and the dense fog, though overshone by a bright star-specked sky, was so chilly that the last talkative passenger had fled to the light and life within.

When three bells—half-past nine—had sounded, and Rowland had given in

A fanciful contemporary recreation of the crash. Note the survivors floating on ice floes, and the fact that the ship is sinking from the port stern!
AUTHOR'S COLLECTION

First photos of the rescued passengers, printed in *The Sphere*.
AUTHOR'S COLLECTION

The *Carpathia*, commanded by Captain Rostron, arrived in New York on April 18 with 703 survivors. AUTHOR'S COLLECTION

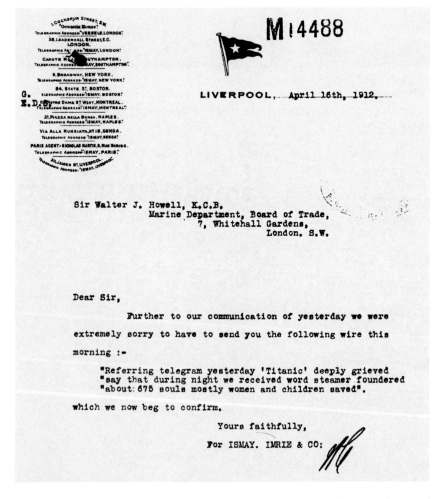

M14488

LIVERPOOL, April 16th, 1912.

Sir Walter J. Howell, K.C.B.
        Marine Department, Board of Trade,
                7, Whitehall Gardens,
                        London, S.W.

Dear Sir,

        Further to our communication of yesterday we were extremely sorry to have to send you the following wire this morning :-

        "Referring telegram yesterday 'Titanic' deeply grieved
        "say that during night we received word steamer foundered
        "about: 675 souls mostly women and children saved".

which we now beg to confirm.

                        Yours faithfully,

                        For ISMAY. IMRIE & CO:

The White Star Line's official letter of confirmation to the British Board of Trade that *Titanic* did, indeed, founder. BRITISH PUBLIC RECORDS

A commemorative
feature honoring
Titanic's victims that
ran in the British
magazine *Punch* after
the tragedy.

TOLL OF THE SEA.

[Dedicated to the memory of the brave men who went down in the *Titanic*, April 15th.]

Tears for the dead, who shall not come again
  Homeward to any shore on any tide!
Tears for the dead! but through that bitter rain
  Breaks, like an April sun, the smile of pride.

What courage yielded place to others' need,
  Patient of discipline's supreme decree.
Well may we guess who know that gallant breed
  Schooled in the ancient chivalry of the sea! O.

[A] victim's body being
[rec]overed from the
[Atl]antic, some two weeks
[aft]er the ship sank.

EXTRA, TUESDAY, MAY 14

SAVED FROM THE TITANIC

ECLAIR'S WORLD SENSATION

MISS DOROTHY GIBSON, a survivor of the sea's greatest disaster, tells the story of the shipwreck, supported by an all-star cast, on the film marvel of the age :: :: :: ::

ART POSTERS, PHOTOS and HERALDS ARE READY

| TUESDAY MAY 14 | ECLAIR FILM CO. FORT LEE, NEW JERSEY Sales Company, Sole Agents | TUESDAY MAY 14 |

Survivor/actress Dorothy Gibson starred in the film *Saved From the Titanic,* which was released one month after the disaster.
AUTHOR'S COLLECTION

Hearses carry away the bodies of victims, which were transported to Halifax.
BRUCE DALE/ NATIONAL GEOGRAPHIC IMAGE COLLECTION

One of the many musical commemorations of the tragedy,
written and published after the sinking. AUTHOR'S COLLECTION

According to *The Sphere*, Captain Smith's last words were "Be British"... or were they?

AUTHOR'S COLLECTION

A postcard advertising *Titanic*'s sister ship. Could *Olympic* and *Titanic* have been switched?

AUTHOR'S COLLECTION

Postcard honoring the
ship's "Heroic Musicians."
What was their last song?
AUTHOR'S COLLECTION

One of the ship's massive
propellers, half buried in
the ocean floor.
EMORY KRISTOF/NATIONAL
GEOGRAPHIC IMAGE COLLECTION

The launching of the ship was meticulously recreated in the block-buster 1997 film *Titanic*.
PHOTOFEST

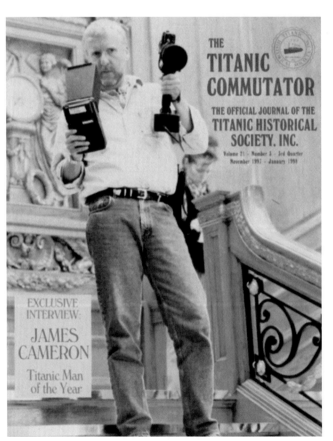

James Cameron and his record-breaking film were honored by *The Titanic Commutator.*
AUTHOR'S COLLECTION

his turn the required call—"all's well"—the first officer left his post and approached him.

"Rowland," he said as he drew near; "I hear you've walked the quarter-deck."

"I cannot imagine how you learned it, sir," replied Rowland; "I am not in the habit of referring to it."

"You told the captain. I suppose the curriculum is as complete at Annapolis as at the Royal Naval College. What do you think of Maury's theories of currents?"

"They seem plausible," said Rowland, unconsciously dropping the "sir"; "but I think that in most particulars he has been proven wrong."

"Yes, I think so myself. Did you ever follow up another idea of his—that of locating the position of ice in a fog by the rate of decrease in temperature as approached?"

"Not to any definite result. But it seems to be only a matter of calculation, and time to calculate. Cold is negative heat, and can be treated like radiant energy, decreasing as the square of the distance."

The officer stood a moment, looking ahead and humming a tune to himself; then saying: "Yes, that's so," returned to his place.

"Must have a cast-iron stomach," he muttered, as he peered into the binnacle; "or else the boats'n dosed the wrong man's pot."

Rowland glanced after the retreating officer with a cynical smile. "I wonder," he said to himself, "why he comes down here talking navigation to a foremast hand. Why am I up here—out of my turn? Is this something in line with that bottle?" He resumed the short pacing back and forth on the end of the bridge, and the rather gloomy train of thought which the officer had interrupted.

"How long," he mused, "would his ambition and love of profession last him after he had met, and won, and lost, the only woman on earth to him? Why is it—that failure to hold the affections of one among the millions of women who live, and love, can outweigh every blessing in life, and turn a man's nature into a hell, to consume him? Who did she marry? Some one, probably a stranger long after my banishment, who came to her possessed of a few qualities of mind and physique that pleased her—who did not need to love her—his chances were better without that—and he steps coolly and easily into my heaven. And they tell us, that 'God doeth all things well,' and that there is a heaven where all our unsatisfied wants are attended to—provided we have the necessary faith in it. That means, if it means anything, that after a lifetime of unrecognized allegiance, during which I win nothing but her fear and contempt, I may be rewarded by the love and companionship of her soul. Do I love her soul? Has her soul beauty of face and the figure and carriage of a Venus? Has her soul deep, blue eyes and a sweet, musical voice? Has it wit, and grace, and charm? Has it a wealth of pity for suffering? These are the things I loved. I do not love her soul, if she has one. I do not want it. I want her—I need her." He stopped in his walk and leaned against the bridge railing, with eyes fixed on the fog ahead. He was speaking his thoughts aloud now, and the first officer drew within hearing, listened a moment, and went back. "Working on him," he whispered to the third officer. Then he pushed a button which called the captain, blew a short blast of the steam whistle as a call to the boatswain, and resumed his watch on the drugged lookout, while the third officer conned the ship.

The steam call to the boatswain is so common a sound on a steamship as to generally pass unnoticed. This call affected another besides the boatswain. A little night-gowned figure arose from under a berth in a saloon stateroom, and, with wide-open, staring eyes, groped its way to the deck, unobserved by the watchman. The white, bare little feet felt no cold as they pattered the planks of the deserted promenade, and the little figure had reached the steerage entrance by the time the captain and boatswain had reached the bridge.

"And they talk," went on Rowland, as the three watched and listened, "of the wonderful love and care of a merciful God, who controls all things—who has given me my defects, and my capacity for loving, and then placed Myra Gaunt in my way. Is there mercy to me in this? As part of a great evolutionary principle, which develops the race life at the expense of the individual, it might be consistent with the idea of a God—a first cause. But does the individual who perishes, because unfitted to survive, owe any love, or gratitude to this God? He does not! On the supposition that He exists, I deny it! And on the complete lack of evidence that He does exist, I affirm to myself the integrity of cause and effect—which is enough to explain the Universe, and me. A merciful God—a kind, loving, just, and merciful God—" he burst into a fit of incongruous laughter, which stopped short as he clapped his hands to his stomach and then to his head. "What ails me?" he gasped; "I feel as though I had swallowed hot coals—and my head—and my eyes—I can't see." The pain left him in a moment and the laughter returned. "What's wrong with the starboard anchor? It's moving. It's changing. It's a—what? What on earth is it? On end—and the windlass—and the spare anchors—and the davits—all alive—all moving."

The sight he saw would have been horrid to a healthy mind, but it only moved this man to increased and uncontrollable merriment. The two rails below leading to the stem had arisen before him in a shadowy triangle; and within it were the deck-fittings he had mentioned. The windlass had become a thing of horror, black and forbidding. The two end barrels were the bulging, lightless eyes of a nondescript monster, for which the cable chains had multiplied themselves into innumerable legs and tentacles. And this thing was crawling around within the triangle. The anchor-davits were many-headed serpents which danced on their tails, and the anchors themselves writhed and squirmed in the shape of immense hairy caterpillars, while faces appeared on the two white lantern-towers—grinning and leering at him. With his hands on the bridge rail, and tears streaming down his face, he laughed at the strange sight, but did not speak; and the three, who had quietly approached, drew back to await, while below on the promenade deck, the little white figure, as though attracted by his laughter, turned into the stairway leading to the upper deck.

The phantasmagoria faded to a blank wall of gray fog, and Rowland found sanity to mutter, "They've drugged me"; but in an instant he stood in the darkness of a garden—one that he had known. In the distance were the lights of a house, and close to him was a young girl, who turned from him and fled, even as he called to her.

By a supreme effort of will, he brought himself back to the present, to the bridge he stood upon, and to his duty. "Why must it haunt me through the years," he groaned; "drunk then—drunk since. She could have saved me, but she chose to damn me." He strove to pace up and down, but staggered, and clung to the rail; while the three watchers approached again, and the little white figure below climbed the upper bridge steps.

"The survival of the fittest," he rambled, as he stared into the fog; "cause and effect. It explains the Universe—and me." He lifted his hand and spoke loudly, as though to some unseen familiar of the deep. "What will be the last effect? Where in the scheme of ultimate balance—under the law of correlation of energy, will my wasted wealth of love be gathered, and weighed, and credited? What will balance it, and where will I be? Myra,—Myra," he called; "do you know what you have lost? Do you know, in your goodness, and purity, and truth, of what you have done? Do you know—"

The fabric in which he stood was gone, and he seemed to be poised on nothing in a worldless universe of gray—alone. And in the vast, limitless emptiness there was no sound, or life, or change; and in his heart neither fear, nor wonder, nor emotion of any kind, save one—the unspeakable hunger of a love that had failed. Yet it seemed that he was not John Rowland, but some one, or something else; for presently he saw himself, far away—millions of billions of miles; as though on the outermost fringes of the void—and heard his own voice, calling. Faintly, yet distinctly, filled with the concentrated despair of his life, came the call: "Myra—Myra."

There was an answering call, and looking for the second voice, he beheld her—the woman of his love—on the opposite edge of space; and her eyes held the tenderness, and her voice held the pleading that he had known but in dreams. "Come back," she called; "come back to me." But it seemed that the two could not understand; for again he heard the despairing cry: "Myra, Myra, where are you?" and again the answer: "Come back. Come."

Then in the far distance to the right appeared a faint point of flame, which grew larger. It was approaching, and he dispassionately viewed it; and when he looked again for the two, they were gone, and in their places were two clouds of nebula, which resolved into myriad points of sparkling light and color—whirling, encroaching, until they filled all space. And through them the larger light was coming—and growing larger—straight for him.

He heard a rushing sound, and looking for it, saw in the opposite direction a formless object, as much darker than the gray of the void as the flame was brighter, and it too was growing larger, and coming. And it seemed to him that this light and darkness were the good and evil of his life, and he watched, to see which would reach him first, but felt no surprise or regret when he saw that the darkness was nearest. It came, closer and closer, until it brushed him on the side.

"What have we hear, Rowland?" said a voice. Instantly, the whirling points were blotted out; the universe of gray changed to the fog; the flame of light to the moon rising above it, and the shapeless darkness to the form of the first officer. The little white figure, which had just darted past the three watchers, stood at his feet. As though warned by an inner subconsciousness of danger, it had come in its sleep, for safety and care, to its mother's old lover—the strong and the weak— the degraded and disgraced, but exalted—the persecuted, drugged, and all but helpless John Rowland.

With the readiness with which a man who dozes while standing will answer the question that wakens him, he said—though he stammered from the now waning effect of the drug: "Myra's child, sir; it's asleep." He picked up the night-gowned little girl, who screamed as she wakened, and folded his pea-jacket around the cold little body.

"Who is Myra?" asked the officer in a bullying tone, in which were also cha-grin and disappointment. "You've been asleep yourself."

Before Rowland could reply a shout from the crow's-nest split the air.

"Ice," yelled the lookout; "ice ahead. Iceberg. Right under the bows." The first officer ran amidships, and the captain, who had remained there, sprang to the engine-room telegraph, and this time the lever was turned. But in five seconds the bow of the *Titan* began to lift, and ahead, and on either hand, could be seen, through the fog, a field of ice, which arose in an incline to a hundred feet high in her track. The music in the theater ceased, and among the babel of shouts and cries, and the deafening noise of steel, scraping and crashing over ice, Rowland heard the agonized voice of a woman crying from the bridge steps: "Myra— Myra, where are you? Come back."

Chapter VII

Seventy-five thousand tons—dead-weight—rushing through the fog at the rate of fifty feet a second, had hurled itself at an iceberg. Had the impact been received by a perpendicular wall, the elastic resistance of bending plates and frames would have overcome the momentum with no more damage to the pas-sengers than a severe shaking up, and to the ship than the crushing in of her bows and the killing, to a man, of the watch below. She would have backed off, and, slightly down by the head, finished the voyage at reduced speed, to rebuild on insurance money, and benefit, largely, in the end, by the consequent advertising of her indestructibility. But a low beach, possibly formed by the recent over-turning of the berg, received the *Titan,* and with her keel cutting the ice like the steel runner of an iceboat, and her great weight resting on the starboard bilge, she rose out of the sea, higher and higher—until the propellers in the stern were half exposed—then, meeting an easy spiral rise in the ice under her port bow, she heeled, overbalanced, and crashed down on her side, to starboard.

The holding-down bolts of twelve boilers and three triple-expansion engines, unintended to hold such weights from a perpendicular flooring, snapped, and down through a maze of ladders, gratings, and fore-and-aft bulkheads came these giant masses of steel and iron, puncturing the sides of the ship, even where backed by solid, resisting ice; and filling the engine- and boiler-rooms with scald-ing steam, which brought a quick, though tortured death, to each of the hundred men on duty in the engineer's department.

Amid the roar of escaping steam, and the bee-like buzzing of nearly three thousand human voices, raised in agonized screams and callings from within the inclosing walls, and the whistling of air through hundreds of open dead-lights as the water, entering the holes of the crushed and riven starboard side, expelled it, the *Titan* moved slowly backward and launched herself into the sea, where she floated low on her side—a dying monster, groaning with her death-wound.

A solid, pyramid-like hummock of ice, left to starboard as the steamer ascended, and which projected close alongside to the upper, or boat-deck, as she fell over, had caught, in succession, every pair of davits to starboard, bending and wrenching them, smashing boats, and snapping tackles and gripes, until, as the ship cleared herself, it capped the pile of wreckage strewing the ice in front of, and around it, with the end and broken stanchions of the bridge. And in this shattered, box-like structure, dazed by the sweeping fall through an arc of sev-enty-foot radius, crouched Rowland, bleeding from a cut in his head, and still holding to his breast the little girl—now too frightened to cry.

By an effort of will, he aroused himself and looked. To his eyesight, twisted and fixed to a shorter focus by the drug he had taken, the steamship was little more than a blotch on the moon-whitened fog; yet he thought he could see men clambering and working on the upper davits, and the nearest boat—No. 24—seemed to be swinging by the tackles. Then the fog shut her out, though her position was still indicated by the roaring of steam from her iron lungs. This ceased in time, leaving behind it the horrid humming sound and whistling of air; and when this too was suddenly hushed, and the ensuing silence broken by dull, booming reports—as from bursting compartments—Rowland knew that the holo-caust was complete; that the invincible *Titan,* with nearly all her people, unable to climb vertical floors and ceilings, was beneath the surface of the sea.

Mechanically, his benumbed faculties had received and recorded the impres-sions of the last few moments; he could not comprehend, to the full, the horror of it all. Yet his mind was keenly alive to the peril of the woman whose appealing voice he had heard and recognized—the woman of his dream, and the mother of the child in his arms. He hastily examined the wreckage. Not a boat was intact. Creeping down to the water's edge, he hailed, with all the power of his weak voice, to possible, but invisible boats beyond the fog—calling on them to come and save the child—to look out for a woman who had been on deck, under the bridge. He shouted this woman's name—the one that he knew—encouraging her to swim, to tread water, to float on wreckage, and to answer him, until he came to her. There was no response, and when his voice had grown hoarse and futile, and his feet numb from the cold of the thawing ice, he returned to the wreckage, weighed down and all but crushed by the blackest desolation that had, so far, come into his unhappy life. The little girl was crying and he tried to soothe her.

"I want mamma," she wailed.

"Hush, baby, hush," he answered, wearily and bitterly; "so do I—more than Heaven, but I think our chances are about even now. Are you cold, little one? We'll go inside, and I'll make a house for us."

He removed his coat, tenderly wrapped the little figure in it, and with the injunction: "Don't be afraid, now," placed her in the corner of the bridge, which rested on its forward side. As he did so, the bottle of whisky fell out of the pocket. It seemed an age since he had found it there, and it required a strong effort of reasoning before he remembered its full significance. Then he raised it, to hurl it down the incline of ice, but stopped himself.

"I'll keep it," he muttered; "it may be safe in small quantities, and we'll need it on this ice." He placed it in a corner; then, removing the canvas cover from one of the wrecked boats, he hung it over the open side and end of the bridge, crawled within, and donned his coat—a ready-made, slop-chest garment, designed for a larger man—and buttoning it around himself and the little girl, lay down on the hard woodwork. She was still crying, but soon, under the influence of the warmth of his body, ceased and went to sleep.

Huddled in a corner, he gave himself up to the torment of his thoughts. Two pictures alternately crowded his mind; one, that of the woman of his dream, entreating him to come back—which his memory clung to as an oracle; the other, of this woman, cold and lifeless, fathoms deep in the sea. He pondered on her chances. She was close to, or on the bridge steps; and boat No. 24, which he was almost sure was being cleared away as he looked, would swing close to her as it descended. She could climb in and be saved—unless the swimmers from doors and hatches should swamp the boat. And, in his agony of mind, he cursed these swimmers, preferring to see her, mentally, the only passenger in the boat, with the watch-on-deck to pull her to safety.

The potent drug he had taken was still at work, and this, with the musical wash of the sea on the icy beach, and the muffled creaking and crackling beneath and around him—the voice of the iceberg—overcame him finally, and he slept, to waken at daylight with limbs stiffened and numb—almost frozen.

And all night, as he slept, a boat with the number twenty-four on her bow, pulled by sturdy sailors and steered by brass-buttoned officers, was making for the Southern lane—the highway of spring traffic. And, crouched in the stern-sheets of this boat was a moaning, praying woman, who cried and screamed at intervals, for husband and baby, and would not be comforted, even when one of the brass-buttoned officers assured her that her child was in the safe care of John Rowland, a brave and trusty sailor, who was certainly in the other boat with it. He did not tell her, of course, that Rowland had hailed from the berg as she lay unconscious, and that if he still had the child, it was with him there—deserted.

Chapter VIII

Rowland, with some misgivings, drank a small quantity of the liquor, and wrapping the still sleeping child in the coat, stepped out on the ice. The fog was gone and a blue, sailless sea stretched out to the horizon. Behind him was ice—a mountain of it. He climbed the elevation and looked at another stretch of vacant view from a precipice a hundred feet high. To his left the ice sloped to a steeper beach than the one behind him, and to the right, a pile of hummocks and taller peaks, interspersed with numerous cañons and caves, and glistening with water-falls, shut out the horizon in this direction. Nowhere was there a sail or steamer's smoke to cheer him, and he retraced his steps. When but half-way to the wreckage, he saw a moving white object approaching from the direction of the peaks.

His eyes were not yet in good condition, and after an uncertain scrutiny he started at a run; for he saw that the mysterious white object was nearer the bridge than himself, and rapidly lessening the distance. A hundred yards away, his heart bounded and the blood in his veins felt cold as the ice under foot, for the white object proved to be a traveler from the frozen North, lean and famished—a polar bear, who had scented food and was seeking it—coming on at a lumbering run, with great red jaws half open and yellow fangs exposed. Rowland had no weapons but a strong jackknife, but this he pulled from his pocket and opened as he ran. Not for an instant did he hesitate at a conflict that promised almost certain death; for the presence of this bear involved the safety of a child whose life had become of more importance to him than his own. To his horror, he saw it creep out of the opening in its white covering, just as the bear turned the corner of the bridge.

"Go back, baby, go back," he shouted, as he bounded down the slope. The bear reached the child first, and with seemingly no effort, dashed it, with a blow of its massive paw, a dozen feet away, where it lay quiet. Turning to follow, the brute was met by Rowland.

The bear rose to its haunches, sank down, and charged; and Rowland felt the bones of his left arm crushing under the bite of the big, yellow-fanged jaws. But, falling he buried the knife-blade in the shaggy hide, and the bear, with an angry snarl, spat out the mangled member and dealt him a sweeping blow which sent him farther along the ice than the child had gone. He arose, with broken ribs, and—scarcely feeling the pain—awaited the second charge. Again was the crushed and useless arm gripped in the yellow vise, and again was he pressed backward; but this time he used the knife with method. The great snout was pressing his breast; the hot, fetid breath was in his nostrils; and at his shoulder the hungry eyes were glaring into his own. He struck for the left eye of the brute and struck true. The five-inch blade went in to the handle, piercing the brain, and the animal, with a convulsive spring which carried him half-way to his feet by the wounded arm, reared up, with paws outstretched, to full eight feet of length, then sagged down, and with a few spasmodic kicks, lay still. Rowland had done what no Innuit hunter will attempt—he had fought and killed the Tiger-of-the-North with a knife.

It had all happened in a minute, but in that minute he was crippled for life; for in the quiet of a hospital, the best of surgical skill could hardly avail to reset the fractured particles of bone in the limp arm, and bring to place the crushed ribs. And he was adrift on a floating island of ice, with the temperature near the freezing point, and without even the rude appliances of the savage.

He painfully made his way to the little pile of red and white, and lifted it with his uninjured arm, though the stooping caused him excruciating torture. The child was bleeding from four deep, cruel scratches, extending diagonally from the right shoulder down the back; but he found upon examination that the soft, unyielding bones were unbroken, and that her unconsciousness came from the rough contact of the little forehead with the ice; for a large lump had raised.

Of pure necessity, his first efforts must be made in his own behalf; so wrapping the baby in his coat he placed it in his shelter, and cut and made from the canvas a sling for his dangling arm. Then, with knife, fingers, and teeth, he partly skinned the bear—often compelled to pause to save himself from fainting with pain—and cut from the warm but not very thick layer of fat a broad slab, which, afer bathing the wounds at a near-by pool, he bound firmly to the little one's back, using the torn night-gown for a bandage.

He cut the flannel lining from his coat, and from that of the sleeves he made nether garments for the little limbs, doubling the surplus length over the ankles and tying in place with rope-yarns from a boat-lacing. The body lining he wrapped around her waist, inclosing the arms, and around the whole he passed turn upon turn of canvas in strips, marling the mummy-like bundle with yarns, much as a sailor secures chafing-gear to the doubled parts of a hawser—a process when complete, that would have aroused the indignation of any mother who saw it. But he was only a man, and suffering mental and physical anguish.

By the time he had finished, the child had recovered consciousness, and was protesting its misery in a feeble, wailing cry. But he dared not stop—to become stiffened with cold and pain. There was plenty of fresh water from melting ice, scattered in pools. The bear would furnish food; but they needed fire, to cook this food, keep them warm, and the dangerous inflammation from their hurts, and to raise a smoke to be seen by passing craft.

He recklessly drank from the bottle, needing the stimulant, and reasoning, perhaps rightly, that no ordinary drug could affect him in his present condition; then he examined the wreckage—most of it good kindling wood. Partly above, partly below the pile, was a steel lifeboat, decked over air-tight ends, now doubled to more than a right angle and resting on its side. With canvas hung over one half, and a small fire in the other, it promised, by its conducting property, a warmer and better shelter than the bridge. A sailor without matches is an anomaly. He whittled shavings, kindled the fire, hung the canvas and brought the child, who begged piteously for a drink of water.

He found a tin can—possibly left in a leaky boat before its final hoist to the davits—and gave her a drink, to which he added a few drops of the whisky. Then he thought of breakfast. Cutting a steak from the hindquarters of the bear, he toasted it on the end of a splinter and found it sweet and satisfying; but when he attempted to feed the child, he understood the necessity of freeing its arms— which he did, sacrificing his left shirtsleeve to cover them. The change and the food stopped its crying for a while, and Rowland lay down with it in the warm boat. Before the day had passed the whisky was gone and he was delirious with fever, while the child was but little better.

Chapter IX

With lucid intervals, during which he replenished or rebuilt the fire, cooked the bear-meat, and fed and dressed the wounds of the child, this delirium lasted three days. His suffering was intense. His arm, the seat of throbbing pain, had swollen to twice the natural size, while his side prevented him from taking a full breath, voluntarily. He had paid no attention to his own hurts, and it was either the vigor of a constitution that years of dissipation had not impaired, or some anti-febrile property of bear-meat, or the absence of the exciting whisky that won the battle. He rekindled the fire with his last match on the evening of the third day and looked around the darkening horizon, sane, but feeble in body and mind.

If a sail had appeared in the interim, he had not seen it; nor was there one in sight now. Too weak to climb the slope, he returned to the boat, where the child, exhausted from fruitless crying, was now sleeping. His unskillful and rather heroic manner of wrapping it up to protect it from cold had, no doubt, contributed largely to the closing of its wounds by forcibly keeping it still, though it must have added to its present sufferings. He looked for a moment on the wan, tear-stained little face, with its fringe of tangled curls peeping above the wrappings of canvas, and stooped painfully down, kissed it softly; but the kiss awakened it and it cried for its mother. He could not soothe it, nor could he try; and with a formless, wordless curse against destiny welling up from his heart, he left it and sat down on the wreckage at some distance away.

"We'll very likely get well," he mused, gloomily, "unless I let the fire go out. What then? We can't last longer than the berg, and not much longer than the bear. We must be out of the tracks—we were about nine hundred miles out when we struck; and the current sticks to the fog-belt here—about west-sou'west—but that's the surface water. These deep fellows have currents of their own. There's no fog; we must be to the southward of the belt—between the Lanes. They'll run their boats in the other Lane after this, I think—the money-grabbing wretches. Curse them—if they've drowned her. Curse them, with their water-tight compartments, and their logging of the lookouts. Twenty-four boats for three thousand people—lashed down with tarred gripe-lashings—thirty men to clear them away, and not an axe on the boat-deck or a sheath-knife on a man. Could she have got away? If they got the boat down, they might have taken her in from the steps; and the mate knew I had her child—he would tell her. Her name must be Myra, too; it was her voice I heard in that dream. That was hasheesh. What did they drug me for? But the whisky was all right. It's all done with now, unless I get ashore—but will I?

The moon rose above the castellated structure to the left, flooding the icy beach with ashen-gray light, sparkling in a thousand points from the cascades, streams, and rippling pools, throwing into blackest shadow the gullies and hollows, and bringing to his mind, in spite of the weird beauty of the scene, a crushing sense of loneliness—of littleness—as though the vast pile of inorganic desolation which held him was of far greater importance than himself, and all the hopes, plans, and fears of his lifetime. The child had cried itself to sleep again, and he paced up and down the ice.

"Up there," he said, moodily, looking into the sky, where a few stars shone faintly in the flood from the moon; "Up there—somewhere—they don't know just where—but somewhere up above, is the Christians' Heaven. Up there is their good God—who has placed Myra's child here—their good God whom they borrowed from the savage, bloodthirsty race that invented him. And down below us—somewhere again—is their hell and their bad god, whom they invented themselves. And they give us our choice—Heaven or hell. It is not so—not so. The great mystery is not solved—the human heart is not helped in this way. No good, merciful God created this world or its conditions. Whatever may be the nature of the causes at work beyond our mental vision, one fact is indubitably proven—that the qualities of mercy, goodness, justice, play no part in the governing scheme. And yet, they say the core of all religions on earth is the belief in this. Is it? Or is it the cowardly, human fear of the unknown—that impels the savage mother to throw her babe to a crocodile—that impels the civilized man to endow churches—that has kept in existence from the beginning a class of soothsayers, medicine-men, priests, and clergymen, all living on the hopes and fears excited by themselves.

"And people pray—millions of them—and claim they are answered. Are they? Was ever supplication sent into that sky by troubled humanity answered, or even heard? Who knows? They pray for rain and sunshine, and both come in time. They pray for health and success and both are but natural in the marching of events. This is not evidence. But they say that they know, by spiritual uplifting, that they are heard, and comforted, and answered at the moment. Is not this a physiological experiment? Would they not feel equally tranquil if they repeated the multiplication table, or boxed the compass?

Millions have believed this—that prayers are answered—and these millions have prayed to different gods. Were they all wrong or all right? Would a tentative prayer be listened to? Admitting that the Bibles, and Korans, and Vedas, are misleading and unreliable, may there not be an unseen, unknown Being, who knows my heart—who is watching me now? If so, this Being gave me my reason, which doubts Him, and on Him is the responsibility. And would this being, if he exists, overlook a defect for which I am not to blame, and listen to a prayer from me, based on the mere chance that I might be mistaken? Can an unbeliever, in the full strength of his reasoning powers, come to such trouble that he can no longer stand alone, but must cry for help to an imagined power? Can such time come to a sane man—to me?" He looked at the dark line of vacant horizon. It was seven miles away; New York was nine hundred; the moon in the east over two hundred thousand, and the stars above, any number of billions. He was alone, with a sleeping child, a dead bear, and the Unknown. He walked softly to the boat and looked at the little one for a moment; then, raising his head, he whispered: "For you, Myra."

Sinking to his knees the atheist lifted his eyes to the heavens, and with his feeble voice and the fervor born of helplessness, prayed to the God that he denied. He begged for the life of the waif in his care—for the safety of the mother, so needful to the little one—and for courage and strength to do his part and bring them together. But beyond the appeal for help in the service of others, not one word or expressed thought of his prayer included himself as a beneficiary. So much for pride. As he rose to his feet, the flying-jib of a bark appeared around the corner of ice to the right of the beach, and a moment later the whole moon-lit fabric came into view, wafted along by the faint westerly air, not half a mile away.

He sprang to the fire, forgetting his pain, and throwing on wood, made a blaze. He hailed, in a frenzy of excitement: "Bark ahoy! Bark ahoy! Take us off," and a deep-toned answer came across the water.

"Wake up, Myra," he cried, as he lifted the child; "wake up. We're going away."

"We're goin' to mamma?" she asked, with no symptoms of crying.

"Yes, we're going to mamma, now—that is," he added to himself; "if that clause in the prayer is considered."

Fifteen minutes later as he watched the approach of a white quarter-boat, he muttered: "That bark was there—half a mile back in the wind—before I thought of praying. Is that prayer answered? Is she safe?"

Chapter X

On the first floor of the London Royal Exchange is a large apartment studded with desks, around and between which surges a hurrying, shouting crowd of brokers, clerks, and messengers. Fringing this apartment are doors and hallways leading to adjacent rooms and offices, and scattered through it are bulletin-boards, on which are daily written in duplicate the marine casualties of the world. At one end is a raised platform, sacred to the presence of an important functionary. In the technical language of the "City," the apartment is known as the "Room," and the functionary, as the "Caller," whose business it is to call out in a mighty sing-song voice the names of members wanted at the door, and the bare particulars of bulletin news prior to its being chalked out for reading.

It is the headquarters of Lloyds—the immense association of underwriters, brokers, and shipping-men, which, beginning with the customers at Edward Lloyd's coffee-house in the latter part of the seventeenth century, has, retaining his name for a title, developed into a corporation so well equipped, so splendidly organized and powerful, that kings and ministers of state appeal to it at times for foreign news.

Not a master or mate sail under the English flag but whose record, even to forecastle fights, is tabulated at Lloyds for the inspection of prospective employers. Not a ship is cast away on any inhabitable coast of the world, during underwriters' business hours, but what that mighty sing-songery announces the event at Lloyds within thirty minutes.

One of the adjoining rooms is known as the Chartroom. Here can be found in perfect order and sequence, each on its roller, the newest charts of all nations, with a library of nautical literature describing to the last detail the harbors, lights, rocks, shoals, and sailing directions of every coast-line shown on the charts; the tracks of latest storms; the changes of ocean currents, and the whereabouts of derelicts and icebergs. A member of Lloyds acquires in time a theoretical knowledge of the sea seldom exceeded by the men who navigate it.

Another apartment—the Captain's room—is given over to joy and refreshment, and still another, the antithesis of the last, is the Intelligence office, where anxious ones inquire for and are told the latest news of this or that overdue ship.

On the day when the assembled throng of underwriters and brokers had been thrown into an uproarious panic the Crier's announcement that the great *Titan* was destroyed, and the papers of Europe and America were issuing extras giving the meager details of the arrival at New York of one boat-load of her people, this office had been crowded with weeping women and worrying men, who would ask, and remain to ask again, for more news. And when it came—a later cable-gram,—giving the story of the wreck and the names of the captain, first officer, boatswain, seven sailors, and one lady passenger as those of the saved, a feeble old gentleman had raised his voice in a quavering scream, high above the sobbing of the women, and said:

"My daughter-in-law is safe; but where is my son,—where is my son, and my grandchild?" Then he had hurried away, but was back again the next day, and the next. And when, on the tenth day of waiting and watching, he learned of another boat-load of sailors and children arrived at Gibraltar, he shook his head, slowly, muttering: "George, George," and left the room. That night, after telegraphing the consul at Gibraltar of his coming, he crossed the channel.

In the first tumultuous riot of inquiry, when underwriters had climbed over desks and each other to hear again of the wreck of the *Titan,* one—the noisiest of all, a corpulent, hook-nosed man with flashing black eyes—had broken away from the crowd and made his way to the Captain's room, where, after a draught of brandy, he had seated himself heavily, with a groan that came from his soul.

"Father Abraham," he muttered; "this will ruin me."

Others came in, some to drink, some to condole—all, to talk.

"Hard hit, Meyer?" asked one.

"Ten thousand," he answered, gloomily.

"Serve you right," said another, unkindly; "have more baskets for your eggs. Knew you'd bring up."

Though Mr. Meyer's eyes sparkled at this, he said nothing, but drank himself stupid and was assisted home by one of his clerks. From this on, neglecting his business—excepting to occasionally visit the bulletins—he spent his time in the Captain's room drinking heavily, and bemoaning his luck. On the tenth day he read with watery eyes, posted on the bulletin below the news of the arrival at Gibraltar of the second boat-load of people, the following:

"Life-buoy of *Royal Age,* London, picked up among wreckage in Lat. 45–20, N. Lon. 54–31 W. Ship *Arctic,* Boston, Capt. Brandt."

"Oh, mine, good God," he howled, as he rushed towards the Captain's room.

"Poor devil—poor damn fool of an Israelite," said one observer to another. "He covered the whole of the *Royal Age,* and the biggest chunk of the *Titan.* It'll take his wife's diamonds to settle."

Three weeks later, Mr. Meyer was aroused from a brooding lethargy, by a crowd of shouting underwriters, who rushed into the Captain's room, seized him by the shoulders, and hurried him out and up to a bulletin.

"Read it, Meyer—read it. What d'you think of it?" With some difficulty he read aloud, while they watched his face:

"John Rowland, sailor of the *Titan,* with child passenger, name unknown, on board *Peerless,* Bath, at Christiansand, Norway. Both dangerously ill. Rowland speaks of ship cut in half night before loss of *Titan.*"

"What do you make of it, Meyer—*Royal Age,* isn't it?" asked one.

"Yes," vociferated another, "I've figured back. Only ship not reported lately. Overdue two months. Was spoken same day fifty miles east of that iceberg."

"Sure thing," said others. "Nothing said about it in the captain's statement—looks queer."

"Vell, what of it," said Meyer, painfully and stupidly: "dere is a collision clause in der *Titan*'s policy; I merely bay the money to der steamship company instead of to der *Royal Age* beeple."

"But why did the captain conceal it?" they shouted at him. "What's his object—assured against collision suits."

"Der looks of it, berhaps—looks pad."

"Nonsense, Meyer, what's the matter with you? Which one of the lost tribes did you spring from—you're like none of your race—drinking yourself stupid like a good Christian. I've got a thousand on the *Titan,* and if I'm to pay it I want to know why. You've got the heaviest risk and the brain to fight for it—you've got to go do it. Go home, straighten up, and attend to this. We'll watch Rowland till you take hold. We're all caught."

They put him into a cab, took him to a Turkish bath, and then home.

The next morning he was at his desk, clear-eyed and clear-headed, and for a few weeks was a busy, scheming man of business.

Chapter XI

On a certain morning about two months after the announcement of the loss of the *Titan,* Mr. Meyer sat at his desk in the Rooms, busily writing, when the old gentleman who had bewailed the death of his son in the Intelligence office tottered in and took a chair beside him.

"Good morning, Mr. Selfridge," he said, scarcely looking up; "I suppose you have come to see der insurance paid over. Der sixty days are up."

"Yes, yes, Mr. Meyer," said the old gentleman, wearily; "of course, as merely a stockholder, I can take no active part; but I am a member here, and naturally a little anxious. All I had in the world—even to my son and grandchild—was in the *Titan.*"

"It is very sad, Mr. Selfridge; you have my deepest sympathy. I pelieve you are der largest holder of *Titan* stock—about one hundred thousand, is it not?"

"About that."

"I am der heaviest insurer; so Mr. Selfridge, this battle will be largely between you and myself."

"Battle—is there to be any difficulty?" asked Mr. Selfridge, anxiously.

"Berhaps—I do not know. Der underwriters and outside companies have blaced matters in my hand and will not bay until I take der initiative. We must hear from one John Rowland, who, with a little child, was rescued from der berg and taken to Christiansand. He has been too sick to leave der ship which found him and is coming up der Thames in her this morning. I have a carriage at der dock and expect him at my office by noon. Dere is where we will dransact this little pizness—not here."

"A child—saved," queried the old gentleman; "dear me, it may be little Myra. She was not at Gibraltar with the others. I would not care—I would not care much about the money, if she was safe. But my son—my only son—is gone; and, Mr. Meyer, I am a ruined man if this insurance is not paid."

"And I am a ruined man if it is," said Mr. Meyer, rising. "Will you come around to der office, Mr. Selfridge? I expect der attorney and Captain Bryce are dere now." Mr. Selfridge arose and accompanied him to the street.

A rather meagerly-furnished private office in Threadneedles Street, partitioned off from a larger one bearing Mr. Meyer's name in the window, received the two men, one of whom, in the interests of good business, was soon to be impoverished. They had not waited a minute before Captain Bryce and Mr. Austen were announced and ushered in. Sleek, well-fed, and gentlemanly in manner, perfect types of the British naval officer, they bowed politely to Mr. Selfridge when Mr. Meyer introduced them as the captain and first officer of the *Titan,* and seated themselves. A few minutes later brought a shrewd-looking person whom Mr. Meyer addressed as the attorney for the steamship company, but did not introduce; for such are the amenities of the English system of caste.

"Now then, gentlemen," said Mr. Meyer, "I pelieve we can broceed to pizness up to a certain point—berhaps further. Mr. Thompson, you have the affidavit of Captain Bryce?"

"I have," said the attorney, producing a document which Mr. Meyer glanced at and handed back.

"And in this statement, captain," he said, "you have sworn that der voyage was uneventful up to der moment of der wreck—that is," he added, with an oily smile, as he noticed the paling of the captain's face—"that nothing occurred to make der *Titan* less seaworthy or manageable?"

"That is what I swore to," said the captain, with a little sigh.

"You are part owner, are you not, Captain Bryce?"

"I own five shares of the company's stock."

"I have examined der charter and der company lists," said Mr. Meyer; "each boat of der company is, so far as assessments and dividends are concerned, a separate company. I find you are listed as owning two sixty-seconds of der *Titan* stock. This makes you, under der law, part owner of der *Titan,* and responsible as such."

"What do you mean, sir, by that word responsible?" said Captain Bryce, quickly.

For answer, Mr. Meyer elevated his black eyebrows, assumed an attitude of listening, looked at his watch and went to the door, which, as he opened, admitted the sound of carriage wheels.

"In here," he called to his clerks, then faced the captain.

"What do I mean, Captain Bryce?" he thundered. "I mean that you have concealed in your sworn statement all references to der fact that you collided with and sunk the ship *Royal Age* on der night before the wreck of your own ship."

"Who says so—how do you know it?" blustered the captain. "You have only that bulletin statement of the man Rowland—an irresponsible drunkard."

"The man was lifted aboard drunk at New York," broke in the first officer, "and remained in a condition of delirium tremens up to the shipwreck. We did not meet the *Royal Age* and are in no way responsible for her loss."

"Yes," added Captain Bryce, "and a man in that condition is liable to see anything. We listened to his ravings on the night of the wreck. He was on lookout—on the bridge, Mr. Austen, the boats'n, and myself were close to him."

Before Mr. Meyer's oily smile had indicated to the flustered captain that he had said too much, the door opened and admitted Rowland, pale, and weak, with empty left sleeve, leaning on the arm of a bronze-bearded and manly-looking giant who carried little Myra on the outer shoulder, and who said, in the breezy tone of the quarterdeck:

"Well, I've brought him, half dead; but why couldn't you give me time to dock my ship? A mate can't do everything."

"And this is Captain Barry, of der *Peerless*," said Mr. Meyer, taking his hand. "It is all right, my friend; you will not lose. And this is Mr. Rowland—and this is der little child. Sit down, my friend. I congratulate you on your escape."

"Thank you," said Rowland, weakly, as he seated himself; "they cut my arm off at Christiansand, and I still live. That is my escape."

Captain Bryce and Mr. Austen, pale and motionless, stared hard at this man, in whose emaciated face, refined by suffering to the almost spiritual softness of age, they hardly recognized the features of the troublesome sailor of the *Titan*. His clothing, though clean, was ragged and patched.

Mr. Selfridge had arisen and was also staring, not at Rowland, but at the child, who, seated in the lap of the big Captain Barry, was looking around with wondering eyes. Her costume was unique. A dress of bagging-stuff, put together—as were her canvas shoes and hat—with sail-twine in sail-makers' stitches, three to the inch, covered skirts and underclothing made from old flannel shirts. It represented many an hour's work of the watch-below, lovingly bestowed by the crew of the *Peerless*; for the crippled Rowland could not sew. Mr. Selfridge approached, scanned the pretty features closely; and asked:

"What is her name?"

"Her first name is Myra," answered Rowland. "She remembers that; but I have not learned her last name, though I knew her mother years ago—before her marriage."

"Myra, Myra," repeated the old gentleman; "do you know me? Don't you know me?" He trembled visibly as he stooped and kissed her. The little forehead puckered and wrinkled as the child struggled with memory; then it cleared and the whole face sweetened to a smile."

"Gwampa," she said.

"Oh, God, I thank thee," murmured Mr. Selfridge, taking her in his arms. "I have lost my son, but I have found his child—my granddaughter."

"But, sir," asked Rowland, eagerly; "you—this child's grandfather? Your son is lost, you say? Was he on board the *Titan*? And the mother—was she saved, or is she, too—" he stopped unable to continue.

"The mother is safe—in New York; but the father, my son, has not yet been heard from," said the old man, mournfully.

Rowland's head sank and he hid his face for a moment in his arm, on the table at which he sat. It had been a face as old, and worn, and weary as that of the white-haired man confronting him. On it, when it raised—flushed, bright-eyed and smiling—was the glory of youth.

"I trust, sir," he said, "that you will telegraph her. I am penniless at present, and, besides, do not know her name."

"Selfridge—which, of course, is my own name. Mrs. Colonel, or Mrs. George Selfridge. Our New York address is well known. But I shall cable her at once; and, believe me, sir, although I can understand that our debt to you cannot be named in terms of money, you need not be penniless long. You are evidently a capable man, and I have wealth and influence."

Rowland merely bowed, slightly, but Mr. Meyer muttered to himself: "Vealth and influence. Berhaps not. Now, gentlemen," he added, in a louder tone, "to pizness, Mr. Rowland, will you tell us about der running down of der *Royal Age*?"

"Was it the *Royal Age*?" asked Rowland. "I sailed in her one voyage. Yes, certainly."

Mr. Selfridge, more interested in Myra than in the coming account, carried her over to a chair in the corner and sat down, where he fondled and talked to her after the manner of grandfathers the world over, and Rowland, first looking steadily into the faces of the two men he had come to expose, and whose presence he had thus far ignored, told, while they held their teeth tight together and often buried their fingernails in their palms, the terrible story of the cutting in half of the ship on the first night out from New York, finishing with the attempted bribery and his refusal.

"Vell, gentlemen, vwhat do you think of that?" asked Mr. Meyer, looking around.

"A lie, from beginning to end," stormed Captain Bryce.

Rowland rose to his feet, but was pressed back by the big man who had accompanied him—who then faced Captain Bryce and said quietly:

"I saw a polar bear that this man killed in open fight. I saw his arm afterward, and while nursing him away from death I heard no whines or complaints. He can fight his own battles when well, and when sick I'll do it for him. If you insult him again in my presence I'll knock your teeth down your throat."

Chapter XII

There was a moment's silence while the two captains eyed one another, broken by the attorney, who said:

"Whether this story is true or false, it certainly has no bearing on the validity of the policy. If this happened, it was after the policy attached and before the wreck of the *Titan.*"

"But der concealment," shouted Mr. Meyer, excitedly.

"Has no bearing, either. If he concealed anything it was done after the wreck, and after your liability was confirmed. It was not even barratry. You must pay this insurance."

"I will not bay it. I will not. I will fight you in der courts." Mr. Meyer stamped up and down the floor in his excitement, then stopped with a triumphant smile, and shook his finger into the face of the attorney.

"And even if der concealment will not vitiate der policy, der fact that he had a drunken man on lookout when der *Titan* struck der iceberg will be enough. Go ahead and sue. I will not pay. He was part owner."

"You have not witnesses to that admission," said the attorney. Mr. Meyer looked around the group and the smile left his face.

"Captain Bryce was mistaken," said Mr. Austen. "This man was drunk at New York, like others of the crew. But he was sober and competent when on lookout. I discussed theories of navigation with him during his trick on the bridge that night and he spoke intelligently."

"But you yourself said, not ten minutes ago, that this man was in a state of delirium tremens up to der collision," said Mr. Meyer.

"What I said and what I will admit under oath are two different things," said the officer, desperately. "I may have said anything under the excitement of the moment—when we were accused of such an infamous crime. I say now, that John Rowland, whatever may have been his condition on the preceding night, was a sober and competent lookout at the time of the wreck of the *Titan.*"

"Thank you," said Rowland, dryly, to the first officer; then, looking into the appealing face of Mr. Meyer, he said:

"I do not think it will be necessary to brand me before the world as an inebriate in order to punish the company and these men. Barratry, as I understand it, is the unlawful act of a captain or crew at sea, causing damage or loss; and it only applies when the parties are purely employees. Did I understand rightly—that Captain Bryce was part owner of the *Titan?*"

"Yes," said Mr. Meyer, "he owns stock; and we insure against barratry; but this man, as part owner, could not fall back on it."

"And an unlawful act," went on Rowland, "perpetrated by a captain who is part owner, which might cause shipwreck, and, during the perpetration of which shipwreck, really occurs, will be sufficient to void the policy."

"Certainly," said Mr. Meyer, eagerly. "You were drunk on der lookout—you were raving drunk, as he said himself. You will swear to this, will you not, my friend? It is bad faith with der underwriters. It annuls der insurance. You admit this, Mr. Thompson, do you not?"

"That is law," said the attorney, coldly.

"Was Mr. Austen a part owner, also?" asked Rowland, ignoring Mr. Meyer's view of the case.

"One share, is it not, Mr. Austen?" asked Mr. Meyer, while he rubbed his hands and smiled. Mr. Austen made no sign of denial and Rowland continued:

"Then, for drugging a sailor into a stupor, and having him on lookout out of his turn while in that condition, and at the moment when the *Titan* struck the iceberg, Captain Bryce and Mr. Austen have, as part owners, committed an act which nullifies the insurance on that ship."

"You infernal, lying scoundrel!" roared Captain Bryce. He strode toward Rowland with a threatening face. Half-way, he was stopped by the impact of a huge brown fist which sent him reeling and staggering across the room toward Mr. Selfridge and the child, over whom he floundered to the floor—a disheveled heap,—while the big Captain Barry examined teeth-marks on his knuckles, and everyone else sprang to their feet.

"I told you to look out," said Captain Barry. "Treat my friend respectfully." He glared steadily at the first officer, as though inviting him to duplicate the offense; but that gentleman backed away from him and assisted the dazed Captain Bryce to a chair, where he felt of his loosened teeth, spat blood upon Mr. Meyer's floor, and gradually awakened to a realization of the fact that he had been knocked down—and by an American.

Little Myra, unhurt but badly frightened, began to cry and call for Rowland in her own way, to the wonder, and somewhat to the scandal of the gentle old man who was endeavoring to soothe her.

"Dammy," she cried, as she struggled to go to him; "I want Dammy—Dammy—Da-a-may."

"Oh, what a pad little girl," said the jocular Mr. Meyer, looking down on her. "Where did you learn such language?"

"It is my nickname," said Rowland, smiling in spite of himself. "She has coined the word," he explained to the agitated Mr. Selfridge, who had not yet comprehended what had happened; "and I have not yet been able to persuade her to drop it—and I could not be harsh with her. Let me take her, sir." He seated himself, with the child, who nestled up to him contentedly and soon was tranquil.

"Now, my friend," said Mr. Meyer, "you must tell us about this drugging." Then while Captain Bryce, under the memory of the blow he had received, nursed himself into an insane fury; and Mr. Austen, with his hand resting lightly on the captain's shoulder ready to restrain him, listened to the story; and the attorney drew up a chair and took notes of the story; and Mr. Selfridge drew his chair close to Myra and paid no attention to the story at all, Rowland recited the events prior to and succeeding the shipwreck. Beginning with the finding of the whisky in his pocket he told of his being called to the starboard bridge lookout in place of the rightful incumbent; of the sudden and strange interest Mr. Austen displayed as to his knowledge of navigation; of the pain in his stomach, the frightful shapes he had seen on the deck beneath and the sensations of his dream—leaving out only the part which bore on the woman he loved; he told of the sleep-walking child which awakened him, of the crash of ice and instant wreck, and the fixed condition of his eyes which prevented their focusing only at a certain distance, finishing his story—to explain his empty sleeve—with a graphic account of the fight with the bear. "And I have studied it all out," he said, in conclusion. "I was drugged—I believe, with hasheesh, which makes a man see strange things—and brought up on the bridge lookout where I could be watched and my ravings listened to and recorded, for the sole purpose of discrediting my threatened testimony in regard to the collision of the night before. But I was only half-drugged, as I spilled part of my tea at supper. In that tea, I am positive, was the hasheesh."

"You know all about it, don't you," snarled Captain Bryce, from his chair, "'twas not hasheesh; 'twas an infusion of Indian hemp; you don't know—" Mr. Austen's hand closed over his mouth and he subsided.

"Self-convicted," said Rowland, with a quiet laugh. "Hasheesh is made from Indian hemp."

"You hear this, gentlemen," exclaimed Mr. Meyer, springing to his feet and facing everybody in turn. He pounced on Captain Barry. "You hear this confession, captain; you hear him say Indian hemp? I have a witness now, Mr. Thompson. Go right on with your suit. You hear him, Captain Barry. You are disinterested. You are a witness. You hear?"

"Yes, I heard it—the murdering scoundrel," said the captain.

Mr. Meyer danced up and down in joy, while the attorney, pocketing his notes, remarked to the discomfited Captain Bryce: "You are the poorest fool I know," and left the office.

Then Mr. Meyer calmed himself, and facing the two steamship officers, said, slowly and impressively, while he poked his forefinger almost in their faces:

"England is a fine country, my friends—a fine country to leave behind sometimes. Dere is Canada, and der United States, and Australia, and South Africa— all fine countries, too—fine countries to go to with new names. My friends, you will be bulletened and listed at Lloyds in less than half an hour, and you will never again sail under der English flag as officers. And, my friends, let me say, that in half an hour after you are bulletened, all Scotland Yard will be looking for you. But my door is not locked."

Silently, they arose, pale, shamefaced, and crushed, and went out the door, through the outer office, and into the street.

Chapter XIII

Mr. Selfridge had begun to take an interest in the proceedings. As the two men passed out he arose and asked:

"Have you reached a settlement, Mr. Meyer? Will the insurance be paid?"

"No," roared the underwriter, in the ear of the puzzled old gentleman; while he slapped him vigorously on the back; "it will not be paid. You or I must have been ruined, Mr. Selfridge, and it has settled on you. I do not pay der *Titan's* insurance—nor will der other insurers. On der contrary, as der collision clause in der policy is void with der rest, your company must reimburse me for der insurance which I must pay to der *Royal Age* owners—that is unless our good friend here, Mr. Rowland, who was on der lookout at der time, will swear that her lights were out."

"Not at all," said Rowland. "Her lights were burning—look to the old gentleman," he exclaimed. "Look out for him. Catch him!"

Mr. Selfridge was stumbling toward a chair. He grasped it, loosened his hold, and before anyone could reach him, fell to the floor, where he lay, with ashen lips and rolling eyes, gasping convulsively.

"Heart failure," said Rowland, as he knelt by his side. "Send for a doctor."

"Send for a doctor," repeated Mr. Meyer through the door to his clerks; "and send for a carriage, quick. I don't want him to die in der office."

Captain Barry lifted the helpless figure to a couch, and they watched, while the convulsions grew easier, the breath shorter, and the lips from ashen gray to blue. Before the doctor or carriage had come, he had passed away.

"Sudden emotion of some kind," said the doctor when he did arrive. "Violent emotion, too. Hear bad news?"

"Bad and good," answered the underwriter. "Good, in learning that this dear little girl was his granddaughter—bad, in learning that he was a ruined man. He was der heaviest stockholder in der *Titan*. One hundred thousand pounds, he owned, of der stock, all of which this poor, dear little child will not get." Mr. Meyer looked sorrowful, as he patted Myra on the head.

Captain Barry beckoned to Rowland, who, slightly flushed, was standing by the still figure on the couch and watching the face of Mr. Meyer, on which annoyance, jubilation, and simulated shock could be seen in turn.

"Wait," he said, as he turned to watch the doctor leave the room. "Is this so, Mr. Meyer," he added to the underwriter, "that Mr. Selfridge owned *Titan* stock, and would have been ruined, had he lived, by the loss of the insurance money?"

"Yes, he would have been a poor man. He had invested his last farthing—one hundred thousand pounds. And if he had left any more it would be assessed to make good his share of what der company must bay for der *Royal Age*, which I also insured."

"Was there a collision clause in the *Titan*'s policy?"

"Dere was."

"And you took the risk, knowing that she was to run the Northern Lane at full speed through fog and snow?"

"I did—so did others."

"Then, Mr. Meyer, it remains for me to tell you that the insurance on the *Titan* will be paid, as well as any liabilities included in and specified by the collision clause in the policy. In short, I, the one man who can prevent it, refuse to testify."

"Vwhat-a-t?"

Mr. Meyer grasped the back of a chair and, leaning over it, stared at Rowland. "You will not testify? Vwhat you mean?"

"What I said; and I do not feel called upon to give my reasons, Mr. Meyer."

"My good friend," said the underwriter, advancing with outstretched hands to Rowland, who backed away, and taking Myra by the hand, moved toward the door. Mr. Meyer sprang ahead, locked it and removed the key, and faced them.

"Oh, mine goot Gott," he shouted, relapsing in his excitement into the more pronounced dialect of his race; "vwhat I do to you, hey? Vwhy you go pack on me, hey? Haf I not bay der doctor's bill? Haf I not bay for der carriage? Haf I not treat you like one shentleman? Haf I not, hey? I sit you down in mine office and call you Mr. Rowland. Haf I not been one shentleman?"

"Open that door," said Rowland, quietly.

"Yes, open it," repeated Captain Barry, his puzzled face clearing at the prospect of action on his part. "Open it or I'll kick it down."

"But you, mine friend—heard der admission of der captain—of der drugging. One good witness will do; two is petter. But you will swear, mine friend, you will not ruin me."

"I stand by Rowland," said the captain, grimly. "I don't remember what was said, anyhow; got a blamed bad memory. Get away from that door."

Grievous lamentation—weepings and wailings, and the most genuine gnashing of teeth—interspersed with the feeble cries of the frightened Myra and punctuated by terse commands in regard to the door, filled that private office, to the wonder of the clerks without, and ended, at last, with the crashing of the door from its hinges.

Captain Barry, Rowland, and Myra, followed by a parting, heartborne malediction from the agitated underwriter, left the office and reached the street. The carriage that brought them was still waiting.

"Settle inside," called the captain to the driver. "We'll take another, Rowland."

Around the first corner they found a cab, which they entered, Captain Barry giving the driver the direction—Bark *Peerless,* East India Dock."

"I think I understand the game, Rowland," he said, as they started; "you don't want to break this child."

"That's it," answered Rowland, weakly, as he leaned back on the cushion, faint from the excitement of the last few moments. "And as for the right or wrong of the position I am in—why, we must go farther back for it than the question of lookouts. The cause of the wreck was full speed in a fog. All hands on lookout could not have seen that berg. The underwriters knew the speed and took the risk. Let them pay."

"Right—and I'm with you on it. But you must get out of the country. I don't know the law on the matter, but they may compel you to testify, You can't ship 'fore the mast again—that's settled. But you can have a berth mate with me as long as I sail a ship—if you'll take it; and you're to make my cabin your home as long as you like; remember that. Still, I know you want to get across with the kid, and if you stay around until I sail it may be months before you get to New York, with the chance of losing her by getting foul of English law. But just leave it to me. There are powerful interests at stake in regard to this matter."

What Captain Barry had in mind, Rowland was too weak to inquire. On their arrival at the bark he was assisted by his friend to a couch in the cabin, where he spent the rest of the day, unable to leave it. Meanwhile, Captain Barry had gone ashore again.

Returning toward evening, he said to the man on the couch: "I've got your pay, Rowland, and signed a receipt for it to that attorney. He paid it out of his own pocket. You could have worked that company for fifty thousand, or more; but I knew you wouldn't touch their money, and, so, only struck him for your wages. You're entitled to a month's pay. Here it is—American money—about seventeen." He gave Rowland a roll of bills.

"Now here's something else, Rowland," he continued, producing an envelope. "In consideration of the fact that you lost all your clothes and later, your arm, through the carelessness of the company's officers, Mr. Thompson offers you this." Rowland opened the envelope. In it were two first cabin tickets from Liverpool to New York. Flushing hotly, he said, bitterly:

"It seems that I'm not to escape it, after all."

"Take 'em, old man, take 'em; in fact, I took 'em for you, and you and the kid are booked. And I made Thompson agree to settle your doctor's bill and expenses with that Sheeny. 'Tisn't bribery. I'd heel you myself for the run over, but, hang it, you'll take nothing from me. You got to get the young un over. You're the only one to do it. The old gentleman was an American, alone here—hadn't even a lawyer, that I could find. The boat sails in the morning and the night train leaves in two hours. Think of that mother, Rowland. Why, man, I'd travel round the world to stand in your shoes when you hand Myra over. I've got a child of my own." The captain's eyes were winking hard and fast, and Rowland's eyes were shining.

"Yes, I'll take the passage," he said, with a smile. "I accept the bribe."

"That's right. You'll be strong and healthy when you land, and when that mother's through thanking you, and you have to think of yourself, remember—I want a mate and will be here a month before sailing. Write to me care o' Lloyds, if you want the berth, and I'll send you advance money to get back with."

"Thank you, captain," said Rowland, as he took the other's hand and then glanced at his empty sleeve; "but my going to sea is ended. Even a mate needs two hands."

"Well, suit yourself, Rowland; I'll take you mate without any hands at all while you had your brains. It's done me good to meet a man like you; and—say, old man, you won't take it wrong from me, will you? It's none 'o my business, but you've been too all-fired good a man to drink. You haven't had a nip for two months. Are you going to begin?"

"Never again," said Rowland, rising. "I've a future now, as well as a past."

Chapter XIV

It was near noon of the next day that Rowland, seated in a steamer-chair with Myra and looking out on a sail-spangled stretch of blue from the saloon-deck of a west-bound liner, remembered that he had made no provisions to have Mrs. Selfridge notified by cable of the safety of her child; and unless Mr. Meyer or his associates gave the story to the press it would not be known.

"Well, he mused, "joy will not kill, and I shall witness it in its fullness if I take her by surprise. But the chances are that it will get into the papers before I reach her. It is too good for Mr. Meyer to keep."

But the story was not given out immediately. Mr. Meyer called a conference of the underwriters concerned with him in the insurance of the *Titan* at which it was decided to remain silent concerning the card they hoped to play, and to spend a little time and money in hunting for other witnesses among the *Titan*'s crew, and in interviewing Captain Barry, to the end of improving his memory. A few stormy meetings with this huge obstructionist convinced them of the futility of further effort in his direction, and, after finding at the end of a week that every surviving member of the *Titan*'s port watch, as well as a few of the others, had been induced to sign for Cape voyages, or had otherwise disappeared, they decided to give the story told by Rowland to the press in the hope that publicity would avail to bring to light corroboratory evidence.

And this story, improved upon in the repeating by Mr. Meyer to reporters, and embellished still further by the reporters as they wrote it up, particularly in the part pertaining to the polar bear,—blazoned out in the great dailies of England and the Continent, and was cabled to New York, with the name of the steamer in which John Rowland had sailed (for his movements had been traced in search of evidence), where it arrived, too late for publication, the morning of the day on which, with Myra on his shoulder, he stepped down the gangplank at a North River dock. As a consequence, he was surrounded on the dock by enthusiastic reporters, who spoke of the story and asked for details. He refused to talk, escaped them, and gaining the side streets, soon found himself in crowded Broadway, where he entered the office of the steamship company in whose employ he had been wrecked, and secured from the *Titan*'s passenger-list the address of Mrs. Selfridge—the only woman saved. Then he took a car up Broadway and alighted abreast of a large department store.

"We're going to see mamma, soon, Myra," he whispered in the pink ear; "and you must go dressed up. It don't matter about me; but you're a Fifth Avenue baby—a little aristocrat. These old clothes won't do, now." But she had forgotten the word "mamma," and was more interested in the exciting noise and life of the street than in the clothing she wore. In the store, Rowland asked for, and was directed to the children's department, where a young woman waited on him.

"This child has been shipwrecked," he said. "I have sixteen dollars and a half to spend on it. Give it a bath, dress its hair, and use up the money on a dress, shoes, and stockings, underclothing, and a hat." The young woman stooped and kissed the little girl with sheer sympathy, but protested that not much could be done.

"Do your best," said Rowland; "it is all I have. I will wait here."

An hour later, penniless again, he emerged from the store with Myra, bravely dressed in her new finery, and was stopped at the corner by a policeman who had seen him come out, and who marveled doubtless, at such juxtaposition of rags and ribbons.

"Whose kid ye got?" he demanded.

"I believe it is the daughter of Mrs. Colonel Selfridge," answered Rowland, haughtily—too haughtily, by far.

"Ye believe—but ye don't know. Come back into the shtore, me tourist, and we'll see who ye shtole it from."

"Very well, officer; I can prove possession." They started back, the officer with his hand on Rowland's collar, and were met at the door by a party of three or four people coming out. One of this party, a young woman in black, uttered a piercing shriek and sprang toward them.

"Myra!" she screamed. "Give me my baby—give her to me."

She snatched the child from Rowland's shoulder, hugged it, kissed it, cried, and screamed over it; then, oblivious to the crowd that collected, incontinently fainted in the arms of an indignant old gentleman.

"You scoundrel!" he exclaimed, as he flourished his cane over Rowland's head with his free arm. "We've caught you. Officer, take that man to the station-house. I will follow and make a charge in the name of my daughter."

"Then he shtole the kid, did he?" asked the policeman.

"Most certainly," answered the old gentleman, as, with the assistance of the others, he supported the unconscious young mother to a carriage. They all entered, little Myra screaming for Rowland from the arms of a female member of the party, and were driven off.

"C'm an wi' me," uttered the officer, rapping his prisoner on the head with his club and jerking him off his feet.

Then, while an approving crowd applauded, the man who had fought and conquered a hungry polar bear was dragged through the streets like a sick animal by a New York policeman, For such is the stultifying effect of a civilized environment.

Chapter XV

In New York City there are homes permeated by a moral atmosphere so pure, so elevated, so sensitive to the vibrations of human woe and misdoing, that their occupants are removed completely from all consideration of any but the spiritual welfare of poor humanity. In these homes the news-gathering, sensation-mongering daily paper does not enter.

In the same city are dignified magistrates—members of clubs and societies— who spend late hours, and often fail to arise in the morning in time to read the papers before the opening of court.

Also in New York are city editors, bilious of stomach, testy of speech, and inconsiderate of reporters' feelings and professional pride. Such editors, when a reporter has failed, through no fault of his own, in successfully interviewing a celebrity, will sometimes send him news-gathering in the police courts, where printable news is scarce.

On the morning following the arrest of John Rowland, three reporters, sent by three such editors, attended a hall of justice presided over by one of the late-rising magistrates mentioned above. In the anteroom of this court, ragged, disfigured by his clubbing, and disheveled by his night in a cell, stood Rowland, with other unfortunates more or less guilty of offense against society. When his name was called, he was hustled through a door, along a line of policemen— each of whom added to his own usefulness by giving him a shove—and into the dock, where the stern-faced and tired-looking magistrate glared at him. Seated in a corner of the court-room were the old gentleman of the day before, the young mother with little Myra in her lap, and a number of other ladies—all excited in demeanor; and all but the young mother directing venomous glances at Rowland. Mrs. Selfridge, pale and hollow-eyed, but happy-faced, withal, allowed no wandering glance to rest on him.

The officer who had arrested Rowland was sworn, and testified that he had stopped the prisoner on Broadway while making off with the child, whose rich clothing had attracted his attention. Disdainful sniffs were heard in the corner with muttered remarks: "Rich indeed—the idea—the flimsiest prints." Mr. Gaunt, the prosecuting witness, was called to testify.

"This man, your Honor," he began excitedly, "was once a gentleman and a frequent guest at my house. He asked for the hand of my daughter, and as his request was not granted, threatened revenge. Yes, sir. And out on the broad Atlantic, where he had followed my daughter in the guise of a sailor, he attempted to murder that child—my grandchild; but was discovered —"

"Wait," interrupted the magistrate. "Confine your testimony to the present offense."

"Yes, your Honor. Failing in this, he stole, or enticed the little one from its bed, and in less than five minutes the ship was wrecked, and he must have escaped with the child in—"

"Were you a witness of this?"

"I was not there, your Honor; but we have it on the word of the first officer, a gentleman —"

"Step down, sir. That will do. Officer, was this offense committed in New York?"

"Yes, your Honor; I caught him meself."

"Who did he steal the child from?"

"That leddy over yonder."

"Madam, will you take the stand?"

With her child in her arms, Mrs. Selfridge was sworn, and in a low, quavering voice repeated what her father had said. Being a woman, she was allowed by the woman-wise magistrate to tell her story in her own way. When she spoke of the attempted murder at the taffrail, her manner became excited. Then she told of the captain's promise to put the man in irons on her agreeing to testify against him— of the consequent decrease in her watchfulness, and her missing the child just before the shipwreck—of her rescue by the gallant first officer, and his assertion that he had seen her child in the arms of this man—the only man on earth who would harm it—of the later news that a boat containing sailors and children had been picked up by a Mediterranean steamer—of the detectives sent over, and their report that a sailor answering this man's description had refused to surrender a child to the consul at Gibraltar and had disappeared with it—of her joy at the news that Myra was alive, and despair of ever seeing her again until she had met her in this man's arms on Broadway the day before. At this point, outraged maternity overcame her. With cheeks flushed, and eyes blazing scorn and anger, she pointed at Rowland and all but screamed: "And he has mutilated—tortured my baby. There are deep wounds in her little back, and the doctor said, only last night, that they were made by a sharp instrument. And he must have tried to warp and twist the mind of my child, or put her through frightful experiences; for he has taught her to swear—horribly—and last night at bedtime, when I told her the story of Elisha and the bears and the children, she burst out into the most uncontrollable screaming and sobbing."

Here her testimony ended in a breakdown of hysterics, between sobs of which were frequent admonitions to the child not to say that bad word; for Myra had caught sight of Rowland and was calling his nickname.

"What shipwreck was this—where was it?" asked the puzzled magistrate of nobody in particular.

"The *Titan*," called out half a dozen newspaper men across the room.

"The *Titan*," repeated the magistrate. Then this offense was committed on the high seas under the English flag. I cannot imagine why it is brought into this court. Prisoner, have you anything to say?"

"Nothing, your Honor." The answer came in a kind of dry sob.

The magistrate scanned the ashen-faced man in rags, and said to the clerk of the court: "Change this charge to vagrancy—eh—"

The clerk, instigated by the newspaper men, was at his elbow. He laid a morning paper before him, pointed to certain big letters and retired. Then the business of the court suspended while the court read the news. After a moment or two the magistrate looked up.

"Prisoner," he said, sharply, "take your left sleeve out of your breast!" Rowland obeyed mechanically, and it dangled at his side. The magistrate noticed, and read on. Then he folded the paper and said:

"You are the man who was rescued from an iceberg, are you not?" The prisoner bowed his head.

"Discharged!" The word came forth in an unjudicial roar. "Madam," added the magistrate, with a kindling light in his eye, "this man has merely saved your child's life. If you will read of his defending it from a polar bear when you go home, I doubt that you will tell it any more bear stories. Sharp instrument— umph!" Which was equally unjudicial on the part of the court.

Mrs. Selfridge, with a mystified and rather aggrieved expression of face, left the court-room with her indignant father and friends, while Myra shouted profanely for Rowland, who had fallen into the hands of the reporters. They would have entertained him after the manner of the craft, but he would not be entertained—neither would he talk. He escaped and was swallowed up in the world without; and when the evening papers appeared that day, the events of the trial were all that could be added to the story of the morning.

Chapter XVI

On the morning of the next day, a one-armed dock lounger found an old fishhook and some pieces of string which he knotted together; then he dug some bait and caught a fish. Being hungry and without fire, he traded with a coaster's cook for a meal, and before night caught two more, one of which he traded, the other sold. He slept under the docks—paying no rent—fished, traded, and sold for a month, then paid for a second-hand suit of clothes and the services of a barber. His changed appearance induced a boss stevedore to hire him tallying cargo, which was more lucrative than fishing, and furnished, in time, a hat, pair of shoes, and an overcoat. He then rented a room and slept in a bed. Before long he found employment addressing envelopes for a mailing firm, at which his fine and rapid penmanship secured him steady work; and in a few months he asked his employers to indorse his application for a Civil Service examination. The favor was granted, the examination easily passed, and he addressed envelopes while he waited. Meanwhile he bought new and better clothing and seemed to have no difficulty in impressing those whom he met with the fact that he was a gentleman. Two years from the time of his examination he was appointed to a lucrative position under the Government, and as he seated himself at the desk in his office, could have been heard to remark: "Now John Rowland, your future is your own. You have merely suffered in the past from a mistaken estimate of the importance of women and whisky."

But he was wrong, for in six months he received a letter which, in part, read as follows:

"Do not think me indifferent or ungrateful. I have watched from a distance while you made your wonderful fight for your old standards. You have won, and I am glad and I congratulate you. But Myra will not let me rest. She asks for you continually and cries at times. I can bear it no longer. Will you not come and see Myra?"

And the man went to see—Myra.

PART IV

Discovering the Tomb
of the *Titanic:*
Dr. Ballard's Epic Triumph

27

THE QUEST OF THE CENTURY

Dr. Robert Ballard's Discovery
of the Wreck of the *Titanic*

> It was one thing to have won—to have found the ship. It
> was another thing to be there. That was the spooky part.
> I could see the *Titanic* as she slipped nose first into the
> glassy water. Around me were the ghostly shapes of the
> lifeboats and the piercing shouts and screams of people
> freezing to death in the water.
>   Our little memorial service lasted five, maybe ten
> minutes. Then I just said, "Thank you all. Now let's get
> back to work."
>
>   —Dr. Robert Ballard's thoughts moments after finding
>   the wreck of the *Titanic*

For 26,644 days the great liner R.M.S. *Titanic* rested peacefully on the
ocean floor, her magnificent body broken in two, her bow buried sixty-
five feet in the earth two-and-a-half miles below the surface of the North
Atlantic. Then, on September 1, 1985, *Titanic*'s sleep was interrupted.

In the summer of 1985, Dr. Robert Ballard, a marine geologist with
the Woods Hole Oceanographic Institution of Massachusetts, and a
French team from IFREMER were exploring the ocean bottom in the
area where the *Titanic* sank. They were using a deep-sea submersible
camera sled—the *Argo*—that was being towed by a U.S. Navy research
vessel, the *Knorr*.

Shortly after midnight early on the morning of Sunday, September 1, 1985, crew member Bill Lange switched *Argo*'s camera from forward-looking to down-looking. Watching the video monitor, he then said one word: "Wreckage." Thus began the *Titanic*'s new era.

The first real piece of the *Titanic* the explorers saw was one of the ship's main boilers. Over the next few days, Ballard and his team used the *Argo* to determine several important facts about the lost liner. One of the most important was that the *Titanic* was upright. They also learned that the first funnel was gone, and that a great deal of the ship seemed to still be intact. This confirmed what many survivors had reported: that the forward funnel had fallen into the water just before the ship went under, nearly hitting Collapsible B, one of the lifeboats that floated off the *Titanic* as she sank and to which Colonel Gracie, Harold Bride, Second Officer Lightoller, and between thirty-five and forty others clung desperately in the icy waters.

Since that memorable day, the *Titanic* has been revisited many, many times. Dr. Ballard himself has returned to the *Titanic* several times; a Russian film crew shooting an Imax film went down to it in 1991; George Tulloch and RMS Titanic have visited the ship too many times to count; and James Cameron went down at least a dozen times as research for his film.

In the past decade, over six thousand *Titanic* artifacts have been recovered from the mile-wide debris field between and around the two halves of the great vessel. So far, everyone involved in expeditions to the *Titanic* seems to draw the line at plundering the interior of the wreck itself . . . but this will likely change now that the debris field is essentially picked clean and interest in the *Titanic* not only continues, but grows significantly as more and more people see Cameron's film and become fascinated with the legend of the ship.

There is a brand-new Renault automobile somewhere in the front cargo hold of the *Titanic.* And on a *Larry King Live* broadcast on Christmas Eve 1997, Dr. Ballard himself proclaimed with certainty that if someone were to go deep enough into the *Titanic,* say, into the boiler rooms or third-class cabins, there would no doubt be human skeletons.

These aspects of the *Titanic* story are irresistible to many, and it is only a matter of time before the wreck is plundered the way the Egyptian tombs have been during the past few decades. The *Titanic* is decaying, and many experts believe that between iron-eating bacteria and the ongoing decomposition of the other materials on the *Titanic* (such as leather and wood) caused by the sea water itself, the great steamer may be nothing but a stain on the ocean floor within a hundred years at most.

Museums routinely put Egyptian mummies on display. Is it that much of a leap to imagine them doing the same with skeletons found inside the *Titanic?* It would be repugnant to mount such an exhibition, but you can be certain that the lines for admission would stretch for miles once the display opened.

Today, Dr. Ballard continues to explore the world's oceans, looking for lost ships. In the fall of 1997, he published a book called *Lost Liners,* and in April 1998 he announced that he would lead an expedition to find and explore the U.S.S. *Yorktown,* the aircraft carrier which was sunk by Japanese torpedoes on June 7, 1942, during the Battle of Midway.

On Tuesday, May 19, 1998, Robert Ballard once again succeeded in pinpointing the burial place of a great, lost sea-going vessel. During an expedition led by the National Geographic Society and commanded by Ballard, the *Yorktown*'s gun emplacement was identified from a videotape shot by a Navy remote submersible vehicle. The National Geographic Society would not reveal the exact location of the wreck, but the expedition had been exploring an area about 1,250 miles west-northwest of Honolulu, Hawaii. Ocean depths there reached close to seventeen-thousand feet, nearly a mile deeper than where the *Titanic* lies. Unlike the *Titanic,* nothing will ever be allowed to be removed from the *Yorktown;* federal law prohibits the disturbance of any Navy wreck.

Interest in the *Titanic* continues unabated. It is one of the most famous ships and *the* most famous ship*wreck* in history, and Dr. Ballard's discovery of the wreck ranks as one of the most significant marine archaeological events of the twentieth century.

The night does, indeed, live on.

FIVE LITTLE-KNOWN FACTS ABOUT ROBERT BALLARD'S DISCOVERY OF THE *TITANIC*

1. Robert Ballard approached Roy Disney to fund an expedition to search for the *Titanic* in 1978. Disney turned him down, telling him, "Because of the enormous capital investment which you require imme-

diately, it is simply not feasible for us to become involved." Ballard had asked Disney for the now-paltry sum of $1.5 million.

2. On the way down to the *Titanic* (a trip which takes about two-and-a-half hours), Ballard and his dive mates usually listened to Vivaldi's *The Four Seasons* on cassette. They would turn the tape off when they got to the wreck so they could record their comments without a "soundtrack."

3. Since there is no toilet on the submersible, Ballard and his diving companions had to urinate in a plastic bottle which they nicknamed HERE, an acronym for Human Endurance Range Extender.

4. One of the most common questions asked of Dr. Ballard after he discovered the wreck was, "Did you see any bodies?" During a 1986 dive, Ballard was horrified to see what he described as "a small, white smiling face" lying on the ocean floor. "For a split second I thought a corpse had actually materialized—and it scared the hell out of me," he wrote in his 1987 book, *The Discovery of the Titanic.* The head turned out to be the ceramic head of a doll of French or German origin. The doll's hair and clothes were long gone, and after his initial reaction, Ballard felt an overwhelming sense of sadness as he wondered who had owned the toy and whether or not the little girl had been one of the survivors. James Cameron used an image of a doll's head lying on the ocean floor in the opening sequence of his 1997 film, *Titanic.*

5. During one of his tours of the *Titanic* wreck, Dr. Ballard noticed reddish-brown stalactites of rust hanging down several feet from the *Titanic*'s railings. These formations were the result of iron-eating bacteria and had never been seen on what Ballard described as "such a massive scale." Ballard coined the term "rusticles" to describe these stalactites, and that is the word that is universally used today when referring to rust formations of this type—on other shipwrecks as well as the *Titanic.*

> The history of the R.M.S. *Titanic,* of the White Star Line,
> is one of the most tragically short it is possible to
> conceive. The world had waited expectantly for its
> launching and again for its sailing; had read accounts of
> its tremendous size and its unexampled completeness and

luxury; had felt it a matter of the greatest satisfaction that such a comfortable and above all such a safe boat had been designed and built—the "unsinkable lifeboat"—and then in a moment to hear that it had gone to the bottom as if it had been the veriest tramp steamer of a few hundred tons; and with it fifteen hundred passengers, some of them known all the world over! The improbability of such a thing ever happening was what staggered humanity.

—Lawrence Beesley, *The Loss of the S.S.* Titanic: *Its Story and Its Lessons* (1912)

28

RMS Titanic's "Big Piece" Debacle

> You can't bring this thing up with no one looking.
> This is theater.
>
> > —George Tulloch, president of RMS Titanic,
> > talking about his attempt to raise a piece of the
> > *Titanic*'s hull to the surface

> The ocean gives no quarter. We failed on this attempt
> because we neglected to carefully coordinate the twenty-
> first-century technology of deep ocean recovery with the
> nineteenth-century technology of winching and rigging.
> We won't make that mistake again.
>
> > —George Tulloch, later

The specifics of trying to raise a piece of the *Titanic* from the ocean floor—the nuts-and-bolts details—are absolutely fascinating. While reading the daily dispatches of George Tulloch's expedition to retrieve a piece of the *Titanic*'s hull in August 1996, I was mesmerized by the facts and awed by the overwhelming complexity of any attempt to perform such a seemingly impossible task.

The four amazing Edison light towers; the eight inflatable floatation bladders filled with lighter-than-water diesel fuel; the desperate plan to tow the piece to a spot closer to shore in a last-ditch effort to save it; all of these details were of intense interest to me. And yet, the truth was that I was allowing myself to actually be *entertained* by this story of adventure and present-day treasure-seeking. In the abstract, it didn't seem so ghoulish.

The title of this chapter does not use the word *debacle* lightly. In hindsight, the attempt to raise a piece of the *Titanic*'s mangled starboard hull as part of a cruise expedition complete with casino gambling and B-list celebrities seems like a blatant contradiction of RMS Titanic's stated intent to maintain the wreck with "respect and dignity." (The casinos did close, though, as a sign of respect, when the *Nadir* reached the site of *Titanic*'s sinking.)

The goal was ambitious. With a price tag of around $17 million attached to the project, the ever-enterprising George Tulloch and company had to scramble to find investors and to raise the necessary capital. One of the ways they did this was to sell two thousand tickets to the event at $5,000 apiece.

The plan was for two luxury cruise ships—the S.S. *Royal Majesty* and the M.V. *Island Breeze*—to accompany Tulloch's salvage vessel, the *Nadir*, to the site where the seventeen-ton Big Piece (as it came to be called) was located, approximately seventy feet east of the *Titanic*'s stern wreckage.

The Big Piece measured twenty feet wide and twenty-four feet long and had been identified by Harland and Wolff's David Livingstone (the 1990s counterpart of *Titanic*'s builder Thomas Andrews) as having been part of the outer wall of two C-deck first-class berths—C79 and C81—the two rooms next-door to the cabin that had been occupied by the British journalist W. T. Stead, editor of the *Review of Reviews*. (At first there was talk that the piece might have actually been part of Stead's cabin wall, but this theory was ultimately discounted.) Stead had been on his way to the United States at the personal request of President Taft, who had asked Stead to give a speech at the upcoming World Peace Conference at Carnegie Hall. Stead perished in the *Titanic*.

Tulloch's cruise ships were equipped with closed-circuit TVs in each cabin so that the guests could monitor the progress of the expedition in relative comfort. If they got bored, though, they could always turn their attention to the Las Vegas-style floor shows on the ships.

The salvage vessel *Nadir* and the submersible *Nautile* were the main players in the ambitious attempt to bring a piece of the *Titanic* up into the sunlight after eighty-four years hidden in the unimaginable darkness on the ocean floor, two-and-a-half miles below the surface. Eight lift bags filled with a total of twenty thousand gallons of diesel fuel borrowed from the *Nadir* were tethered to the Big Piece with twenty-five tons of steel chain. Each bag had a lift capability of three and a half tons, so the prevailing thinking was that the Big Piece's seventeen or so tons of weight would be no problem for the eight bags to lift. Unless . . .

Well, it turned out that there were several "unlesses" when it came to Tulloch's mission. The first potential problem was the estimated weight of the Big Piece. The Piece had been carefully measured and had been estimated to weigh between fifteen and eighteen tons—but everyone knew that it could be heavier. If its weight neared twenty tons, the eight lift bags were not going to be able to move it.

Another possible problem was the "mud slurp" factor. If the Piece was buried too deep (a real possibility), the suction created by the mud would increase the lift requirement substantially enough, in fact, that the chains could quickly snap, allowing the Piece to just settle back into the mud on the ocean floor.

Then there was the actual task of raising the Piece to the surface. Even though the fuel-filled lift bags should have been able to rise slowly to the surface with the Big Piece dangling beneath them, some scientists on the expedition feared that the bags would raise the Piece most of the way and then just stop. Why? Because the bags might hit a warm-water thermocline, a water layer separating the colder, heavier deep water from the warmer, lighter water closer to the surface. If the bags hit one of these layers, their lifting power would essentially be neutralized and the bags and the Big Piece would simply float around the Atlantic, "holding hostage hundreds of thousands of dollars of equipment, and a good bit of the *Nadir*'s fuel" (in the words of expedition crew member Steve Allison).

On Thursday, August 29, the green-and-red flotation bags broke the surface of the Atlantic with the Big Piece dangling two-hundred feet beneath them. Because of worsening weather conditions at the time, the decision was made to tow the Piece to the Grand Banks off the coast of Newfoundland, where the water depth was only two-hundred-fifty to three-hundred feet. There, divers could repair the rigging and ultimately raise the Big Piece in New York Harbor in front of TV cameras and the astonished eyes of those lucky enough to get a spot near the water, where they could actually see a piece of the *Titanic* rise from the sea.

Good plan—if it had worked.

Moving slowly at 2 knots, the *Nadir* began its slow trek to shallower waters. However, the weather got worse and the waves got rougher, and ultimately the chains holding the Big Piece simply couldn't take the stress. They broke at 3:00 A.M. on Friday, August 30. The Big Piece—a part of the *Titanic* that had first been ripped from the body of the great liner, and then, after eighty-four years, unceremoniously jerked from its resting place on the sea bottom—planed slowly down to the ocean floor, ultimately landing upright, ten miles from the site of the *Titanic*.

Antisalvage *Titanic* lovers were ecstatic, interpreting Tulloch's failure as a message from beyond to leave *Titanic* alone. The crew of the *Nautile* eventually cut loose the six flotation bags that were still attached to the Big Piece and recovered the fuel from them for the *Nadir*'s tanks. Before they left the site, they dropped a plaque onto the Piece that read, "I will come back. G. Tulloch." (And he did. In August 1998, Tulloch's RMS Titanic expedition "*Titanic* '98" successfully raised the Big Piece from the ocean floor. See the Epilogue, page 399, for complete details on this and other accomplishments of this expedition.)

Serious historical archaeological study is one thing; carnivallike exploitation of what is undeniably a gravesite is quite another. When I first heard of Tulloch's plans to raise a portion of the *Titanic*'s hull as part of a "cruise package," my immediate reaction was, "What in the name of heaven is he thinking?" The *idea* of the original project was a valid one, and the potential findings could have been of great significance, but the execution of the mission was tacky, insensitive, and offensive in the worst possible way.

The *perception* of an action is oftentimes more important than the actual carrying out of that action. If Tulloch had simply raised the money on his own by seeking participation from private investors, foundations, and even corporate sponsorship, and then gone out and done the best he could to recover the hull piece, odds are that there probably would not have been much outcry against him and his company.

29

DR. ROBERT BALLARD
VS. GEORGE TULLOCH
Titanic Differences

During one of Dr. Robert Ballard's lectures and book-signings that I attended in the winter of 1998, Dr. Ballard used his forum to speak deprecatingly of RMS Titanic president George Tulloch. Ballard passionately spoke out against any attempts to raise the *Titanic,* and was also quite negative about salvage expeditions to the wreck, stating (and I'm paraphrasing) that he didn't think the responsibility for the great liner—and ownership of all the artifacts recovered from her—should be in the hands of some car dealer from Connecticut.

Thus, the battle rages on. Whose side are *you* on?

Dr. Ballard discovered the *Titanic*'s remains in 1985 and was immediately against disturbing its rest in any way other than photographically. In fact, Ballard felt so strongly about this that for a time he refused to reveal the exact location of the *Titanic*'s resting place. Ballard believes that salvaging artifacts from the *Titanic* is akin to grave-robbing, and that the wreck should be considered a sacred memorial to those lost in the disaster.

Tulloch, on the other hand, believes that salvaging artifacts from the wreck furthers historical knowledge and makes great contributions toward the preservation of the memory of the lost liner. He has vowed never to sell artifacts he recovers from the site (other than the $10 pieces of *Titanic* coal he sells to raise money for future expeditions) and there have been several traveling exhibitions of *Titanic* artifacts over the past decade or so, all of which boast enormous attendance and tremendous media attention.

However noble such sentiments sound, it cannot be denied that George Tulloch is not averse to capitalizing in other ways on the *Titanic* and her legend. At the end of March 1998, a furniture manufacturing company called Classic Leather of Hickory, North Carolina, officially announced that they would be selling authentic reproduction furniture from the *Titanic* in a line called "The RMS Titanic Artifact Collection." The line included bedroom furnishings from first-class staterooms as well as chairs and other pieces from the First Class Dining Saloon and the First-Class Smoking Lounge. The company did not announce final prices, but it was expected that a first-class smoking chair would sell for $800 to $900; a parlor club chair for $1,000; and a dining room table for between $2,900 and $3,900. The line had been tested during the Christmas 1997 holidays by offering a leather deck chair for $795 in the J. Peterman catalog. Ron Freeman, Classic Leather's director of business development, told the press, "The chair did great, and that's why we decided to go forward with the line." The furniture was offered through a *Titanic* licensing deal with George Tulloch's company, RMS Titanic, signed in the spring of 1997.

This is the type of blatant commercializing of the *Titanic* that angers and offends many *Titanic* buffs who believe that the ship is a grave site— a tomb for the 1,523 lost when she sank—and should not be desecrated, commercialized, or exploited in any way.

So, who's right?

Here is a look at some of the comments that have been made about the ultimate fate and treatment of the *Titanic* wreck and everything on and around her. You can make up your own mind as to who to side with.

Dr. Ballard "When I sailed away from the *Titanic* wreck site in 1986, I did so with the reasonable hope that the ship's last resting place would be left undisturbed." (from the epilogue to the 1995 edition of his book *The Discovery of the Titanic*)

George Tulloch "Our philosophy at RMS Titanic echoes the thoughts of the *Titanic*'s designer and builder, Thomas Andrews, as he expressed them in his 1910 Christmas card: 'It is not what you say, it is not what you think, it is not what you feel. It is what you do.' RMS Titanic is dedicated to preserving and protecting the memory of the *Titanic* with dignity and respect." (from the epilogue to the RMS Titanic–sponsored book *Titanic: Legacy of the World's Greatest Ocean Liner*)

Millvina Dean, *Titanic* survivor "If they want to make money, I don't honestly mind." (from *People,* May 19, 1997)

Eva Hart, *Titanic* survivor "[*Titanic* salvagers are] fortune hunters, vultures, pirates." (from *Civilization,* December 1997/January 1998)

Edward Kamuda, president of the Titanic Historical Society "The wreck is a grave site. There's nothing that can be learned there that's worth disturbing the site. There's no reason to do this except for greed." (from *Civilization,* December 1997/January 1998)

George Tulloch "When you're in the *Nautile,* working in slow motion, and you know it's costing you five dollars a second, that sharpens your concentration." (from a British television documentary)

Walter Lord, author of *A Night to Remember* "To me, the mystique of the *Titanic* was one of the wonderful things about it—the mystique of not knowing what happened once it slipped beneath the waves. And they've certainly ended that. Pulling these things up out of the water, you take away the mystery." (from *Civilization,* December 1997/January 1998)

George Tulloch "There's hardly a day goes by that I don't say to myself, life would be so much easier if we could sell [the *Titanic* artifacts]. But there's a real problem with selling them. And the real problem is, it's wrong." (from *Civilization,* December 1997/January 1998)

John Whitehead, Media Service, The U.S. Commemorative Fine Art Gallery "Official and authentic *Titanic* historical items are finally being made available to the public for a very limited period of time and while certain supplies last. These historic items are being made available by the U.S. Commemorative Fine Art Gallery, a division of SCI. SCI, along with RMS Titanic, Inc., financed and carried out the now famous *Titanic* Expedition and Cruise, as seen on the Discovery Channel and a *National Geographic* television special." (from a full-page ad in the January 5, 1998, issue of *USA Today*)

(The items being offered for sale [each were $19, all five for $47] were copies of the passenger and crew log; the only known photographs taken by Father Brown aboard the *Titanic*; an exact reproduction of a newspaper found at the wreck site; historical photos of four of the living survivors at a first-ever meeting in 1996; and pieces of the *Titanic* coal recovered from the *Titanic*'s debris field.)

In 1997, George Tulloch joined forces with Time-Life and the Discovery Channel to create and publish a book about the *Titanic* called *Titanic: Legacy of the World's Greatest Ocean Liner*.

If you put aside any negative feelings you may have about the actions and motivating philosophy of Tulloch and RMS Titanic, there is no denying that the book is magnificent—and important. It contains hundreds of gorgeous photos and illustrations of the *Titanic* and the artifacts retrieved from her debris field, and it makes an important contribution to the library of works about the *Titanic* and her history. Sure, it also serves as a $35 hardcover public relations package for RMS Titanic, Inc., but for *Titanic* buffs, it is a glorious compilation.

Dr. Ballard also published a book about his involvement with the *Titanic. The Discovery of the Titanic: Exploring the Greatest of All Lost Ships*, was published in 1987, and to date it has sold well over one million copies. I do not recall reading in the book Dr. Ballard stating that he would be refusing royalties so as not to exploit the *Titanic*. On the other hand, monies earned from Tulloch's book supposedly went toward funding future expeditions to the *Titanic*. To many, this blatant irony illustrates the difficulty in attempting to define—with certainty—what is *Titanic* exploitation and what is legitimate commercial enterprise.

The debate continues. James Cameron made money off the *Titanic* from his movie. Dr. Ballard had no problem with this and was actually interviewed with Cameron after the film was released.

George Tulloch, on the other hand, tries to further our knowledge of the *Titanic* through his many salvage trips to the site, and is loathed by the antisalvage faction of *Titanic* buffs.

I have problems with both the antisalvage and the prosalvage points of view, and for me, I guess it all boils down to the issue of respect. I don't have any problem with Dr. Ballard getting rich off a book about his discovery of the *Titanic*. I would just prefer that he take a somewhat less strident position about other commercial exploitation of the great ship and her memory.

I also have no problem with RMS Titanic being the salvor in possession of the wreck and everything on it. George Tulloch seems to be sincere in his passion for the ship and will probably, in the long run, be viewed as a careful caretaker of the *Titanic*. I just wish he would tone down the carnival aspects of many of his endeavors and show the wreck and its victims a little more respect.

The discovery of the *Titanic* in 1985 raised some difficult questions, especially for the families of her victims. These questions have many answers, and it is up to each student of the *Titanic* to decide what is personally acceptable and, perhaps more importantly, what is not.

DR. ROBERT BALLARD was the marine geologist and forty-two-year-old head of the Woods Hole Oceanographic Institute's Deep Submergence laboratory in 1985, when he and his team made their first expedition to find the *Titanic*. Dr. Ballard has since gone on to find and explore other wrecks, including the aircraft carrier the *Yorktown* and the *Titanic*'s sister ship, the *Brittanic*. Ballard has also written several books about his endeavors, including the 1997 book, *Lost Liners*.

GEORGE TULLOCH was the owner of the largest BMW dealership in the United States when he sold out his share in his early thirties and moved to Florida to wait tables at a restaurant at Disney World. When he was forty-three, he moved back to Greenwich, Connecticut, and became a partner in his old car dealership. When he heard about plans to salvage the *Titanic,* he ended up raising more than $2 million to finance a 1987 expedition to the wreck. He eventually formed RMS Titanic, Inc., and was granted sole salvage rights to the wreck. Today, he mostly concentrates on raising money for more expeditions to the wreck site.

30

THE R.M.S. *TITANIC*
INTERNATIONAL MARITIME MEMORIAL
ACT OF 1985
(S 450RR–450RR-6)

Here is the text of the law written to protect the *Titanic* from being "disturbed" by salvage operations. Considering the fact that over six-thousand items from the *Titanic* have been salvaged from her debris field in the past decade or so, it might be worth asking if the International Maritime Memorial Act of 1985 ever actually achieved its stated purpose.

(a) Findings

The Congress finds that:
(1) the R.M.S. TITANIC, the ocean liner which sank on her maiden voyage after striking an iceberg on April 14, 1912, should be designated as an international maritime memorial to the men, women, and children who perished aboard her;
(2) the recent discovery of the R.M.S. TITANIC, lying more than twelve thousand feet beneath the ocean surface, demonstrates the practical applications of ocean science and engineering;
(3) the R.M.S. TITANIC, well preserved in the cold, oxygen-poor waters of the deep North Atlantic Ocean, is of major national and international

cultural and historical significance, and merits
appropriate international protection;

(4) the R.M.S. TITANIC represents a special opportunity
for deep ocean scientific research and exploration.

(b) Purposes

The Congress declares that the purposes of sections
450rr to 450rr-6 of this title are:

(1) to encourage international efforts to designate the
R.M.S. TITANIC as an international maritime
memorial to those who lost their lives aboard her
in 1912;

(2) to direct the United States to enter into
negotiations with other interested nations to
establish an international agreement which will
provide for the designation of the R.M.S. TITANIC
as an international maritime memorial, and protect
the scientific, cultural, and historical
significance of the R.M.S. TITANIC;

(3) to encourage, in those negotiations or in other
fora, the development and implementation of
international guidelines for conducting research
on, exploration of, and if appropriate, salvage of
the R.M.S. TITANIC;

(4) to express the sense of the United States Congress
that, pending such international agreement or
guidelines, no person should physically alter,
disturb, or salvage the R.M.S. TITANIC in any
research or exploratory activities which are
conducted.

PART V

Titanic 1997:
From Mexico to Broadway

31

THE STORY OF *TITANIC*

James Cameron's Quest to Make the Ultimate *Titanic* Movie

[T]he most compelling reason that I wanted to do something about the *Titanic* was that in my research of it I got infused with the emotionalism of the tragedy. It really just struck me as this magnificent, incredibly sad, very emotional occurrence which was real and which was well understood and which, in a way, couldn't have been better. It was as if history wrote a great novel for us, and it was all right there. I thought there was an opportunity to do a film that captured the emotionalism, somehow, by using a kind of nonhistoric technique. In a way, it's a little bit heretical, but [it's] the idea that you use characters which are fictional to create an emotional reality for the audience, and then use that as a way into an emotional experiencing of the shipwreck, as opposed to one that was perfectly detailed, minute by minute, historically, but only that.

> —James Cameron, talking to Ken Marschall in the
> January 1988 issue of the *Titanic Commutator,* the
> official journal of the Titanic Historical Society

During his many promotional interviews for *Titanic,* director James Cameron told over and over the story of pitching the movie to Twentieth Century–Fox and yet, the saga never got stale. Why? Because the sheer impossibility of the tale made it all the more fascinating.

Cameron told the studio that he wanted to make a movie that would cost "north of" $100 million; that would run over three hours (which meant that theaters could only show it a limited number of times each day); that would be an elaborate historical period piece (meaning *scads* of costly costumes); that would not be able to use big-name stars because of the added expense they would incur, as well as the age of the characters; and that had absolutely no possibility for a sequel or merchandise tie-in products. Oh . . . and one more thing. Everyone already knows the end of the story.

This pitch had a lot "not to like" in it, and Cameron knew it. But this was, after all, James "*Aliens-Terminator 2-True Lies*" Cameron doing the pitching, and so Twentieth Century–Fox paid attention. They eventually expressed enough interest in the idea that Cameron decided to write a film treatment of his story. Cameron's *Titanic* film treatment—a gripping, one-hundred-sixty-nine-page epic—is what sealed (the movie) *Titanic*'s fate.

In a 1998 interview with Charlie Rose, Cameron said that the studio executives who read his *Titanic* treatment told him that they *hated* that they liked it so much, because now they knew they would have to go ahead and make the movie. And thus began a three-year odyssey that included a dozen trips to the bottom of the Atlantic to film the actual *Titanic*; building a replica of the great liner—at an amazing 92 percent scale—in Baja, Mexico; an arduous seven-month shoot for the cast (which included many of the cast and crew ending up in the hospital because someone deliberately laced their food with an hallucinogenic drug); Cameron giving back to the studio his director's salary and profit participation in order to complete the film (which ended up ultimately being delayed for almost six months); and a three-hour, fifteen-minute movie that went on to become the highest-grossing picture in history; and a movie that would win eleven Academy Awards, tying *Ben Hur* for the most Oscars ever won.

The movie's soundtrack became the biggest-selling movie soundtrack of all time, and within a couple of months of *Titanic*'s December 19, 1997, release, Leonardo DiCaprio, Kate Winslet, and James Cameron became members of the rabidly sought-after, A-list, Hollywood elite.

DiCaprio's salary grew tenfold—from $2.5 million for *Titanic* to a projected $25 million for his next picture (after the already-completed

The Man in the Iron Mask), and instant books on the young heartthrob appeared within weeks of the movie's release.

Kate Winslet went from being a relatively unknown British actress accustomed to making small films in the "Jane Eyre School of Film-making" to being an actress with a name recognizability factor equal to or surpassing that of actresses with decades more experience (and many more films) to their credit. Suddenly Winslet had a worldwide following, and was appearing on more magazine covers than a *Titanic* fan could keep track of. Web sites devoted to her sprang up overnight, and the tabloids devoted page after page to her love life, her up-and-down weight, and the relentless rumors about whether or not she and DiCaprio were really lovers during the making of *Titanic*. (Both Winslet and DiCaprio have consistently denied that they were, and they both sound credible.)

There were several catalysts that all worked in concert to convince James Cameron that he really wanted to do a film about the *Titanic* tragedy.

The first was simply watching the 1958 film *A Night to Remember* (based on Walter Lord's book) one night when he had nothing else to do. Watching that film planted the seed for Cameron. He had learned a little bit about the *Titanic* after meeting Dr. Robert Ballard in 1988 while doing research into deep-sea exploration for his 1989 movie, *The Abyss*. *A Night to Remember* got Cameron thinking about how the telling of the story of the *Titanic* would be different today with what is now known about the wreck, and by using advanced computer imaging techniques for the production.

According to Cameron, while all these ideas were percolating in his mind, he came across a copy of Don Lynch and Ken Marschall's defini-tive history of the *Titanic*, the spectacular book *Titanic: An Illustrated History*. After looking through this volume, Cameron told Ken Marschall in the *Titanic Commutator*, "the vividness of the imagery that you cre-ated made me realize that, with all the great new digital composite tech-nology that we have, we could actually realize those [paintings]. We could put people into those images, moving people, bring that to life. And that was exciting from a technical standpoint. So it all just kind of swarmed around in this soup stock of my creative unconsciousness for a while."

For Cameron, what "sealed the deal," so to speak, was receiving an invitation to a screening of the Imax film *Titanica*. Seeing the wreck so vividly in that acclaimed documentary made Cameron realize that he, too, could use actual footage of the *Titanic*, but in a *fictional* story, and, from that point on, it was just a matter of arranging the financing and rebuilding the *Titanic* from the ground up—simple things like that. (Oh, and also making his movie *True Lies* between the time he committed to a deal with the Russians to use their submersibles for the movie and actually writing the *Titanic* treatment.)

Titanic was originally scheduled for a summer 1997 release, but it was decided (with not a little bit of grumbling from the studio) that it would be pushed to December. As work on the film continued though 1996 and early 1997, everything ended up costing more than originally budgeted. "A lot of the overages on the picture," Cameron told Ken Marschall, "were attributable to things like the electrical budget and the transportation budget, things that weren't necessarily obvious going in. We never did anything that we didn't plan. We didn't build anything that we hadn't budgeted for. It's just that everything wound up costing more than we thought it was going to."

The budget overruns on the film resulted in Twentieth Century–Fox bringing in Paramount Pictures as a partner to help defray some of the astronomical costs of the production. After the film's budget broke the $100 million mark, Paramount signed on for $65 million—capped—in a deal that probably ended up being one of the most lucrative investments the studio ever made. As production continued, however, even $165 million wasn't enough to finish the film, and for a time there was even talk of pulling the plug on the epic—something Cameron absolutely refused to even consider. One story claims that Cameron told the studio that the only way they could cut his movie to prevent further outlays was to take the film away from him. He also told them that the only way they would be able to take his movie away from him was to kill him.

Now that's commitment, eh?

Cameron then reportedly stormed out of the meeting, and *Titanic*'s fate was, subsequently, a question mark.

After everyone's tempers cooled, Cameron came back to the table with a revolutionary offer. He would personally give up a total of approximately $30 to $35 million—his $10 million director's fee and the $25 or so million he could conceivably earn in profit participation on the film—in order to complete the movie the way he wanted to. Twentieth Century–Fox agreed, Cameron signed over his cut of *Titanic*, and the film was finally released on December 19, 1997.

As of the April 15, 1998, anniversary of *Titanic*'s sinking, *Titanic* had grossed worldwide in excess of $1.2 billion, and its projected total gross (after its video release and cable and network airings) would probably be close to $2 billion.

In late April 1998, a rumor circulated that Cameron would be receiving a bonus from Twentieth Century–Fox and Paramount for a sum somewhere between $75 and $110 million. Cameron later told the media that he would be taking a year off before tackling any new projects.

In March 1998, the Associated Press reported that a twelve-year-old Italian girl named Gloria from the town of Caselfranco Emilia had seen the movie *Titanic* every day since it had opened in December, and that she planned on continuing to attend the nine o'clock feature in the only movie theater in town, probably for as long as the movie played there. Gloria, who also had cats named Jack and Rose, was enamored with Leonardo DiCaprio's character of Jack Dawson and told the local newspaper *La Repubblica* that "Jack is cuter than Leo, and it's for real, it's a true story. That's what makes it so beautiful." The paper also reported that the theater had stopped charging Gloria for admission and was even saving a special seat for her each evening. Gloria's mother said she had no problem with her daughter's "hobby": "She's not doing anything bad."

Titanic's studios and James Cameron would more than likely agree.

TITANIC: THE LOST SCENES

I don't think I would have tried to take anyone's place. But if I saw the boats being launched half full, I think I would have gone into the cold water. There were four people who did what I like to think I'd have been smart enough to do, which is wait until the boats rowed away, then dive off the ship and swim over to a boat.

—James Cameron, *Esquire*, December 1997

There are serveral incarnations of a movie before it ends up on the screen. First, there is the *film treatment*, which looks like a movie script except that usually the scenes are not numbered and much of the dialogue is merely described but not provided.

James Cameron's treatment for *Titanic* is a one hundred sixty-nine-page monster that was the starting point for the shooting script he used to make the movie. In fact, Cameron's treatment is what convinced Twentieth Century–Fox to greenlight the project.

After selling the treatment, Cameron then wrote a *script* with more detailed scenes and dialogue, polishing and revising until he ended up with a final shooting script that became the bible of *Titanic*'s production.

There were approximately forty scenes from Cameron's *Titanic* film treatment that did not make it into the final film. It is probable that all or most of these "lost scenes" were actually shot for the movie and were deleted during editing for time and/or story flow. Cameron has said that he would someday like to release a Director's Cut of *Titanic* with anywhere from twenty to forty minutes of deleted material added back in. (He has released Director's Cuts of several of his earlier films, most notably *Terminator 2*.)

Cameron's Director's Cut of *Titanic* will likely generate some interesting debate since some of the eliminated scenes, if they had been included in the film, would have changed the final version of *Titanic*'s story somewhat.

- A crass line from Louis Bodine about Depends (adult diapers) following Rose's arrival, was cut from the film, as was a sequence focusing quite a bit on Daniel Marvin and his new bride. Also, J. Bruce Ismay's query in the Palm Court Restaurant about Freud was not a part of the original treatment.

- Jack's "air in my lungs" speech was quite different from the version that made it onto celluloid, and Rose's "so serious" comment (during the nude drawing scene) may actually have been a Kate Winslet ad-lib.

- A lengthy scene in the frantic wireless room was cut as was a scene in which a panicked Ismay confronts Fifth Officer Lowe.

- In the last scene, we are told that Rose lies "warm in her bunk. . . . She is very still. She could be sleeping, or something else." We then return with Rose to the *Titanic* where she and Jack meet again, except that in the final film, Rose goes *up* the staircase instead of Jack coming *down,* and the camera then pans up to the skylight of the grand staircase, as Jack and Rose's souls fly together into the light.

Comparing two different versions of such an important film is a fascinating exercise and illustrates quite dramatically the many changes a screenplay goes through before finally making it to your local cineplex. *Titanic* is a masterpiece in its final form and James Cameron made the changes he needed to in order for the film to work.

Perhaps the most significant change from Cameron's original version to the final film is Jack Dawson's joyous "I'm the king of the World" shout, which was *not* a part of Cameron's original treatment. Although as James Cameron (and his billions of *Titanic* viewers) now know, it *should* have been!

TITANIC BLUNDERS

The man who makes no mistakes does not usually make anything.

—Edward Phelps

Even a $200 million movie isn't perfect, as this list of *Titanic* blunders illustrates. But before you come down on me for nit-picking a masterpiece, let me assure you that this section is meant to be *fun,* and not to impugn James Cameron or his crew. The chronicling of historical events is a precarious endeavor, if only because facts can be checked. It is impossible to be completely accurate when working in nonfiction (trust me, this I know from firsthand experience) and these tiny bloopers are, in the big picture, trivial and irrelevant.

Still there's no denying that they sure are fun to pick out when watching a movie, and thus, this list is included with the best intentions and in a spirit of adulation. After all, if we didn't love *Titanic* as much as we all obviously do, we sure as hell would not spend the time to *study* it, now would we?

These goofs are listed chronologically and notated by the time at which they appear in the film, give or take a few seconds.(Set your VCR counter to zero as soon as the studio logo appears on-screen.) Special thanks to all who helped with this section, including the fine folks at the Internet Movie Database (imdb.com—put it on your "Favorites" list); Molly Brown biographer Kristen Iversen; *Last Dinner on the Titanic* authors Rick Archbold and Dana McCauley; and my brother Paul.

- During the opening newsreel footage, as the camera pans across the *Titanic*'s bow, a strip of land can be seen above the railing at a place where there should only be open sea.

- At :11, as Rose and Lizzy watch CNN's report about Brock Lovett's *Titanic* expedition, Cameron's camera crew can be seen very briefly reflected in Rose's TV.

- At :15, Rose tells Lovett and the others that the "Heart of the Ocean" pendant "was a dreadful heavy thing" and that she "only wore it this once" (referring to the time she wore it while posing naked for Jack). Later, though, we see Cal Hockley present Rose with the necklace and put it around her neck, making the number of times she wore it actually *two* instead of one.

- At :23, in the poker scene prior to the *Titanic*'s departure from Southampton, Jack Dawson's cards are briefly seen. Although some of his hand is obscured, three of the cards look like a 5, an 8, and a 4. Jack then draws *one* card and claims his winnings— tickets to America on the *Titanic*— with a full house. The only way he could have filled a full house, however, is if he already had two pair, which does not appear to be the case from the cards briefly visible.

- At :27, Jack and Fabrizio enter their steerage cabin and their bunks can be seen. The pipe frames supporting the bunks have set-screw speed-rail fittings, a pipe-fitting technique that apparently was not developed until 1946, thirty-five years after *Titanic* was constructed.

- At :28, Old Rose tells the *Keldysh* crew, "At Cherbourg a woman came aboard named Margaret Brown . . . but we all called her

Molly." Margaret Brown was *never* referred to as "Molly" until after her death. Kristen Iversen, author of a comprehensive 1998 biography of Molly Brown, told me, "Margaret Tobin Brown was never known as Molly; that was an invention of Hollywood. In fact, most of what people know of her life is from the Debbie Reynolds movie [*The Unsinkable Molly Brown*, 1964], which was ninety-nine percent pure invention!"

- At :29, Captain Smith and First Officer Murdoch are standing on the bridge in front of and to the right of the wheelhouse. The captain tells Murdoch, "Take her to sea Mister Murdoch. Let's stretch her legs." The sun is clearly to the left since the left side of Captain Smith's and Murdoch's faces are brightly lit. In the next scene, we see Murdoch entering the wheelhouse and his shadow is in *front* of him, meaning the sun is now *behind* him, which would put it to the *right* of Captain Smith, which is impossible.

- At :29, the gauges in the engine room are shown fitted with sweated tubing fittings. This plumbing procedure had not yet been developed in 1911, and at that time threaded brass fittings were still in use.

- At :33, Thomas Andrews, Molly Brown, Rose, Cal, and Ruth gather for lunch in the Verandah Café and Palm Court. In a memorable scene, Cal orders Rose's meal, telling the steward they'll "both have the lamb. Rare, with very little mint sauce." According to original White Star Line and *Titanic* menus from the period (reprinted in this volume), lamb with mint sauce was only available for dinner. The luncheon menu offered grilled mutton chops. Another possible blunder is having the group eating lunch in the Palm Court itself. According to the book *Last Dinner on the Titanic,* "There were actually two Verandah cafés, one on each side of the deck house just aft of the smoking room . . . Just how much use these rooms received as actual cafés is open to question. One of them seems to have been adopted primarily as a playroom for first-class children. But presumably, passengers could always order a snack or a cup of hot bouillon from an obliging steward."

- At :39, in response to Rose's question about the temperature of the water, Jack tells her, "Freezing. Maybe a couple of degrees over." The water temperature that night was actually a couple of degrees *below* freezing, although Jack may not have known this, and so calling this a blooper might be a bit of a stretch.

- At :39, Jack asks Rose if she's ever been to Wisconsin, and then tells her that when he was a boy, he and his father used to go ice fishing on Lake Wissota. Lake Wissota is a manmade lake that was not built until 1917.

- At :48, during the scene on the promenade deck the morning after Rose's failed suicide attempt, a hill with a building on it can be seen above Jack's left shoulder, which would mean the building (and the hill!) was floating somewhere in the North Atlantic.

- At :53, Jack tells Rose that he went to the "pier in Santa Monica" and drew portraits for ten cents. Construction of the Santa Monica Pier began in 1916, four years after the *Titanic* sank.

- At :54, spit miraculously appears on Jack's chin as he turns to meet Ruth and her lady friends. There was no spit on his face when he was facing the railing, and then after he turned, a glob was visible on the lower right of his chin. This is the glob that Molly Brown signals him to wipe off.

- At :56, camera equipment can be glimpsed (very) briefly reflected in the glass windows of the door held open for Jack as he arrives for his big dinner with the swells.

- At :59, Molly asks Jack if he'd care to escort a lady to dinner. He says, "Why, certainly," and she takes his arm. But then in the next scene, Jack and Molly can be seen still standing apart. Also, at 1:00, as Jack, Molly, and Rose approach John Jacob Astor (Molly calls out to him, "Hey, Astor!"), only Rose is on Jack's arm; Molly is seen walking by herself.

- At 1:13, Rose, Ruth, Cal, Molly and many other first-class passengers attend a worship service and sing the hymn, "Eternal Father, Strong to Save," (also known as "The Navy Hymn"). The two verses the group sing in the movie, however, were not written until 1937 by Robert Nelson Spencer, so the odds are against them all knowing the words in 1912. (The worshipers also sang a verse that began, "Lord, guard and guide the men who fly/Through the great spaces in the sky," which was written by Mary Hamilton in 1915.)

- At 1:14, Jack is prevented by stewards and Cal's valet Lovejoy from entering the First-Class Dining Room because he held a third-class ticket and his presence there was not "appropriate" (according to Lovejoy). Actually, the worship services held on the Titanic at 10:30 A.M. on Sunday, April 14, were open to all the passengers on the ship.

- At 1:20, a lighting error occurs in the scene when Rose "flies" from the ship's bow. From the *Internet Movie Database*: "During the scene when Rose 'flies' from the ship's bow, the sunlight is clearly falling almost exactly straight across the ship from left to right. On the evening of the 14th, early on in a 'Great Circle' voyage course, the ship would be sailing somewhere slightly between WSW and SW; the lighting in the movie would indicate that the sun is between SSE and SE, when it actually would have been between W and WNW." Also, Rose and Jack's faces are lit from obviously different angles during the scene.

- At 1:22, Bodine is wearing a white T-shirt and vest when earlier he had been wearing a "Smiley face with a bullet hole in his fore-head" T-shirt. Since Rose has been talking continuously, either this is a mistake, or Bodine left the imaging shack while Rose was telling her story to go change, which is highly unlikely, consider-ing the passion he obviously possessed for the whole *Titanic* legend.

- At 1:25, Rose pays Jack for her drawing with a dime some claimed was a *Roosevelt* dime, which would have been an error, since Roo-sevelt dimes had not yet been minted in 1912. The coin seen in the film, however, is now believed to actually be a *Barber* dime, which was minted between 1892 and 1916.

- At 1:26, an obviously older man's hands draws Rose. (They are actually the hands of director James Cameron, who was the artist responsible for the finished sketches.)

- At 1:27, a blood blister under Jack's thumbnail that had been visible earlier in the drawing scene miraculously disappears (because these were now probably DiCaprio's hands).

- At 1:29, it can clearly be seen that Captain Smith is wearing soft contact lenses, a convenience which would not be available for another fifty-nine years.

- At 1:31, Rose gives Lovejoy the finger and, contrary to blooper spotters' contention that this was anachronistic, the middle-finger gesture had been in use (meaning what it has always meant) since the late 1800s.

- At 1:31, Jack and Rose run through Boiler Room No. 6 to evade Lovejoy and then enter the cargo hold, where they find the Renault that they ultimately put to very good use. The only problem with this sequence of events is that there was no door on the *Titanic* that opened onto the cargo hold from Boiler Room No. 6, and even if there were, Jack and Rose would have ended up in a baggage hold *next door* to the hold where the Renault was stored.

- At 1:32, camera equipment can be briefly glimpsed reflected in the brass panel on the front of the Renault Jack and Rose make love in.

- At 1:38, just as the the *Titanic* is seconds away from striking the iceberg, First Officer Murdoch runs onto the bridge and bumps into Second Officer Lightoller, making him spill his tea. In reality, Lightoller was asleep in his bunk when the *Titanic* collided with the iceberg. In the chapter "Collision With an Iceberg" from his book *Titanic*, Lightoller wrote, "I was just about ready for the land of nod, when I felt a sudden vibrating jar run through the ship . . . I instantly leaped out of my bunk and ran out on deck, in my pajamas; peered over the port side, but could see nothing there; ran across to the starboard side, but neither was there anything there, and as the cold was cutting like a knife, I hopped back into my bunk." Lightoller remained in his bunk for the next half hour until summoned by Fourth Officer Boxhall.

- At 1:49, Harold Bride begins sending out the C.Q.D. distress signal on Captain Smith's order, yet what he clicks out is reportedly not intelligible Morse code.

• At 1:52, Jack is handcuffed to a pipe in the master-at-arms' office, which is shown as having a porthole. On the *Titanic,* however, the master-at-arms' office was actually an interior room on E deck, between cabins E201 and E1, at the end of Scotland Road. Jack would have had to have been in cabin E2 in order to have a porthole.

• At 1:53, bandleader Wallace Hartley assembles his musicians on the deck as the lifeboats are loaded and tells them, "Like the captain said, nice and cheery." Most of the histories of the *Titanic* have Hartley independently gathering his orchestra to play on deck as the lifeboats are loaded. Having the order to play come directly from Captain Smith is dubious at best.

• At 1:58, from outside the ship, we see the handcuffed Jack peering through the porthole in the master-at-arms' office. The porthole is seen as being completely below water, and yet a minute later, in a scene inside the room, the water line is visible several inches below the top of the porthole.

• At 2:03, Rose uses the heavy brass nozzle of a fire hose to break the glass of a cabinet containing a fire axe. Our Rose does a very good job of smashing out almost all of the glass in the door, leaving the axe completely exposed. However, in the next scene (only a split second later), as Rose is seen pulling the axe out of its holder, most of the glass is still in the door, including the top section of the door which has red lettering on it (that probably says something like, "In Case of Fire Break Glass").

• At 2:08, in the scene where Andrews confronts Lightoller about lowering the boats half full, visible breath from both men is present throughout the scene, except when Lightoller tells Andrews that they were not sure of the weight and were afraid that the boats would buckle. Since breath was digitally added to these exterior scenes, this seems to have been an omission.

• At 2:28, Rose and Jack come upon Thomas Andrews in the First-Class Smoking Lounge. Andrews is standing in front of the fireplace staring at the painting hung above it. On the *Titanic,* this painting was a work called *Approach to Plymouth Harbor,* painted especially for the *Titanic* by Norman Wilkinson. No photographs of this work exist, however, so in the film, a painting of New York Harbor was used instead. Also in this scene, Andrews's life belt is seen draped across the back of a sofa. It has been traditionally accepted that Andrews's life belt lay strewn across a card table as he stood awaiting his—and his *Titanic*'s—death.

- At 2:30, when Captain Smith enters the wheelhouse to await his death, the ship's telegraph is set to "Full Reverse" instead of "All Stop" (the handle straight up in the air), which was the order Smith had given at around 1:40.

- At 2:36, Cal escapes in a solid-bottom lifeboat that floats off as the *Titanic* goes down. In reality, none of the *Titanic*'s sixteen wood-bottom lifeboats floated off the ship. Two of the collapsible lifeboats floated off; the others were all lowered by ropes.

- At 2:53, Fifth Officer Lowe's voice echoes as he calls out to any of those still alive and afloat in the Atlantic. It is impossible for a voice to echo in the middle of the ocean unless there is something solid nearby off of which its sound can bounce.

- At 3:00, Rose is shown staring up at the Statue of Liberty from aboard the *Carpathia*. For her to be seeing the statue as she does, she supposedly would have had to have been standing on land.

- At 3:01, a close-up of the Statue of Liberty's torch is shown and it is the restored, post-1986 gold-leaf version, instead of the original amber stained-glass torch that was in use in 1912.

TITANIC: MUSIC FROM THE MOTION PICTURE

"Music to drown by. Now I know I'm in first class."
—Tommy Ryan, from the movie *Titanic*
(played by Jason Barry)

James Horner's score for *Titanic* is all I had hoped and prayed it would be and much more. It deftly leaps from intimacy to grandeur, from joy to heart-wrenching

sadness and across the full emotional spectrum of the film
while maintaining a stylistic and thematic unity. And most
importantly, he has made us one with Jack and Rose,
feeling the beat of their hearts as they experience the kind
of love we all dream about, but seldom find.

—James Cameron, from his liner notes
for the *Titanic* soundtrack

A music lover I know was surprised to learn that the *Titanic* soundtrack
was released on the Sony Classical label. "It's from a *movie*," he
protested, defining in four words the problem with eclectic creations like
Horner's *Titanic* compositions.

Is the soundtrack actually classical music? Well, no, it isn't; and yet
there are moments when the influence of Dvorak and Mahler can definitely be heard.

Is Horner's music, instead, New Age? A case can be made that New
Age (or perhaps, World Music?) is the category that best defines the
sound and "feel" of many of the fifteen tracks on the CD. In fact, James
Cameron specifically asked James Horner to listen to the music of New
Age songstress Enya as he was preparing to write the score, telling him
that he wanted an "Enya" feel to the music. Horner delivered on this
request and, in fact, "Southampton" (the second single released from
the soundtrack) could easily fit on any one of Enya's many albums.

Regardless of the label or labels used to describe James Horner's
evocative *Titanic* music, though, the bottom line is that the CD crossed
all barriers when it came to its purchasers: *Everyone* seemed to be buying
the soundtrack, and, even more amazingly, people were actually listening
to the entire CD, from the mournful Irish pipe opening of "Never an
Absolution" through the stately "Hymn to the Sea." Granted, many
people programmed their CD players so that the Celine Dion cut would
repeat a few times, but all of the soundtrack was embraced by *Titanic*
fans, and their devotion to the music (and their desire to relive the movie
experience) made the CD the biggest selling soundtrack in history.

In the spring of 1998, it was reported that the same teenage girls
who were seeing the movie over and over were also getting together
and having soundtrack listening parties at which a game was played to

see who cried first as the music carried them vicariously through Jack and Rose's story once again.

"We had no idea that it was going to do as well as it's done, in the same way the movie company didn't know it was going to do so well at the box office," said Peter Gelb, of Sony Classical.

By early April 1998, sales of the soundtrack had topped five million copies, according to the record industry research firm Soundscan. In fact, the soundtrack sold 847,662 copies during the week of Valentine's Day 1998, which was the fifth highest one-week sales total racked up by any CD since Soundscan began keeping records, in 1991.

One of the most popular cuts on the CD (and a smash hit on its own) was the aforementioned Celine Dion power ballad "My Heart Will Go On." James Cameron had adamantly told composer Horner that under no circumstances did he want a pop song playing over the end credits of *Titanic*. Horner at first resigned himself to this restriction, and yet, he could not resist putting together a song anyway. Horner and lyricist Will Jennings crafted a beautiful ballad based on instrumental themes Horner had written for the soundtrack (most notably the lovely melody for "Rose").

Horner then asked his friend, Canadian superstar Celine Dion, to cut a demo track of the song that he could take to Cameron. Celine agreed, but was a little nervous because of the secrecy surrounding the project. She added to her edginess by drinking two cups of coffee before recording the song (she usually drank only water) and later told *Entertainment Weekly*, "I couldn't control my voice. I was shaking and sweating; I could hear my knees." Dion also broke down in tears three-quarters of the way through the recording session because of the almost unbearable sadness attached to the song.

All of this emotional trauma paid off, however. "I'm glad I felt that way, because look what happened," Dion told *Entertainment Weekly*. Dion's caffeine-fueled recording of the song (the one on the soundtrack, not the slicker version on her own CD, *Let's Talk About Love*) literally drips with heartfelt emotion, and it convinced James Cameron to not only include it on the soundtrack CD, but to also allow it to be played over the movie's ending credits, something he swore he'd never do.

"It was mind-boggling how that song so captures the essence of Rose's character," Glen Brunman, executive director of Sony Music Soundtrax, told the Associated Press after the single became such a huge success. "You don't often have a melody that comes to define so much that was experienced. The song gives voice to the feelings throughout the movie."

James Horner, who won two Academy Awards for his work on *Titanic,* found a couple of other ways to capitalize on the movie's popularity. In the spring of 1998, Sony Music announced that James Horner and an orchestra would tour and perform the score to the movie, and, in the early fall of 1998, a second *Titanic* soundtrack would be released. This would contain music by the Irish band Gaelic Storm (seen in the movie in the steerage party scenes), as well as new *Titanic* music (composed by Horner and "inspired" by the film). The sequel CD also included versions of songs performed by the ship's orchestra as the ship was sinking, and a recording of "My Heart Will Go On" which included dialogue from the film. ("Southampton" also included dialogue from the movie.)

"Every time I have a conversation with a film company, they are trying to find a way of emulating or duplicating the success of *Titanic,*" Peter Gelb told the Associated Press.

The Tracks

1. "Never an Absolution" (3:03)
2. "Distant Memories" (2:24)
3. "Southampton" (4:02)
4. "Rose" (2:52)
5. "Leaving Port" (3:26)
6. " 'Take Her to Sea, Mr. Murdoch' " (4:31)
7. " 'Hard to Starboard' " (6:52)
8. "Unable to Stay, Unwilling to Leave" (3:57)
9. "The Sinking" (5:05)
10. "Death of *Titanic*" (8:26)
11. "A Promise Kept" (6:03)
12. "A Life So Changed" (2:13)
13. "An Ocean of Memories" (7:58)
14. "My Heart Will Go On" (love theme from *Titanic,* performed by Celine Dion) (5:11)
15. "Hymn to the Sea" (6:26)

CREDITS

Music composed and conducted by James Horner
Album produced by James Horner
Supervising music editor: Jim Henrikson
Music editor: Joe E. Rand
Assistant music editor: Lesley Langs
Music recorded and mixed by Shawn Murphy at Todd-AO Scoring Stage,
    Studio City, California
Assistant engineers: Andy Bass, David Marquette
Music preparation: Bob Bornstein
Orchestra contractor: Sandy De Crescent
Orchestrations by James Horner
Additional orchestrations by Don Davis

Vocals by SISSEL

Featured Instrumental Soloists:
    Simon Franglen
    Tony Hinnigan
    James Horner
    Randy Kerber
    Eric Rigler
    Ian Underwood

"My Heart Will Go On" (love theme from *Titanic*)
Music by James Horner
Lyrics by Will Jennings
Performed by Celine Dion
Produced by James Horner and Simon Franglen

FILM INDUSTRY AWARDS AND NOMINATIONS FOR *TITANIC*

Okay, so James Cameron shouting "I'm the king of the world" after *Titanic* won its 11th Academy Award was a *little* tacky, but can you blame him? Vindication, after all, *does* have a name, and his name is Oscar.

Here is a listing of all the major nominations and awards bestowed upon *Titanic*.

ACADEMY AWARDS

BEST ART DIRECTION AND SET DECORATION: Michael Ford (set decorator), Peter Lamont (art director)
BEST CINEMATOGRAPHY: Russell Carpenter
BEST COSTUME DESIGN: Deborah Lynn Scott
BEST DIRECTOR: James Cameron
BEST EFFECTS, SOUND EFFECTS EDITING: Tom Bellfort, Christopher Boyes
BEST EFFECTS, VISUAL EFFECTS: Thomas L. Fisher, Michael Kanfer, Mark A. Lasoff, Robert Legato
BEST FILM EDITING: Conrad Buff IV, James Cameron, Richard A. Harris
BEST MUSIC, ORIGINAL DRAMATIC SCORE: James Horner
BEST MUSIC, SONG: James Horner (music), Wilbur Jennings (lyrics), for the song "My Heart Will Go On," performed by Celine Dion
BEST PICTURE: James Cameron and Jon Landau, producers
BEST SOUND: Tom Johnson, Gary Rydstrom, Gary Summers, Mark Ulano

NOMINATED

BEST ACTRESS: Kate Winslet
BEST MAKEUP: Greg Cannon, Tina Earnshaw, Simon Thompson
BEST SUPPORTING ACTRESS: Gloria Stuart

AMERICAN CINEMA EDITORS

NOMINATED

BEST FEATURE FILM

AMERICAN SOCIETY OF CINEMATOGRAPHERS

OUTSTANDING ACHIEVEMENT IN CINEMATOGRAPHY IN THEATRICAL RELEASES: Russell Carpenter

BLOCKBUSTER ENTERTAINMENT AWARDS

FAVORITE ACTOR IN A DRAMA: Leonardo DiCaprio
FAVORITE ACTRESS IN A DRAMA: Kate Winslet

FAVORITE SUPPORTING ACTOR IN A DRAMA: Billy Zane
FAVORITE SUPPORTING ACTRESS IN A DRAMA: Kathy Bates

BOGEY AWARDS, GERMANY

BOGEY AWARD: *Titanic*

BROADCAST FILM CRITICS ASSOCIATION AWARDS

BEST DIRECTOR: James Cameron

NOMINATED

BEST PICTURE

CHICAGO FILM CRITICS ASSOCIATION AWARDS

BEST CINEMATOGRAPHY: Russell Carpenter
BEST ORIGINAL SCORE: James Horner

NOMINATED

BEST DIRECTOR: James Cameron
BEST PICTURE

DIRECTORS GUILD OF AMERICA

OUTSTANDING DIRECTORIAL ACHIEVEMENT IN MOTION PICTURES:
James Cameron

FLORIDA FILM CRITICS CIRCLE AWARDS

BEST CINEMATOGRAPHY: Russell Carpenter
BEST FILM

GOLDEN GLOBE AWARDS

BEST DIRECTOR—MOTION PICTURE: James Cameron
BEST MOTION PICTURE—DRAMA
BEST ORIGINAL SCORE—MOTION PICTURE: James Horner

BEST ORIGINAL SONG—MOTION PICTURE: James Horner (music), Will Jennings (lyrics), for the song "My Heart Will Go On"

NOMINATED

BEST PERFORMANCE BY AN ACTOR IN A MOTION PICTURE—DRAMA: Leonardo DiCaprio
BEST PERFORMANCE BY AN ACTRESS IN A MOTION PICTURE—DRAMA: Kate Winslet
BEST PERFORMANCE BY AN ACTRESS IN A SUPPORTING ROLE IN A MOTION PICTURE: Gloria Stuart
BEST SCREENPLAY—MOTION PICTURE: James Cameron

GOLDEN LAUREL AWARDS

MOTION PICTURE PRODUCER OF THE YEAR: James Cameron and Jon Landau

GOLDEN SATELLITE AWARDS

BEST DIRECTOR OF A MOTION PICTURE: James Cameron
BEST MOTION PICTURE—DRAMA: James Cameron, Jon Landau
BEST MOTION PICTURE ART DIRECTION: Peter Lamont
BEST MOTION PICTURE COSTUME DESIGN: Deborah Lynn Scott
BEST MOTION PICTURE FILM EDITING: Conrad Buff IV, James Cameron, Richard A. Harris
BEST MOTION PICTURE SCORE: James Horner
BEST ORIGINAL SONG IN A MOTION PICTURE: James Horner (composer), Will Jennings (lyricist), for the song "My Heart Will Go On," performed by Celine Dion

NOMINATED

BEST ACTOR IN A MOTION PICTURE—DRAMA: Leonardo DiCaprio
BEST ACTRESS IN A MOTION PICTURE—DRAMA: Kate Winslet
BEST MOTION PICTURE CINEMATOGRAPHY: Russell Carpenter
BEST MOTION PICTURE SCREENPLAY—ORIGINAL: James Cameron
BEST VISUAL EFFECTS IN A MOTION PICTURE: Robert Legato

LOS ANGELES FILM CRITICS ASSOCIATION

BEST PRODUCTION DESIGN: Peter Lamont

SCREEN ACTORS GUILD

OUTSTANDING PERFORMANCE BY A FEMALE ACTOR IN A SUPPORTING ROLE:
Gloria Stuart (tied with Kim Basinger for *L. A. Confidential*)

NOMINATED

OUTSTANDING PERFORMANCE BY A CAST

OUTSTANDING PERFORMANCE BY A FEMALE ACTOR IN A LEADING ROLE:
Kate Winslet

WRITERS GUILD OF AMERICA

NOMINATED

BEST SCREENPLAY WRITTEN DIRECTLY FOR THE SCREEN: James Cameron

32

A FIRST-CLASS CAST

> I wept flood buckets. Absolute buckets. It made it seem
> completely worth it. It's fantastic thinking that I've been
> such a big part of it, and it's probably going to go down
> in history. If anything, it almost frightens me.
>
> —Kate Winslet after first seeing *Titanic*
> (*Rolling Stone*, March 1998)

Titanic resurrected the career of a thirties film siren and transformed two young actors into global silver-screen superstars. For those interested in other films by the seven members of *Titanic*'s main cast, here is a selected look at these fine actors' filmography. (Also, see the section "*Titanic* Cast and Credits" for a complete listing of the entire cast of *Titanic*.)

Leonardo DiCaprio (Jack Dawson) *Critters 3* (1991); *This Boy's Life* (1993); *What's Eating Gilbert Grape* (1993); *The Basketball Diaries* (1994); *The Quick and the Dead* (1994); *Total Eclipse* (1995); and *The Man in the Iron Mask* (1998).
FILM CLIP: In 1998, after *Titanic* made DiCaprio a worldwide star of enormous magnitude, copies of his 1995 film *Total Eclipse* were reportedly pulled from video stores all across the country because the movie contained full frontal nude scenes of DiCaprio. When *Playgirl* magazine announced that they would be publishing stills from the film, DiCaprio sued to prevent them from printing these suddenly embarrassing pix.

Kate Winslet (Rose DeWitt Bukater)   *Heavenly Creatures* (1994); *A Kid in King Arthur's Court* (1995); *Sense and Sensibility* (1995); *Jude* (1996); *Hamlet* (1996); and *Hideous Kinky* (1998).

FILM CLIP: Kate Winslet smokes like a fiend, admits that picking her feet is a typical evening activity, and is inordinately proud of what she describes as her "big, huge flappers" (she's talking about her aforementioned tootsies). She also battles constantly with her weight (an early nickname for her in her 185-pound days was "Kate Weighs-a-Lot"); and she told James Cameron and his crew that during *Titanic's* flooded corridor scene, "if it suddenly looks like *Jaws*, the movie, it's my fault." "Think of it," she told *Rolling Stone*, "seven months, seven periods." The same month that *Titanic* opened, the "celebrity nudity" magazine *Celebrity Skin* published several full frontal nude photos of Winslet from her obscure 1996 film, *Jude.*

Billy Zane (Caledon Hockley)   Most prominent films include *Back to the Future* (1985); *Critters* (1986); *Back to the Future, Part 2* (1989); *Dead Calm* (1989); *Memphis Belle* (1990); *Orlando* (1992); *Posse* (1993); *Silence of the Hams* (1993); *Tombstone* (1993); *The Phantom* (1996); *Taxman* (1998); and *Susan's Place* (1999).

FILM CLIP: In the spring of 1998, Oprah Winfrey had James Cameron and some of the cast of *Titanic* on her daytime talk show, and when Billy Zane was introduced, he walked out carrying a baby doll and mischievously threw it at Cameron. Also, in 1986, in one of his earliest acting roles, Billy Zane appeared in the horror film *Critters*. Five years later, Zane's *Titanic* costar Leonardo DiCaprio would later appear in the second sequel to *Critters* (*Critters 3*). In early 1998, Zane completely shaved his head and made a number of media appearances (including Howard Stern's radio program and E! show, and the *Live With Regis and Kathie Lee* show) completely bald and wearing sunglasses.

Kathy Bates (Margaret "Molly" Brown)   Most prominent films include *Straight Time* (1978); *Come Back to the Five and Dime, Jimmy Dean, Jimmy Dean* (1982); *The Morning After* (1986); *Men Don't Leave* (1989); *Roe vs. Wade* (1989); *Dick Tracy* (1990); *Misery* (1990); *White Palace* (1990); *At Play in the Fields of the Lord* (1991); *Fried Green Tomatoes* (1991); *Prelude to a Kiss* (1992); *Dolores Clai-*

borne (1994); *North* (1994); *Diabolique* (1996); and *The Late Shift* (1996).

FILM CLIP: Even though no one actually referred to Kathy Bates's *Titanic* character Margaret Brown as Molly until well after her death, Bates's portrayal of the flamboyant and earthy Colorado millionairess Molly Brown is one more in a string of brilliant performances by the Oscar winning actress (for *Misery*). Adding to her performance was the fact that Bates bears an absolutely uncanny resemblance to the actual Molly Brown.

Frances Fisher (Ruth DeWitt Bukater)   Most prominent films include *Can She Bake a Cherry Pie?* (1983); *Patty Hearst* (1988); *Lucy and Desi: Before the Laughter* (1991); *Unforgiven* (1992); and *The Stars Fell on Henrietta* (1994).

FILM CLIP: In March 1998, Frances Fisher took the syndicated entertainment show *Access Hollywood* on a tour of the Rosarito compound where *Titanic* had been filmed. The ship was gone, the massive tank was drained, and there was an air of sadness surrounding the place as she walked through the many locations where scenes from the movie had been filmed. But since Twentieth Century–Fox had built the studio facility for repeated use, the production buildings and trailers were still standing and in use. When Fisher took the cameras into the makeup trailer, she broke into tears because, revealingly, *that* was where the cast and crew had spent the most time together—not on the sets during shooting.

Bernard Hill (Capt. Edward J. Smith)   Most prominent films include *The Bounty* (1984); *Shirley Valentine* (1989); and *Mountains of the Moon* (1990).

FILM CLIP: In April 1998, Bernard Hill hosted a new television documentary about the *Titanic* called *Titanic: Secrets Revealed*, in which new information about the watertight doors was revealed. (See chapter 21.) Interestingly, Hill seems to have taken sides in the Ballard vs. Tulloch, antisalvage vs. prosalvage debate that continues to rage about the fate of the *Titanic*. At the conclusion of the documentary, Hill praised George Tulloch's organization, RMS Titanic, for maintaining the *Titanic*'s legacy with dignity and respect. This was something of a surprise, since James Cameron seems to be firmly on the side of the antisalvage faction of *Titanic* Rivet Heads. (Cameron consulted Don Lynch and Ken Marschall for the making of the film and appeared with Dr. Ballard after the film opened.) It must be assumed that even though Hill worked for Cameron, his position regarding the wreck is prosalvage.

Gloria Stuart (Old Rose)   Most prominent films include *The Old Dark House* (1932); *The Invisible Man* (1933); *Roman Scandals* (1933); *The Poor Little Rich Girl* (1936); *Rebecca of Sunnybrook Farm* (1938); *It Could Happen to You* (1939); *The Three Musketeers* (1939); *The Two Worlds of Jenny Logan* (1979); and *My Favorite Year* (1982). FILM CLIP: Gloria Stuart was eighty-seven years old when she was nominated for an Academy Award for Best Supporting Actress for her performance as the one hundred one-year-old Rose in *Titanic*, making her the oldest actor ever nominated for an Oscar. Not too bad after a hiatus from acting of sixty years or so (except for a couple of small roles in between), eh?

IN THEIR OWN WORDS: CAMERON, DICAPRIO, WINSLET, AND ZANE TALK ABOUT *TITANIC*

Here is a sampling of some of the things Cameron and prominent cast members had to say about the making of the most expensive—and most successful—movie of all time (these quotes are taken from the electronic press kit sent to the media upon the film's release.)

JAMES CAMERON

Before James Cameron could create characters from 1912, he had to understand the people of 1912. Here he talks about what it was like to live in that halcyon, pre–World War I, pre-*Titanic* era:

The sense was that they were in this shining, golden upward spiral of progress and that everything was only going to get better and better and nicer and nicer. Now we have electric light, and we have subways, and we have flying machines, and we have transatlantic travel through the power of steam—which is what the *Titanic* represents—and the telephone had just been invented, and movies were brand new, and people were excited by that; [and] the recording of music for the first time, wireless telecommunication. All of these things, which we, of course, take utterly for granted, were new at that time. So there was this tremendous optimism and this tremendous excitement.

What did the sinking of the *Titanic* actually mean? Here, Cameron discusses the deeper truths that can be revealed from a study of the disaster—and by looking at the human arrogance that caused it:

> We [must] understand and absorb the message of the warning against putting our faith optimistically in technology, and more importantly, putting our faith optimistically in the application of technology by flawed human systems, because it was really human failures that sank the *Titanic*, not the ship itself. The technology itself was fine. It was the state of the art at that time. *Titanic* was a well-made ship. It's hard to criticize its mode of fabrication. It was just piloted into an iceberg in the middle of the ocean. It wasn't meant to survive that, so there are many, many metaphors that can be gleaned from the *Titanic* and that, I think, accounts for [the] continuing fascination for the public at large with a disaster that happened eighty-five years ago.

Here, Cameron explains his thought process regarding re-creating the *Titanic*'s sinking:

> So we've got the wreck, we know what it looks like, we've been there, we've photographed it. And we've got what people said they saw as it sank. And I drew lines between those two things and that's what the film represents.

Cameron reads history for enjoyment, and here he explains the critical leap of empathy students of history need to make in order for the past to fascinate us the way he believes it should:

> The second you realize that it was real people who had the same emotions that we do, who felt the same pain, the same joy, the same love, that we feel right now, that they just expressed it in different words and different phrases and they dressed funny . . . the second you get that, then history becomes very, very interesting.

LEONARDO DICAPRIO

Leonardo DiCaprio had to give a great deal of thought as to how to bring Jack Dawson to life, and here he reveals that Jack's memorable sensitivity was anything but spontaneously arrived at:

He definitely senses interest from her [Rose's] standpoint, but I don't think Jack would be the type of guy that imposes [himself] or pressures her to go for something that she isn't comfortable with. And I think he . . . gives her the space, and allows her to make that decision on her own.

Many have said that working with James Cameron can be a surreal experience, and it seems as though Leonardo DiCaprio agrees wholeheartedly with that assessment:

[The stern was] completely vertical, and we were just sitting there, and all of a sudden I see Jim on a crane going up, with the whole night sky [around him], going another hundred feet in the air with his camera, [and] sort of leaning over . . . with the camera right above me. And I'm looking up at him and I just asked myself, how did I get here? What sort of turns did I make in my life to be *here*, at this present moment? Just looking at the whole situation was completely surreal. It was completely bizarre.

James Cameron may make headlines for the technical aspects of his many films, but to his cast, he is also unquestionably a dedicated "actors'" director. Here DiCaprio discusses working with Jim:

Jim is certainly unlike anybody I've ever worked with. I think he really not only understands the technical side of how to make something look *unbelievable*, but throughout all his films, he's really had a lot of concentration on performances, too. But, at the same time, he's *extremely* demanding.

KATE WINSLET

If there's *anyone* who should know what English people should look like, it's an English actress, right? Here, Kate Winslet talks about the authenticity of *Titanic*'s Southampton boarding scene.

[When] the boarding scene at Southampton begins . . . it looks *extraordinary*. It looks so real, I couldn't believe it. And the number of people . . . I'd never done *anything* where there'd been so many extras before. And everyone looked so *real*, they looked so *English*; I mean it really did.

Here Kate Winslet reveals that she also gave a great deal of thought to Rose and Jack's relationship before she started filming their many scenes together:

They share so much of the same sort of passion for so many different things in life—which he already has. And she is aspiring to have those things, but they're in her dream world, and [yet] they're right in front of her. And she falls in love with him, *and* with them, and goes with it.

Titanic was the first film in which two actresses were nominated for Academy Awards for playing the same character. Here, Kate Winslet talks about meeting the woman who would be playing the "older" her:

> I was desperate to know who was going to be playing the older me, and I was told it was Gloria Stuart. It was just fascinating to me to meet this lady who had so much to talk about. She'd known so many incredible people. She was great friends with the Marx Brothers, and she was showing me pictures of herself and things that she'd done and people that she'd met and telling me tremendous stories about naughty things she'd got up to, and she had so much life and so much exuberance and the same passion for this film as I had.

BILLY ZANE

Here Billy Zane—the wealthy *Titanic* villain we loved to hate—talks about how impressed he was with the Academy Award–winning interior set decoration for *Titanic:*

> The interior set decorating is just to die for; it's fantastic. There's so much detail in the molding and the fabrics. And apparently some of the carpet that was in the dining room was actually spun off of the original pattern from the company that made the carpeting for the *Titanic,* which is pretty impressive.

Titanic was an extremely long shoot, and here Billy Zane gives credit where credit is due . . . to the long-suffering extras!:

> We had the most dedicated corps of extras, who put up with what it took to make this movie, which was long hours in the cold, in the water, standing around, emoting, screaming, running, hiding, jumping. And the spirit was just incredible.

Here Billy Zane discusses the meaning of "Jimspeak," which also might explain why *Titanic*'s budget went, ahem, a tad over budget:

> On the page it says, "Cal looks over the railing to see Boat 14 be lowered into the water." Now, in "Jimspeak," that means basically,

"All right, now give me five hundred people and sixty technical elements working." It was full-on, and that's the case with every scene. There's always something amazing going on beyond what was, certainly, written in brief.

TITANIC CAST AND CREDITS

Release Date: Friday, December 19, 1997
Produced by: Twentieth Century–Fox, Lightstorm Entertainment, and Paramount Pictures
MPAA Certification: PG-13
MPAA Reasons: Rated PG-13 for disaster-related peril and violence, nudity, sensuality, and brief language.
Languages: French, English, German, Swedish
Running Time: 195 minutes
Sound Mix: DTS 70mm, DTS, Dolby Digital, SDDS
Distributed by: Twentieth Century–Fox
Effects by:
  Digital Domain (special visual effects and digital animation)
  4-Ward Productions
  Matte World Digital
  Pacific Titles and Optical (additional visual effects)
  POP Film
  Perpetual Motion Pictures (additional visual effects)
  Banned From the Ranch Entertainment
  Video Image (additional visual effects)
  CIS Hollywood
  Donald Pennington, Inc.
  Cinesite
  Title House (additional effects)
  Digiscope (additional visual effects)
  Hammerhead Productions, Inc.
  Industrial Light and Magic
  Light Matters, Inc.
  USA 1997 Color (DeLuxe)
Advertising Copy Tag Lines:
  Collide with destiny.
  Nothing on Earth could come between them.
Also Known As: *Planet Ice* (1996) (fake working title)
Directed by: James Cameron

CAST

Leonardo DiCaprio	Jack Dawson
Kate Winslet	Rose DeWitt Bukater
Billy Zane	Cal Hockley
Kathy Bates	Molly Brown
Frances Fisher	Ruth DeWitt Bukater
Bernard Hill	Capt. Edward J. Smith
Jonathan Hyde	J. Bruce Ismay
Danny Nucci	Fabrizio De Rossi
David Warner	Spicer Lovejoy
Bill Paxton	Brock Lovett
Gloria Stuart	Old Rose
Victor Garber	Thomas Andrews
Suzy Amis	Lizzy Calvert
Lewis Abernathy	Lewis Bodine
Nicholas Cascone	Bobby Buell
Dr. Anatoly M. Sagalevitch	Anatoly Milkailavich
Jason Barry	Tommy Ryan
Ewan Stewart	First Officer Murdoch
Ioan Gruffudd	Fifth Officer Lowe
Jonathan Phillips	Second Officer Lightoller
Mark Lindsay Chapman	Chief Officer Wilde
Richard Graham	Quartermaster Rowe
Paul Brightwell	Quartermaster Hitchens
Ron Donachie	Master-at-Arms
Eric Braeden	John Jacob Astor
Charlotte Chatton	Madeleine Astor
Bernard Fox	Col. Archibald Gracie
Michael Ensign	Benjamin Guggenheim
Fannie Brett	Madame Aubert
Jenette Goldstein	Irish Mommy
Camilla Overbye Roos	Helga Dahl
Linda Kerns	Third-Class Female Passenger
Amy Gaipa	Trudy Bolt
Martin Jarvis	Sir Duff Gordon
Rosalind Ayres	Lady Duff Gordon

Rochelle Rose	Countess of Rothes
Jonathan Evans-Jones	Wallace Hartley
Brian Walsh	Irish Man
Rocky Taylor	Bert Cartwell
Alexandrea Owens	Cora Cartwell
Simon Crane	Fourth Officer Boxhall
Edward Fletcher	Sixth Officer Moody
Scott G. Anderson	Lookout Frederick Fleet
Martin East	Lookout Lee
Craig Kelly	Marconi Operator Harold Bride
Gregory Cooke	Marconi Operator Jack Phillips
Liam Tuohy	Chief Baker Joughin
James Lancaster	Father Byles
Elsa Raven	Ida Strauss
Lew Palter	Isidor Strauss
Reece P. Thompson III	Irish Little Boy
Laramie Landis	Irish Little Girl
Alison Waddell	Cal's Crying Girl
Amber Waddell	Cal's Crying Girl
Mark Rafael Truitt	Yaley
John Walcutt	First-Class Husband
Terry Forrestal	Chief Engineer Bell
Derek Lea	Leading Stoker Barrett
Richard Ashton	Carpenter John Hutchinson
Sean M. Nepita	Elevator Operator
Brendan Connolly	Scotland Road Steward
David Cronnelly	Crewman
Garth Wilton	First-Class Waiter
Martin Laing	Promenade Deck Steward
Richard Fox	Steward No. 1
Nick Meaney	Steward No. 2
Kevin Owers	Steward No. 3
Mark Capri	Steward No. 4
Marc Cass	Hold Steward No. 1
Paul Herbert	Hold Steward No. 2

Emmett James	First-Class Steward
Christopher Byrne	Stairwell Steward
Oliver Page	Steward Barnes
James Garrett	*Titanic* Porter
Erik Holland	Olaf Dahl
Jari Kinnunen	Bjorn Gunderson
Anders Falk	Olaus Gunderson
Martin Hub	Slovakian Father
Seth Adkins	Slovakian Three-Year-Old Boy
Barry Dennen	Praying Man
Vern Urich	Man in Water
Rebecca Jane Klingler	Mother at Stern
Tricia O'Neil	Woman
Kathleen S. Dunn	Woman in Water
Romeo Francis	Syrian Man
Mandana Marino	Syrian Woman
Van Ling	Chinese Man
Bjorn	Olaf
Dan Pettersson	Sven
Shay Duffin	Pub Keeper
Greg Ellis	*Carpathia* Steward
Diana Morgan	News Reporter
Ferenc Szedlák	String Ensemble Member (The I Salonisti Ensemble)
Werner Giger	String Ensemble Member (The I Salonisti Ensemble)
Thomas Füri	String Ensemble Member (The I Salonisti Ensemble)
Lorenz Hasler	String Ensemble Member (The I Salonisti Ensemble)
Béla Szedlák	String Ensemble Member (The I Salonisti Ensemble)
Kris Andersson	Dancer

Bobbie Bates..	Dancer
Aaron James Cash....................................	Dancer
Anne Fletcher	Dancer
Ed Forsyth...	Dancer
Andie Hicks...	Dancer
Scott Hislop..	Dancer
Stan Mazin	Dancer
Lisa Ratzin...	Dancer
Julene Renee..	Dancer
James Cameron..	Brief cameo in steerage dance scene (uncredited)
Aimee Amanda Garten............................	Young Female First-Class Passenger (uncredited)
Jo Lynn Garten	Older Female Second-Class Passenger (uncredited)
Don Lynch...	Man Playing With Top With Child (uncredited)
Francisco Váldez......................................	Man Being Combed for Lice (uncredited)
Peter J. White...	Third Officer Groves (uncredited)

Written by: James Cameron
Cinematography: Russell Carpenter
Music: James Horner
Production Design: Peter Lamont
Costume Design: Deborah Lynn Scott (as Deborah L. Scott)
Film Editing: Conrad Buff IV, James Cameron, Richard A. Harris
Produced by: James Cameron, Pamela Easley (associate); Al Giddings (coproducer); Grant Hill (coproducer); Jon Landau; Sharon Mann (coproducer); Rae Sanchini (executive)

33

Returning to *Titanic*

Bringing the Past to Life
With State-of-the-Art Special Effects

A rigorous philosophy of absolute correctness permeated
every department, from Set Design and Construction,
through Decorating, Props, Wardrobe, Hairdressing, and
Visual Effects. In addition to how things looked, every
nuance of human behavior had to be examined. How
people moved, how they spoke, their etiquette, how the
ship's crew would have performed its routine and
emergency duties . . . all these things had to be known
before a single scene could be staged.

> —James Cameron, from his foreword to
> *James Cameron's Titanic*

Pictures Under Pressure

Before James Cameron started work on *Titanic*, he made a series of
twelve dives to the real *Titanic*, at a cost to Twentieth Century–Fox of
around $3 million. After Cameron completed his twelfth dive to the
wreck, he realized that he had spent more time with the ship than had
any of her ill-fated passengers or crew. Cameron wanted footage of the
wreck to use in his planned *Titanic* movie and he also wanted to see for
himself what the doomed leviathan looked like, sitting there in two

pieces on the ocean floor, the bow stately and grave; the stern, a crumpled mass of twisted steel.

To prepare for the dives, model makers at Digital Domain, the effects company founded by Cameron, along with Scott Ross and Stan Winston, constructed a twelve-foot-long model of the *Titanic* for Cameron to use as a reference. The model was just the first of many incarnations of the *Titanic* that would be built—both in the real world and in the confines of cyberspace—in order to fulfill Cameron's vision of recreating *Titanic* on-screen—with a verisimilitude never before achieved on film.

There were two big problems attached to Cameron's goal of capturing authentic *Titanic* footage on film for use in his movie, and both ultimately required that groundbreaking equipment actually be built for the dives. The first problem was somehow giving Cameron access to areas of the ship where the large Russian submersible *Keldysh,* commissioned for the dives, would not fit. This required building a revolutionary tethered, remotely operated vehicle (ROV), in which a video camera could be mounted. The ROV would be able to glide around the *Titanic*'s deck and also enter the ship if it came across an accessible entranceway. Cameron knew that actual footage of the interior of the *Titanic* would be a priceless addition to the film.

The other problem was the camera that would go inside the ROV. It had to be a custom-designed camera that would allow a standard film load to last twice as long as it would in a standard format. (You can't reload a camera two-and-a-half miles below the surface.) Even with this doubling, though, the actual run time of a film load was only fifteen minutes.

At the depth at which Cameron would be shooting, the pressure was 6,600 pounds per square inch. To handle this kind of pressure, the glass that covered the front port of the ROV's titanium camera housing had to be seven inches thick. Even with this thickness, the danger of the glass failing was something engineer and camera designer Mike Cameron, James Cameron's brother, thought about constantly. James Cameron explained to *Cinefex* magazine that if the glass port failed, "water would race down inside of the tube, probably exceeding hypersonic velocity before it reached the back of the housing and demolish the camera down to a molecular level. Worse, the stainless steel end cap would then blow off with the kinetic energy of a cannon shell and go right through the sphere of the submarine. So our lives depended on that glass not shattering."

For safety, Mike Cameron instructed his brother to never have the back end of the camera housing pointing towards the sub. "Mike," James replied, "the back of the housing is *always* going to be pointing toward the sub, because the camera's going to be pointing *away* from the sub. That's the whole idea!"

Fortunately, Mike Cameron's thick glass performed beautifully and his brother got the footage he wanted, some of which is seen in the final film. In an interview with Larry King, Cameron talked about which real *Titanic* footage he used, noting that it can easily be determined which scenes of the ship are of the model and which are of the actual wreck: Any scenes that have both the wreck and the ROV in it were done on a model. (They would have needed two remotely-operated cameras to get both in one shot.) Any scenes of just the wreck alone are of the real *Titanic*.

FIRST THOUGHTS

After Cameron's dives, he and producer Jon Landau began to think about how they were actually going to depict the *Titanic* on-screen.

"We were faced with a unique dilemma," Landau told *Cinefex*. "We had to show a pristine ship sailing the ocean, and then we had to show it sinking. If we had to deal with only one of these elements, it would have been a hundred times easier—but we were faced with both."

James Cameron initially believed that in order for the movie to look real, they would have to shoot out on the open sea. He decided to look into building a massive *Titanic* set on a great tanker and shooting off the shores of Poland or Sweden because of the rich light in those locations. At first Poland looked so promising that Cameron and Landau actually talked to shipbuilders in Gdansk about constructing their talked-about "sea-going" *Titanic* set.

In concert with their plans for constructing the "presinking" *Titanic*, they began to discuss ways of shooting the sinking. Prior cinematic attempts to show the foundering of the great vessel ultimately fell short when it came to visual believability. Earlier filmmakers had always used models, and the sinking usually looked like you were watching a toy boat sink in a big tank. Cameron would have none of that. He was adamant that the sinking not be done solely with miniatures. He wanted to be able to show the actors on the ship as it went down.

Since the "portable" set atop the tanker was still how they planned to show the ship during the first few days of its voyage, they figured they would have to dismantle this structure after shooting these scenes and reassemble it in a tank where they could then submerge it. The biggest problem with this plan was that the largest tank facility in the world—on the island of Malta in the Mediterranean—was too small. They did give thought to modifying the Malta tank to fit their needs, but that would have involved Twentieth Century–Fox investing a lot of money in someone else's facility, and then walking away from it at the end of shooting. Cameron and Landau then considered filling an abandoned quarry or pit mine with water, but that idea was rejected as well.

As is often the case with seemingly insurmountable problems, though, leaps of creative brainstorming often provide a solution, and this time it was Digital Domain's groundbreaking work with "digital water" that gave them their answer.

They began to consider the possibility that maybe they didn't have to shoot the scenes of the ship at sea actually out at sea. And the studio also made it clear that if they were going to invest big bucks in a stage and tank facility, it would be nice to end up with a permanent Twentieth Century–Fox asset at the end of the day.

A BIG DECISION

The decision was finally made to purchase land, build a tank facility and studio compound, and construct a (nearly) full-size *Titanic* that would be made to appear out to sea when necessary through the magic of Digital Domain's new computer-generated water. The final result was that Cameron's epic film would be made, and Twentieth Century–Fox would end up with a superb studio facility that could be used for future film projects. (Some industry insiders estimate the cost of the digital effects in *Titanic* to be over 30 percent of the film's $200 million budget—or around $60 million.)

In June 1996, Twentieth Century–Fox bought a forty-acre parcel of land near Rosarito, Mexico, thirty miles south of San Diego on the Baja,

California, peninsula. The site consisted of one hundred acres, and Fox optioned the remaining sixty acres for possible future expansion. Principal photography on *Titanic* was scheduled to begin in September 1996, and thus the "one hundred-day studio" was constructed on the site—in, amazingly, about a hundred days.

The entire facility ultimately consisted of four stages:

Stage 1 was a massive 8½-acre tank (it had three water depths—3½ feet, 15 feet, and 40 feet) fronting the ocean in which the *Titanic* copy would be built and sunk. Cameron and company had a twenty-five-foot model of the *Titanic* built in order to determine the exact position of this enormous set. Cameron used lipstick cameras to figure out shots and see what the ship would look like against the ocean background. It was decided to face the ship to the north into the area's prevailing winds so that the smoke from the three functional funnels would stream backwards, making the ship look like it was barreling along at 20 or so knots.

Stage 2 was a smaller thirty-foot-deep tank in which the First-Class Dining Saloon was built. During the sinking scenes, this set allowed the dining saloon to be lowered into the water, providing a truly realistic rendering of the actual event.

Stages 3 and 4 were smaller and more conventional sets that were used for many of the other scenes set in the interior of the ship.

For the exterior of the ship, they ended up building the four funnels, the bridge, the boat deck, the boat deck's promenade deck, the forward and aft well decks, and the poop deck. They did not build the forecastle deck (the fo'c'sle), and Cameron later realized that they probably should have, since it took more time and money to shoot around the fact that it wasn't there than it would have cost to actually have built it. According to Cameron, "it turned out to be more of a pain in the ass not to have built it than to have built it."

The final constructed ship was 10 percent smaller than the original *Titanic*. They cut out eighteen-foot slices between each of the smokestacks and also removed a twenty-foot slice from the poop deck. They also reduced the size of the masts and smokestack funnels, and slightly reduced the size of the sixteen wooden lifeboats and the Wellin lifeboat davits so that everything would line up as it did on the original *Titanic*. (Cameron hired the Wellin Co., the firm that built the davits for the original *Titanic*, to build the davits for his cinematic *Titanic*. Davits are the pulley devices used to lower lifeboats to the water.)

The final ship was approximately 775 feet long (the real *Titanic* was

882½) and was in two sections, joined between the second and third funnels. Also, Cameron's crew built only the starboard (right) side of the ship and later "flopped" the film (as in a mirror image) for scenes requiring them to show the port (left) side of the ship.

The final ship required five hundred Mexican and American workers to build, and yet, after it was completely painted and essentially finished, to everyone's horror, it still looked like a model on film. According to supervising art director Charles Lee, "I tell you, after building something seven hundred feet long, we were pretty damned determined it was *not* going to look like a model." They decided that the problem was with the portholes: They looked too uniform and appeared fake-looking on film.

This was remedied with some truly creative thinking on the part of Lee and his team. They scanned photographs of the interior rooms of the *Titanic* and her sister ship the *Olympic* into a computer, colorized them, blew them up to fit specific portholes, and then placed them digitally behind the ship's portholes—in most cases precisely where they would have been on the actual ship. The result was breathtaking and gave the ship the realistic look they were all initially hoping for.

The majority of the film would ultimately be shot on this life-size *Titanic* and its surrounding stages, except for a few scenes on the Atlantic off the coast of Nova Scotia for the scenes of the *Keldysh* at sea; a few interiors shot in a converted warehouse in Halifax (for the *Keldysh*'s imaging shack and lab scenes); and a couple of days in Malibu for the scenes of Rose at home.

Cameron also did a one-day shoot aboard the S.S. *Lane Victory* (he chartered it for the day) to shoot authentic bow and stern wakes which would later be incorporated into Digital Domain's many digital water-effects shots.

TITANIC'S UNFORGETTABLE MOMENTS

There are countless images and scenes in *Titanic* where we truly believe we are seeing something impossible: How in the name of heaven, our rational mind wonders, was James Cameron able to travel back in time and record what we are seeing now? Where, in fact, do you buy a time machine these days anyway? How much do they cost? About $200 million??

The visual impact of *Titanic* is astonishing and will be studied for years to come. When filmgoers learn after the fact that almost all of the ocean seen in the movie is computer-generated and that hundreds of the people on the *Titanic*'s deck were likewise created digitally, it becomes a challenge to figure out what is real and what is not.

Some of the scenes in the movie are so realistic, people begin to question their own sanity when told that none of what they saw as real actually existed in reality. L.A. screenwriter James Cole (*Last Rung on the Ladder*, *Stereopticon*) was one of many in the industry who were very impressed with Cameron's recreation of the *Titanic:* "As the film began, I figured I'd be able to spot all the effects shots," he told me. "But once the submersibles crested *Titanic*'s bow and shined their lights on the wreck, I realized it wasn't going to be that easy. At first I'd think, 'There. That has to be the miniature,' then a second later I'd be unsure."

For many people, it's the engine room scene that is the last straw. The scenes in the engine room are so realistic that some find it impossible to fathom how such verisimilitude could be created on a computer screen and with miniature models. One young guy I know could not stop talking about the giant pistons in the engine room, wondering how they built them.

The scene in question lovingly depicts the *Titanic*'s engine room immediately after Captain Smith gives the order, "Take her to sea, Mr. Murdoch." (In fact, in the script, the sequence that includes the engine room scenes is titled "Ode to *Titanic*.")

This scene was a combination of live foreground elements, a partially raised platform and scaffold set with green-screen walls, composited with a full miniature set, all digitally composited to blend everything together seamlessly. The engine room scene is truly one of the most impressive sequences in the film. And yet, it is just one of many.

Here is a ranking—in order of visual impact, overall memorability, and sheer beauty—of the dozen most unforgettable scenes in *Titanic*. Note: This list is ranked in reverse order; therefore, the last scene description you will read is the one I consider to be the most memorable in the movie.

12. **The Face in the Bow** I'm not even sure this image was intentional, but the first time we see the front hull of the *Titanic* wreck (from Brock Lovett's submarine), a ghostly face can be

made out in the shape of the bow and in the fittings on the hull plates. Regardless of whether or not the bow was digitally enhanced to provide an eerie subliminal kick, or this is how the bow really looks, it is, indeed, quite something to see.

11. **The *Titanic* Seen Through the Pub Window**   The effects for this scene (the scene in which Jack wins his *Titanic* tickets in a "lucky hand of poker") were done almost solely with miniatures and photographic special effects, and yet the end result is seamless. Neither the pub (as a building) nor the *Titanic* in this scene are real, but the sequence works beautifully. A seventeen-foot wide photo blowup of Digital Domain's forty-foot *Titanic* model was mounted on rigid backing and used as a backdrop for the photographing of the miniature pub set. This scene is truly an example of how simple it can be to cheat reality—when you know what you're doing, that is.

10. **The Collision With the Iceberg**   The collision was done solely with green-screen effects and by having members of Cameron's visual team dump ice on the deck after the ship hit the berg. Even though it's a little dark, this scene works amazingly well considering it was done completely on a soundstage.

9. **The Grand Staircase**   *Titanic*'s Grand Staircase, which extended from the boat deck down to the D Deck First Class Reception Room, was recreated for the movie in meticulous detail. The scenes in the movie involving the staircase are memorable for two reasons: first, the accuracy of the replica is a brilliant achievement in set design; and second, because Cameron and company completely destroy the beautiful structure as *Titanic* goes under. The scene where the glass dome topping the staircase explodes as ninety thousand gallons of water pour down the stairs is breathtaking. And the brief image seen later of a drowned woman floating in the flooded staircase, her nightgown gently billowing beneath her, is both poignant and terrifying in its finality.

8. **The Flooding of the Corridors**   There were several corridor flooding scenes in *Titanic,* and they are all impressive, but the most memorable one is the sequence in *Titanic*'s third hour in which we see Jack and Rose being chased down a hallway by an enormous wall of water. This scene was extremely dangerous,

and James Cameron did not want to put Leonardo DiCaprio and Kate Winslet at risk, so stunt doubles were used for the scene. (As visual effects supervisor Adam Howard acknowledged, "Obviously, they couldn't put the leads in there," noting that "even the stunt doubles were being slammed into walls.") But in the final version of this scene, we actually see the faces of Jack and Rose (DiCaprio and Winslet) as they desperately try to escape the monstrous flood of sea water pouring down the corridor behind them. This effect was achieved by digital face replacement, the first time, according to Howard, "where face replacement is right in your face." (Prior to *Titanic,* this technique had only been used for distance shots or scenes where the face of the actor was partially obscured.)

Kate Winslet's face was the most difficult to replace because Rose is facing the camera face-on for the entire shot. Winslet's cinematic face replacement ultimately consisted of almost fifty individual pieces of film. A big problem with this scene was that Kate Winslet's stunt double was much heavier than the actress, and the contours of her face and neck did not match Winslet's at all. In addition, each strand of Kate Winslet's hair also had to be replaced individually for the scene, and digital water had to be added to hide transitions. Howard ultimately ended up spending close to two months on this scene, one that lasts less than thirty seconds in the final film. "This was among the hardest shots I've ever done," he told *Cinefex,* "and I've been doing this kind of work for seventeen years."

7. **The Dolphins**   Of the several dolphins seen cavorting in front of *Titanic*'s bow as she steams through the Atlantic, only one (the one on the left of the shot) is real. All the others are computer generated and were carefully designed to blend perfectly with the live dolphin. Hammerhead Production's Jamie Dixon was at first adamantly opposed to using computer generated dolphins but finally agreed to when he realized it would be the only way to get the multiple dolphins that Cameron wanted into the scene.

Apparently uncertain of his initial results, Dixon sent a videotape of his dolphins footage to James Cameron without telling the director which of the animals were real and which were com-

puter generated. Cameron approved the footage without comment, and Dixon then knew that his computer generated dolphins were fine.

6. **The First "Reveal" of the Ship**   A "reveal" shot is when the
image dissolves from one scene to another, "revealing" something for the first time to the viewer. The first "reveal" of
Titanic—from the modern wreck to the brand-new ship docked
in Southampton in 1912—is beautifully executed and reportedly
was a very difficult shot to pull off.

Visual effects supervisor Rob Legato talked about this shot in
a December 1997 interview with *Cinefex* magazine: "That first
transition to 1912 was one of our toughest shots in the film,
not only because it was intrinsically difficult—which it was—but
because it was the first reveal of the ship and we wanted it perfect. The transformation was fairly straightforward. Erik Nash
shot both the wrecked ship and the clean ship using the same
motion control move, and then our digital team did a morph-
dissolve kind of thing to transition between them. There were
hundreds of people on the new ship—some of them 2-D and
the rest computer generated—pretty elaborate stuff. The hardest
part of the shot, however, was that almost nothing in it was
real—which was also true of our other shots in the sequence."

5. **The Sinking**   The sinking of the *Titanic* as depicted in *Titanic*
is the most realistic rendering of the disaster to date, and the
most amazing segment of the sinking sequence are the scenes
atop the stern where Jack and Rose cling precariously to the railing as people fall to their deaths all around them. These scenes
were shot using a combination of green-screen, model photography, and computer-generated passengers. The poop deck of
Cameron's near-life-size *Titanic* model was rigged so that it
could be tilted from level to 90 degrees in mere seconds, and
Cameron used an extremely long tower crane to shoot the scene
from above. The results are stunning and provide us with what
has to be a fairly accurate depiction of what the people who
remained on the *Titanic*'s deck must have seen and experienced
as the stern reared up and then plummeted straight down at a
speed of between 20 and 30 knots.

One of the survivors who lived through this horrible event

described the final plunge as like being on an elevator ride, but in Cameron's film, we actually see—through the eyes of Jack and Rose—precisely what that must have felt like. For this scene, stunt people actually let go and plummeted two hundred feet down the length of the deck, and we see them bouncing off capstans and other pieces of deck equipment before plunging into the water. We also see people falling off the stern behind the *Titanic* and, in one gruesome scene, we watch as a man falls off the poop deck, bounces off one of the *Titanic*'s gigantic (and now exposed) propellers (with a cringe-inducing "clang") and then splashes into the frigid water of the North Atlantic.

To film this scene, Cameron created what came to be described as the Nerf set, since everything was covered in soft foam that had been painted to look like steel. Cameron has a zero tolerance policy when it comes to safety on his sets, and on *Titanic,* there were only three minor injuries sustained by stunt people during filming. The tilting poop deck sequence was one of the most technically complex scenes to shoot, and Cameron's stunt people even went so far as to utilize training equipment designed to train paratroopers. This entire sequence no doubt played a role in *Titanic* winning Academy Awards for Best Visual Effects and Best Film Editing.

4. **The Departure From Southampton** This sequence is one of *Titanic*'s most impressive, and yet it was created entirely in postproduction using models, digital people, digital water, and other tricks of the trade. Even after watching it dozens of times, I still cannot see the "man behind the curtain," so to speak. Some fans have suggested that having a little sailboat cruising in the waters a few yards away from the *Titanic* as she departs Southampton is terribly unrealistic: In the real world, *Titanic*'s wake would have engulfed and probably destroyed the little boat and killed everyone aboard. If this is true (is it?), it is the only flaw in an otherwise wondrous scene.

3. **The Engine Room and Boiler Room Scenes** In *Titanic* there are several sequences set in her cavernous engine and boiler rooms, and they are all astonishing. Almost all of what we see in these scenes is not real. The engine room was created using partial real-world sets (mainly for the foreground of the scenes),

miniatures, computer animation, and green-screen motion control photography. One problem the effects team had when it came to bringing Cameron's scripted engine room scenes to life was that no photographs exist of the *Titanic*'s engine room. They had to work from Harland and Wolff blueprints of the *Titanic* and the *Olympic*, and yet even these documents did not answer questions about the placement of controls and other details. For research, *Titanic*'s Second Unit Director Steve Quale went on the *Queen Mary* and visited her engine room. He then tried to subtract two or three decades of technological advancement in order to come up with an engine room that was as close to *Titanic*'s original as they could conceive. Quale also visited the *Jeremiah O'Brien*, a decommissioned but still-functioning World War II Liberty ship berthed in San Francisco Bay. This visit was extremely helpful because, as he told *Cinefex*, "The *Jeremiah O'Brien* is one of the last reciprocating engine ships still operable. It has the same triple expansion engines the *Titanic* did—only much smaller—so I was able to see how all of these physical elements worked and determine how the whole reversing engines sequence should take place."

Many steamship aficionados have praised *Titanic* for the accuracy of the reversing engines sequence Quale mentioned. Why? Because the sequence in the film correctly depicts only the starboard and port screws (propellers) turning when the reversing engines are engaged. The middle screw did not turn when in reverse mode. Another factor adding to the reality of the engine room scenes was the use of handheld cameras to shoot the manic activity after the ship hits the iceberg. The tumult of the actual events is enhanced by the kinetic nervousness of the camera rushing through the room, climbing stairs, and running across catwalks.

2. **The "Ode to *Titanic*" Flyovers**   These scenes are the ones that leave people gasping due to their enormous sweep and incredible reality. The ship, when seen in its entirety in a gigantic, seamless, fluid flyover, has a presence it has never before achieved on-screen. Many people I spoke to about the film, after seeing Cameron's all-encompassing, loving look at the ship as seen from the air, assumed that Cameron had actually built the

Titanic from scratch, took it out to sea, and then flew around it in a helicopter—probably dangling half out the door with his camera—in order to capture these images. Sorry, Charlie, but these "full-body" shots were all done in postproduction using digital water, a giant tower crane, and countless other computer effects (for smoke from the funnels, people on the decks, wind, etc.).

The full-view scenes of *Titanic* at sea are state-of-the-art visual special effects at their absolute best. Cameron makes excellent use of these sequences for story development as well (lest we forget during all this talk of effects that *Titanic* also tells a story). His first flyover is after Jack's "I'm King of the World" shout to the universe; the second, after Rose's "I'm flying!" scene.

1. **The Dissolve to the Wreck** This is the scene that everyone talks about, and it is so brilliantly executed it almost takes you out of the movie for a moment as you reflect upon what you just saw. Jack makes Rose climb up onto the *Titanic*'s bow railing with her eyes closed. He then extends her arms and tells her to open her eyes. She gasps at the vista before her. "I'm flying!" she exclaims. They kiss, and then the camera slowly pulls back to show the two young lovers locked in an embrace on the bow of the *Titanic* in 1912. The light begins to change, and eerily, rusticles begin to form on the bow railing. For a terrible moment, Jack and Rose are actually seen standing together *on the sunken bow* of the *Titanic* wreck, but then they disappear, and all we see is the *Titanic*'s bow, as it now exists two-and-a-half miles beneath the sea. This sequence ends with Old Rose looking at the *Titanic* wreck in the video monitor aboard the *Keldysh*. In the book *James Cameron's Titanic*, writer Ed Marsh notes, "This elegant transition in time and memory . . . combines many levels of story, character, and emotion into one image and is the result of Cameron and Digital Domain's vision to extend the boundaries of visual effects in the service of storytelling." This scene was aligned and tracked frame by frame to achieve a smooth transition, and it is the single most memorable sequence in the movie.

34

THE MOST SUCCESSFUL MOVIE OF ALL TIME?

A *Titanic* Balance Sheet

Here is a look at *Titanic*'s profit and loss sheet, according to the *Wall Street Journal* and other sources. All figures are approximate and are provided to give you an idea of the kind of once-in-a-century money *Titanic* is making. When you factor in the undeniable truth that in the arts, failure is the rule, the success of *Titanic* is that much more amazing.

Titanic is the number one box office earner on a dollar-for-dollar basis, but when earnings of older films are adjusted for inflation, *Titanic* makes the Top Ten, but *E.T.: The Extraterrestrial* and *Gone With the Wind* still lead the pack.

REVENUES

Domestic theatrical	$ 550,000,000	(as of 4/25/98)
Foreign theatrical	1,200,000,000	(projected)
Domestic video	360,000,000	(projected)
Foreign video	216,000,000	(projected)
Domestic network and pay TV	60,000,000	
Foreign TV	65,000,000	(projected)
Total:	$2,451,000,000	

COSTS

Production and interest	$ 235,000,000
Cost of prints	27,000,000
Worldwide marketing costs	115,000,000
Video marketing and production costs	242,000,000
Residuals and participation	52,000,000
Studio interest and distribution costs	105,000,000
Total:	$ 776,000,000

Projected Worldwide Net Profit: $1,675,000,000

VARIETY LOOKS AT TITANIC'S IMPACT ON THE 1912 MOVIE BOX OFFICE

Four days after the Titanic sank, Variety, the "Show Business Bible" of Hollywood, looked at how the tragedy was affecting box office receipts across the United States. They published an article on page four of the Saturday, April 20, 1912, issue titled "Paralyzing Titanic Terror Casts Pall Over Theatres." Here are some excerpts from that somewhat jaded, elitist, and irreverent article. Isn't it the quintessential definition of irony that today, seven decades after the Titanic foundered, the success of James Cameron's movie is being warmly embraced by Hollywood? I guess the establishment's perspective is a tad different when a disaster is good for Hollywood, eh?

"[After the sinking], business of all kinds was practically suspended and the attendance at the theatres of all classes suffered materially. The first half of the week it was impossible to arouse any spontaneous humor at the various musical and comedy shows, which partook very much of the nature of funeral services."

"With the stories of the survivors and other harrowing accounts of grief that will be constantly in the papers for the next week, it is expected the theatres will continue to suffer in attendance and appreciation until the frightful Titanic Terror commences to dim."

"[At the Winter Garden Theater], about the middle of the show, the male members of a box party stepped out for a drink. On their return, one, with almost unpardonable stupidity [gave a *Titanic* passenger's sister] some sort of information as to the probable fate of her brother. As almost anybody else might have foreseen, she promptly dropped into a dead faint, almost precipitating a panic in the music hall."

"The only known theatrical person onboard the *Titanic* besides Henry B. Harris was Charles Williams, said to be a former dancing partner of *Hello George*'s John Scott. He was reported to be among the survivors from the second cabin . . ."

"Cancellations commenced to flood the steamship agencies after it became known the *Titanic* had gone down. It is expected that ocean travel will be very light this season, with only those going across called there upon business."

"Several theatrical people who had made reservations for space are undecided whether to go. A number have said they will cancel, going to the mountains or seashore instead."

35

TITANIC: A NEW MUSICAL

Sail on, sail on
Great ship *Titanic!*
—"Godspeed Titanic" from
Titanic: A New Musical

There are many emotional moments in *Titanic: A New Musical,* and it is understandable why it has been one of the most successful Broadway musicals in quite some time since its opening on April 23, 1997, at the Lunt-Fontanne Theater in New York City. In fact, *Titanic: A New Musical* is so popular it even has its own newsgroup on the Internet (alt.buybroadway.titanic).

One of *Titanic*'s heart-wrenching moments includes the scene when the third-class passengers, who had previously sung "I Must Get on That Ship" in anticipation of boarding *Titanic* for their long-awaited journey to America (where "the streets are paved with gold"), reprise the song in act 2—only this time they sing about getting on a lifeboat. Another extremely powerful moment is during the finale, when the survivors' lost loved ones—victims of the *Titanic*'s foundering—rejoin them onstage to sing "Godspeed Titanic" with *its* poignant line, "Pray the journey's sound, till your port be found." (By the way, the song "Godspeed Titanic" has one of those chill-inducing, incredibly majestic melodies made all the more dramatic knowing the outcome of the "godspeed" wishes bestowed upon the R.M.S. *Titanic.*)

One of the most interesting numbers in the musical is the song "The Blame," which takes place in act 2 after the collision with the iceberg. Writer Peter Stone and lyricist Maury Yeston have the characters of

J. Bruce Ismay, Thomas Andrews, and Captain Smith furiously hurling accusations at each other in an attempt to exonerate their own actions and absolve themselves of blame for the imminent sinking. At first, Ismay is hopeful that the ship will not sink ("Possibly she won't go down/Possibly she'll stay afloat/Possibly all this could come to an end on a positive note") until Andrews bluntly informs him that he knows "certain things" and that the ship will, indeed, sink unless she can sprout wings. Ismay then lashes out at Andrews, asking him: If he knew so much, why didn't he know enough to prevent this? He then horribly shouts out, "This is your work, Mr. Andrews! You have done us in!" Ismay, ever the pragmatist, also informs Andrews that "if someone must take the blame, it is you!"

Captain Smith then wonders aloud if a ship will come and save them, and after Andrews tells him that the hull is "hemorrhaging," Ismay again attacks, telling Smith, "There stands the captain who sailed us straight into disaster!" Andrews then defends the captain, asking Ismay, "Pray, who urged him to go faster?" and then the captain also sticks up for himself, asking Ismay, "Who called for speed and to break every record?"

Ismay fires back with his own accusatory questioning, asking Smith, "Who ignored warnings of icebergs when sighted?" and then, to Andrews, "Who, sir, refused to extend up the bulkheads?" (As Andrews rightly responds, it was Ismay himself who refused to extend the bulkheads above E deck in order to make more room for first-class staterooms.)

The argument continues, with Smith accusing Ismay of undermining the position of the captain and insisting that they land sooner than planned; Ismay accusing Smith of not posting enough lookouts and taking a course too far north for the season; and Andrews accusing Ismay of demanding a ship that was both the largest *and* the fastest.

At the conclusion of this powerful number, though, after all the desperate charges are hurled back and forth, Captain Smith steps forward and accepts full responsibility: "There's only one captain," he sings, "and I was in charge . . . this is my ship, no one else's . . ."

Titanic: A New Musical celebrated its one-year anniversary on April 23, 1998, and its continued success was in part due to the success of James Cameron's movie, which transformed *Titanic* fever into an all-out global *Titanic* epidemic. Granted, the musical is a far different experience than the movie, but it is nonetheless a brilliant rendering of the *Titanic* story, all the more amazing when we realize that the tale is told in a mere forty songs and seventy-three minutes of performance.

Titanic: A New Musical succeeds in the extremely difficult task of synthesizing countless elements of an undeniably grand epic into a musical experience that, yes, tells the story, but also does not diminish its gravity because of its musical format.

In one early review, a critic complained that none of *Titanic*'s songs had you humming them on the way out of the theater. Rubbish. The songs in *Titanic* are engaging and do a superb job of moving the story along while also being extremely entertaining. After only one hearing, the melodies of "I Must Get on That Ship," "Lady's Maid," "No Moon," and especially "Godspeed Titanic" were most definitely imprinted on this listener's brain.

On June 2, 1997, at the 1997 Tony Awards held at Radio City Music Hall, *Titanic: A New Musical*, won five awards:

Best Musical
Best Original Score—Music and Lyrics by Maury Yeston
Best Book of a Musical—Peter Stone
Best Orchestrations—Jonathan Tunick
Best Scenic Design—Stewart Laing

The praise for *Titanic* has been effusive and frequent. Ken Mandelbaum, writing in *Playbill On-Line,* said, "*Titanic* is by far the season's best score, one you'll want to hear again and again, and it's beautifully preserved." The Associated Press said the musical had "a striking score," and the *New Yorker* was similarly impressed: "*Titanic* leads the fleet of spring musicals! *Titanic* manages to be grave and entertaining, somber and joyful; little by little you realize that you are in the presence of a genuine addition to American musical theater." David Messineo, editor of *Sensations Magazine,* wrote, "*Titanic: A New Musical* is a remarkable accomplishment."

On September 8, 1997, *People* magazine gave the original cast CD a rave, writing, "It takes guts to write a musical about the century's most infamous disaster, yet Broadway's *Titanic* unflinchingly sails forth with its cargo of epic themes aboard what was the earth's largest man-made moving object, until it suddenly stopped moving on April 15, 1912. The

Tony Award–winning Maury Yeston score is big and moving too, influenced by the moody *Sweeney Todd,* and the rich orchestration relies little on the cheap-sounding synthesizers that mar such contemporaries as *Les Miserables* and *The Phantom of the Opera.* Yeston's lyrics, somber but not mawkish, steady the course (one inspired touch: Yeston imagines the ship's designer frantically redrawing his blueprints to make the sinking liner unsinkable once more, on paper). This *Titanic,* at least, is shipshape."

THE MUSICAL NUMBERS, SETTINGS, AND PERFORMERS OF *TITANIC:* A NEW MUSICAL

The action takes place between April 10 and 15, 1912. All characters and events are based on facts.

ACT ONE

1. Overture/Prologue: "In Every Age"—Thomas Andrews

The Launching

SCENE:
Southampton, England, The Ocean Dock;
Wednesday, April 10, 1912; 6:00 A.M.

2. "How Did They Build Titanic?"—Stoker Frederick Barrett
3. "There She Is"—Barrett, Radioman Harold Bride, Lookout Frederick Fleet, and Crewmen

SAME SCENE:
8:00 A.M.
"Loading Inventory"—Stevedore, 3rd Officer Pitman, 2nd Officer Lightoller, 4th Officer and Navigator Joseph Boxhall, Quartermaster Robert Hitchens, Captain Edward J. Smith, 1st Officer William Murdoch, Crewmen, Bellboy

SAME SCENE:
10:00 A.M.
"The Largest Moving Object"—J. Bruce Ismay, Captain Smith, Thomas Andrews

4. "I Must Get on That Ship"—Pitman, Kate Murphey, Kate McGowan,
   Kate Mullins, 3rd Class Passengers, Charles Clarke, Edgar
   Beane, Alice Beane, Caroline Neville, 2nd Class Passengers
5. "The 1st Class Roster"—Pitman, Alice Beane, Passengers

SCENE:

Aboard R.M.S. *Titanic*: 12:00 noon

6. "Godspeed Titanic"—Full Company

SCENE:

Boiler Room No. 6

7. "Barrett's Song"—Stoker Frederick Barrett

SCENE:

The Bridge

8. "To Be a Captain"—1st Officer William Murdoch

SCENE:

The 3rd Class Commissary

9. "Lady's Maid"—Kate McGowan, Kate Murphey, Kate Mullins,
   Four 3rd Class Men, German Man, Italian Man and Woman,
   Jim Farrell

SCENE:

The 1st Class Dining Saloon

10. "What a Remarkable Age This Is!"—1st Class Steward Etches, Male
    1st Class Passengers, Female 1st Class Passengers, Millionaires,
    Millionaires' Wives, Staff

SCENE:

The Radio Room, on the Boat Deck
Late Saturday Night

11. "The Proposal"/"The Night Was Alive"—Frederick Barrett,
    Harold Bride

SCENE:

The Upper Promenade ("A") Deck
Sunday Morning, April 14

12. "Hymn"/"Doing the Latest Rag"—Passengers, Bandmaster Wallace
    Hartley and His 2-Man Ensemble, 1st Class Passengers
13. "I Have Danced"—Alice Beane, Edgar Beane

SCENE:

The Crow's Nest, 10:30 p.m.

14. "No Moon"—Frederick Fleet

SCENE:

The 1st Class Deck

"No Moon" (continues)—Ida Straus, Isidor Straus

SCENE:

The 3rd Class Deck

"No Moon" (continues)—Jim Farrell, Kate McGowan

SCENE:

On the Bridge, 11:00 p.m.

"No Moon" (continues)—Capt. Smith, Lightoller, Murdoch

SCENE:

The Crow's Nest and the Bridge

"No Moon" (continues)—Fleet, Smith, Lightoller, and Murdoch

SCENE:

The 2nd Class Deck

"No Moon" (continues)—Caroline Neville, Charles Clarke

SCENE:

The 1st Class Smoke Room

"No Moon" (continues)—Mrs. Cardoza, The Major,
John Jacob Astor, Wallace Hartley

15. "Autumn"/Finale—Wallace Hartley, Mrs. Cardoza, The Major

SCENE:
The Crow's Nest and the Boat Deck
"Autumn"/Finale (continues)—Frederick Fleet, Fleet's Personnel,
Passengers, Harold Bride, Frederick Barrett, Thomas Andrews

SCENE:
The Collision, a tableau

END OF ACT ONE
(15 Minute Intermission)

ACT TWO

SCENE:
The Upper Promenade ("A") Deck
The 1st Class Grand Salon, Sunday Morning, 12:03 A.M.
16. "Dressed in Your Pyjamas in the Grand Salon"—1st Class
Passengers, Etches, Stewards, John Thayer, Benjamin
Guggenheim, Alice Beane

SCENE:
The Radio Room, 12:16 a.m.
17. "The Blame"—Bruce Ismay, Thomas Andrews, Capt. Smith

SCENE:
The Boat Deck
18. To the Lifeboats:
"Getting in the Lifeboat"—Marion Thayer, John Thayer
"I Must Get on That Ship" (reprise)—Murdoch, Lightoller, Isador
Straus, Ida Straus, Steward, John Jacob Astor, Alice Beane,
Bellboy, George Widener, Charles Clarkes, All Passengers
"Lady's Maid" (reprise)—Jim Farrell, Kate McGowan
"The Proposal"/"The Night Was Alive" (reprise)/Canons—Barrett,
Bride, Company, Andrews, Ship's Officers
19. "We'll Meet Tomorrow"—Barrett, Charles Clarke, Full Company

SCENE:
The Upper Promenade Deck, "A" Deck 2:01 a.m.
20. "Still"—Isidor Straus, Ida Straus

SCENE:

The Boat Deck

21. "To Be a Captain" (reprise)—Etches

SCENE:

The 1st Class Smoke Room, "A" Deck, 2:16 a.m

22. "Mr. Andrews' Vision"—Thomas Andrews

23. Epilogue: "In Every Age" (reprise)/Finale—Harold Bride, All
   Survivors, The Company, Offstage Voices, Full Company

FINAL CURTAIN

PRODUCTION NOTES

Story and Book by Peter Stone
Music and Lyrics by Maury Yeston
Directed by Richard Jones
Choreography by Lynne Taylor-Corbett
Sets and Costumes by Stewart Laing
Lighting by Paul Gallo
Sound by Steve Canyon Kennedy
Orchestrations by Jonathan Tunick
Music Supervision and Direction by Kevin Stites
Music Coordinator, John Miller
Technical Supervisor, Aurora Productions
Action Coordinator, Rick Sordelet
Production Stage Manager, Susan Green
Executive Producer, Dodger Management Group
Associate General Manager, Robert C. Strickstein
Presented by Dodger Endemol Theatricals, Richard S. Pechter, and the
   John F. Kennedy Center for the Performing Arts
At the Lunt-Fontanne Theater

ORCHESTRA

Conductor: Kevin Stites
Associate Conductor: Matthew Sklar
Assistant Conductor: Nicholas Archer

Original Cast Soundtrack Recorded
on April 27, 1997, at the Hit Factory's Studio 1, New York City

ORIGINAL CAST

Officers and Crew of R.M.S. *Titanic*

Capt. E. J. Smith .... John Cunningham
1st Officer William Murdoch .... David Costabile
2nd Officer Charles Lightoller .... John Bolton
3rd Officer Herbert J. Pitman .... Matthew Bennett
Frederick Barrett, Stoker............................. Brian d'Arcy James
Harold Bride, Radioman.............................. Martin Moran
Henry Etches, 1st Class Steward.................. Allan Corduner
Frederick Fleet, Lookout .... David Elder
Quartermaster Robert Hitchens.................... Adam Alexi-Malle
4th Officer Joseph Boxhall........................... Andy Taylor
Chief Engineer Joseph Bell .... Ted Sperling
Wallace Hartley, Orchestra Leader .... Ted Sperling
Bandsman Bricoux....................................... Adam Alexi-Malle
Bandsman Taylor .... Andy Taylor
Stewardess Robinson.................................... Michele Ragusa
Stewardess Hutchinson .... Stephanie Park
Bellboy .... Mara Stephens

PASSENGERS ABOARD R.M.S. *TITANIC*

1st Class Passengers

J. Bruce Ismay .... David Garrison
Thomas Andrews .... Michael Cerveris
Isidor Straus.. Larry Keith
Ida Straus.. Alma Cuervo
John Jacob Astor .... William Youmans
Madeline Astor .... Lisa Datz
Benjamin Guggenheim .... Joseph Kolinski
Mademoiselle Aubert.................................... Kimberly Hester
John B. Thayer .... Michael Mulheren
Marion Thayer... Robin Irwin
George Widener.. Henry Stram
Eleanor Widener .... Jody Gelb

Charlotte Cardoza .... Becky Ann Baker
J. H. Rogers .... Andy Taylor
The Major .... Matthew Bennett
Edith Corse Evans .... Mindy Cooper
Also . . . Melissa Bell, Jonathan Brody, David Elder, Erin Hill,
John Jellison, Peter Kapetan, Theresa McCarthy, Charles McAteer,
Drew McVety, Jennifer Piech, Clarke Thorell, Kay Walbye

2nd Class Passengers

Charles Clarke... Don Stephenson
Caroline Neville .... Judith Blazer
Edgar Beane .... Bill Buell
Alice Beane... Victoria Clark
Also . . . Melissa Bell, John Bolton, Jonathan Brody,
Mindy Cooper, David Costabile, David Edler, John Jellison,
Peter Kapetan, Drew McVety, Kay Walbye

3rd Class Passengers

Kate McGowen... Jennifer Piech
Kate Murphey.. Theresa McCarthy
Kate Mullins .... Erin Hill
Jim Farrell... Clarke Thorell
Also . . . Adam Alexi-Malle, Becky Ann Baker, Melissa Bell,
Matthew Bennett, Jonathan Brody, Mindy Cooper, Alma Cuervo,
Lisa Datz, Jody Gelb, Kimberly Hester, Robin Irwin,
John Jellison, Peter Kapetan, Larry Keith, Joseph Kolinski,
Drew McVety, Michael Mulheren, Charles McAteer,
Ted Sperling, Mara Stephens, Henry Stram, Andy Taylor,
Kay Walbye, William Youmans

"STEAMER TITANIC"

Largest and most luxurious in the World. Launched at Belfast Ireland, May 1911. Length 882 ft. 6 in. Displacement 66,000 tons. On her maiden trip struck a mammoth iceberg on Sunday, April 14th at 10.25 P. M. in 41° 49 minutes, north latitude-50° 14 minutes, West longitude. The worst disaster known in Marine History. Sunk at 2.20 A. M. April 15 1912, with a loss of over 1500 lives.

PART VI

The Immortal *Titanic* Saga: The Legend Lives On

THE RAREST *TITANIC* COLLECTIBLE IN EXISTENCE?

Shortly before the R.M.S. *Titanic* left Southampton on April 10, 1912, on its maiden voyage, three of its deck benches were removed from the ship to make room for deck equipment. The benches were brought to the White Star Line offices in Southampton, and one of them was given to a Vicar (an Anglican clergyman in charge of a parish) who had close personal connections with members of the White Star organization. It remained in his possession for decades.

In the late 1990s, the Vicar's family sold his *Titanic* deck bench (Onslow's in London handled the sale) and it was purchased by a representative of the J. Peterman Co., which then allowed it to be displayed as part of the *Titanic* exhibit in St. Petersburg, Florida, until May 15, 1998.

In the J. Peterman spring 1998 catalog, the Vicar's *Titanic* deck bench was offered for sale, complete with documentation authenticating its genesis and history. The price? $188,000.

The bench's descriptive catalog copy, which was signed by J. Peterman, concluded with "Serious collectors only pls."

I should say so.

TITANIC RESURRECTION?

From the Associated Press:
April 6, 1998:

US, SWISS TO BUILD *TITANIC* REPLICA

NEW YORK (AP)—A Swiss-U.S. partnership said it will build a $500 million, full-size replica of the *Titanic* and have it ready for the 90th anniversary of the ship's sinking.

"It cannot sink," assured Walter Navratil, president of the Swiss-based development company White Star Line Ltd., in Monday's *New York Post.*

Navratil said the oil-fueled steamer will make a Southampton, England–New York round trip in April 2002. The ship will pause in the North Atlantic 560 miles off Newfoundland, where 1,500 passengers died on April 15, 1912.

Tickets will cost $10,000 to $100,000, organizers said. After the voyage, the ship will serve as a pleasure cruiser.

The developers said they copyrighted the name "R.M.S. Titanic" with the Institute for Intellectual Property in Switzerland last week.

"We thought now would be the right moment, because the whole world is keen on *Titanic,*" said Annette Voelcker, spokeswoman for G&E Business Consulting and Trust, the Swiss-based developer and the chief shareholder in the project.

But don't worry.

"It will have modern equipment to detect icebergs," she added.

The original ship cost $10 million in 1912. The project's U.S. partner is Titanic Development Corp. of Las Vegas.

April 8, 1998:

SOUTH AFRICANS PLAN *TITANIC* REPLICA

JOHANNESBURG, South Africa (AP)—A South African-based company announced plans Wednesday to build a replica of the *Titanic* by the end of next year, well ahead of a competing Swiss-U.S. partnership.

The public relations firm Saatchi & Saatchi said RMS Titanic Shipping Holdings of South Africa hired it to handle the account for the new *Titanic* project.

The ship will be built in Durban, on South Africa's east coast, and make its maiden voyage on December 29, 1999, according to Saatchi & Saatchi.

It said RMS Titanic Shipping Holdings secured the exclusive rights to build the replica from Harland and Wolff Holdings, which it said owned the original plans for the *Titanic*.

It said the replica would be built to the exact specifications of the original liner but include modern amenities such as air conditioning, satellite television and safety technology.

On Monday, the Swiss-U.S. partnership said it would spend $500 million on its replica of the *Titanic*.

Walter Navratil, president of the White Star Line Ltd., said the oil-fueled steamer would make a Southampton, England–New York round trip in April 2002. The ship would pause in the North Atlantic, where 1,500 passengers died when the original Titanic went down on April 15, 1912.

Tickets will cost $10,000 to $100,000, organizers said. After the voyage, the ship will serve as a pleasure cruiser.

Titanic has become the highest-grossing film of all time and won 11 Academy Awards, tying *Ben Hur* for the all-time record.

The proposed Swiss-U.S. and South African–U.S. *Titanic* replicas were soon joined by two others. In late April 1998, it was announced that a company called Voyager Titanic Exhibition, which was based in Dusseldorf, Germany, had trademarked the name RMS Titanic in Germany, France, Switzerland, Spain, Belgium, the Netherlands, and Luxembourg. According to Harland and Wolff's chief engineer Jim Lee, however, Voyager's efforts had been ambitious, but only on paper as of spring 1998. "[They are] not quite out of the gate yet," said Lee, and there were no details as to a planned launch date or when they actually planned on starting construction.

The fourth *Titanic* replica planned was a $30 million, one-sixth-scale ship (about 150 feet from bow to stern) intended to be used as a non-profit business and tourism center by a Belfast-based company called North Star Holdings. The company behind this smaller version of the great vessel claimed moral superiority over the other, more commercial ventures. "People forget this was a major tragedy," said Mark Blackburne, head of North Star. He also blasted the other developers as "profiteers."

The South African–based company (see the second news story on previous page) tried to block out the other builders by acquiring exclusive access to Harland and Wolff—and their original *Titanic* plans. According to Jim Lee, though, this was wishful thinking on the part of the company. "If people come up with the funding," he told the *New York Post* in April 1998, "we'll write a contract with them."

The Swiss-U.S. company faced its own legal problems after announcing their ambitious plans to have a brand-new *Titanic* launched by 2002, the ninetieth anniversary of the ship's sinking. This company, which legally christened itself White Star Lines Ltd., was threatened with a lawsuit by the Cunard Line, which claimed ownership of the name White Star Line since the 1930s, when they bought the name from International Mercantile Marine, the original owner of the *Titanic*.

When asked by the *New York Post*'s Laura Italiano to comment on this unprecedented boom in *Titanic* "resurrections," Harland and Wolff's Jim Lee was laconic: "Whether the world needs four *Titanics* or not is something else, isn't it?"

Indeed.

EPILOGUE

August 1998:
The "Big Piece" Triumph and "*Titanic* Live"

> It is so immense, so beautiful, so devastated. You are
> seeing things that you only read about, and to actually see
> where all of these events took place is a profoundly
> moving experience.
>
> —*Titanic* historian Charles Haas

August 1998 was one of the most important months in the history of *Titanic* research, with George Tulloch and RMS Titanic's second try to raise the Big Piece from the bottom of the Atlantic. It was a resounding success.

Two years after the Big Piece debacle (see chapter 28), Tulloch exonerated his actions during his previous P. T. Barnumlike first expedition of trying to raise the seventeen-ton piece of *Titanic*'s hull. Apparently responding to the critical drubbing he took for the disrespectful tastelessness of his first try, Tulloch's *Titanic* '98 expedition did not include gawking sightseers, casino gambling, floor shows, or any other hint of the partylike atmosphere surrounding his first attempt.

This time it was pure science—unadulterated maritime archaeological research—and Tulloch succeeded (for the most part) in turning a debacle into a triumph.

DATELINE, AUGUST 12, 1998

Even though the *Titanic* '98 expedition left Boston harbor on July 30, 1998 and began issuing reports the first day, the first in-depth media

399

coverage of the expedition for the public was a one-hour NBC *Dateline* special called "Raising the *Titanic*" that aired on Wednesday, August 12, 1998.

Titanic '98 had several mission goals, but the one that was probably the most important to George Tulloch was the recovery of the Big Piece, the hull piece he had had in his grip, but then lost, in August 1996.

On Monday, August 10, 1998, the Associated Press reported that the Big Piece had, indeed, been recovered from the ocean floor and was in the possession of RMS Titanic. A second press announcement followed the next day in which George Tulloch said, "We at RMS Titanic, Inc. are extraordinarily pleased to recover this immense piece of *Titanic*'s history today. While the *Titanic* can never be resurrected, this section from *Titanic*'s hull will serve as a dramatic monument to *Titanic*'s memory for eternity. My profound thanks are extended to the team of engineers and scientists whose skills and expertise have made this recovery operation a success."

So the world knew with certainty that the Big Piece was now out of the water for the first time in eighty-six years.

But *Dateline*'s one-hour "Raising the *Titanic*" special two days later did not reveal the resurrection immediately. Instead it treated the question of whether or not Tulloch and company succeeded with tantalizing quips that held viewers until the final two minutes of the program in which footage of the Big Piece being lifted up out of the water was finally shown.

Dateline's reason was to provide exclusive coverage of the recovery of the Big Piece, so they built the entire hour "special" around that event, repeatedly teasing the viewer with quetions as to whether or not the expedition team would actually succeed in its quest.

Even though Tulloch greatly toned down the "show biz" tone of the expedition, NBC picked up the ball and treated the events leading up to the recovery, as well as the ultimate resurrection of the Big Piece, like an episode of *Unsolved Mysteries*. But network TV is network TV and the three major networks never met an opportunity for hype they didn't like.

The show called the *Titanic* "a legend entombed on the ocean floor"; described the expedition as an "unprecedented mission" (conveniently forgetting the 1996 attempt), and encouraged viewers to "watch history being made."

Anchor Stone Phillips also said that the purpose of the mission was to solve the "lingering mystery of why *Titanic* sank" (I thought that the ship hit an iceberg and filled with water), and correspondent Sarah James used phrases like "incredible odyssey" and was actually allowed to travel down to the site of the Big Piece in the *Nautile*.

It is well known that the Discovery Channel and NBC have aligned themselves with George Tulloch and RMS Titanic in order to have exclusive video and print rights to the group's salvage efforts. Thus, there was an implicit bias on the part of NBC's coverage of the expedition, evidenced by such comments:

* At one point correspondent Sarah James stated that George Tulloch was "brought on board by the French" in order to ensure that the recovered *Titanic* artifacts were preserved properly and made available to the public. This makes it sound as though the French sought out the best man they could find to protect the artifacts, again conveniently forgetting that Tulloch aggressively pursued salvor-in-possession rights to the wreck and everything on it.
* Later, James also said that "Tulloch has pledged not to sell any of the artifacts but his company does make money selling *Titanic* memorabilia and from ticket sales to [*Titanic*] exhibits." Technically true, but omitting the fact that it has been reported (perhaps incorrectly?) that legally Tulloch *cannot* sell *Titanic* artifacts and thus, if that is true, then his pledge may be just a tad disingenuous.
* In a halfhearted attempt at journalistic balance, the argument that Tulloch's salvage efforts are a "violation of an underwater tomb" is brought up and Tulloch is asked why shouldn't clothing and other artifacts recovered from the debris field be returned to the descendants of the rightful owners. Tulloch's answer—which actually makes a whole lot of sense—is to answer the question with a question: Who do you give the stuff to? Which cousin? Which grandniece?
* The point is then made that if Tulloch had not acquired total rights to the wreck, *Titanic* would probably have suffered the same fate as that of other shipwrecks, which is to be picked clean by treasure hunters and scavengers. In all fairness, I completely agree with him on this point. If it was not *illegal* for anyone else to salvage *Titanic*, any group with the money to rent a *Nautile* or a comparable submersible would be down there ripping off railings and tearing the wreck to pieces.
* Near the end of the special, correspondent Bob McKeown states that George Tulloch's "personal mission" is "to help all of us better understand the storied vessel lost on that night to remember." It must be noted that antisalvage proponents are not pleased at all that George Tulloch has presumed to take upon himself such a mantle of responsibility regarding the memory of R.M.S. *Titanic*.

Aside from all this, the *Dateline* special did provide some new information other than its coverage of the recovery of the Big Piece.

Dateline introduced us to South Carolina teacher Bill Willard, the inventor of the small remote-controlled camera dubbed "T-Rex," short for *Titanic* Remote Explorer. When Willard met one of the 1996 team's members at a convention he asked him why they hadn't gone inside the wreck and taken pictures. When he was told a camera that small didn't exist, he asked if he built it, would they use it. He did, and they did. (Or so they planned. The T-Rex [named "Robin"] was still not working properly when NBC aired their special.)

Dateline also revealed for the first time that the Big Piece was confirmed to be part of the port side C-deck suite C-86 (not C-79 and C-81 as previously thought), that had been occupied by Mr. and Mrs. Walter Douglas of Minneapolis, returning from a vacation in Europe. *Dateline* tracked down Mrs. Douglas's grandniece (Mr. Douglas went down with the ship) and read a poem Mrs. Douglas had written about the sinking of the *Titanic*.

"*TITANIC* LIVE"

A full-page ad in the Friday, August 14, 1998 *USA Today* trumpeted the Discovery Channel's "*Titanic* Live" special on Sunday, August 16, 1998 and invited *Titanic* buffs to "Be there at the moment of discovery as robotic cameras, deep-sea submersibles and satellite relays take you 2½ miles beneath the ocean's surface in a daring attempt to explore *Titanic* live!" The ad also cautioned us that "conditions will dictate" what we actually saw during the live broadcast, but there is no denying that the expedition's agenda was as grand as *Titanic*'s Grand Staircase itself.

Titanic '98 planned on exploring live the following sites:

- The third-class hallways where it has been rumored gates were locked to keep steerage passengers from getting to the lifeboats;
- the boiler rooms in the stern, to determine whether or not boilers exploded, the hull imploded, or both;
- the Marconi room, in an attempt (reportedly funded by the Marconi Foundation) to recover the actual Marconi wireless apparatus used to send out the *Titanic*'s pleas for help;
- the bow at the mudline where the *Titanic* struck the iceberg, to visually record the first actual pictures of the iceberg damage to the ship's hull.

The hype-heavy special started off by telling us that during the two hours, the expedition team would be "sorting out truth from legend, fact from folklore," and the entire broadcast was anchored by NBC's Bob McKeown and Sarah James (both had also anchored the *Dateline* special "Raising the *Titanic*" earlier in the week), buttressed by introductions and comments from John Siegenthaler back in the Discovery Channel's studio.

For the most part, the fiber optics and satellite technology worked flawlessly and the only glitches and jarring moments came when Sarah James tried to talk over Paul Matthias's comments from the *Nautile* down at the *Titanic* site. There was a slight delay in communicating with the sub and so when James didn't allow Matthias to completely finish his comment, there were moments of dead silence as each waited for the other to say something.

Featured prominently in the broadcast were George Tulloch, P. H. Nargeolet, and other members of RMS Titanic as well as Harland and Wolff's David Livingstone, naval architect Bill Garzke (see chapter 25 on *Titanic*'s flawed rivets for more from Garzke), and *Titanic* historians and authors Charles Haas and John Eaton. Microbiologist Dr. Roy Cullimore was also onboard to discuss the effects the rusticles (iron-eating bacteria) were having on the structural integrity of the ship. (The general feeling is that the *Titanic*—in a period of ninety years or less—will be reduced to little more than a stain on the floor of the Atlantic.)

"*Titanic* Live" consisted of six prepared segments, interspersed with live broadcasts from the *Nautile* and interviews with the principals on the deck of the *Ocean Voyager*.

Of the six, the "Heart of *Titanic*" segment provided the most amazing video of the interior of the wreck. The tiny T-Rex ROV Robin (now up and running) showed us:

- Captain E. J. Smith's bathroom, complete with shots of the Captain's shower head and his bathtub (which Haas ludicrously described as needing a good cleaning);
- the officers' quarters;
- the Marconi Room wireless cabin, complete with a shot of a piece of wireless apparatus;
- the interior of J. Bruce Ismay's Cabin B-54, reached via the Grand Staircase;
- a light fixture and a chandelier;

- a B-Deck Reception Room;
- Cabin B-51, with its fireplace visible;
- Ismay's cabin door, wash basin and chair;
- safety bars leading to (fencing off?) a third-class Recreation Room;
- G Deck;
- piles of canvas mail bags covered with what looked like pink shag carpeting but which was actually an unknown undersea life form;
- some intact first-class cabin windows;
- the skylight of the Marconi Room;
- a Marconi junction box.

Other live underwater footage of the *Titanic* consisted of the wreckage of the stern (taken by Paul Matthias in the *Nautile*), and footage showing a starboard engine pump, boilers, cylinder no. 2 of the port side reciprocating engine, and other general footage of the mangled stern section of the ship (showed by Matthias).

All of this footage (plus the earlier video of the bow, the forward mast, the crow's nest hatchway, and the wheelhouse telemotor mounting) almost made sitting through all the other hype and the rehashing of previously seen materials worth it.

However, we *must* separate the *Titanic* '98 mission from the "*Titanic* Live" broadcast.

Even though George Tulloch made what is probably the single most tasteless *faux pas* during this broadcast that I have ever heard during a *Titanic* exploration, there is no denying that the recovery of the Big Piece, the implementing of the year-long "rusticle" experiment (in which various metals were placed on the ocean floor to see which metal best resists rusticle formation, in the hopes of using that sort of metal in future ship-building endeavors), plus the amazing exterior and interior footage recorded during the mission all make this a monumentally important scientific event. The *faux pas* I am referring to occured during one of Sarah James's conversations with Paul Matthias down in the *Nautile*. She asked Tulloch if he would like to say something to the underwater explorer, and Tulloch eagerly said he would. He then said to Matthias, "I hope I don't have to tell Gail [Matthias's wife] that you're sleeping at the bottom of the ocean tonight." Tulloch was actually referring to the weather holding up for *Nautile*'s ascent, but it came across as extremely inappropriate, considering that they were exploring a wreck that many consider a tomb where more than fifteen hundred people *still* "sleep" at the bottom of the ocean. It is this kind of unthinking and disrespectful remark that has infuriated many of *Titanic*'s antisalvage proponents.

Regarding the prosalvage versus antisalvage argument, I think Charles Haas made a very good argument defending his and Tulloch's efforts over the past decade or so. Now that we know for certain that *Titanic* is disintegrating, there will come a time when the artifacts recovered, video footage, and photographs taken of the wreck are all the world has left of the great liner. That truly is an important consideration and makes a strong argument for chronicling the wreck in as detailed a manner as possible before the inevitable happens. Whether you agree with Haas and Tulloch or not, there is no denying that if they were not doing what they are doing, our knowledge of *Titanic* and her passengers and crew would be far less complete.

I feel that it's also necessary to say a few words about the anchors of this broadcast. Bob McKeown and Sarah James are undoubtedly professionals . . . but they are also obviously not serious *Titanic* aficionados. *Titanic* '98 was an assignment for them and thus, I got the sense that they crammed for the event, much the way a college student who didn't crack a book for a whole semester tries to learn the entire course over the weekend before finals.

This kind of sudden and overwhelming immersion in a subject often results in hyperbole, especially in the attempt at communicating the importance and momentousness of the event being covered.

Sarah James was especially guilty of this, commenting that the *Titanic*'s victims were a "crucible" and that "they were us." Later, speaking of *Titanic*'s legend, she said that "we plotted her with the longtitude and the latitude of our imaginations." Earlier in the broadcast, Bob McKeown told us that we were "watching something that no one has ever seen before." Well, I suppose that's *technically* correct but the hype factor seemed a tad too much. Even John Siegenthaler poured it on, describing the broadcast as "an unprecedented event in television" that was making "broadcast history." I guess the video footage from the Moon didn't make the cut, eh? The concluding remarks by the anchors were even worse.

"*Titanic* Live" was an important event in the history of *Titanic* exploration. But it seems to have been a little too slick for most of the *Titanic* faithful. Following the broadcast, the *Titanic* Internet newsgroups were flooded with postings about the show and the reviews were almost over-whelmingly negative. In fact, the occasional poster who claimed to have enjoyed the broadcast was immediately attacked and accused of being an RMS Titanic public relations shill.

Overall, the broadcast was well worth watching, but throughout its two hours, I kept wondering how *National Geographic* would have tackled the same project.

I suspect the results would have been somewhat different.

APPENDIX A
TITANIC RESOURCES

MOVIES AND TV

1912 *Saved From the Titanic* (silent)
1929 *Atlantic* (feature film)
1943 *Titanic* (Nazi propaganda film)
1953 *Titanic* (feature film)
1956 *A Night to Remember* (NBC/Kraft; made for TV)
1958 *A Night to Remember* (feature film)
1979 *S.O.S. Titanic* (ABC; made for TV)
1980 *Raise the Titanic* (feature film)
1996 *Titanic* (CBS; made-for-TV miniseries)
1997 *Titanic* (feature film)

Titanic-Related Episodes of TV Series and Films With a Titanic Cameo

1958 *One Step Beyond:* "April 14th" (TV episode)
1964 *The Unsinkable Molly Brown* (feature film)
1966 *The Time Tunnel:* "Rendezvous With Yesterday" (TV episode)
1971 *Night Gallery:* "Lone Survivor" (TV episode)
1976 *Upstairs Downstairs* (BBC-TV series)
1979 *Time Bandits* (feature film)
1982 *Voyagers:* "Voyagers of the Titanic" (TV episode)
1985 *Ghostbusters 2* (feature film)
1995 *No Greater Love* (made-for-TV movie)

DOCUMENTARIES

The Final Voyage (1960)
S.O.S. Titanic (1979)
Titanic: A Question of Murder (1983)
Return to the Titanic (1986)
Titanic: The Nightmare and the Dream (1986)
National Geographic, Secrets of the Titanic (1987)

National Geographic, Search for Battleship Bismarck (1990)
I Witness Video, Eva Hart (1992)
Treasures of the Titanic (1992)
Titanica (1993)
Titanic: Treasures of the Deep (1993)
The Making of a Night to Remember (1994)
National Geographic, Last Voyage of the Lusitania (1994)
Titanic: The Legend Lives On (1994)
Echoes of Titanic (1997)
Titanic: Anatomy of a Disaster (1997)
Titanic: Collide With Destiny (1997)
Titanic Remembered (1997)
Titanic: Breaking New Ground (1998)
Titanic: Secrets Revealed (1998)

BOOKS

Nonfiction

Archbold, Rick, and McCauley, Dana. *Last Dinner on the Titanic: Menus and Recipes From the Legendary Liner.* New York: Hyperion, 1997.

Ballard, Robert. *Finding the Titanic.* New York: Cartwheel Books, 1993.

Ballard, Robert, with Archbold, Rick. *The Discovery of the Titanic.* New York, Toronto: Warner Books, Madison Press, 1987.

Beesley, Lawrence. *The Loss of the Titanic: Its Story and Its Lessons.* New York: Houghlin Mifflin, 1912.

Behe, George. *Titanic: Psychic Forewarnings of a Tragedy.* Cambridge, England: Patrick Stephens, 1987.

Biel, Steven. *Down With the Old Canoe: A Cultural History of the Titanic Disaster.* New York, W. W. Norton, 1996.

Bonsall, Thomas E. *Titanic.* New York: Gallery, 1987.

Booth, John, and Coughlan, Sean. *Titanic: Signals of Disaster.* Westbury: White Star, 1993.

Bown, Mark, and Simmons, Roger. *R.M.S. Titanic: A Portrait in Old Picture Postcards.* Shropshire, England: Brampton, 1987.

Boyd-Smith, Peter. *Titanic: From Rare Historical Reports.* 1st ed. Southampton: Brooks, 1992; Southampton: Steamship, 1994 (2nd ed.).

Braynard, Frank O. *Story of the Titanic Postcards: Twenty-four Ready-to-Mail Cards.* New York: Dover Publications, 1988.

Brown, Rustie. *The Titanic, the Psychic, and the Sea.* Lomita, Calif.: Blue Harbor, 1981.

Bryceson, Dave. *The Titanic Disaster: As Reported in the British National Press April–July 1912.* New York: Norton, 1997.

Bullock, Shan F. *A Titanic Hero: Thomas Andrews, Shipbuilder.* Riverside,

Conn.: Seven C's Press, 1973 (reprint of an edition published in Dublin in 1912 by Maunsel Press).

Butler, Daniel Allen. *Unsinkable: The Full Story of RMS Titanic.* Mechanicsburg, Penn.: Stackpole Books, 1998.

Clarke, Arthur. *Ghost From the Grand Banks.* New York: Bantam Doubleday Dell, 1990.

Cohen, Leo. *Titanic Revisited.* La Jolla, Calif.: L. Cohen, 1984.

Conklin, Thomas. *The Titanic Sinks!: Disaster as Media Event.* New York: Random House, 1997.

Conrad, Joseph. *Notes on Life and Letters.* London and Toronto: J. M. Dent and Sons Ltd., 1921.

Cooper, Gary. *The Man Who Sank the Titanic?: The Life and Times of Captain Edward J. Smith.* Stoke-on-Trent, England: Witan, 1992.

Costello, Philip. *Titanic.* Portsmouth, Hampshire, England: Titanic Products, 1985.

Davie, Michael. *Titanic: The Death and Life of a Legend.* New York: Knopf, 1987.

Eaton, John P., and Haas, Charles A. *Titanic: The Story in Pictures.* Wellington, England: Stephens, 1986.

_____. *Titanic: Destination Disaster: The Legend and the Reality.* New York: Norton, 1987.

_____. *Titanic: Triumph and Tragedy.* New York: Norton, 1986.

Everett, Marshall, ed. *The Wreck and Sinking of the Titanic: The Ocean's Greatest Disaster: A Graphic and Thrilling Account of the Greatest Floating Palace Ever Built Carrying Down to Watery Graves More Than 1,500 Souls.* Chicago: L. H. Walter, 1912.

Friedlander, Robert. *Titanic.* (Translated by Erna McArthur). London: Secker, 1938.

Gardiner, Robin, and van der Vat, Dan. *The Riddle of the Titanic.* London: Weidenfeld and Nicolson, 1995.

_____. *The Titanic Conspiracy: Cover-Ups and Mysteries of the World's Most Famous Sea Disaster.* Secaucus, N.J.: Citadel Press, 1996.

Gardner, Martin, ed. *The Wreck of the Titanic Foretold?* New York: Prometheus, 1998.

Garrett, Richard. *Atlantic Disaster: Titanic and Other Victims of the North Atlantic.* Auburn, Wash.: Seven Hills, 1986.

Gibbs, Philip. *The Deathless Story of the Titanic.* London: Lloyd's Weekly News, 1912.

Gracie, Col. Archibald. *The Truth About the Titanic.* New York: Mitchell, Kennerly, 1913 (reprint published as *Titanic: A Survivor's Story* by Chicago Academy Press, 1996).

Harrison, Leslie. *Defending Captain Lord: A Titanic Myth, Part Two.* Worcestershire, England: Images Publications, 1996.

———. *A Titanic Myth: The Californian Incident.* London: William Kimber, 1986.

Heyer, Paul. *Titanic Legacy: Disaster as Media Event and Myth.* Westport, Conn.: Praeger, 1995.

Hilton, George W. *Legacy of the Titanic.* Stanford, Calif.: Stanford University Press, 1995.

Hoffman, William, and Grimm, Jack. *Beyond Reach: The Search for the Titanic.* New York: Beaufort Books, 1982.

Hyslop, Donald; Forsyth, Alastair; and Jemima, Sheila, eds. *Titanic Voices: Memories From the Fateful Voyage.* New York: St. Martin's Press, 1997.

Kuntz, Tom, ed. *The Titanic Disaster Hearings: The Official Transcripts of the 1912 Senate Investigation.* New York: Pocket Books, 1998.

Lightoller, Commander C. H. *Titanic and Other Ships.* London: Nicholson and Watson, 1935.

Lloyd's Weekly News. *The Deathless Story of the Titanic: Complete Narrative With Many Illustrations.* London: Lloyd's Weekly News, 1912 (reprint: London: Lloyd's of London Press, 1985).

Lord, Walter. *The Night Lives On.* New York: William Morrow, 1986.

———. *A Night to Remember.* New York: Holt, Rinehart, and Winston, 1955.

Lynch, Donald. *Titanic: An Illustrated History.* New York: Hyperion, 1992.

MacInnis, Joseph. *Titanic: In a New Light.* Charlottesville, Vir.: Thomasson-Grant, 1992.

Marcus, Geoffrey. *The Maiden Voyage.* New York: Viking Press, 1969.

Marsh, Ed. *James Cameron's Titanic.* New York: HarperPerennial, 1997.

Marshall, Logan, ed. *The Sinking of the Titanic.* Philadelphia: John C. Winston Co., 1912.

Mauro, Philip. *The Titanic Catastrophe and Its Lessons.* London: Morgan and Scott, 1912.

Mowbray, Jay H. *Sinking of the Titanic: Most Appalling Ocean Horror With Graphic Descriptions of Hundreds Swept to Eternity Beneath the Waves.* Harrisburg, Penn.: Minter Co., 1912.

Neil, Henry. *Wreck and Sinking of the Titanic.* Chicago: Homewood Press, 1912.

O'Connor, Richard. *Down to Eternity.* New York: Fawcett, 1956.

Padfield, Peter. *The Titanic and the Californian.* New York: John Day Co., 1965.

Pellegrino, Charles R. *Her Name, Titanic: The Untold Story of the Sinking and Finding of the Unsinkable Ship.* New York: McGraw-Hill, 1988.

Pellow, James, with Kendle, Dorothy. *A Lifetime on the Titanic: The Biography of Edith Haisman.* London: Island Books, 1995.

Quinn, Paul J. *Titanic at Two A.M: An Illustrated Narrative With Survivor Accounts.* New York: Fantail, 1997.

Random House. *Titanic: The Official Story April 14–15, 1912.* New York: Random House, 1997.

Reade, Leslie. *The Ship That Stood Still: The Californian and Her Mysterious Role in the Titanic Disaster.* New York: Norton, 1993.

Robertson, Morgan, and Stevenson, Ian. *The Wreck of the Titan: The Paranormal Experiences Connected With the Sinking of the Titanic.* Cutchogue, N.Y.: Buccaneer Books, 1991.

Rose, Alan. *Build Your Own Titanic.* New York: G. P. Putnam, 1981.

Rostron, Capt. Arthur. *Home From the Sea.* New York: Macmillan, 1931.

Russell, Thomas H. *Sinking of the Titanic.* Chicago: Homewood Press, 1912.

Shipbuilders magazine. *Ocean Liners of the Past: Olympic and Titanic.* Cambridge, England: Patrick Stephens, Ltd., 1976 (reprint of the magazine's 1911 editions).

Spignesi, Stephen J. *The Complete Titanic: From the Ship's Earliest Blueprints to the Epic Film.* Secaucus, N.J.: Birch Lane Press, 1998.

Stenson, Patrick. *"Lights": The Odyssey of C. H. Lightoller.* New York: Norton, 1984.

Thayer, John B. *The Sinking of the S.S. Titanic: April 14–15, 1912.* Philadelphia: John B. Thayer, 1940.

Tibbals, Geoff. *The Titanic: The Extraordinary Story of the "Unsinkable" Ship.* New York: Reader's Digest, 1997.

Ticehurst, Brian J. *Titanic Passenger Miss Kate Buss of Sittingbourne.* Kent, England: B&J Printers, 1995.

———. *Titanic's Memorials, Worldwide: Where They Are Located: A Listing of the Memorials and Grave Sites/Stones of Both Titanic Victims and Survivors.* Southampton: B&J Printers, 1996.

Tyler, Sidney. *A Rainbow of Time and Space: Orphans of the Titanic.* Tucson, Ariz.: Aztek Corporation, 1981.

Wade, Wyn Craig. *Titanic: End of a Dream.* New York: Penguin, 1986.

Walker, J. Bernard. *An Unsinkable Titanic: Every Ship Its Own Lifeboat.* New York: Dodd, Mead, 1912.

Wels, Susan. *Titanic: Legacy of the World's Greatest Ocean Liner.* New York: Time-Life, 1997.

Winocour, Jack, ed. *The Story of the Titanic: As Told by Its Survivors.* (Lawrence Beesley, Archibald Gracie, C. H. Lightoller, Harold Bride). New York: Dover, 1960.

Young, Filson. *Titanic.* London: G. Richard, 1912.

Fiction

Bainbridge, Beryl. *Every Man for Himself.* London: Duckworth, 1996.
Bass, Cynthia. *Maiden Voyage.* New York: Bantam Books, 1997.
Brown, Richard. *Voyage of the Iceberg.* New York: Beaufort Books, 1983.
Chipperfield, Joseph E. *The Story of a Great Ship: The Birth and Death of the Steamship Titanic.* New York: Roy Publications, 1959.
Cussler, Clive. *Raise the Titanic!* New York: Viking Press, 1976.
Finney, Jack. *From Time to Time: A Novel.* New York: Simon and Schuster, 1995.
Peck, Richard. *Amanda/Miranda.* New York: Viking, 1980.
Precht, Robert. *Titanic.* New York: Dutton, 1940.
Robertson, Morgan. *Futility, or the Wreck of the Titan.* Secaucus, N.J.: Citadel Press, 1998 (in *The Complete Titanic: From the Ship's Earliest Blueprints to the Epic Film,* by Stephen J. Spignesi).
Seil, William. *Sherlock Holmes and the Titanic Tragedy: A Case to Remember.* New York: Inbook, 1996.
Stanwood, Donald. *The Memory of Eva Ryker.* New York: Coward McCann and Geoghegan, 1987.
Steel, Danielle. *No Greater Love.* New York: Bantam Doubleday Dell, 1991.
Ziavras, Charles. *Titanic Interlude.* Lowell, Mass.: Ithica Press, 1983.

Poetry

Ball, Richard. "The Last Voyage of the Titanic." Milton, Ind.: Gazebo Books, 1968.
Cronin, Anthony. "R.M.S. Titanic." Dublin, Ireland: Raen Arts Press, 1981.
Dixon, J. Qallan. "Wreck of the Steamship Titanic." Buffalo, N.Y.: Sovereign Publishing, 1912.
Drew, Edwin. "The Wreck of the Titanic: Treated in Verse." London: W. Nicholson and Sons, 1912.
Greeley, Horace. "The Wreck of the Titanic: A Poem." Brooklyn, N.Y.: Donald Sinclair, n.d.
Hardy, Thomas. "The Convergence of the Twain." New York: Prometheus, 1998 (in *The Wreck of the Titanic Foretold?* ed. by Martin Gardner).
Howell, J. A. "The Great Ship Titanic and Its Disaster." Richwood, W.V.: Yew Pine Independent Print, 1913.
MacFie, Ronald Campbell. "The Titanic: An Ode of Immortality." London: E. MacDonald, 1912.
Pratt, E. J. "The Titanic." Toronto: Macmillan, 1935.

Root, E. Merrill. "Of Perilous Seas" (including "When Man's Great Ship Went Down"). Francestown, N.H.: Golden Quill Press, 1964.

Stahl, C. Victor. "The Sinking of the Titanic and Other Poems." Boston: Sherman, French and Co., 1915.

Children's Books

Ballard, Robert. *Exploring the Titanic.* New York: Scholastic, 1988.

Blos, Joan. *The Heroine of the Titanic: A Tale Both True and Otherwise of the Life of Molly Brown.* New York: Morrow, 1991.

Boning, Richard. *Adventures at Sea.* Baldwin, N.Y.: Dexter and Westbrook, 1978.

_____. *Titanic* (Incredible Series). Baldwin, N.Y.: Dexter and Westbrook, 1974.

Brewster, Hugh. *Inside the Titanic: A Giant Cut-Away Book.* Illustrated by Ken Marschall. New York: Little, Brown, 1997.

Bunting, Eve. *S.O.S. Titanic.* San Diego, Calif.: Harcourt Brace, 1996.

Cooke, Arthur Owens. *A Day in the Shipyard.* New York: Hodder and Stoughton, 1911.

Donnelly, Judy. *The Titanic, Lost . . . and Found.* New York: Random House, 1987.

Gormley, Beatrice. *Back to the Titanic!* Denver: Apple, 1994.

Hamilton, Sue L. *Royal Mail Steamship Titanic.* Bloomington, Minn.: Abdo and Daughters, 1988.

Henkel, Virginia. *Letters From the Past.* Petone, N.Z.: Nelson Price Milburn, 1989.

Kent, Deborah. *The Titanic* (Cornerstones of Freedom Series). Danbury, Conn.: Children's Press, 1993.

Rawlinson, Jonathan. *Discovering the Titanic* (Great Adventure Series). Vero Beach, Fla.: Rourke Enterprises, 1988.

Sloan, Frank. *Titanic* (a First Book Series). New York: Watts, 1987.

Spedden, Daisy, and Stone, Corning. *Polar the Titanic Bear.* Boston: Little, Brown, 1994.

Stacey, Thomas. *The Titanic* (World Disaster Series). San Diego: Lucent, 1989.

Tanaka, Shelley. *On Board the Titanic: What It Was Like When the Great Liner Sank.* Richmond Hill, Ontario: Scholastic Canada, 1996.

Wallace, Jim. *Terror on the Titanic* (Choose Your Own Adventure, No. 169). New York: Bantam, 1996.

Williams, Barbara. *Titanic Crossing.* New York: Dial Books for Young Readers, 1995.

MAGAZINES

Here is a listing of some selected magazine coverage of the discovery of the *Titanic*, and *Titanic*, the movie. Many of these magazines featured their *Titanic* story on their cover. There are, in addition to these periodicals, hundreds of journals around the world that have published stories about *Titanic* (both the historical event and the movie), but it would require a separate volume to list those and this is not intended to be such a bibliography. Instead, this is meant to serve as a guide for those interested in some recent and important periodical coverage of the ship and the film.

Al Majalla (Saudi Arabia; January 1998)
American Cinematographer (December 19, 1997)
Celebrity Skin (December 1997)
Cine Live (France; January 1998)
Cinefex (December 1997)
Cinema (Germany; January 1998)
Civilization (December 1997)
Computer Graphics World (January 1998)
Cracked (March 1998; May 1998)
Empire (England; February 1998)
Entertainment Weekly (October 24, 1997; November 2, 1997; November 7, 1997; December 12, 1997; December 19, 1997; January 9, 1998; January 23, 1998; February 6, 1998; March 13, 1998; March 20, 1998; 1998 Oscar edition)
Esquire (December 1997)
Film Comment (January/February 1998)
Film Review (England; January 1998; February 1998)
Gente (Italy; February 1998)
Globe (January 13, 1998; March 24, 1998; March 31, 1998)
Gold Series: Leo and Titanic (March 1998)
Le Figaro (France; January 1998)
Life (June 1997)
Linux Journal (February 1998)
Make-Up Artist (February 1998)
Movieline (December/January 1997/1998; March 1998)
National Geographic (December 1985; December 1986)
National Review (December 23, 1996)
Naval History (October 1996)
New Tekniques (December 1997)
Newsweek (September 16, 1985; September 23, 1985; February 23, 1998)
Nouvel Observateur (France; February 1998)
Panorama (Italy; February 1998)

Paris Match (France; February 12, 1998)
People (May 19, 1997; January 26, 1998)
Popular Mechanics (January 1986; September 1998)
Popular Science (February 1995)
Porthole (January 1998)
Premiere (France; January 1998; December 1997)
The Red Herring (January 1998)
Roadshow (Japan; February 1998)
Rolling Stone (March 5, 1998)
Science (September 27, 1985)
Sea Classics (February 1998; March 1988)
Smithsonian (August 1986)
Theatre Crafts International (January 1998)
Time (August 11, 1986; September 16, 1985)
Time Out (England; December 1997)
TV Hits (England; January 1998)
US (January 1988)
U.S. News and World Report (September 16, 1985; September 23, 1985; July 28, 1986; August 11, 1986)
Vanity Fair (January 1998; March 1988)
Veja (Spain; January 1998)
Wired (February 1998)
Written By (December 1997)

ORGANIZATIONS

If you were going to join only one *Titanic* historical society, do yourself a favor and join the first organization on the list below, the Titanic Historical Society, Inc. (THS), based in Massachusetts. Their official publication, the *Titanic Commutator,* is alone worth the annual membership fee. If you do join, you will be in good company: Don Lynch, Ken Marschall, and Dr. Robert Ballard are all members of the THS (as is your humble author), and the entire organization works very hard to maintain the memory of the *Titanic* in a dignified, yet historically accurate manner. Their catalog of books, videos, audiotapes, posters, and other *Titanic* memorabilia is a wonder to behold. The society's annual convention attracts the elite of the world of *Titanic* aficionados—including *Titanic* survivors—and the society even has its own museum, located, in, of all places, the rear of a jewelry store.

As to the other organizations, I have had no personal contact with anyone associated with these groups, but provide their addresses (which may or may not be current) for those interested in learning more about them.

Titanic Historical Society
P.O. Box 51053 (208 Main Street)
Indian Orchard, MA 01151
(413) 543-4770

Titanic International, Inc.
P.O. Box 7007
Freehold, NJ 07728

The British Titanic Society
P.O. Box 401
Hope Carr Way
Leigh, Lancashire
WN7 3WW England

The Titanic Society of Ireland
The Anchorage
Coast Road
Malahide Co.
Dublin, Ireland

The Shannon Ulster Titanic Society
Adam Bell
8 Knockdene
Bangor, Co. Down
Northern Ireland
BT20 4UZ6AE

The Ulster Titanic Society
32 Heatherstone Road
Bangor, Co. Down
Northern Ireland
BT19 6AE

The Steamship Historical Society of America
300 Ray Drive
Suite No. 4
Providence, RI 02906
(401) 274-0805

The Titanic Society of South Africa
P.O. Box 1880
Rottenville, 2130
Johannesburg
South Africa

MEMORABILIA SOURCES

Titanic memorabilia often walks a fine line. When do *Titanic* "souvenirs" cross that line and become disrespectful and inappropriate? The *Titanic* sinking was, after all, a terrible disaster in which over 1,500 people lost their lives. Many consider the wreck a gravesite and regard *Titanic* memorabilia as offensive as Holocaust or slavery souvenirs.

Nevertheless, there is a huge market for *Titanic* items, and for those interested in what is available, there are two important sources, the Titanic Historical Society and the J. Peterman Company.

The Titanic Historical Society

The Titanic Historical Society publishes a catalog of *Titanic* books and merchandise that is a gold mine of *Titanic* information. Profits from sales go to help maintain the superb quality of the society's official publication, the *Titanic Commutator*, and also to help defray other organizational expenses, thereby allowing the society to keep membership dues very reasonable (most members pay around $25, which, considering the caliber of the *Commutator* and the other services provided by the society, is quite inexpensive).

Contact the THS at the address provided above in the "Organizations" section.

THS's catalog of Titanic items includes the following:

- Audiocassettes and CDs of *Titanic* survivor accounts
- Videotapes of *Titanic* documentaries
- *Titanic* books, including reprints of rare 1912 volumes, officer and survivor biographies, passenger and crew lists, children's books, books about the *Californian* controversy, and official *Titanic* documents
- Audiocassettes and CDs of *Titanic* songs and music
- 1912 newspaper reproductions
- Histories of related subjects, including several volumes about the invention of wireless radio communication
- Authentic reproductions of White Star Line flags, badges, brochures, booklets, and other items
- *Titanic* postcard sets, many of which reprint original 1912 postcards
- *Titanic* and White Star Line stationery, note cards, and envelopes
- Reprints of authentic *Titanic, Olympic, Brittanic, Homeric, Carpathia, Adriatic, Andrea Doria,* and *Empress of Ireland* deck plans
- *Titanic* posters, lithographs, fine art prints, and photos, including many Ken Marschall works, as well as prints and photos signed by *Titanic* survivors, such as Millvina Dean and Winnifred Quick Van Tangerloo
- *Titanic* and White Star Line T-shirts, caps, jewelry, and watches

- Novelties such as *Titanic* jigsaw puzzles, writing pens, key chains, magnets, and needlepoint patterns
- Back issues of the *Titanic Commutator*

The J. Peterman Company

The J. Peterman Co., the Lexington, Kentucky, mail-order firm immortalized on *Seinfeld* (Elaine writes catalog copy for the company) and known for quirky little mini-stories about their merchandise, also sells *Titanic* merchandise, but their line is markedly different from the items offered by the Titanic Historical Society.

The company got into the "*Titanic* business" in the fall of 1997 when they began offering authentic props and other items from James Cameron's movie. This initial foray into the world of *Titanic* fandom far exceeded their expectations (they sold out of almost everything, almost immediately, including very expensive costumes and other items from the movie) and in their spring 1998 catalog (which had "More TITANIC" prominently displayed on the cover), they expanded their offerings by adding authentic *Titanic* artifacts to their line. Even though artifacts recovered from the wreck cannot legally be sold, reproductions of *Titanic* items were eagerly sought after, and J. Peterman capitalized on this hunger by commissioning replicas of *Titanic* artifacts and also by buying some extremely rare *Titanic* items that could be sold legally. (See the section in this chapter called "The Rarest Titanic Collectible in Existence?")

The J. Peterman Company worked with George Tulloch's group, RMS Titanic, to include "exact reproductions of items salvaged by RMS Titanic, Inc., which has sole rights to the recovery." They also offered "a limited number of astonishing props and costumes from . . . *Titanic*." (The catalog also stated that "Actual artifacts from the *Titanic* aren't for sale at any price," but that they were "being preserved by RMST for permanent display for future generations.")

Here is a selected listing of some of J. Peterman's *Titanic* merchandise, which was separated from the rest of the catalog in a special four-page section titled "Ship of Dreams" (amount in parentheses are the prices the items sell for, not their face value):

- *Titanic* framed tickets with stubs ($250)
- *Titanic* wicker wingback chair and sofa ($3,500)
- Original *Titanic* posters signed by James Cameron ($95—at the request of James Cameron, half of the proceeds from the sale of these posters went to the National Multiple Sclerosis Foundation)
- R.M.S. *Titanic* stationery set ($45)

- "Captain Smith's" coat ($5,000—worn by Bernard Hill in *Titanic*)
- *Titanic* anchor ($25,000—a fiberglass thirteen-foot tall replica of the actual *Titanic* anchor)
- *Titanic* flatware, framed ($375—used in the movie)
- *Titanic*-era $20 gold standard bills (sold for $350—used in the movie)
- *Titanic* folding leather chair ($795—replica of a *Titanic* chair)

The J. Peterman Co. also offered the authorized replica of Rose's "La Coeur da Mer" (Heart of the Ocean) necklace for $198, which is rather expensive for a rhodium-plated chain and mounting, with synthetic diamonds. Fans thought otherwise, however, and by the April 15, 1998, anniversary of *Titanic*'s sinking, the company had sold over four thousand of these necklaces. "This is far and away the best *Titanic* seller," J. Peterman's Arnie Cohen told *USA Today*. "Between now and June 1, we think we'll sell more than ten thousand."

NEWSGROUPS AND E-DIGESTS

Internet newsgroups are essentially cyberspace bulletin boards where people with like interests can post messages, questions, FAQs (Frequently Asked Questions files), and also respond to others on the newsgroup. Individual messages are called subjects, and a message with its resultant responses are called threads.

E-Digests, on the other hand, are compilations of postings and responses that are e-mailed to subscribers of the digest daily.

For *Titanic* buffs, there are two newsgroups and one E-Digest worth your attention:

Newsgroups

alt.history.ocean-liners.titanic   This is a historic newsgroup that looks at the ship and the sinking, along with everything relevant to the history of the *Titanic*. Some of the postings are extremely informative and boast a high level of knowledge; many are naive questions by posters who are visiting the site for the first time. There is ongoing debate on this newsgroup about such issues as Murdoch's suicide, the fate of the *Titanic*'s lifeboats, and even whether or not there was an Egyptian mummy in *Titanic*'s cargo hold.

Shortly after the movie *Titanic* was released, in December 1997, many movie fanatics began posting on alt.history.ocean-liners.titanic, eager for dialogue about the film. Some of the longtime members of the newsgroup were angered by this kind of digression, and their outcry contributed to the establishment of a newsgroup devoted to the movie.

alt.movies.titanic   This is the newsgroup devoted to James Cameron's movie, *Titanic*. The postings are frequent and consist of talk about favorite scenes, and rumors about things like the video release and edited versions of the film in other countries. For a time, there were ongoing threads about the Heart of the Ocean replicas and the position of the movie on the all-time earnings list. This newsgroup gets a lot of "I Love Leonardo DiCaprio" postings, as well as frequent postings about where to find nude photos of Kate Winslet on the net. Between the two, alt.movies.titanic is the less serious of the *Titanic* newsgroups.

E-Digests

titanic-discuss@silverquick.com   This is a daily digest of questions, comments, and files about the *Titanic* that is e-mailed only to subscribers. The postings average between ten and one hundred a day and can be quite a chore to keep up with on a daily basis. A lot of information is provided in this digest, however, and might be worth subscribing to (it's free) if you consider yourself a very serious *Titanic* aficionado who wants a great deal of information from fellow Rivet Heads. This informative digest can also be subscribed to at their Web site. Point your browser to http://www.silverquick.com/titanic.htm The *Titanic Discuss Digest* is owned by Mark Taylor, a serious *Titanic* scholar who provides a valuable resource at no cost for those who want to learn more about the history of the *Titanic*. Mark can be reached at met@mindspring.com

WEB SITES

There are too many *Titanic*-related Web sites to even keep track of, so the best way to access *Titanic* information (both historical and movie-related) is to do a search on the World Wide Web for the word *Titanic* and then stand back. A few excellent search engines for this task are www.excite.com, www.hotbot.com, www.infoseek.com, and, of course, that old faithful, www.yahoo.com

To save a little time, however, here are the URLs of some important and interesting *Titanic* sites. Any of these are well worth a visit.

http://www2.titanic1.org/titanic1/
(The Titanic Historical Society)
http://www.titanicmovie.com
(The official *Titanic* movie site)
http://www.titanic-online.com
(The RMS Titanic, Inc., site)
http://www.lib.virginia.edu/cataloging/vnp/titpref.html
(Reprints of *Titanic*-era news stories)
http://www.geocities.com/Hollywood/Hills/3162/titanic_webring.html
(A *Titanic* Web ring with links to other sites)
http://www.discovery.com/DCO/doc/1012/world/specials/titanic/
   titanicopener.html
(*Titanic: Raising a Legend* live online from the Discovery Channel)
http://www.si.edu/resource/faq/titanic.htm
(Entry on the *Titanic* from the Encyclopedia Smithsonian)
http://www.mediature.com/titanic/
(*Titanic* page from Macedon Mediature, Inc.)
http://www.niweb.com/dnet/dnetnAvo/
(International Titanic Convention page from the Ulster Titanic Society)
http://octopus.gma.org/space1/titanic.html
(*The Grave of the Titanic,* from the Gulf of Maine Aquarium)
http://www.frenchbulldog.org/ardesign/titanic
(Includes an interview with *Titanic* survivor Eva Hart)

Here are a couple of other sites worth checking out:

http://www.titanicinternational.org
http://www.sstitanic.com

APPENDIX B
TITANIC'S CARGO MANIFEST

I have always found distracting the traditional way that the *Titanic*'s cargo was listed in the many *Titanic* books published over the years. The shipper's name was always listed first, and then the items they were shipping as cargo on the *Titanic*. It occurred to me that the most interesting aspect of the *Titanic*'s cargo manifest was *what* was shipped, not *who* was shipping it. Thus, for the first time, here is a listing, in alphabetical order, of all the goods listed on the *Titanic*'s cargo manifest.

By listing the contents of the manifest in this manner, this vast quantity of goods becomes much more accessible and easier to read. Also, by reading down the list of goods shipped on the *Titanic*, we get a glimpse and deeper insight into life in the early 1900s.

Cargo Goods	Quantity	Shipper
Alarm apparatus	15 cases	Maltus and Ware
Anchovies	75 cases	Acker, Merrall and Condit
Argols[1]	33 bags	Holder of original bill of lading
Athletic goods	34 cases	A. G. Spaulding and Bros.
Auto	1 case	W. E. Carter
Auto parts	1 case	G. Prost
Beans	3 cases	J. Munro and Co.
Biscuits	25 cases	Wakem and McLaughlin
Biscuits	7 cases	T. Leeming and Co.
Books	5 cases	T. Meadows and Co.
Books	2 cases	Thomas and Pierson
Books	9 cases	American Express Co.
Books	2 cases	Brasch and Rothenstein
Books	3 cases	Snow's Express Co.
Books	10 cases	J. B. Lippincott and Co.
Books	5 cases	American Shipping Co.

[1] Argol is a crude tartar deposited in wine casks during aging.

Cargo Goods	Quantity	Shipper
Books	35 cases	Adams Express
Books	1 case	Davies, Turner and Co.
Books	2 cases	G. W. Sheldon and Co.
Books	5 cases	Adams Express Co.
Books	3 cases	Wells, Fargo and Co.
Books	5 cases	Tice and Lynch
Books and lace	2 cases	G. T. Mathews and Co.
Boots	2 cases	Adams Express Co.
Brandy	110 cases	H. Hollander
Briar Pipes	3 cases	U.S. Export Co.
Brushware	1 case	Park and Tilford
Brushware	1/2 case	Calhoun, Robbins and Co.
Brushware	1 case	Victor and Achiles
Brushware	1 case	Cauvigny Brush Co.
Buchu	8 bales	Order
Buchu	5 bales	Holder of original bill of lading
Bulbs	3 cases	J. M. Thorburn and Co.
Bulbs	1 case	R. F. Downing and Co.
Butter	12 cases	N.Y. and Cuba SS Co.
Calabashes[2]	16 cases	Holder of original bill of lading
Camera and stand	8 cases	American Express Co.
Candles	1 package	American Motor Co.
Canvas	1 case	American Express Co.
Capers	12 bundles	J. Munro and Co.
Champagne	63 cases	F. B. Vandegrift and Co.
Cheese	1 case	American Express Co.
Cheese	70 bundles	Judas Bernard and Co.
Cheese	30 bundles	American Express Co.
Cheese	50 bundles	F. X. Baumert and Co.
Cheese	190 bundles	Rathenberger and Co.
Cheese	50 bundles	Haupt and Burgi
Cheese	40 bundles	Sheldon and Co.
Cheese	50 bundles	C. Percival
Cheese	50 bundles	C. D. Stone and Co.
Cheese	30 bundles	Phoenix Cheese Co.
Cheese	10 bundles	P. H. Petry and Co.
Cheese	15 bundles	Reynolds and Dronig
Cheese	15 bundles	Order

[2] A calabash is a gourd whose hard shell is used as a utensil, such as a bottle.

Cargo Goods	Quantity	Shipper
China	1 cask	Tiffany and Co.
Cloth	1 case	Pitt and Scott
Clothing	1 case	Carbon Machinery Equipment Co.
Cognac	15 cases	C. A. Van Renssaller
Cognac	2 cases	American Express Co.
Coney skins[3]	3 cases	Broadway Trust Co.
Confectionery	6 cases	Adams Express Co.
Cork	6 bales	Wakem and McLaughlin
Cotton	2 cases	Nottingham Lace Works
Cotton	4 cases	Leo J. Rosenthal Co.
Cotton	1 case	Tice and Lynch
Cotton laces	12 cases	H. B. Claflin and Co.
Cotton laces	1 case	Calhoun, Robbins and Co.
Cottons	7 cases	Sherman Sons and Co.
Cottons	20 cases	Mills and Gibb
Cottons	1 case	B. Altman and Co.
Cretonne[4]	1 case	R. H. Sterns and Co.
Crude rubber	31 packages	Order
Dragon's blood[5]	76 cases	Brown Bros and Co.
Dried fruit	8 cases	N.Y. and Cuba SS Co.
Drug sundries	5 cases	Park and Tilford
Earth	1 barrel	American Express Co.
Effects	1 package	American Express Co.
Eggs	1 case	Wells, Fargo and Co.
Elastic cords	1 case	P. C. Kuyper and Co.
Elastics	1 case	American Express Co.
Elastics	1 case	G. W. Sheldon and Co.
Embroidery	4 cases	Holder of original bill of lading
Engine packing	1 case	R. F. Downing and Co.
Factice	14 cases	Order
Feathers	1 case	Young Bros.
Feathers	11 cases	Morris Goldster
Feathers	4 cases	Holder of original bill of lading
Felt	1 case	R. F. Downing and Co.

[3] Coney skins are rabbit skins.

[4] Cretonne is a strong unglazed cotton or linen cloth used especially for curtains or upholstery.

[5] Dragon's blood is a resin from the fruit of a palm used for coloring varnish and in photoengraving.

Cargo Goods	Quantity	Shipper
Films	1 case	N.Y. Motion Picture Co.
Films	6 cases	American Express Co.
Films	1 case	C. B. Richard
Filter paper	41 cases	E. Fouger
Fish	75 bales	Strohmeyver and Arpe
Fish	10 bundles	J. Munro and Co.
Fishes	5 cases	Order
Flowers	2 cases	Judkins and McCormick
Frames	1 bag	Tice and Lynch
Furniture	3 cases	Wm. Baumgarten and Co.
Furniture	2 cases	Thomas and Pierson
Furniture	2 cases	Wells, Fargo and Co.
Glassware	2 barrels	American Express Co.
Gloves	1 case	Mills and Gibb
Gloves	1 case	Marshall Field and Co.
Gloves	1 case	A. M. Tolson and Co.
Gloves	1 case	Speilman Co.
Goat skins	79	Holder of original bill of lading
Golf balls	1 box	G. W. Sheldon and Co.
Gramophone	1 case	American Express Co.
Grandfather clocks	2 cases	Order
Gum	3 cases	Brown Bros and Co.
Gum	13 cases	Order
Gum	14 casks	Order
Gutta-percha[6]	100 bags	Baring Bros and Co.
Hair nets	3 cases	R. Sanger and Co.
Hair nets	1 case	Rush and Co.
Hair nets	4 packages	Order
Hardware	2 cases	Thomas and Pierson
Hat leather, etc.	2 cases	M. J. Corbett and Co.
Hats	1 case	Adams Express Co.
Hatters' fur	10 cases	Order
Hogshead[7] vinegar	2 cases	N.Y. and Cuba SS Co.
Horsehair	2 cases	Order
Hosiery	4 cases	American Express Co.
Hosiery	1 case	James Jacobson

[6] Gutta-percha is a tough plastic substance from the latex of several Malaysian trees that resembles rubber but contains more resin and is used in insulation and in dentistry.

[7] A hogshead is a large cask or barrel, usually holding from 63 to 140 gallons.

Cargo Goods	Quantity	Shipper
Hosiery	3 cases	Thomas Meadows and Co.
Instruments	5 cases	G. W. Sheldon and Co.
Iron jacks	1 case	R. F. Downing and Co.
Ironware	1 case	International Trading Co.
Jute bagging	30 rolls	Order
Lace collars	2 cases	Brasch and Rothenstein
Lace goods	1 case	Gallia Textile Co.
Lace tissue	1 case	G. H. Cobb
Laces	1 case	Naday and Fleischer
Laces	1 case	H. Mallouk
Laces	8 cases	Bardwill Bros.
Leather	1 case	P. C. Kuyper and Co.
Leather	3 bales	Adams Express Co.
Leather	3 cases	A. Wimpfheimer and Co.
Leathers	2 cases	Order
Linens	2 cases	P. K. Wilson and Sons
Linoleum	856 rolls	Witcombe, McGrachlin and Co.
Linoleum	4 rolls	Adams Express Co.
Liquor	1 case	Acker, Merrall and Condit
Liquor	190 cases	P. W. Engs and Sons
Liquor	1 case	Moquin Wine Co.
Liquors	2 cases	Order
Machinery	1 case	G. W. Sheldon and Co.
Machinery	1 crate	Aero Club of America
Machinery	1 case	Davies, Turner and Co.
Machinery	18 cases	Alfred Suter
Meal	1 case	R. F. Downing and Co.
Melons	10 boxes	Dujardin and Ladnick
Merchandise	25 cases	American Express Co.
Merchandise	1 case	Davies, Turner and Co.
Merchandise	2 parcels	American Express Co.
Merchandise	1 case	F. B. Vandegrift and Co.
Merchandise	1 parcel	S. Budd
Merchandise	1 parcel	Lemke and Buechner
Merchandise	1 case	G. S. Nicholas and Co.
Merchandise	1 case	G. A. Walker
Merchandise	18 cases	American Express Co.
Merchandise	20 bundles	J. Munro and Co.
Mercury	2 barrels	American Express Co.
Mixed vegetables	10 cases	J. Munro and Co.
Mushrooms	107 cases	Knauth, Nachod and Kuhne

Cargo Goods	Quantity	Shipper
Mushroooms	22 cases	J. Munro and Co.
Mushroooms	25 cases	Nichols Austin
Mussels	225 cases	Acker, Merrall and Condit
Notions	1 case	Davies, Turner and Co.
Oil	18 cases	N.Y. and Cuba SS Co.
Oil	38 cases	Moquin Wine Co.
Old oak beams	A quantity	American Express Co.
Olive oil	25 cases	Nichols Austin
Olives	25 cases	J. Munro and Co.
Opium	4 cases	Order
Orchids[8]	8 cases	Maltus and Ware
Orchids	11 cases	Maltus and Ware
Ostrich feathers	12 cases	Holder of original bill of lading
Packed packages	1 case	American Express Co.
Pamphlets	1 case	Wells, Fargo and Co.
Pamphlets	1 case	Knauth, Nachod and Kuhne
Parcel	1	E. H. Van Ingen and Co.
Parchment	1 case	T. Meadows and Co.
Paste	8 cases	American Express Co.
Peas	15 cases	J. Munro and Co.
Peas	13 cases	J. Munro and Co.
Pens	4 cases	Spencerian Pen Co.
Periodicals	12 packages	G. E. Stechert and Co.
Periodicals	10 packages	International News Co.
Photos	1 case	Davies, Turner and Co.
Pictures	1 case	Davies, Turner and Co.
Pictures, etc.	2 cases	Oelrichs and Co.
Plants	1 case	American Express Co.
Plants	30 cases	Hempstead and Sons
Plants	1 case	Wells, Fargo and Co.
Potatoes	1,196 bags	Chas Pape and Co.
Potatoes	318 bags	J. P. Sauer and Co.
Potatoes	1,962 bags	Order
Preserves	25 cases	Schall and Co.
Preserves	6 cases	N.Y. and Cuba SS Co.

[8] These nineteen cases of orchids (five hundred all told) were bound from India to California via the *Titanic*. They were of a rare variety not yet introduced on the Pacific coast and growers there were eagerly awaiting their arrival—until they received the news that the flowers had been shipped to them on the *Titanic*.

Cargo Goods	Quantity	Shipper
Preserves	3 cases	Lazard Freres
Printed matter	1 case	Aero Club of America
Printed matter	4 cases	Pitt and Scott
Printed matter	4 cases	Davies, Turner and Co.
Printed matter	2 cases	U.S. Export Co.
Printed matter	3 cases	American Express Co.
Printer's blankets	4 cases	Fuchs and Lang Manufacturing Co.
Prints	3 cases	American Express Co.
Rabbit hair	1 case	Order
Rabbit hair	15 cases	Brown Bros. and Co.
Raw feathers	1 case	A. I. Simon and Co.
Raw feathers	7 cases	Order
Raw silk	8 bales	Order
Refrigeration apparatus	11 cases	Anderson Refrigeration Machinery Co.
Ribbons	2 cases	J. G. Johnson Co.
Rough wood	35 bags	H. Blechoff and Co.
Rubber	68 cases	Baring Bros and Co.
Rubber	11 bales	National City Bank of New York
Rubber	134 cases	Arnold and Zeiss
Rubber goods	1 case	American Express Co.
Salt powder	60 cases	S. Stern
Samples	3 boxes	T. Meadows and Co.
Samples	2 cases	American Express Co.
Sardines	25 cases	Lazard Freres
Sardines	246 cases	Order
Scientific instruments	1 case	U.S. Export Co.
Sero fittings	1 case	American Express Co.
Sheep skins	3 bales	Holder of original bill of lading
Shelled walnuts	100 cases	Brown Bros. and Co.
Shelled walnuts	11 cases	Heidelbach, Ickelheimer and Co.
Shelled walnuts	100 bales	Brown Bros. and Co.
Shelled walnuts	300 cases	First National Bank of Chicago
Shelled walnuts	150 cases	Order
Shells	5 cases	Kronfeld, Saunders and Co.
Silk	2 cases	Order
Silk crepe	3 cases	Spielman Co.
Silk goods	1 case	Flietmann and Co.
Silk goods	3 cases	J. A. Blum
Silk goods	3 cases	T. Tiedman and Sons

Cargo Goods	Quantity	Shipper
Silk goods	1 case	F. Costa
Silver goods	1 case	Tiffany and Co.
Skins	1 bale	Thorer and Praetorius
Skins	5 packages	M. Cohen Bros
Skins	1 case	Engle Gross Co.
Skins	1 bale	Lazard Freres
Skins	4 bales	J. Gillman
Skins	2 packages	Dublin, Morris and Kornbluth
Skins	8 bales	Order
Skins	8 bales	Order
Skins	8 packages	Order
Skins	1 case	Order
Skins	3 bales	Holder of original bill of lading
Soap	6 cases	F. R. Arnold Co.
Soap	2 cases	Adams Express Co.
Soap perfume	3 cases	Crown Perfume Co.
Speedometer	1 case	American Express Co.
Sponges	117 cases	Lasker and Bernstein
Stationery	2 cases	Tice and Lynch
Sticks	28 bags	Rawstick and H. Trading Co.
Straw	4 bales	Isler and Guve
Straw	53 packages	Isler and Guve
Straw braids	1 case	American Express Co.
Straw goods	13 bales	H. W. Peabody and Co.
Straw hats	4 cases	Lustig Bros
Straw hats	3 cases	American Express Co.
Sundries	1 case	U.S. Export Co.
Surgical instruments	1 case	International Trading Co.
Syrups	25 cases	P. W. Engs and Sons
Syrups	10 cases	Order
Tea	437 casks	Wright and Graham Co.
Tea	285 casks	Order
Tea	200 packages	Order
Tennis balls	3 cases	R. F. Downing and Co.
Test cords	3 cases	U.S. Export Co.
Tin tubes	1 case	Adams Express Co.
Tissues	3 cases	Order
Tissues	3 cases	Muser Bros
Tissues	3 cases	Manhattan Shirt Co.
Tissues	3 cases	American Express Co.
Toothpaste	1 case	Park and Tilford

Cargo Goods	Quantity	Shipper
Tulle[9]	1 case	P. H. Petry and Co.
Tulle	2 cases	A. S. Metzger
Tulle	61 cases	P. K. Wilson and Son
Tweed	1 case	American Express Co.
Vegetables	3 cases	Order
Velvets	1 case	Rusch and Co.
Velvets	1 case	A. V. Heyliger
Vermouth	6 cases	Geo F. Dubois
Vinegar	19 cases	N.Y. and Cuba SS Co.
Whiskey	1 cases	Wells, Fargo and Co.
Window frames	3 cases	Order
Wine	1 case	Wakem and McLaughlin
Wine	42 cases	Wakem and McLaughlin
Wine	10 bundles of 2 cases	N.Y. and Cuba SS Co.
Wine	16 hogsheads	Geo. C. DuBois
Wine	185 cases	H. Hollander
Wine	10 hogsheads	C. A. Van Renssaller
Wine	50 cases	Acker, Merrall and Condit
Wine	4 cases	Geo F. Dubois
Wine	3 barrels	Holder of original bill of lading
Wool fat	17 packages	Shieffelin and Co.
Woollens	1 case	E. H. Van Ingen and Co.
Woollens	3 cases	Milbank, Leaman and Co.

[9] Tulle is a sheer, often stiffened silk usually used for veils, evening dresses, or ballet costumes.

PHOTO ACKNOWLEDGMENTS

All photos and illustrations, unless otherwise noted, are taken from the collection of the author.

Page xiv, 392: Postcard White Star Liner, *"Titanic"*
Pages xx–xxi: Cross section of *Titanic*'s B, C, and D decks
Page 12: Front page of the *Report of Survey of an Immigrant Ship*
Page 20: *Olympia* sailing schedule
Page 21: Dinner menu
Page 46, left: Second-class breakfast menu. Right, luncheon menu
Page 47: Specimen of a Third-class Bill of Fare
Page 53: Postcard showing the Morse code for S.O.S. and C.Q.D. that were sent out from *Titanic*'s wire room
Page 54: Postcard illustrating *Titanic*'s first contact with the iceberg
Pages 54–57: Details from the report of the British Board of Trade Inquiry's *Report on the Loss of the "Titanic"*
Page 90: Notice of Macy's closing for the day due to the death of Mr. and Mrs. Straus
Page 103: Cover of the British Board of Trade Inquiry's *Report on the Loss of the "Titanic"*
Page 118: Newspaper clipping of telegram of condolence from King George
Page 119: Postcard illustrating the tragedy of the sinking
Page 121: Cover of the published findings of the Hearing Before a Subcommittee of the U.S. Senate
Page 164: The infamous iceberg that was struck by the *Titanic*
Page 176: Chart indicating ice barrier and nearby ships
Page 185: Postcard illustrating the lowering of the lifeboats
Page 199: Front page of *The Evening Sun,* April 15, 1912
Page 208: Postcard showing mechanism by which lifeboats were lowered
Pages 210–211: Front page of the *Boston Daily Globe,* April 16, 1912
Page 218: Front page, same day, of the evening edition of the *Boston Daily Globe*
Page 222: Sworn statement from Margaret "Molly" Brown
Page 234: Postcard of an oceanic view of the R.M.S. *Titanic*
Page 254: Memorial Postcard
Pages 382–383: Spread from the CD booklet to Broadway's *Titanic: A New Musical*

ABOUT THE AUTHOR

Stephen J. Spignesi specializes in popular culture subjects, including television, film, contemporary fiction, and historical biography. He has written several authorized entertainment books and has worked with Stephen King, Turner Entertainment, the Margaret Mitchell Estate, Andy Griffith, Viacom, and other entertainment industry personalities and entities on a wide range of projects. Spignesi has also contributed essays, chapters, articles, and introductions to a wide range of books.

Spignesi's books have been translated into several languages, and he has also written for *Harper's, Cinefantastique, Saturday Review, Mystery Scene, Gauntlet,* and *Midnight Graffiti* magazines; as well as the *New York Times,* the *New York Daily News,* and the *New Haven Register.* Spignesi also appeared as a Kennedy family authority in the 1998 *E!* documentary, *The Kennedys: Power, Seduction, and Hollywood.*

In addition to writing, Spignesi lectures on a variety of popular culture subjects and teaches writing in the Connecticut area. He is the founder and editor in chief of the small press publishing company, the Stephen John Press, which recently published the acclaimed feminist autobiography *Open Windows: The Autobiography of Charlotte Troutwine Braun.*

Spignesi is a graduate of the University of New Haven and lives in New Haven with his wife, Pam, and their cat, Carter, named for their favorite character on *ER.*